World Yearbook of Education 2005

What is the role of education in developing global knowledge and culture?
What is its relationship with the new knowledge economy?
Is there scope for resistance to globalization or nationalism?

The volume deals with two major and apparently opposing forces within education and society: globalization and nationalism.

Globalization is often considered in economic terms – of continued growth of international trade and a concentration of wealth in corporate hands – yet it also encompasses technological, political and cultural change. The *World Yearbook of Education 2005* explores the role of the education sector in our globalized knowledge economy, and considers the political implications of this in terms of monopolarity and the cultural consequences of homogenization and Americanization.

The other strand of this study – nationalism – remains a persistent force within education and society in all parts of the world, and this volume examines the extent to which it can fuel conflict at all levels through prejudice and intolerance. Concentrating on the epistemological consequences of nationalism, leading international thinkers examine the extent to which it is reflected in the curricula of schools and universities around the world.

Finally, the complex relationship between globalization and nationalism is explored, and contributors analyse the part that educational institutions and practices play in forming both agendas. A wide range of perspectives are employed, including post-colonial discourse, classical economics and sociological theory.

Nationalism and globalization are both ongoing processes, and this volume makes a case for the central role of education in both – through its potential to influence change and to act as a benevolent force in shaping a global community.

David Coulby is Professor of Education and Head of International Activities at Bath Spa University College. His research interests cover areas of the sociology and politics of knowledge and culture. His most recent book (with Crispin Jones) is *Education and Warfare in Europe* (Ashgate, London).

Evie Zambeta is Assistant Professor on Education Policy at the University of Athens. Her main research interests include analysis of education politics and identity politics. She has published widely on education and policy, and her most recent book is *School and Religion* (Themelio, Athens).

World Yearbook of Education Series

379
COU

BOOK NO: 1867124

1867124

This book is due for return on or before the last date shown below.

World Yearbook of Education 2005

Globalization and nationalism in education

**Edited by
David Coulby and
Evie Zambeta**

RoutledgeFalmer
Taylor & Francis Group

LONDON AND NEW YORK

First published 2005 by RoutledgeFalmer
2 Park Square, Milton Park, Abingdon, Oxon OX14 4RN

Simultaneously published in the USA and Canada
by RoutledgeFalmer
270 Madison Ave, New York, NY 10016

RoutledgeFalmer is an imprint of the Taylor & Francis Group

© 2005 David Coulby, Evie Zambeta and individual contributors

Typeset in Palatino by
Florence Production Ltd, Stoodleigh, Devon
Printed and bound in Great Britain by
MPG Books Ltd, Bodmin, Cornwall

British Library Cataloguing in Publication Data
A catalogue record for this book is available from
the British Library

Library of Congress Cataloging in Publication Data
A catalog record for this book has been requested

ISBN 0–415–34858–7
ISSN 0084–2508

Contents

Contributors

Nafsika Alexiadou is a lecturer at the University of Keele (UK). Her areas of research and publication include policy and practice in education, social exclusion and European education policy developments, and qualitative methodology.

Leslie Bash graduated in sociology and subsequently taught in primary and secondary schools in England, following which he moved into higher education, gaining a doctorate in comparative education. He has research interests in and has written on aspects of education policy, teacher education, urban education and the links between ethnicity, nationhood and education systems. More recently, his work has focused on globalization and intercultural encounter in education. Currently, he is Principal Lecturer in Education and programme leader for the professional doctorate in education (Ed.D.) at Anglia Polytechnic University (APU), where he teaches sociology of education and intercultural education at undergraduate level and supervises a significant number of students on APU's international Ph.D. programme.

Christopher Blake, Ph.D. is Vice President for Academic Affairs at Mount St Mary's University, Maryland. Previously, he was Professor of Education, Director of Teacher Education and Chair of the Department of Education at Mount St Mary's, and prior to that Associate Dean of the Graduate School at Towson University in Baltimore. His interests include the role of ethnography in teachers' experiences and the politicization of educational research as a tool of macro reform agendas.

David Coulby is Professor of Education and Head of International Activities at Bath Spa University College. His research interests cover areas of the sociology and politics of knowledge and culture. His most recent book (with Crispin Jones) is *Education and Warfare in Europe* (London, Ashgate).

Philip Garner is Professor of Education at Nottingham Trent University. He has published widely and led large research projects in the area of the education of children perceived to have special educational needs, with particular reference to inclusion.

Jagdish Gundra is the UNESCO Professor of Intercultural Education at London University Insititute of Education. He has published widely in the areas of intercultural education and human rights.

Crispin Jones is Emeritus Reader in Education at the University of London Institute of Education. He has been a Series Editor of the *World Yearbooks of Education* since 1994.

Lisbeth Lundahl is a professor at the Department of Child and Youth Education, Special Education, and Counselling, and vice rector at Umeå University in Sweden. Her main research interests are contemporary education politics and youth matters in historical and comparative perspectives. Her earlier research has primarily concerned the educational strategies of powerful social actors (the Conservative Party and the labour market organizations, respectively) in Sweden. Youth politics and young people in between school and work are focused in one of her recent projects, the politics and micropolitics of decentralized education in another.

Zane Ma Rhea has 13 years of teaching experience spanning primary, university, government and corporate education. Her teaching experiences have been shaped by the context of her employment, as a primary schoolteacher in a remote *anangu* (aboriginal) desert school, as a lecturer at various universities, as a workplace educator for Australian corporations and as a programme leader for international skills development short courses. Her areas of research interest include the leadership and management of diversity in education and industry, and theorizing and understanding the impact of the commodification of knowledge and how this shapes the incorporation of indigenous knowledge in education. Of central importance is the role being played by Western-style education in the preservation of local, traditional and indigenous lifeways.

Suchitra Narayan is a special education consultant in Cochin, India. She has participated in a range of international projects, including initiatives relating to the cross-cultural transferability of teaching approaches to support inclusive education.

Jenny Ozga is Director, Centre for Educational Sociology, Moray House School of Education, University of Edinburgh (since 2001) and was previously Dean of Social Sciences, Keele University. Jenny Ozga's main research interests are in education policy. Her current research includes work on social inclusion policies, and on Education and Youth Transitions across the UK. She is also involved in a project on Knowledge Transfer in Education Research. She has a developing interest in Research-policy Relationships in Europe in the context of the emergent European Research Area. Her recent publications include: 'Modernising Education Governance in England and Scotland: Devolution and Control' (with

N. Alexiadiou, *European Research Journal*, 2002); *Policy Research in Educational Settings: Contested Terrain* (Buckingham, Open University Press, 2000); 'Education Policy in the United Kingdom: The Dialectic of Globalisation and Identity' (*Australian Educational Researcher*, 2000); 'Les Zones d'action educative et la modernisation de l'adminstration chargée des affaires scolaires en Angleterre' (with D. Pye, *Revue Française de Pedagogie*, 2000); 'Modernising Education Governance: Some Intra-national (UK) Comparisons' (*European Educational Research Journal*, 2000).

Terri Seddon is Professor of Education at Monash University and Director of the Centre for Work and Learning Studies. She has longstanding interests in social and historical analysis of education and educational change. She is currently researching the changing politics of education and training which accompanies the cross-sectoral blurring of boundaries and marketized education and training reform. Her research has focused on post-compulsory education and, over the last ten years, adult and vocational education and training. She has published four books: *Reshaping Australian Education: Beyond Nostalgia* (with Lawrence Angus, 2000); *Pay, Professionalism and Politics: Reforming Teachers? Reforming Education?* (1996); *Context and Beyond: Reframing the Theory and Practice of Education* (1993); and *A Curriculum for the Senior Secondary Years in Australia* (with Christine Deer, 1992).

Masako Shibata currently lectures on intercultural issues and teacher-education courses in Doshisha University and others on a part-time basis. Most of her research is historically based and centres on the role of education as a political institution in the processes of the construction, destruction and reconstruction of states, education and international conflict, and education and powerful national and political beliefs. Among many aspects of the role of education, she has developed a particular interest in the search for national identity, not as the mission of the state alone, but as the dynamics of the popular perceptions of 'national pasts'. After completing her doctoral study in the Institute of Education, University of London, she published a number of articles in the academic literature, e.g. 'Can the Japanese Change Their Education System?' and 'Educational Policy Borrowing: Historical Perspectives' (in press).

Evie Zambeta is an Assistant Professor on Education Policy at the University of Athens. Her main research interests include analysis of education politics and identity politics in the Greek and European education systems. Her most recent book is *School and Religion* (Athens, Themelio).

Series editors' introduction

This volume on *Globalization and Nationalism in Education* follows on from last year's *Yearbook* on *Digital Technology, Communities & Education*. Like that volume, it addresses rapidly changing technical and social phenomena and assesses their impact on education. More than that volume, but like many of its predecessors, this book brings together a huge social process with its associated theorizing and places them alongside developments in schools and universities as they become more aspects of production than consumption. The authors have to handle the shifting perspective from global economic and political forces to curricular and organizational changes in institutions.

The volume, like others in the series, draws on a wealth of different national perspectives. This is important not only in providing analyses of different institutional contexts, but also in drawing on differences in the ways in which globalization and its impact on education is being perceived and theorized in different states.

An important theme of the book is the trend towards the globalization of knowledge. This is manifested in many ways, the most evident perhaps being the shift to English as the first foreign language throughout the world. The authors also draw attention to the globalization of medical diagnosis of special educational needs and to the globalization of the notion of the superiority of European civilization and its origins in Classical Greece. Asked on one occasion what he thought of European civilization, Gandhi replied that he thought it would be a good idea.

The volume introduces authors who will play a significant part in the future of the *World Yearbooks of Education*. Jenny Ozga, Terri Seddon and Evie Zambeta will be taking on roles as Series Editors and Editors in the future. We wish them well.

David Coulby and Crispin Jones
Bath, 2004

Introduction

Trends in globalization

David Coulby and Evie Zambeta

This volume deals with two major and apparently opposing forces within education and society, globalization and nationalism.

Globalization is seen in primarily economic terms with the increase in international trade and the concentration of wealth into corporate hands. The political implications of this in terms of monopolarity and the cultural consequences in terms of homogenization and Americanization are also examined. Educational institutions themselves are part of this process of globalization because of their central role in the development of the knowledge economy (discussed in Chapters 1 and 2). Chapter 9 analyses the social and epistemological consequences of the emergence of the knowledge economy for teaching and education. Chapter 8 analyses the global homogenization of the categories of special educational needs and the idealization of the policy of inclusion.

Nationalism remains a persistent force within education and society in all parts of the world (as explored in Chapters 3, 4 and 13). The volume recognizes the extent to which this fuels conflict at all levels through racism, religious conflict, prejudice against refugees and ultimately warfare. It concentrates on the epistemological consequences of nationalism as this is reflected in the curricula of schools and universities.

The volume attempts to explore the conflict between these two forces of globalization and nationalism. It also seeks to develop theoretical positions within which educational institutions and practices can be understood to participate in both the forces and the conflict. It does this within the understanding of post-colonial discourse theory (see Chapters 13 and 14) as well as more classical economic and sociological positions. Education itself is becoming globalized and is an essential component of the wider process. The volume, therefore, examines the technologies and knowledge characteristics which underpin this process.

A core example which the volume uses in terms of a globalized epistemology and consequent curricular impact is that of Greece. The activities, achievements and modes of organization of fourth-century Athens have had an astonishing impact on what is perceived to be knowledge, government and beauty in large parts of the world. The volume

2 David Coulby and Evie Zambeta

examines this achievement in detail (in Chapters 10 and 11) as a colonial construct in the case of Greece itself, and then Europe and the wider world. The fabrication of Greece presents a potent example of the globalization of history, ethics, politics and culture.

The volume concludes by recognizing nationalism and indeed colonialism as ongoing processes. It assesses the importance of educational institutions within a globalized economy. It recognizes the importance of education in generating change at the level of the individual consciousness and asks how far this provides any agency for resistance against the two forces which the book has discussed.

As has been noted, globalization is a primarily economic phenomenon which is largely facilitated by encompassing changes in technology. Globalization also has, however, political and cultural aspects. These aspects are obviously interrelated, so the headings used below are offered as a mode of discussion rather than an explanatory typology. This chapter discusses these trends in turn and concludes with an introduction to anti-globalization movements and thinking. Though in this analysis globalization is by no means treated as an uncontested concept, it is nevertheless considered as a set of overwhelming processes that are being witnessed in contemporary societies.

Economic trends

One set of arguments that identify a pattern of economic globalization concern the absolute increase in world trade. Goods, capital, people and ideas are seen to be moving in greater quantities and with greater speed between ever expanding areas of the globe. In fact the empirical basis of this contention has been contested with economic historians pointing to the *belle époque* period before the First World War as a time of even greater economic integration than that of the early twenty-first century (Held and McGrew, 2000b; Held and McGrew, 2002; Hobsbawm, 1962, 1987, 1994).

While on one hand globalization is perceived as an enhancement of global interdependence, there is much scepticism as to the extent to which this phenomenon is now more evident than it used to be in the *belle époque* period at the end of the nineteenth century, when the big empires were giving way to the so-called nation-states. There is a substantial literature however arguing that 'globalisation is a myth' (such as in Held and McGrew, 2002b), while the real political agenda is that of a creation of a global market which enhances capitalism and generates Americanization and neoliberal policy. This argument suggests that the phenomenon which is now perceived as globalization is a continuity in the development of capitalist relations rather than a genuinely new stage of capitalism. Despite this scepticism, there is less ambiguity with regard to the fact that we are witnessing a process of growing linkage between different national economies and societies. For those who see the historical argument as inadequate to explain the present, globalization is not a synonym for imperialism. While imperialism has been considered as a political, geographical and economic expansion that led to internationalization, globalization affects the whole range of human activity, within and beyond the boundaries of the nation-state (Kotzias, 2003).

The present internationalization of the economy and the market is, however, qualitatively different from that of the *belle époque*. Indeed the major patterns of world trade are not currently represented by increased movement across all states of the globe but rather by enhanced trade between the triadic economic powers of Japan, the USA and the European Union (EU) (Photopoulos, 2002). Furthermore, those opposed to globalization emphasize that its benefits have largely accrued to the triad states. Although a few states have managed to leap in the post-First World War period to the status of more economically developed countries (MEDCs) – Singapore, South Korea, Taiwan and, to a lesser extent, Malaysia and Thailand – the actual gap between the richest and poorest people in the world has actually increased steadily during this period. If globalization is happening it is resulting in an enhancement of global economic inequality. Many states have seen their relative and absolute economic status decline in the period of globalization: Zimbabwe, Argentina, Venezuela, Brazil, Romania and Bulgaria. At the same time the numbers of people living in absolute poverty have reduced in the last quarter of a century due primarily to the growing prosperity of India and China with their vast populations (Wolf, 2003).

There are two trends which less disputably point towards a shift to economic globalization: first, the movement towards an international organization of production, distribution and consumption; and, second, the increasing importance of economic and trade-related issues in international affairs. Classic examples of the globalization of production, distribution and consumption are training shoes or cars. But the process may be seen also in the generation of less tangible assets such as films, non-governmental organization (NGOs) or university Masters' programmes. A car may be designed in the UK, with its machine tools and assembly production units designed and built in Germany, and its actual assembly taking place in São Paulo or Shenzhen. An advertising and marketing strategy is then put together in New York featuring a Russian model or Brazilian footballer to support the car's ultimate distribution in the EU and North America. A specialist Master's programme in the application of information and communication technology (ICT) to geophysics may be developed jointly by two universities in the UK and the USA. In fact the target student group for this programme is mainly outside both these countries. It sets up an international pattern of recruitment especially from South Asian countries. A few years down the track it has introductory (pre-Masters') courses in place in institutions in Thailand, China and Indonesia. One of these actually then becomes a centre for the main programme, sending its lecturers to the UK and USA universities on Ph.D. programmes. At this point the degree course has become both a global venture and a significant element in world trade.

This process was previously seen as a 'new international division of labour' (Frobel *et al.*, 1988); however, Castells has argued that it is not a straightforward process of exporting simple manufacturing functions to less economically developed countries (LEDCs) (Castells, 1989, 1996, 1997, 1998). Rather, particular areas within MEDCs and LEDCs take on functions of design, capitalization, manufacture and distribution without any particular hierarchy. That is not to assert that some regions and states are not richer than others: Nagoya, Munich and southern California represent remarkable concentrations of wealth. But elements of impoverishment are to be found in these areas too. Those regions in both LEDCs and MEDCs which are excluded from this process of the advanced division of labour experience high levels of economic marginalization and impoverishment: this applies as much to the rust belt of the USA as to rural western China.

To turn to the second issue of the increased importance of trade-related issues in international affairs, this has obviously been consolidated by the completion of the Uruguay round and the formation of the World Trade Organisation (WTO) in 1994 (Wilkinson, 2002). Impoverishment and debt have led many LEDCs to seek assistance from the World Bank. This has often been conditional upon the adoption of structural adjustment policies which have entailed the reduction of public spending on areas such as health and education and the privatization of nationally owned facilities such as power, telephones or water distribution (Hertz, 2001). While this has given countries such as Kenya or the Philippines an appearance of enhanced capitalism, it has actually served to increase both inequality and actual impoverishment in these states. The effects of globalization in such states has been radically to transform both local economic conditions and also the nature of domestic politics. In the triad states the impact of trade on international relations has involved the exacerbation of trade disputes and their referral to the WTO. Thus between the EU and the USA there are currently major disputes concerning agricultural subsidies, steel subsidies, genetically modified foods, which the EU refuses to import, and hormone-fed beef which again the EU will not touch. So far these disputes have led not only to WTO arbitration but also to the threatened imposition of trade bans on luxury imports from the EU by the USA. The possibility of serious trade wars between the triad states is emerging. The WTO sought to incorporate yet another tranche of economic activity within its reach (Kelk and

Worth, 2002), but at the Cancun meeting in 2003 these proposals were rejected and indeed the future of the whole Doha round was thrown into jeopardy. The crucial grouping of China, Brazil and India may suggest the beginning of organized international resistance to Western (triad) enforced globalization.

There is, of course, a sense in which actual trade wars are already happening. Recent events in Iraq have served to put the control of the world's second biggest oilfield in the hands of the USA and the UK. While this may not have been motivated by short-term gain, medium-term control of this resource was surely the main reason for intervention (Rampton and Stauber, 2003; Ritter and Pitt, 2002; Traynor, 2003). Similarly, military intervention by the USA in Panama and Columbia has been intended to control the trade of the second most valuable global commodity, illegal drugs.

The broadening in the unequal distribution of power and wealth and the monopolarity which characterizes the processes of globalization lead to much scepticism with regard to its actual meaning. It is argued that the economic policy which is adopted in most of the states world-wide is in fact a neoliberal political agenda rather than an irresistible imperative of globalization. The attack on public services at an international level is interpreted as an ideological position and not as an inevitable choice (Negreponti-Delivanis, 2001; Vergopoulos, 1999). These policies are usually legitimized on the basis of the widely recognized need to raise the economy's potential for competitiveness on a global scale. However, for the opponents of the neoliberal agenda, the policy which underpins the competitiveness of the economy mainly serves the end of capital accumulation while it undermines the position of labour.

As a few commodities become crucial to economic success, developments in technology mean that knowledge is becoming an increasingly important element both in world trade and in economic power (Burton-Jones, 1999; Etzkovitz and Leydesdorff, 2001; Neef, 1998; Stewart, 1997; Thurow, 1999; Witchit Srisa-an, 2000). A country's position in the global competitive economic environment is largely dependent on its capacity to develop a growth strategy that allows it to participate in the international arena through highly specialized products whose share in global trade increases. It should be noted, however, that despite the ongoing process of de-industrialization since the 1970s, 57 per cent of global economic transactions still represents industrial products. Car manufacturing may not be a knowledge-intensive activity any more, compared to nanotechnology for instance, but cars continue to be desirable consumer goods in the global market. Nevertheless, certain countries, such as Singapore or Finland, have managed to change their place in the global economy and become more competitive through investment in the knowledge base of their economy and the production of highly specialized new technology. In this technology, automation system design and global marketing, for instance, are emerging as more significant elements within the knowledge economy than the simple bulk manufacture of products such as cars.

The first list of important knowledge areas for trade is relatively obvious:

- ICT technology and programmes;
- pharmaceuticals;
- military technology;
- aerospace;
- materials technology and nanotechnology;
- genetic engineering.

A second list of at least equally important knowledge processes and creations may be less evident:

- international legal services (almost exclusively based on the eastern seaboard of the USA) (Gabel and Bruner, 2003);
- fashion and design (one of the UK's most economically significant exports to Japan);
- music;
- television, film and computer games;
- marketing and advertising;
- university level education (Davis, 2003).

The development of the knowledge economy is discussed in Chapters 1 and 2; at this point it is only necessary to note that the capacity for knowledge generation and utilization may be as economically significant to a state or region (Silicon Valley, Cambridge University and Science Park) as a major manufacturing capacity or extractive capacity.

The final point to emphasize in terms of economic trends (and indeed to cultural trends) is that the process is not only one way from MEDCs to LEDCs. The Bangalore region of India is already an important site for the development of specialist software and other ICT services as well as relocated call centres serving the UK. Taiwan has more sophisticated chip production facilities than any state in the EU. Cairo and Mumbai, as well as Hollywood and London, are important sites in the production and distribution of film and television (Crane *et al.*, 2002). The development of the network society allows the emergence of a new hierarchy not only between states, but also between urban environments and clever regions that do not always belong to the triad states (Chalaris, 2003). Parts of New Delhi, Rio and Lagos can be competitive partners in this new social geography of difference. China's economic emergence, symbolized by its joining the WTO in 2002, is resulting in the focusing of design, manufacture and distribution in centres such as Shanghai,

Shenzen and Hong Kong. This economic potential is related to the fact that China has achieved a massive growth rate within the last decade which is also depicted in the explosion of the numbers of Chinese students who attend highly ranked universities around the world (Negreponti-Delivanis, 2001).

Technological trends

Technological trends concern principally developments in ICT and transportation. These trends and their associated characteristics are dealt with in Chapter 1. In some ways it is the developments in technology that have facilitated the economic trends outlined above. It was innovations in ICT that enabled electronic financial transactions to be made, thereby allowing trading in shares, currencies, commodities, futures and other more complex products to take place at lightning speed across the globe. The establishment of three major exchanges in New York, London and Tokyo means that these massive flows of capital are carried on on a twenty-four-hour basis. Further developments have allowed the international outsourcing of functions as various as design, call centres, accountancy, publishing, and undergraduate and postgraduate study.

Developments in transportation have been apparently less dramatic in the final third of the twentieth century. Three important trends need to be identified as they are influential on the economic and cultural changes outlined above: first, the current and incipient expansion of air travel; second, the selective but substantial investment in high speed trains; and, third, the reduction in the price of sea freight. Air travel has become available more widely and cheaply. There is a current expansion in the size and number of airports as well as the general lengthening of runways needed to accommodate the new, huge Airbus. For all the virtual exchanges of communication represented by ICT developments, there is also an increase in the number and frequency and, to a lesser extent, distance of people moving. These movements represent more than myopic tourism; they are also the entrepreneurs of the global economy keeping in contact with their market, suppliers, agent and partners as well as the students and other knowledge entrepreneurs seeking a profit by moving information and skills from one site to another. High-speed trains offer the possibility of moving many more people almost equally as fast as jet travel and directly from city centre to city centre. The large investment they represent is perhaps a predictor of the future growth areas of the global economy. In the past this was certainly the case of the Shinkansen running down the east coast of Honshu from Tokyo, through Osaka to Hiroshima. Recent high-speed links include those from Hamburg to Berlin, from Shanghai to Pudong and from the Channel Tunnel to Marseilles. The Japanese experimental maglev train has reached 361 miles per hour in trials. Third, and finally, containers and bulk shipping have led to a substantial reduction in the cost of sea freight. Thus, a bottle of Australian or Chilean wine can now be bought in English supermarkets for the price of its French competitor. All these three technological developments have unprecedented effects and potential in the transformation of the basis of the economy and the mode of human transactions.

Political trends

For many exponents of globalization theory, the major impact of globalization has been in the weakening of the state itself. Many transnational corporations (TNCs) now have a larger annual income than many states. The list of the world's largest economies shows, not unexpectedly, the USA, Japan, Germany, the UK and France as the first five. China is already sixth and rising. At number 21, though, the organization is not a state but a company, ExxonMobil, just ahead of Turkey at 22. Then follows Wal-Mart, then Austria. A country such as Portugal comes in at number 48, well behind Ford, BP and Toyota (Gabel and Bruner, 2003).

The power of the TNCs originates from their existence in the market place rather than in geographical space. The boundaries and jurisdiction of the state are no longer determinants of the practices of these massive corporations. With their ability to mobilize vast resources, and their wide technological and knowledge capacity, they are able to be innovative and act at a speed and scale far beyond most states and at a rate the world has never seen before (Gabel and Bruner, 2003). Indeed, this is one of the crucial differences between the *belle époque* and the present time. The major issue is not whether the number of the TNCs increases, which of course is happening (in 1914 there were 3,000 multinational corporations (MNCs), whereas in 2000 there were 63,000), but the power they exercise. In the 1990s the 500 top-listed MNCs had under their control 70 per cent of global trade, 80 per cent of total foreign investment and 30 per cent of the global GDP (Photopoulos, 2002). At the same time inequality is increasing both within and between states.

Many states have had to surrender elements of their domestic policy when they seek financial assistance from the World Bank. Smaller states desperate for foreign direct investment will establish tax-free trade zones, offer subsidies or long tax holidays to potential investors and often turn a blind eye to illegal labour exploitation practices and pollutive and degenerative environmental misuse (Klein, 2001, 2002). Indeed this competition to attract the investment of large TNCs is by no means confined to small, economically weak states: competition between the states of the EU for new investment in manufacturing, such as Japanese or US car plants, or in large cultural/recreative facilities, such as Euro Disney, can be vigorous and long-lasting. Some theorists have gone as far as to describe 'Captive states' (in this case the UK) (Monbiot,

2001), where political power is no longer held by formal governments responsible to the electorate.

The role of the state, in the context of globalization, is contested. While there is strong evidence that international organizations such as the Organisation for Economic Cooperation and Development (OECD), the WTO and the International Monetary Fund (IMF) have the power directly to intervene and control the growth strategies of some states, at the same time the state remains the mediating institution of political control. Nevertheless, the power of states could be perceived as being hollowed out in significant ways. Global governance is considered as 'multilayered' (Held and McGrew, 2002b) because it is constituted by and through a complexity of several agents and distinct governing mechanisms which operate at different levels:

- the suprastate (such as the United Nations (UN) system, the OECD, the World Bank or the IMF);
- the regional, such as the EU, the North American Free Trade Agreement (NAFTA), the Southern Common Market in Latin America (MERCOSUR), The Association of Southeast Asian Nations (ASEAN) (see next paragraph for details);
- the transnational (i.e. the TNCs or the anti-globalization movement);
- the sub-state (such as local government or corporate interests); in some contexts the sub-state is of high visibility as the power of nationalism provokes division in Spain, Belgium, the Soviet Union, Yugoslavia, Czechoslovakia, Russia (Chechnya), Iraq, Indonesia (East Timor) and the United Kingdom.

The parallel function and interconnection of these different layers of governance act as major constraints which are sandwiching the state. Global governance, however, develops a variable geometry in which the regulatory capacities of certain agencies or the relative power of certain states vary significantly. While Kenya or Latvia are highly vulnerable to the impacts of global institutions, China is highly resistant and the USA, as the single hyperpower, virtually invulnerable. The role of the latter, in particular, is of vital importance in the shaping of the international economic and political order, a role that has been performed either by the USA's paralysing absence or enthusiastic involvement in certain procedures. The WTO, for example, owes its creation to post-Second World War efforts to develop a liberal compromise for managing the global economy, an attempt that has been indisputably steered by the USA (Wilkinson, 2002).

The emerging system of global governance is thus characterized by spheres of authority with compliance-generating capacities (Rosenau, 2002). During the past decades, and especially after the end of the Cold War, there has been an immense reconfiguration of power and authority that has led to a new complex mode of governing. Domestic policies usually involve negotiation between the state and diverse agencies of both a public and private nature located within and beyond the state. In this process the state becomes the steering mechanism which facilitates globalization. It should be noted, however, that the state may have a strategic role but not necessarily the dominant one (Held and McGrew, 2002b). While national government, however, derives legitimacy through constitutional frameworks and representation systems, global governance lacks accountability. (For further analysis of the complexities of global governance see Chapter 5.) Questions of legitimacy, such as who rules, in whose benefit, by what mechanisms, and for what purposes, are of crucial importance and feed public discontent regarding politics. Global politics, for instance, seem to be more energetic with regard to performing what has been defined as humanitarian or anti-'terrorist' wars than combating hunger, poverty, Aids or global warming (Pogge, 2001). Furthermore, there is much scepticism regarding whether global, regional, national or local rules should prevail as the regulatory principles. To what extent corporations, local or national governments are eligible to decide on waste or water resources management, pollution regulations or public health issues remains disputed. The extent to which global governance can be legitimized on principles that claim universal validity is a problematic issue (Charalambis, 1998).

The emergence of international (sometimes called regional) organizations is a trend which apparently serves to weaken the role of the state. The EU is obviously the most developed of these. It now encompasses not only a barrier-free trade and labour area but, for most of its members, a single currency, the euro. The adoption of the European Declaration of Human Rights as binding legislation in all 25 countries has resulted in a further level of subordination of individual states as European legislation now takes precedence over domestic law in all countries for many areas of policy. A parallel economic regional organization, NAFTA, comprising Canada, the USA and Mexico, is gathering influence and importance. There are discussions being held to expand it into the whole of the American continent. This development is being vigorously resisted by local (and, not least, anti-globalization) groups in many states of South America, such as Brazil and Venezuela. A parallel organization (ASEAN) has emerged in Southeast Asia. As these regional groups both expand to include new states and strengthen and deepen their internal regulation, then the authority of individual states is inevitably diminished.

The implications of this for democratic government are nowhere more stark than in the EU, where democratic deficit has led to national opposition, in countries as varied as Ireland and Sweden, and general voting apathy (Banchoff and Smith, 1999; Christiansen *et al.*, 2001; Featherstone and Kazamias, 2001; Siedentop, 2000). Furthermore, the dominant ideas of flexibility in the labour market and workfare, as well as the deregulation strategies in social policy, associated with both the EU and NAFTA are greeted with scepticism on the part of those social groups who see social rights as an integral part of citizenship and of the European social heritage. Social policy in particular is considered as a foundation stone of cohesion in the European social space. (For a detailed discussion of the reconstruction of social policy within the European space see Chapter 7.) While the average quality of living in the EU countries is improving, at the same time there is an increase in those social groups who are threatened by social exclusion. Moreover, there are serious discrepancies among the EU countries with regard to the level of welfare provision and public spending on social policy (Korres and Tsombanoglou, 2003). Exponents of European integration argue that a different vision of welfare presupposes the reconsideration of the representation mechanisms with regard to the different social groups (Ananiadi, 2003). Existing discrepancies however, in terms of both power and wealth, will become even wider following the European enlargement. Under the fourth EU Support Framework, some of the till recently lagging regions will find themselves being considered as rich enough in comparison with the new member states. European integration is presented in the EU political discourse as a highly desirable and uncontested political goal. It nevertheless presupposes a vast redistribution of resources and an immense commitment on the part of the richest states and peoples of Europe, a process which cannot be accomplished through a top-down mode of governance. While EU integration is presented as a quite optimistic goal, democratic deficit emerges as a harsh political reality. (For further discussion of the EU and its role in education, see Chapter 6.)

Another political trend has been the reduction in interstate war in the final third of the twentieth century. This has been accompanied by the ending of the Cold War and a reduction in superpower conflict (Reynolds, 2001). This has been replaced by internal conflicts, insurrections, repressions and civil wars (Zaire, Rwanda, Sudan, Chechnya, Northern Ireland, Tibet, East Timor, Kashmir and Yugoslavia). One of the major factors fuelling these internal conflicts has been the resurgence of nationalism. Indeed this has emerged as one of the most potent forces in contemporary politics even where it has not resulted in open warfare. Nationalism can be a driving force of the state even when other values are ostensibly advocated, as with communism in China, Islam in Indonesia or democratic pluralism in Turkey. Of course one person's freedom-fighting independence movement (in Aceh, Palestine or Georgia) is another person's terrorist trying to break down the stability and control of the central state (Anderson, 1983; Appadurai, 1990; Reynolds, 2001). Since the attacks on the New York World Trade Center and the Pentagon in Washington in 2001 the control of the definition of terrorism has become one of the crucial political powers. To be able to legitimate one's enemies as terrorists, especially within the terminology and accompanying power distribution of the USA, is to provide a state with crucial support in the (often brutal) suppression of internal opposition (e.g. Chechnya and Palestine).

Indeed, the most important political trend at the beginning of the twenty-first century has been the emergence of the USA as a single and unchallengeable hyperpower. No other state can summon a fraction of the military might of the USA in terms of either advanced technology, annual expenditure or global reach. Despite chauvinistic posturing from France, Germany and Belgium, the EU will be in no position to challenge this power in the foreseeable future. Indeed one component in the monopolar position of the USA is its network of military and economic alliances which embrace states as different as Turkey, the UK and Japan. Among the remarkable features of the 2003 Iraq War were not only the ease and speed with which it was won by the USA with the assistance of only one major ally, but the inability of the international community to organize any effective resistance to the invasion. At the regional level the Arab states were split by their variable alliances with the USA. At the international level the UN proved utterly ineffective in the face of determined hyperpower resolution.

This impacts on economic globalization to the extent that the process is seen as being beneficial mainly to the USA and to the TNCs based there (Stiglitz, 2002). The World Bank is largely controlled by the USA and it is clear that decisions that have impoverished LEDCs have also served to benefit American TNCs. The WTO is also increasingly being brought under the control of American corporate interests so that domestic political decisions can be challenged where they seem to endanger the accumulation of TNC profit. The US government itself usurps its monopolar position to ignore international treaties such as those on environmental protection and child labour. It uses its economic strength to wage unequal trade wars against countries such as Iraq, Libya and Cuba. As will become apparent in the next section, there is a case that globalization is actually only code for Americanization.

Cultural trends

A case can be made that there is a developing trend towards the global homogenization of culture. Films and television products are increasingly important as aspects of culture. They are watched for longer periods by more people in more countries. While the diversified production in this area has been noted, and to this could be added the international popularity of, for instance, Brazilian soap operas, increasingly the production and distribution is centring on the USA and particularly southern California. Because American television programmes such as *Friends* are distributed globally, they can be sold in any one country at an apparently cheap rate. Thus, it is much more economic for a television station in Latvia or Paraguay to purchase American programmes and either add dubbing or subtitles than it is to produce indigenous programming in the local language/s (Crane *et al.*, 2002). Because of the interconnected references between television and film programming and their links to fast food, books, toys, computer games, music and other merchanting, the popularity of one programme or product can be used to enhance that of another.

A similar case can be made with regard to food consumption, one of the most important of cultural practices. Chinese cities, for instance, are replete with outlets for American fast food: McDonald's, Kentucky Fried Chicken and Pizza Hut. It is remarkable that a country such as China with its rich, varied and historical cuisine should have been colonized by outlets for expensive, fatty trash. The spread of Coke as the family drink of choice in countries like Japan repeats the same regrettable trend. Indeed, the global spread of these products has led commentators to write about the McDonaldization of society (Ritzer, 1993).

Cultural and economic activity, as the examples above show, are not readily separable. Fast food and fizzy drink franchises, television pro-grammes and films, pop music, books (about half the global total of which are published in one city, London) and magazines, design and other cultural products form important and increasing components of the international export trade (Lash and Urry, 1994). Overwhelmingly these products originate in the USA. These products themselves lend glamour to other more durable exports from fashion goods to armaments. McDonald's features a Hollywood movie as part of its international marketing campaign. The movie features particular youth fashions as well as music. Branding of products can be mutually reinforcing through a range of cultural activities and associated advertising tie-ins.

Some commentators have characterized this international movement and choice of cultural products and activities as postmodernity, a condi-tion within which the individual selects her/his individual culture from the infinite multiplicity which is globally on offer (Arnonowitz and Giroux, 1991; Coulby and Jones, 1995; Usher and Edwards, 1994). The wider cultural implications of this are explored in Chapter 14. At this stage it is only necessary to note that education at all levels is deeply implicated here (Burbules and Torres, 2000; Green, 2002; Kazamias, 2003; Kress, 1996; Stromquist and Monkman, 2000). The curricula of schools and universities are also a cultural selection: the question arises as to the extent to which these are or should be influenced either by the processes of globalization or the solipsism of individual preference. Of course a pre-eminent issue here is the increasing prevalence of the English language, reflected not least in school and university curricula. This is a major concern of many of the chapters in this volume. English has become a compulsory subject in almost all education systems. Given the dominance of the English language in the internet, media, journals and books, global trade and business, it is quite possible that people will tend not to learn any foreign language other than English. Accordingly they tend to use even their own language less in highly specialized or academic contexts, a condition which might result in substantial linguistic and cultural impoverishment, especially with regard to the less spoken languages of the world. (For a full discussion of language issues in the context of globalization, including the prospects of language extinction, see Chapter 12.) English linguistic dominance is sometimes presented as endangering the global cultural heritage or the tradition of certain cultures. On the other hand some of the less spoken languages, for example Greek, which has no direct connection with any other language, present an impressive resistance, as its recent creativity in poetry and literature shows (SECE, 2003).

This example shows that, despite the appearance of Americanization, as mentioned in the section above, cultural movement is far from a one-way street. Even in the example of food, it is clear that gastronomic trends move from East to West as well as from West to East. Indian restaurants are ubiquitous in the UK, even in quite small towns, and are gradually appearing across the EU. Chinese restaurants are even more widely spread. Up-market Japanese restaurants are also achieving popularity in some areas of the EU and the USA. Chinese and Hong Kong films have broken into Western distribution networks as yet unpenetrated by Mumbai and Cairo. Immigration, either that of the cosmopolitan elites, or that of economic immigrants, brings with it greater fusion in food, fashion, music and culture in general. Immigration challenges both nationalism and the Americanization of culture since it develops the dynamics of identity and acts as a major facilitating factor towards hybridity (Hall *et al.*, 1992) Although the United States occupies a primary position, this is hardly the same in cultural terms as it is in political. The developing trend is characterized more by cultural exchange, fusion and hybridity than cultural domination (Bhabha, 1990; Bhabha, 1996; Young, 1990; Young, 1995). (Chapter 13 shows that, in some cases, globalization may facilitate the renegotiation of the concept of nationhood itself, to acknowledge oppressed or long-silenced identities and cultures.) However, the fact that the English language dominates in most of the global exchanges has dramatic impact on the type of the hybrid produced. Furthermore, English, as well as education of course, has become the key that allows access to the network society and global culture.

The ubiquity of English and the homogenization of international culture are one side of the coin. A postmodern plurality of cultures can lead to wider internationalization and tolerance. Where populations experience a diversity of culture in terms of art, music and writing as well as food and films, this can result in cosmopolitan tolerance and inclusion as well as in the less positive reinforcement of small nationalisms and racism. This polarization between nationalism and cosmopolitanism is perhaps the extreme choice with which globalization confronts societies, not least their education systems.

Anti-globalization

This refers here not to those theorists who do not accept that the process of globalization is actually occurring, but rather to those activists and writers who acknowledge that it is happening and are doing what they can to oppose and resist it (Bruno and Karliner, 2002; Klein, 2002; Photopoulos, 2002; Wilkinson and Hughes, 2002). The first thing to be said about this trend is that it in no way represents a systematic movement. Indeed, an antipathy to system, grand narratives and global solutions is one of the few things that its various proponents have in common. In some ways the anti-globalizationists represent a congruence of small-scale issue groups:

- eco-protesters or those concerned with access to pure water;
- those seeking rights for small nations or for exploited rural or tribal people;
- those seeking a reduction in global inequality and poverty, sometimes focusing on children's health, prostitution or the treatment of HIV/Aids;
- those opposed to the injustices imposed by particular brands such as Nike, Esso or Nestlé;
- those pursuing better rights and pay for workers both in the MEDCs and in the maquiladoras;
- those opposed to the particular institutions of global capitalism: the World Bank, the IMF, the WTO, NAFTA and the EU;
- those concerned that the politics of a particular state or even of the UN itself are being corrupted or incorporated by corporate interest.

It is these groups who first came to the world's attention in 1999 with the protests on the streets of Seattle and later, in 2001, to violent, indeed murderous, state opposition in Genoa.

Although a motley collection of groups, the nature of the protest does actually constitute a coherent critique of globalization. Corporations are recognized as having more power than many states with dire consequences in terms of labour conditions (poverty, health, child labour, attacks on trade unions) and environmental degradation. Corporations are not responsible in any one state and capital is footloose and mobile.

The consequence of this is that states increasingly seek to attract corporations rather than to control them. They are engaged in a 'race to the bottom' in terms of offering tax incentives and control of the workforce and above all low pay (Stiglitz, 2002). Corporations have undue influence on the media and reportage in many states, not least the USA where large conglomerates often include newspaper and media outlets. Rupert Murdoch has a deal with China which facilitates his bland news channels plus the insipid CNN, while banning the BBC. One corporation thus maintains a control over the information access of 1.2 billion people. International organizations – especially the WTO, but increasingly the UN itself – are dominated by corporate interests and can overthrow the decisions of democratically elected governments (Hertz, 2001). Democratic institutions have become marginalized both by TNCs and by regional governments such as the EU. Involved in these protests is a strong anti-Americanism (and perhaps anti-UK and anti-EU feeling). American foreign policy in the previous century is seen as being dominated by the interests of (American) capitalism, not by the spread of democracy.

Notice that activism is an essential part of this perspective, as democratic institutions are seen to be failing. This is sometimes linked to falling turnouts at local, national and international (EU) elections. For these protesters and their theorists, protest is the only remaining form of participation in national and international decision-making. These protests focus on meetings of the rich countries at the OECD, on the annual May Day workers' gatherings and on local opposition to the expansion of motorways, airport or (US) military facilities. Although often closely coordinated via email and the internet and controlled via cellular phones at the time of the protest, this does not imply any overall organizational structure. The structure is itself web-like and postmodern with many different organizations each with their own nodes in loose interconnectivity one with another. The only overarching organizations are the World Social Forum and the European Social Forum, annual gatherings of activists, which are characterized by the multiplicity of their agenda.

This chapter has introduced the theme of globalization and used examples from education to demonstrate the relevance of this theme to the *World Yearbook*. It is on education that succeeding chapters more explicitly focus. Chapter 3 introduces the theme of nationalism and shows how this is linked to and in contradiction with globalization. Chapter 4 explores the issue of nationalism in depth in the case of Japan and its education system and wider culture. The volume thus examines the complex issue of to what extent educational institutions and systems are agents or victims of the process of globalization and the power of nationalism.

References

Ananiadi, M. (2003) Social Europe and Flexibility, in E. Katsoulis, M. Ananiadi and S. Ioannidis (eds) *Globalisation: Economic, Political and Cultural Aspects.* Athens: Sideris, pp. 319–46.

Anderson, B. (1983) *Imagined Communities: Reflections on the Origin and Spread of Nationalism.* London: Verso.

Appadurai, A. (1990) Disjuncture and Difference in the Global Cultural Economy, in M. Featherstone (ed.) *Global Culture: Nationalism, Globalisation and Modernity.* London: Sage.

Arnonowitz, S. and Giroux, H. A. (1991) *Postmodern Education: Politics, Culture and Social Criticism.* London: Routledge & Kegan Paul.

Banchoff, T. and Smith, M. E. (1999) *Legitimacy and the European Union: The Contested Polity.* London: Routledge.

Bhabha, H. K. (ed.) (1990) *Nation and Narration.* London and New York: Routledge.

Bhabha, H. K. (1996) Culture's In-Between, in S. Hall and P. Du Gay (eds) *Cultural Identity.* London: Sage, pp. 53–60.

Bruno, K. and Karliner, J. (2002) *earthsummit.biz: The Corporate Takeover of Sustainable Development.* Oakland, CA: Food First Books.

Burbules, N. C. and Torres, C. A. (eds) (2000) *Globalisation and Education: Critical Perspectives.* New York and London: Routledge.

Burton-Jones, A. (1999) *Knowledge Capitalism: Business, Work and Learning in the New Economy.* Oxford and New York: Oxford University Press.

Castells, M. (1989) *The Informational City: Information Technology, Economic Restructuring and the Urban-Regional Process.* Oxford: Blackwell.

Castells, M. (1996) *The Information Age: Economy, Society and Culture. Volume 1: The Rise of the Network Society.* Oxford: Blackwell.

Castells, M. (1997) *The Information Age: Economy, Society and Culture. Volume 2: The Power of Identity.* Oxford: Blackwell.

Castells, M. (1998) *The Information Age: Economy, Society and Culture. Volume 3: End of Millennium.* Oxford: Blackwell.

Chalaris, G. (2003) Globalisation and the Network Society, in E. Katsoulis, M. Ananiadi and S. Ioannidis (eds) *Globalisation: Economic, Political and Cultural aspects.* Athens: Sideris, pp. 417–39.

Charalambis, D. (1998) *Democracy and Globalisation.* Athens: Karagiorgas Foundation.

Christiansen, T., Jorgensen, K. E. and Wiener, A. E. (2001) *The Social Construction of Europe.* London: Sage.

Coulby, D. and Jones, C. (1995) *Postmodernity and European Education Systems: Centralist Knowledge and Cultural Diversity.* Stoke on Trent: Trentham.

Crane, D., Kawashima, N. and Kawasaki, K. (eds) (2002) *Global Culture: Media, Arts, Policy and Globalisation.* New York and London: Routledge.

Davis, T. M. (2003) *Atlas of Student Mobility.* New York: Institute of International Education.

Etzkovitz, H. and Leydesdorff, L. (eds) (2001) *Universities and the Global Knowledge Economy: A Triple Helix of University–Industry–Government Relations.* London and New York: Continuum.

Featherstone, K. and Kazamias, G. (eds) (2001) *Europeanisation and the Southern Periphery.* London: Frank Cass.

Frobel, F. *et al.* (1988) *The New International Division of Labour*. Cambridge: Cambridge University Press.

Gabel, M. and Bruner, H. (2003) *Global Inc: An Atlas of the Multinational Corporation*. New York: The New Press.

Green, A. (2002) *Education, Globalisation and the Role of Comparative Research*. London: Institute of Education, University of London.

Hall, S., Held, D. and McGrew, T. (eds) (1992) *Modernity and its Futures*. Cambridge: Polity Press.

Held, D. and McGrew, A. (eds) (2000) *The Global Transformations Reader: An Introduction to the Globalization Debate*. Cambridge: Polity Press.

Held, D. and McGrew, A. (2002a) *Globalisation/Anti-Globalisation*. Cambridge: Polity Press.

Held, D. and McGrew, A. (eds) (2002b) *Governing Globalisation*. London: Polity Press.

Hertz, N. (2001) *The Silent Takeover: Global Capitalism and the Death of Democracy*. London: William Heinemann.

Hobsbawm, E. (1962) *The Age of Capital 1848–1875*. London: Weidenfeld & Nicolson.

Hobsbawm, E. (1987) *The Age of Empire 1875–1914*. London: Weidenfeld & Nicolson.

Hobsbawm, E. (1994) *Age of Extremes: The Short Twentieth Century 1914–1991*. London: Michael Joseph.

Kazamias, A. (2003) Globalisation and Paedeia in the New Kosmopolis: Hubris or Blessing? Reflections on Greece. *Comparative and International Education Review*, 1: 13–42.

Kelk, S. and Worth, J. (2002) *Trading it Away: How GATS Threatens UK Higher Education*. Oxford: People and Planet.

Klein, N. (2001) *No Logo*. London: Flamingo.

Klein, N. (2002) *Fences and Windows: Dispatches from the Front Lines of the Globalization Debate*. London: Flamingo.

Korres, G. and Tsombanoglou, G. (2003) Social Policy and Cohesion: Review of Outcomes and Impacts, in R. Panagiotopoulou, S. Koniordos and L. Maratou-Alibranti (eds) *Globalisation and Contemporary Society*. Athens: EKKE, pp. 153–73.

Kotzias, N. (2003) *Globalisation: The Historical Thesis, the Future and the Political Meaning*. Athens: Kastanioti.

Kress, G. (1996) Internationalisation and Globalisation: Rethinking a Curriculum of Communication. *Comparative Education (Special Number 18)*, 22(2): 185–96.

Lash, S. and Urry, J. (1994) *Economies of Signs and Space*. London: Sage.

Monbiot, G. (2001) *Captive State: The Corporate Takeover of Britain*. London: Pan Books.

Neef, D. (ed.) (1998) *The Knowledge Economy*. Boston, MA: Butterworth-Heinemann.

Negreponti-Delivanis, M. (2001) *Conspiring Globalisation*. Athens: Papazisi.

Photopoulos, T. (2002) *Globalisation, the Left and Inclusive Democracy*. Athens: Ellinika Grammata.

Pogge, T. W. (ed.) (2001) *Global Justice*. Oxford: Blackwell.

Rampton, S. and Stauber, J. (2003) Trading on Fear. *Guardian Weekly*, pp. 32–9.

Reynolds, D. (2001) *One World Divisible: A Global History Since 1945*. Harmondsworth: Penguin.

Ritter, S. and Pitt, W. R. (2002) *War on Iraq: What Team Bush Doesn't Want You to Know*. London: Profile Books.

Ritzer, G. (1993) *The McDonaldization of Society*. Thousand Oaks, CA: Pine Forge Press.

Rosenau, J. (2002) Governance in a New Global Order, in D. Held and A. McGrew (eds) *Governing Globalisation*. London: Polity Press, pp. 70–86.

SECE, K. G. S. (2003) *Cultural Identities and Globalisation*, Conference proceedings. Athens: Endelecheia.

Siedentop, L. (2000) *Democracy in Europe*. London: Penguin.

Stewart, T. A. (1997) *Intellectual Capital: The New Wealth of Organisations*. London: Nicholas Brearley Publishing.

Stiglitz, J. (2002) *Globalisation and its Discontents*. London: Penguin.

Stromquist, N. P. and Monkman, K. (eds) (2000) *Globalisation and Education: Integration and Contestation across Cultures*. Lanham: Rowman & Littlefield.

Thurow, L. (1999) *Creating Wealth: New Rules for Individuals, Companies and Countries in a Knowledge-Based Economy*. London: Nicholas Brearley Publishing.

Traynor, I. (2003) The Privatisation of War. *The Guardian*, 10 December, pp. 1–2.

Usher, R. and Edwards, R. (1994) *Postmodernism and Education*. London: Routledge.

Vergopoulos, K. (1999) *Globalisation: The Great Chimera*. Athens: Nea Synora – A. Livani.

Wilkinson, R. (2002) The Contours of Courtship: The WTO and Civil Society, in R. Wilkinson and S. Hughes (eds) *Global Governance: Critical Perspectives*. London: Routledge, pp. 193–211.

Wilkinson, R. and Hughes, S. (eds) (2002) *Global Governance: Critical Perspectives*. London: Routledge.

Witchit Srisa-an (2000) Universities and the International Knowledge Enterprise, in G. Neave (ed.) *The Universities' Responsibilities to Society: International Perspectives*. Oxford: Pergamon, pp. 141–9.

Wolf, M. (2003) Economic Globalisation: An Unfinished Revolution. *Financial Times Special Report: The World 2003*, 23 January, p. III.

Young, R. (1990) *White Mythologies: Writing History and the West*. London: Routledge.

Young, R. J. C. (1995) *Colonial Desire: Hybridity in Theory, Culture and Race*. London: Routledge.

Part I

Globalization and the knowledge economy

1 The knowledge economy
Technology and characteristics

David Coulby

Introduction

A change is taking place in the global economy. It is simultaneously becoming more internationalized and more centred on knowledge. As always when there are changes in the economy, there will be resulting changes in society and not least in education. But the current tranche of rapid and wide-ranging changes actually involves knowledge, the subject of education itself. To this extent schools and university curricula ought to be at the forefront of the implementation of these developments (Burton-Jones, 1999; Etzkovitz and Leydesdorff, 2001; Neef, 1998; Witchit Srisa-an, 2000). This chapter examines, among other things, the extent to which this is actually the case. The chapter begins the exploration of the development of the knowledge economy as a central educational feature of the processes of globalization described in the Introduction. The emergence of the knowledge economy brings together many of the characteristics of globalized education itemized in Chapter 3. This chapter and the next explore globalization and education, especially higher education, from the perspective of a description and analysis of the knowledge economy. The nature of this focus means that they are primarily dealing with education in the MEDCs and especially in the triad states of Japan, the USA and the EU.

This chapter attempts, in the first part, to spell out what the significant technological changes actually are and will be and to outline, in a preliminary way, some of their impacts on knowledge, especially at university level. In the second part it attempts to look, not to the obvious infrastructural implications or indeed to the curricular changes commensurate with rapid digital development (these are taken up in Chapter 2), but rather to the ways in which technological changes have intellectually impacted within educational institutions and beyond. These characteristics of the knowledge economy may give insights into the wider changes that technology is inscribing on patterns of teaching, learning and research.

The everyday impact of digital technology on education is so deep and widespread that it is easy to ignore some of the more subtle epistemological and institutional changes. The ongoing need for new technology in schools and universities has added a significant new call on their budgets. This is not simply a matter of buying grey boxes. The electrical and networking cabinet needs to be in place and computers are often only a small part of the cost of an ICT suite. Furthermore, skilled teachers and technicians are needed to maintain and upgrade these networks as well as to teach their manifold applications to pupils and students. This makes schools and universities important consumers as well as producers in the knowledge economy. Schools and universities are running more ICT courses and incorporating more elements of ICT into a wide and increasing range of programmes and subject teaching.

In a sense, these technical changes appear straightforward and in need of little explanation. But the development, say, by UK universities of foundation courses in remote Chinese cities is also in large part a product of the knowledge economy. They, along with universities from the USA, Australia and New Zealand, are able to do this on a large scale and with considerable impact both on the career opportunities of students in Shenyang and on the financial well-being of those anglophone universities. What are the technological arrangements and characteristics that make these changes possible? How are the international patterns of knowledge and especially higher educational knowledge, their mode of organization and their discursive strategies of self-justification being transformed in these processes?

The chapter raises post-Marxist questions about the extent of technological determinism with regard to social and epistemological changes. Technical developments inevitably affect education. Once steam engines came into general use then people needed to be taught, at the workplace or in schools or universities, how best to manufacture, maintain and utilize them. Further, they needed to be taught how to develop the technology and how to apply it to an increasing range of activities of production, consumption and distribution. The general spread of mathematics, science and technology teaching, the introduction of technical apprenticeships and the opening of university engineering departments followed the spread of the various waves of the Industrial Revolution into almost all states (Hobsbawm, 1962, 1975, 1987). The industrial system and its associated division of labour impacted on the shape of society in a similarly widespread fashion. These movements were not only one-way. As educational institutions developed in sophistication they were able to impact back on the technology through research and development of products and practices. Similarly, the social organization of capitalism, especially in its association with urbanization (King, 1990), created the need for further technical developments in areas such as mass transportation and mass communication. The social implications of the

Industrial Revolution were vast and irreversible. Its educational implications, although more gradual and less shocking, were also of major significance. The impact of the technologies described in this chapter is taking place in many areas of production, distribution, consumption and control. Educational institutions are a prime site of these changes, the speed of which is much more rapid than earlier impacts of technological development.

The focus of this chapter on the characteristics of the knowledge economy allows it to emphasize the ways in which cultural practices and institutions, not least schools and universities themselves, have served to mediate the raw technology. To this extent the roles of schools and universities in the knowledge economy and the nature of the characteristics identified here are components of significant social and cultural change, as the technological innovations that have accompanied globalization, variously mediated, impact on wide areas of human thought and behaviour. Of course there are areas of education, such as some school curricular systems, as well as other aspects of society, which are either unaffected by the forces of globalization or actively resistant to them. These are considered in Chapters 3, 4, 10 and 11 as the second theme of this volume, that of nationalism, is taken up. This volume suggests that state-sponsored nationalism is a major factor in the formation of curricular systems, especially at school level. These nationalist curricula may actually inhibit the ability of school systems to adapt to the knowledge economy. This adaptation is then a further manifestation of the conflict between tradition and modernity within educational institutions.

Technological changes and the knowledge economy

This section concentrates on four technological changes. Three are relatively new: the internet, mobile telephony and satellite broadcasting and telephony. One, international jet travel, is currently in apparent resurgence. The wider aspects of the spread of ICT (that is, beyond the internet) and its associated applications are not explored in depth. (They form the topic of the *World Yearbook of Education 2004.*) These four technologies, with their capacity for ready international communication, are more obviously associated with globalization. This is not to deny the impact of other areas of technological change, especially those associated with ICT, on globalization and education. Indeed, these are considered in other chapters in this volume, such as Chapter 2.

The *internet* is now a key component of school and university life experienced on a daily basis by pupils, teachers, students and academics in a growing number of states. The British Library catalogue, Eurostat, central and local government databanks and archives, digital journals, satellite imagery: the list of resources is exhaustive and rapidly growing. In many cases the quality as well as the quantity of data is outstanding.

It is frequently updated at a speed that can only be competed with by weekly journals like *New Scientist*. The speed of getting to and working on the web has increased dramatically especially for those working in hub institutions such as universities, but broadband telephony is making practicable and rapid access ever more widely available.

It is little more than a truism to say that, in the triad states, ICT, and particularly the internet, have brought about a sequence of transformations of universities in terms of teaching, learning, research, use of resources and indeed physical layout and appearance. Similar transformations are taking place in schools but at a much slower pace. This slowness may be the consequence of the large financial investment required or it may, as is suggested in Chapter 2, be because school curricular systems are actually resistant to these transformations. Because of the great expense of the provision, ICT has probably steepened the hierarchy between universities both within national systems and internationally. Digital deficit can disadvantage institutions as well as families. Those institutions that do not have waiting suites of machines ready for students to log on will be increasingly less popular. Again, this distinction is less important in schools, where other hierarchies and privileges of provision, associated with class and 'race', remain firmly in place.

Mobile phones appear to be changing both the means and the mode of communication. The amount of disposable income now spent on telephony (more than on entertainment for UK students), the development of text and text language, and the unapologetic intrusion of the phones into so many areas of social, domestic and intellectual life, all point to a transformation of the conceptualization of conversation. Third-generation mobiles have brought net-to-phone access in a way previously problematic. While this technology is still far from perfect in Europe, in Japan mobile phones are a principal way of accessing the net, especially for young people. Websites have been redesigned so that they are easy to read and use on the limited displays of mobile phones.

Furthermore, these machines will soon interface with computers in the way that some hand-held machines now do, providing easily updated, portable databases and communication records. The convergence of mobiles with computers, digital cameras and video, digitalized music and speech programmes, email and the internet allows new potentials in data recording, access and interchange, as well as in social and political control. It expands the nature and amount of data that can be stored and retrieved (photos and video, speech and music are now part of this technology) and vastly increases its accessibility. The personal computer or the local area network then become the repository of data, images and sounds which can then be accessed and updated via mobile devices for purposes of work and leisure. Costs are likely to continue to reduce in an industry that sees itself as being at the forefront of globalization.

This should make this technology available to a wider group of people in a larger number of states. Finally, mobile telephony, like the internet, is a technology that seems to be particularly attractive and transparent to young people. As such, it is becoming part of the school and university life despite the control regimes of secondary schools and the conservatism of some academics.

Satellite technology involves telephony as well as broadcasting, though it is the latter that is discussed here. Again, the amount of available material and its accessibility are striking: hundreds of channels in a range of languages available 24 hours a day around the world, some as free access, some as subscription and some as pay to view. At present there is apparently little controlling principle beyond profit, but this does not mean universal poor quality. This is not to disregard the poor quality of Sky's broadcasting as well as its almost global monopoly. The 'voice-of-America' discourse of CNN similarly hardly assists an internationalist view of current issues. (Sky's Fox News hit previously uncontemplated levels of bias during the second Iraq War with American tanks filmed advancing towards Baghdad to the accompaniment of 'The Star-Spangled Banner'). Indeed, some of the pernicious effects of poor-quality digital broadcasting (Scott-Clark and Levy, 2003) form a sub-theme of several chapters in this volume. But other sides of satellite broadcasting are less easy to dismiss. There is worldwide access to news beyond CNN and from a variety of national and indeed religious perspectives; there are specialist channels for information as well as entertainment; and there are increasing numbers of non-English language channels. Many of these channels are provided as a public service and are free to view. In this area too there is convergence with computers, email and the internet, currently largely mediated by DVDs with their vast storage capacity, opening up new academic as well as commercial possibilities.

Jet travel is not a new technology but one currently resilient on the basis of unsustainably low petrol prices resulting from recent discoveries of new oil deposits. That these discoveries will in fact not extend the life of the fossil fuel economy (to be measured in decades, still, not centuries) has not discouraged the enthusiasm of airlines, aircraft manufacturers, airport authorities or indeed passengers. In Europe, low-cost air travel subsidized by artificially low fuel prices and struggling regional airports has led to a boom in flying as middle-class couples in Frankfurt and Bristol take weekend breaks in Barcelona and Prague. New airports, runways, terminals, rapid transit links and the Jumbo Airbus A380 are all recently developed or in the process of planning. The new Hong Kong airport, completed just before the territories became part of the People's Republic, is now a major national and international hub for the rapidly developing Shenzen and Guangzhou industrial areas of southeast China. Heathrow now has a rapid transit to Paddington railway station; a fifth terminal as big as all the existing four put together is being built; and a third runway is planned. The resurgence of jet travel is mentioned alongside the newer technologies just described because it is germane to the theme of internationalization mentioned in the final section of this chapter.

Aspects of these technologies are cultural as well as material. They are themselves major items of consumption and they have influenced lifestyles and leisure as well as the organization of the workplace and educational institutions. The web, mobiles, laptops and international travel are indeed fashion items. The market for at least the last three focuses on glamour. Advertisements for one of these technologies often feature another. The web has changed the way in which people shop and play as much as the way in which they learn. Mobile phones have changed the very basis of human conversation and, along with email, have expanded the extent and quantity of communication and indeed the ways in which human beings relate to one another. Satellite broadcasting is spreading and increasing the ways in which television has transformed leisure and recreation and become for many – for better or worse – the main element of their culture.

This stress on new technologies is not to imply that globalization has brought about a total technological transformation. Old communication technologies, like traditionalist knowledge, and indeed like its associated nationalism, survive and, in some cases, prosper. Books, newspapers, magazines and journals are thriving both in terms of the expanding range of titles and specializations and in terms of the absolute increase in sales. Whether this vitality will continue under pressure from increased hours of television watching and digitalized entertainment and information gathering remains to be seen. In the triad states at least, museums and exhibitions expand, both in number and (selective) popularity. Terrestrial television seems set to survive in many states and satellite reception has still not completed global coverage. These terrestrial broadcasters are often state-controlled and state (nation)-supporting. Political interest in controlling television broadcasting (in Italy, say, or China) may be as vested as the not unrelated political control of traditionalist knowledge.

Characteristics of the knowledge economy

Characteristics here implies the common features, or better the modes of organization, of the knowledge and the knowledge economy brought about by, or at least with, these technological transformations. These knowledge characteristics are important to understanding the transformations in education and more general patterns of communication and discourse brought about by the rapid introduction of new technology, four components of which have been identified in the last section.

The economic transformations of globalization brought about alongside the development of these technologies have been outlined in the Introduction. The knowledge economy is not exclusively technologically determined but mediated by these economic transformations and their associated social, cultural and political changes. In these terms the knowledge economy may then be seen as an important epistemological aspect of globalization. Some knowledge characteristics, of course, remain, for the moment, unchanged: elitist hierarchies of educational institutions and parallel (but not fixed) hierarchies of knowledge.

The remainder of this chapter is concerned with identifying and analysing four characteristics of this knowledge economy: accessibility, superabundance, marketization and internationalization.

Accessibility obviously characterizes the new epistemology. It is not just the amount of data now available (discussed next under *superabundance*), but the ease with which it can be accessed. And data here of course is meant in its widest interpretation. Large and ever increasing amounts of data are available internationally, at home, at work and on the move. This ease of access raises in new forms the issues concerning curricular selection on the one hand and, by no means unconnected, political censorship on the other. If photocopiers were one of the causes of the downfall of the Soviet Union, how long could it have survived the internet and satellite television? The People's Republic of China attempts to ban the BBC news channels and even its website. Such political attempts to restrict knowledge are likely to prove increasingly futile. Broadcasts can be jammed, but the web is more difficult to restrict and, once someone has the web, they of course have access to the broadcasts.

The criteria in the selection and restriction of knowledge become increasingly visible not least in higher education. Modularization and student choice are only one aspect of this. High-achieving students, with their access to the internet, are increasingly aware of the ways in which university knowledge is truncated by disciplinary boundaries, workplace expectations and constraints in terms of time and equipment. Open access to knowledge problematizes the arbitrariness of curricular selection. For schools and, especially, further and higher education the possibilities for open and distance learning (ODL) are considerably enhanced by accessibility. The paper-free module has already arrived and the paper-free degree is on the way. The implications of technologically geared ODL stretch beyond the mode of delivery. Universities are currently addressing the issue of whether course materials should be lodged within secure areas of their websites or whether they should be open to all, staff, students and the general public. This debate is increasingly addressed in terms of wide access, open discourse and the transparency (or opacity) of university knowledge. In the face of accessibility, some universities and academics have retreated to the posture of clerical defenders of the sacred and secret knowledge. There are of course economic as well as theological and political considerations to the control of accessibility and these are identified in the conclusion to this chapter.

The second characteristic of the knowledge economy is *superabundance*: of information, analysis, entertainment; of discourse, images, music and communication; and of meaning and meaninglessness, truth and error. In the prison camp at Pisa, and en route to St Elizabeth's Mental Hospital in Washington, Ezra Pound declared that 'civilisation is individual'. This is one of those brilliant statements (returned to in Chapter 14) that is entirely true and at the same time entirely false. It is true to a psychologist, say, and yet false to a sociologist obviously. The superabundance of knowledge can lead to a particularistic, individual epistemology where knowledge is not even relativistic (again, see Chapter 14) or anarchic but actually solipsistic. The limits of postmodernity are stretched here. The following by no means exhaustive list gives a range of personalized files:

- the databases and diaries stored in *Outlook*;
- the bibliographies and disk lists kept in, say, *Endnote*;
- music files stored either from compact disks or downloaded from the web;
- the 'favourite' websites stored and filed in each individual's browser,
- collections of photographs related to family and/or profession;
- films, personal video clips and multimedia archives.

These serve to store and codify individual knowledge so that it can be instantly retrieved and so that one element can complement and combine with others in the composition of, say:

- an email letter to an academic, commercial or recreational reference group;
- a school assignment;
- a video diary;
- a multimedia marketing presentation;
- or a personal website.

The personal website indeed is the best evidence of the massification of Pound's individual civilization. As print media are increasingly digitalized, the possibilities of the endless syntheses and recommodifications of individual civilization are being infinitely enhanced.

An alternative response to superabundance is that it can also lead to the opposite of individual knowledge, rather to the deliberate cultivation of the currently popular and the widely accepted. In this scenario texts and media, preferably written by a television 'personality', photogenic daughter of an ex-premier or by a fashion model or football star, take on a life of their own and the subject matter – a cookbook or popular music programme – becomes less important than the popularised wrapping. This wrapping is accepted not because each individual viewer or reader actually subscribes to the admiration of the 'celebrity' concerned, but rather because the very popularity itself makes the commodity desirable. The same popularity principle can be applied to the choice of primary school, and to university courses, restaurants, pairs of jeans and soap operas. In this second response to superabundance fashionability becomes an epistemological principle. This may not be radically new but it is unprecedentedly pervasive and widespread.

Paradoxically, people appear to be operating both these apparently contradictory responses to the epistemology of superabundance simultaneously. The response is both to cultivate the minutiae of individualistic civilization and to follow the current popular cult of reading, viewing or sport coverage. It is possible that there is a class dimension to these two responses. The educated and affluent might tend more to the infinite, fetishistic discriminations of individual civilization, while the less privileged accept the commodified 'celebrity' culture of the mass market.

The third and related characteristic of the knowledge economy concerns the way in which knowledge is increasingly subjected to the globalized forces of *marketization*. Popularity is the measure of success: the number of hits on a website, the number of sales of an academic book or the number of applicants for a school or for a university course. Again, the issue of fashion can be important: a popular television series can boost the numbers of students applying for university courses in veterinary sciences or psychology. By contrast, if students do not want them, they close. While physics and genetics in the UK have been making important theoretical breakthroughs, many university departments in these subjects have actually closed for lack of applicants (Fazackerley, 2003). Science departments in the UK have actually polarized across the last three decades. The most prestigious departments remain highly competitive and selective but, beyond the top three or four universities, science is the easiest subject in which to obtain a place.

Advertisements on local radio and on the sides of buses, reception tables for students at the start of the academic year at international airports, and Chinese government attempts to limit the number of educational official agents, all proclaim that higher education is in the market place, and increasingly in the international market place. The discrete exhibition of primary children's artwork in the doctor's surgery, the well-practised dance routine at the local carnival and the timely press release to the city newspaper proclaim a similar if less voracious market for schools. In England (but not, any longer, in Scotland or Wales) league tables are available at national level for all educational institutions from infant schools to university departments (MacLeod and Lipsett, 2003). Accessibility has given parents, pupils, students and, for that matter, teachers and academics, greater transparency in selecting which knowledge and which institutions to favour. This selection itself is increasingly conducted, especially at postgraduate level, on an international basis. Marketization implies slightly more than a market in education. (Government quotas such as maximum school numbers or, at university level, *numerus clausus* policies in particular subjects usually impair any notion of a perfect market in education.) Marketization further suggests that what parents at school level want and, especially, students at university level want will rapidly become institutionalized knowledge — for example, a foundation degree in aromatherapy was created and began in a UK university in September 2002.

The fourth and final characteristic identified within the knowledge economy is *internationalization*. Knowledge and culture at all levels, from supermarket food to financial data analysis, is becoming increasingly internationalized. English supermarkets carry a bewildering diversity of choice in balsamic vinegars. The Japanese language editions of *The Wall Street Journal* and *The Financial Times* compete for their elite readers. The following commodities and activities, from an almost infinite variety, all operate at an international level:

- sport, especially football;
- glossy magazines from *The Economist* to *Cosmopolitan*;
- fast food outlets;
- films from Hollywood, Mumbai and Cairo;
- university courses in terms of both recruitment, especially but by no means exclusively in anglophone countries, and curriculum content;
- automobile design, racing, construction, marketing and recycling;
- the Catholic Church.

Indeed, apart from its casual amusement level, this list itself is banal precisely because so many activities and products are international. While the positive side of this can be the richness associated with cosmopolitan culture, the negative side concerns globalization and the homogenizing McDonaldization discussed in the Introduction. Either way, serious investment cannot be expected in a new training shoe or a new MBA unless an international market is anticipated. With few, though remarkable exceptions (Royal Ministry of Education Research and Church Affairs (Norway), 1997), this internationalization is not a phenomenon at school level in terms of either pupil admissions or curricular content. The dichotomy between schools and universities with regard to their involvement in the knowledge economy is explored in Chapter 2.

It is in terms of recruitment and content that the internationalization of higher education is at its most visible (Burton-Jones, 1999; van Rooijen *et al.*, 2003; Witchit Srisa-an 2000). Universities in the anglophone countries (the UK, the USA, Ireland, Canada, Australia and New Zealand) now recruit not only from each other but also on a global basis (Davis, 2003). There is competition not only at an institutional level but also between entire systems as Australia and the UK in particular conduct vigorous campaigns of international recruitment (British Council, 2004). Germany (where higher education is still free), the Netherlands and France have begun to enter this market. This multi-million-pound enterprise has led many students to study outside their own countries. At undergraduate level these students represent diverse subjects and levels of attainment. At postgraduate level, however, where they are increasingly concentrated, they are a more homogeneous group, consisting of high attainers as well as the very wealthy and studying subjects such as science, engineering, design, economics and management. The long-term consequences for the sender countries of having their future elites educated in anglophone universities are yet to be assessed. Some of the possibilities of this form of internationalization are discussed in terms of post-colonialism in Chapter 14.

In terms of degree content it might be thought that the consequences of internationalization might be more progressive with a more cosmopolitan and intercultural approach adopted to curriculum selection. To a certain extent this trend can be identified. Against this there is some homogenization in higher educational content, which has accelerated with the demise of Soviet knowledge in 1991. Economics, politics, philosophy and indeed sociology are now seen in a more unified and constrained way. Similarly, with the expansion of the Western clinic, medicine is increasingly seen from only this perspective (see Chapter 8). Above all, the spread of the English language, not only as a first foreign language but also as the language of instruction for international classes and also in some science, engineering and business degree courses, is a homogenizing influence in the internationalization of higher education. Non-anglophone countries are increasingly developing modules or even whole academic years where a range of subjects is taught in English. This facilitates exchange within Europe under the SOCRATES scheme (so that Greek undergraduates can be taught about Danish history and culture in English) as well as encouraging more international recruitment.

Conclusion

The globalization of finance and the internationalization of knowledge have taken place simultaneously. But this does not necessarily mean that either one has caused the other. Rather, the technologies described in the first section of this chapter have facilitated both just as each has assisted the development of the other. As knowledge and finance become increasingly entwined (the knowledge economy) they begin to impact more directly and more forcefully on each other than has been the case in the past. The research needed to produce third-generation mobiles or Eurofighters could not be conducted without substantial private investment. The conflict between universities and corporations over copyrights within genetic engineering reveals, among other things, the extent to which scientific and financial interests are mutually supportive and destructive.

At this point it may be possible to see that the anti-globalization protesters who currently seem to grace every gathering of world leaders are not just a collection of young hooligans who have failed to recognize that capitalism is now the only show in town. The relationship between (capitalist) finance and (capitalist) knowledge and who has the ability to control these in whose interests are precisely and accurately the issues of contestation. One strand of anti-globalization protest is founded on opposition to restricted and homogenized knowledge in schools and universities as well as in the media (Bruno and Karliner, 2002; Burbules and Torres, 2000; Hertz, 2001; Kelk and Worth, 2002; Klein, 2001, 2002; Monbiot, 2001; Sardar and Davies, 2002; Wolf, 2003).

Political actors have also played their part in the process of internationalization not least with regard to higher education. ERASMUS, SOCRATES and TEMPUS programmes have provided an impulse for the Europeanization of students, universities and their courses and research agenda. The Norwegian government provides generous grants for students to study abroad as well as premiums for students who come to Norway. One and a half million Chinese students have sought degrees in other countries in the last ten years. This is partly due to the concerns of one-child Chinese families to invest in the little emperors and little empresses, but it is also due to an absolute shortfall of university places in the People's Republic. The restrictive policies in higher education in other countries such as Greece have led to similar student exports (more accurately described as knowledge and skills imports). At the other end of the market some states, as mentioned above, actively seek to recruit students internationally. In the case of the UK the contribution of universities to the knowledge economy is, in one respect, quite straightforward: fees derived from international students represent a highly successful 'export', worth about seven billion pounds per year to the economy.

This example again emphasizes that internationalization is partly to do with the spread of English as a global second language and this has certainly facilitated the process in many regions. But internationalization involves more than the English language, more indeed than the globalization of the knowledge economy itself. Hybridity and fusion in many forms and domains are increasingly actively pursued within and outside educational institutions. The modes of analysis of post-colonial discourse theory are applied to increasingly wide areas of university intellectual activity. Postmodern cultural products and modes of analysis are gradually achieving curricular acceptance and critical acclaim at school as well as university level. And the homogenizing effects of internationalization are not totally achieved, not even in universities. There may be only one science but there are still many medicines as well as many musics.

References

British Council (2004) *Educating UK: Positioning for Success*. Consultation document. London: British Council.

Bruno, K. and Karliner, J. (2002) *earthsummit.biz: The Corporate Takeover of Sustainable Development*. Oakland, CA: Food First Books.

Burbules, N. C. and Torres, C. A. (eds) (2000) *Globalisation and Education: Critical Perspectives*. New York and London: Routledge.

Burton-Jones, A. (1999) *Knowledge Capitalism: Business, Work and Learning in the New Economy*. Oxford and New York: Oxford University Press.

Davis, T. M. (2003) *Atlas of Student Mobility*. New York: Institute of International Education.

Etzkovitz, H. and Leydesdorff, L. (eds) (2001) *Universities and the Global Knowledge Economy: A Triple Helix of University–Industry–Government Relations*. London and New York: Continuum.

Fazackerley, A. (2003) Science Dies Out in English 'Deserts', *Times Higher Educational Supplement*, 11 July, p. 56.

Hertz, N. (2001) *The Silent Takeover: Global Capitalism and the Death of Democracy*. London: William Heinemann.

Hobsbawm, E. (1962) *The Age of Capital 1848–1875*. London: Weidenfeld & Nicolson.

Hobsbawm, E. (1975) *The Age of Revolution 1789–1848*. London: Weidenfeld & Nicolson.

Hobsbawm, E. (1987) *The Age of Empire 1875–1914*. London: Weidenfeld & Nicolson.

Kelk, S. and Worth, J. (2002) *Trading it Away: How GATS Threatens UK Higher Education*. Oxford: People and Planet.

King, A. D. (1990) *Urbanism, Colonialism and the World Economy: Cultural and Spatial Foundations of the World Urban System*. London: Routledge & Kegan Paul.

Klein, N. (2001) *No Logo*. London: Flamingo.

Klein, N. (2002) *Fences and Windows: Dispatches from the Front Lines of the Globalization Debate*. London: Flamingo.

MacLeod, D. and Lipsett, A. M. (2003) Tested to Destruction. *Guardian Education*, 15 July, p. 9.

Monbiot, G. (2001) *Captive State: The Corporate Takeover of Britain*. London: Pan Books.

Neef, D. (ed.) (1998) *The Knowledge Economy*. Boston, MA: Butterworth-Heinemann.

Royal Ministry of Education Research and Church Affairs (Norway) (1997) *Core Curriculum for Primary, Secondary and Adult Education in Norway*. Oslo: National Centre for Educational Resources.

Sardar, Z. and Davies, M. W. (2002) *Why Do People Hate America?* Cambridge: Icon Books.

Scott-Clark, C. and Levy, A. (2003) Fast Forward into Trouble. *Guardian Weekend*, 14 June, pp. 14–20.

van Rooijen, M., Jones, D. R. and Adam, S. (2003) *The Multinational University* (EAIE occasional paper 15). Amsterdam: European Association for International Education (EAIE).

Witchit Srisa-an (2000) Universities and the International Knowledge Enterprise, in G. Neave (ed.) *The Universities' Responsibilities to Society: International Perspectives*. Pergamon: Oxford, pp. 141–9.

Wolf, M. (2003) Economic Globalisation: An Unfinished Revolution. *Financial Times Special Report: The World 2003*, 23 January, p. III.

2 The knowledge economy
Institutions

David Coulby

Knowledge economy institutions: general

As described in Chapter 1, changes to the globalized economy mean that it is becoming simultaneously more internationalized and more centred on a superabundance of widely accessible knowledge. Castells ties economic and social change more directly to technology than was attempted in the previous chapter. More than many theorists of globalization, he is convinced of the magnitude of the transformation that globalization represents: 'at the end of the twentieth century, we are living through one of those rare intervals in history. An interval characterised by the transformation of our "material culture" by the works of a new technological paradigm organised around information technologies' (Castells, 1996, p. 29). As always, when there are changes in the economy, there will be resulting changes in society (as discussed in the Introduction) and not least in education. But the current tranche of rapid and wide-ranging changes actually involves knowledge, albeit marketized knowledge, the subject of education itself. To this extent schools and university curricula ought to be at the forefront of the implementation of these developments. This chapter examines, among other things, the extent to which this is actually the case, and whether a new relationship between knowledge and the global market place has developed in these traditionalistic institutions.

The chapter provides a different focus on the knowledge economy by initially looking at changes which are taking place at the level of investment, production, distribution and consumption and the new skills necessary to the implementation of these changes. It then considers knowledge itself as an item of world trade. Finally, it considers universities and schools separately since their responses to the emergence of the knowledge economy appear to be markedly different.

The new skills, which are of great value in the market place, involve the ability to place components of knowledge together in a meaningful and profitable way. (This section draws on the essays in Neef, 1998.)

They are not the old style skills of one-off design where a brilliant prototype can proceed to production. They involve the ongoing modification
and improvement of the product and its development to whole new sets
of applications – consider the progress from MS DOS to the latest version
of Windows. The second set of skills are those required to understand
how a given product or set of services can be utilized and sold in a
variety of contexts. This is not merely a matter of sales and marketing:
it requires a genuine and detailed knowledge of the customer's business
and how it can be improved. It can indeed involve knowing the customer's business better than they know it themselves. The skills concern
the identification of opportunities and the implementation of innovation.
Universities, for instance, choose a software package to control student
choices in a modular scheme, but are then shown how adaptations to
the same software can help them track the payment of student fees
and the control of library stock. The third set of skills concerns problem
identification and solution conventionally associated with entrepreneurialism. It is the skill to be able to see the combination of market
opportunity, line of financing and range of technical applications and
facilities that will bring about not so much a new product as a whole
new and expanding range of consumption opportunities. Rather than
being financiers or conventional managers, people with such skills are
managers of ideas. These are the skills needed to develop, finance and
launch the English Premiere League, say, or a new digital broadcasting
corporation or the Eurofighter or a themed holiday resort.

The globalized economy that is based on these skills is effectively one
where services have replaced goods. The actual manufacture, even of
complex machines, is of decreasing importance. 'In 1984, 80 percent of
the cost of a computer was in its hardware, 20 percent in software; by
1990, the proportions were just the reverse' (Reich in Neef, 1998, p. 48).
High profit enterprises in the emerging knowledge economy are thus
involved in services: 'the specialised research, engineering, and design
services necessary to solve problems; the specialised sales, marketing,
and consulting services necessary to identify problems; and the specialised strategic, financial, and management services of brokering the first
two' (p. 50). Within such an economy managers are no longer responsible principally for people but for the gathering, organization and
evaluation of knowledge.

The knowledge needed to sustain and develop such enterprises and
to train and update such managers is, in two important ways, international. First, it is being generated and reproduced in a multitude
of centres around the world; these are principally in the triad states
but also in places such as South Korea and Singapore (Castells, 1989,
1996, 1997, 1998). Second, the centres where it is developed and reproduced (universities certainly, but also the research and development
branches of transnational corporations and of state governments) are

internationalized in terms of their staffing, their students and researchers and their curricula and knowledge and research projects. Knowledge, like finance, people and goods and services is involved in international flows (Lash and Urry, 1994).

The production, evaluation and exchange of knowledge are increasingly important global economic activities, to the extent that knowledge may be becoming the world's most important and valuable trading commodity. In response to this, the triad states and others are attempting, with varying degrees of determination, to transform themselves into smart states. This aspiration towards the smart state (Blunkett, 1999) obviously has profound implications for the curricula of schools and universities. At one level it is obvious enough to assert that knowledge is an important trading commodity. Nor is this a new phenomenon. Knowledge of silk-weaving or of rubber-tapping has moved across the world, making and marring fortunes in the process. From the beginning of the Industrial Revolution, if not earlier, the knowledge of the skilled mechanic has had its global market as the worldwide spread of Scottish engineers well testifies. But this process has now both widened and deepened with the globalization of the economy and the superabundance of knowledge. It now applies to an exceedingly wide range of types of expertise from nuclear physics to the staging of grand opera. The number of skills and areas of expertise within even one activity, such as banking, marketing or genetic engineering, has also expanded dramatically.

Knowledge has emerged as a major trading commodity in the globalized economy. Knowledge and knowledge-based processes both underpin material production and are themselves becoming ever more important aspects of production and consumption. Knowledge of armament developments, pharmaceutical production and medical techniques are highly sought after across the world. Design, and subsequently marketing, of clothing, cars or food can be more remunerative than their actual manufacture or sale. The add-on value of 'aestheticisation' (Lash and Urry, 1994), often located in triad centres such as London, New York or Milan, generates greater profits than the actual mass manufacture of the commodities concerned which often takes place in LEDCs. The media and publications industries now look to global, multimedia production with a string of associated, franchised products. The design of software and operating and filing systems and the convergence of ICT, broadcasting and telephony, described in Chapter 1, have facilitated the mushrooming of global monopolies. The economies of some of the states of the EU and of the USA are gradually shifting to this knowledge production and reproduction. Important institutions in this knowledge economy include:

- television, music and film studios, often operating on a small-scale, franchised basis;

- publishing houses, including the production of the proliferating specialist magazines on themes such as sport, computing and leisure;
- research and development facilities, especially in ICT, genetics, pharmaceuticals and systems design;
- fashion houses and associated designer labels with large-scale marketing industries which can attach them to a whole bundle of products and activities;
- finance houses and law and accountancy firms, increasingly concentrated and operating on an international basis;
- specialist journal and conference networks, including those associated with higher education;
- not least, schools, colleges, universities and research institutes.

Of course, all of these themselves have consumption implications, from local area networks and sound studio equipment to exotic restaurants, which further the shift towards the quaternary, knowledge economy (Zukin, 1988, 1991, 1995).

The movement of pupils and students about the world means that schools and, much more significantly, universities, are themselves traders in knowledge as a commodity. There is stiff competition between universities in the anglophone countries to attract students from other states. These universities, either directly through campuses or franchise arrangements with other institutions, or indirectly through agencies, have significant marketing facilities in states as various as Malaysia, India and Greece. The English language more than the standards of the universities in the anglophone states means that they are attractive to students from a global market place. It is the high fees charged to such students, much more than any policy towards internationalization, which makes them so attractive (for references see Chapter 1). At undergraduate and Master's level, as well as in the form of Ph.D.s, universities are selling knowledge on a world market. A previous Secretary of State for Education and Employment in the UK cited 'the education and training industry' as 'earning' seven billion pounds per year in 'exports' (Blunkett, 1999) for that country.

There are at least two distinct aspects to the emergence of this knowledge economy which are important to states and their educational institutions. First, there is the amount of knowledge which a particular state can generate via its business institutions, research centres and universities; the relevance of this knowledge to the processes of production, distribution and consumption; and the extent to which this knowledge is marketable and renewable. While the relevant areas of knowledge in the past have included finance, industrial production, technology and medicine, in the present and the future they will also increasingly concern the development and application of ICT, genetics and aesthetics. Second, there is the relative quantity of this super-abundant knowledge which the workforce of a given society can mobilize in economic activity; and the extent to which any state has succeeded in becoming a 'smart' society. In the first category the USA is obviously a state that has been successful in generating large amounts of productive knowledge. It is more difficult to point to a successful example in the second category, though Singapore and Finland seem to be doing better than the USA or the other European states in educating a large proportion of their populations to a high degree of productivity within the knowledge economy.

Educational institutions in the knowledge economy: vocational training and universities

In the USA and Western Europe, the shift to globalization and the knowledge economy has been accompanied by anxiety about the curriculum, especially that of schools and vocational training institutions. The form of this anxiety has frequently been a perception of a dissonance between the nature of the school and/or vocational curriculum on the one hand and the needs of the workplace on the other in terms of particular knowledge, skills and demeanour. The exception here has long been Germany, where the vocational education system is widely admired. Smith, for instance (in Neef, 1998) cites Thurow as seeing the education of those who do not go to university as being 'the German secret weapon' (p. 231). He believes that:

> after you get through a German apprenticeship training program, you're simply the best educated person in the world at your level. They turn out an absolutely world-class worker, and it allows them to make very sophisticated products, use very sophisticated machine tools, and operate technologies at levels that the rest of the world finds impossible to operate.
>
> (p. 231)

Smith and other commentators, perhaps too readily, link this strength in training to the success of the German economy. The story is of course more complicated, referring to patterns of investment, post-war renewal and the fact that Germany's economy remains much more concentrated on manufacture than those of the UK, France or the Netherlands (Marsden and Ryan, 1995). Furthermore, the unemployment rate in Germany at nearly 10 per cent is currently twice that of the USA, the UK or Finland. Nevertheless, the importance of the commitment of German industry and commerce to the maintenance of the high-quality apprenticeship scheme is almost universally admired and envied.

Nevertheless, the UK presents the paradigm case for anxiety about dissonance between school curriculum and economic needs. Policies introduced as a consequence of this anxiety in the UK and other triad states have included:

- attempts by states to centralize and control the curriculum;
- an emphasis on (often narrowly defined) vocational skills;
- a stress on basic skills of literacy and numeracy, which has been accompanied in both the UK and the USA by a restatement of traditionalistic values ('back to basics');
- a renewed emphasis on social skills and social ceremonies (graduation day), the techniques of deference and demeanour.

The response to globalization has been to attempt to make the curricula of schools and vocational institutions more relevant to those skills and practices apparently needed in the workplace (Bash and Green, 1995).

These 'reforms' might have served to supply appropriately trained and quiescent workers into a productive sector that had been substantially deskilled, but in the globalized economy many of these kinds of jobs have departed for LEDCs anyway. The stress on vocationalism is counter-cyclical, producing skilled workers for jobs that no longer exist. It is more accurately seen as an advanced form of social control of unemployed young people (Bash *et al.*, 1985) than as a meaningful curricular intervention in the globalized economy. Furthermore, at the higher and expanding level of the economy this trend towards the basics can be seen as counterproductive in that it fails to recognize the emerging processes and practices of the knowledge economy. The skills needed for this knowledge economy may be to some degree vocational, in computer-assisted design, in music technology or in ICT itself, but, where this is the case, it is higher education, rather than schools and vocational institutions, which is supplying the specialized personnel. In more generic terms the skills of the knowledge economy concern: research; risk-taking and opportunism; multimedia presentation; software application; team-building; intercultural and international understanding; English for purposes of both production and consumption; networking across professions and countries; and a persona which is simultaneously corporate and individually distinctive in terms of cultural consumption. Rather than schools or vocational colleges, these are more readily identifiable as the skills taught by higher education institutions, where arts, humanities and social sciences courses continue to proliferate, and where ICT is rapidly penetrating all areas of work. The global expansion of higher education institutions in the last 30 years has accompanied and to a certain degree facilitated the expansion in employment prospects for people with this range of skills.

Universities are indeed essential institutions of the knowledge economy. Interestingly, this is by no means an exclusively science-centred phenomenon: indeed, in the UK, 60 university science departments have closed down in the last ten years (Fazackerley, 2003) because so few students wish to take these courses at undergraduate level. Certainly technology and ICT departments are generating many of the skills of the knowledge economy but this is also the case in the never-more-popular arts and humanities courses and in the social sciences and creative arts. The modularization of higher education and the implementation of government imperatives, via the various quality maintenance arrangements (Cowen, 1996), have assisted in this process. Thus, courses on graphic design are as likely to include modules on marketing as on the Renaissance; sociology degrees will include modules investigating strategies used by the mass media or by advertising, as well as introducing students to the works of Durkheim and Weber. At the same time, whole new degree subjects are being opened up, such as interactive multimedia, creative music technology, brand management or international tourism management. These developments are facilitated by the steady expansion of student numbers and the associated increase in academic staff, often younger people with technological, commercial or aesthetic backgrounds.

Furthermore, universities are themselves one of the major sites not only of preparation for the knowledge economy but of its actual practice. Knowledge processes of many university departments, characterized by the development and expansion of knowledge itself, by the procedures of hypothesis and experimentation, by rehearsal, redrafting and revision, and by interdisciplinarity and fusion are actually conducive to the activities of the knowledge economy. It is in university research departments that many developments and innovations in science and technology are first made: ICT and genetics being obvious current examples. 'The two sources of the Net, the military/science establishment and the personal computing counterculture, did have a common ground: the university world' (Castells, 1996, p. 355). This is not to imply that these processes are exclusively progressive or benign: this would appear to be as far from the case with regard to the commercial applications of genetic technology as it was in earlier phases with regard to armament and pharmaceutical development. The wider critique of globalization cannot be placed in abeyance when considering the adaptation of universities to the knowledge economy.

There are many further examples of universities' direct engagement with the knowledge economy. University departments have a great impact on design and style in matters as diverse as architecture, shoe fashion, websites and theatrical direction. University publishing houses and specialist journals play an important part in disseminating the recent productions of the knowledge economy. Universities are important users of the worldwide web for both the construction and dissemination of research. It is hard to imagine a series of institutions more influential on the development and reproduction of the knowledge economy than universities.

The next section of this chapter goes on to consider the considerable impact that ICT is having on universities, one of the most significant manifestations of the knowledge economy and one of the areas of highest impact between globalization and educational institutions.

Universities and information and communication technology

The emerging political and academic discourse on the knowledge economy (Burton-Jones, 1999; Etzkovitz and Leydesdorff, 2001; Neef, 1998; Stewart, 1997; Thurow, 1999; Witchit Srisa-an 2000) largely ignores the fact that it is a revised version of human capital theory. This theory, popular among those in development education in the 1960s and 1970s, optimistically suggested that, by investing in the education systems of LEDCs, the skill and knowledge levels of their populations would improve and their economies resultantly take off. Events proved the limitations of this theory (see the critique in Karabel and Halsey (1977)), not least in sub-Saharan Africa. Yet proponents of the knowledge economy also tie together educational investment and achievement with economic growth.

Perhaps now, though, there is a third new factor in terms of technical innovation that was not present in the earlier formulation of human capital and which makes the argument less facile and more credible. The argument of the proponents of the knowledge economy is that ICT has the power to transform the economies of states. This implies not the reproduction of knowledge and thereby wealth as in the old human capital theory, but rather the actual *production* of technological knowledge and both wealth and wealth potential within higher education institutions. The universities and research institutes are not ancillary to the knowledge economy; they are actually central to it. They are producing not expertise for an existing manufacturing infrastructure but, rather, this actual infrastructure itself. They are producing skills that the workplace does not yet know that it needs. To this extent they are counter-cyclical in a positive rather than vocationalistic (see the last section), negative way: they are producing skills and knowledge for the economy of tomorrow rather than that of yesterday. Graduates with high-level ICT skills have the capacity to generate wealth (and/or savings) in a wide range of commercial contexts. Their capacity to generate new databases or communications networks, for instance, is itself, within this theory, as much the creation of wealth as the manufacture of a car or the drilling of oil. Similarly, the technical development of the processes and products of the knowledge economy, including those of consumption as well as production and distribution, also take place within some universities as well as within commercial organizations. Indeed the distinction between universities and commercial organizations has in this context outlived its usefulness.

So far, the impact of ICT has been on MEDCs and whether it will work as a means of reducing poverty in LEDCs remains to be seen. There are, however, now clear indications that Malaysia and India, for example, see the possibility of prosperity through the knowledge economy: indeed ICT jobs are already being exported from the UK to especially the Bangalore region of India. Given the nature of the technology there is no reason, unlike during the Industrial Revolution, why its spread should be limited to areas contiguous to its origin. The geographical spread of the ICT economy is not limited by the scale or speed of the steam railway.

The changes that have been brought about in universities by the impact of ICT influence almost all their functions. The impact of ICT has added a heavy, often unacknowledged burden on to the budgets of universities. This concerns first the purchase and renewal of costly equipment. In order to establish a workroom of 20 networked computers, a university first has to make over a room which was probably previously timetabled, with associated opportunity costs. This room then has to be established in terms of furniture, lighting, ventilation and carpets. Power points and network points then have to be installed. The cost of this set-up is usually more than the subsequent purchase of the equipment: computers, printers, scanners and so on. This equipment, however, normally needs to be renewed within three years due to progress within the technology. Purchase of software is also a considerable expense. As well as annual site licences to Microsoft, specialist software in, for example, computer-assisted design, architecture or statistics for social sciences can be highly expensive. The development of computers within universities has necessitated the employment of additional technical staff in order to purchase, install and maintain equipment as well as to induct students, and often academics, into its correct use. The combined impact of these costs has put pressure on other areas of university budgets. In the UK this has contributed to worsening student–teacher ratios, the reduction in full-time, permanent members of staff as a proportion of the workforce and the casualization of the academic profession.

The introduction of ICT into the management of universities has led to the systematic monitoring of students in terms of registration, payment of fees, credit and grade accumulation, library, students union and ICT records. Programmes such as SITS have in turn led to the subsequent facilitation of modular and credit accumulation and transfer modes of programme delivery. The maintenance of accurate, up-to-date student records in large, complex modular programmes would be impossible without interactive database systems. The technology actually defines the type of degree programmes that many universities are able to offer and that students increasingly follow at postgraduate as well as undergraduate level.

Developments in the technology have also facilitated systematic monitoring of universities themselves. In part, this has made simpler the compilation of records that have always needed to be kept in terms of student numbers and budgets. However, the development of university ICT took place against another trend in universities: the desire by central government and its associated agencies to measure performance (Cowen, 1996). This practice in the UK currently involves scrutinies that grade the qualities of a university's teaching and research (as separate exercises) in all its academic areas. Computerised databases then allow this information to be correlated with, for instance, spending on library provision or numbers of staff employed in an area, in a (largely spurious) endeavour to assess the extent to which university departments provide 'value for money'. The compilation and correlation of these data also facilitate the fabrication of league tables so popular with journalists and, to be fair, their readers. These normally take the form of subject disciplines, such as the top ten sociology departments but the *Guardian* recently managed to compile a league table of all 123 UK universities in terms of their overall performance in all their subject areas. Actually, since the University of North London refused to participate, there were only 122 on the table. That Cambridge, London and Oxford were at the top of the list came as a surprise to few academics.

The development of the new technology has led to the need to teach specifically ICT courses at all levels. Undergraduate and postgraduate courses in all aspects of ICT – systems engineering, software design, networking, electronics – are booming in popularity in the triad states and beyond. Universities have brought into existence completely new departments and degree courses. Since much of the research into ICT is also conducted within universities, this achievement was perhaps not as difficult as might have been supposed. Nevertheless it represents some agility in adjusting institutional priorities.

However, it is not only in ICT departments that significant changes have been needed; it has also been necessary to bring ICT into all other academic areas. The study of geography for instance has been transformed by digital mapping, satellite images and internet access to huge demographic databases. Similar radical changes have taken place in creative writing and music, as well as in architecture, psychology and mathematics. It would scarcely be an overstatement to say that the introduction of ICT has transformed the entire nature of university knowledge in the last 20 years. This is particularly significant in that it has taken place in institutions hardly renowned for their flexibility or willingness to change. Indeed, certain aspects of the European university curriculum, theology, say, or classics, would appear to have changed exceedingly slowly over the centuries. It is this rapid responsiveness to changes in ICT that have made (some) universities in Europe and the USA key institutions in the knowledge economy.

ICT is now also frequently used in European universities as a mode of course delivery. At its most mundane, this involves PowerPoint presentation with its numbingly familiar format and its requirement for another tranche of expensive equipment in the shape of laptops and projection. In terms of more complex pedagogy it involves the placing of teaching material, readings and hypertext links on an intranet or on the web. Student assignments and dissertations can be dispatched, marked and moderated via the net. The creation of web pages by students and the placing of material on the net are increasingly a component of assignments. The ability to communicate rapidly with large amounts of information to students in distant locations has facilitated an increase in the quantity and quality of ODL (see Chapter 1). The technology coincides with EU policy (European Commission, 1996, 2002; European Commission Directorate-General for Education and Culture, 2002) and that of many states which have been enthusiastic about ODL as a means of widening (and cheapening) participation in higher education.

In terms of individual students, the onset of ICT has led to increased pressure on their budgets because of the need to purchase independent systems, modems and internet access as well as machines and printers. For some courses in universities in the USA and the UK, the possession of a personal computer is a prerequisite of registration. The impact of ICT on familiar patterns of access to higher education has only been to reinforce existing patterns of stratification. The term digital deficit has been coined to characterize those families where children do not have access to up-to-date ICT provision at home and who are consequently further disadvantaged in their educational progress. The technology is frequently praised for its capacity to liberate speech and ideas. In terms of social equality it may only serve to exacerbate existing patterns.

Turning to academic careers, there has been a need for rapid staff development across a whole range of areas: generic and subject-specific software packages, web access and previously lowly keyboard skills. Despite the ageing workforce of universities in most triad states, these skills appear largely to have been developed. For younger academics, as noted above, ICT seems to be an ever more important component of their professional presentation. Personal and research group web pages, international academic contacts and collaborations maintained by email and conferences, laptops for the use of mobile academics, computerized networked diaries and mobile phone calls to research contacts and funding bodies are all part of the emergent academic career. The characteristics of superabundance, accessibility and internationalization are seen in few careers as evidently as those of university academics and researchers in the elite institutions of the triad.

Finally, there have been radical changes in the relationship between the university and the workplace. Universities are no longer simply providing skilled personnel, but rather, in some cases, are responsible for developing large parts of the technology. Important developments in hardware, software and applications take place in universities and related research institutes as well as in the ICT companies themselves.

The changes resulting from ICT are, of course, not the only trends affecting higher education. Most importantly perhaps, the linked trends to raise the level of participation and simultaneously reduce the unit cost per student are responsible for major changes in many universities (Coulby, 2002). This section of the chapter presents an ideal type, even an idealized version, of change in universities. Nevertheless, after decades, in some cases centuries, of slow change, many are now adapting rapidly to both the new technology and new social and political expectations. As part of this adaptation many triad universities are themselves becoming important institutions within the knowledge economy.

Education and the knowledge economy: schools

As producers and reproducers of knowledge, it is the universities rather than the schools that have responded most readily and substantially to the needs of the knowledge economy. As mentioned above, it is on schools, particularly in the USA and the UK, that commentators, including those concerned with the knowledge economy itself, and politicians have centred their anxiety. Neef writes: 'Unfortunately, in the US and Britain, particularly, there are indications that the education and training infrastructure necessary to provide these knowledge based skills broadly throughout the population is becoming both inadequate and inappropriate for the knowledge-based economy' (1998, p. 9). He and others link this to the likelihood of unemployment and marginalization for a significant section of the population, while, by contrast, those educated in the skills of the knowledge economy continue to thrive.

Rosecrance (also in Neef, 1998) draws attention to the lack of investment in schooling in some states, in particular to the low salaries paid to teachers. He contrasts that with the salaries paid in Switzerland (about twice that in the UK, France or the USA) with the implication that higher salaries will attract better skilled teachers and thus help develop superior schools. The failure of schools to address the needs of the knowledge economy may come to be matched by a shift of education to the private sector. Davis and Botkin (in Neef, 1998) believe that corporations rather than states are making the changes in education necessary for the knowledge economy. They lament the fact that school systems:

are lagging behind the transformation that is evolving outside them, in the private sector at both work and play, with people of all ages. Over the next few decades, the private sector will eclipse the public sector as our predominant educational institution.

(p. 164)

While the strengths identified in universities in the previous sections will probably tend to falsify this bold hypothesis, it certainly highlights the extent of the weaknesses perceived in the school system.

If there is a lack of contact between schools, but not so much universities, and the needs of the knowledge economy then there are at least two sets of reasons. The first concerns the widespread tendency towards centralizing the school curriculum. The second concerns the education, status and remuneration of the teaching force. In both these sets of reasons, which are discussed in the remainder of this chapter, ICT is a contributory element. Before addressing these arguments, however, it is necessary again to eschew any facile, economistic link between schools and society. Transformation of the school curriculum on its own is hardly a sufficient cause to bring about economic restructuring. This is well stated by Carnoy and Fluitman:

> Despite the apparent consensus around the supply-side, skill mismatch argument, the supporting evidence for it is extremely thin, especially in terms of improved education and more and better training solving either the problem of open unemployment (Europe) or the problem of wage distribution (US). It is much more convincing, we argue, that better education and more training could, in the longer run, contribute to higher productivity and economic growth rates.
>
> (Quoted in Castells, 1996, p. 274)

The school and university curricula do not directly control the size or the nature of the workforce. They may, however, have a long-term and indirect effect on the pattern of inward and outward investment, the nature of economic activity, the place that workers play within it and the level of their employability and remuneration.

There is a lack of articulation then, to return to the main argument, between the centralizing curricula of school systems and the associated deskilled and downgraded teaching profession on the one hand and the needs of the emerging knowledge economy on the other. This chapter concludes by considering, first, centralized school curriculum systems and, second, the status of the school teaching profession in relation to the knowledge economy.

The state control of school knowledge appears not to be bringing it into closer harmony with the current and future needs of the workplace.

As noted earlier, the curricula espoused by those taking control of the school curriculum are more relevant to previous phases of European economic development than to the knowledge economy. At this point it is perhaps possible to consider the tension between the two topics of this volume: globalization and nationalism. The political motivation behind the maintenance or introduction of centralized, state-controlled curricular systems at school level is actually more to do with the reproduction of a narrowly conceived national identity than it is with meeting the needs of the globalized economy. While the technical, informational and social skills of the globalized workplace may be remarkably lacking from these systems, there are only too many examples of the inclusion of nationalistic language, history and social studies teaching (Coulby, 2000; Phillips, 1998; Suroor and Behal, 1998; Tawakkul, 1999). The school curriculum, far from opening up to the forces either of globalization or of intercultural internationalism, has retreated into a defence of a parochially defined national identity. It may be that the pressures of globalization (migration, the penetration of international media, the visible presence of 'foreign' TNCs) have in some way contributed to this attempt at a defence of a narrowly conceived national identity.

More generally, the point has been made that centralized national curricular systems tend to generate, or at least maintain, nationalist curricula. The political discourse on standards (Department for Education and Employment, 1997; Department for Education and Skills, 2002a, 2002b), combined with the impulsion towards traditional, nationalist values and culture in the back-to-basics movement of the early 1990s in the UK and the USA. This explicitly reactionary agenda appeared to be taking place in an economic vacuum. The school curriculum, but not that of universities, was being shifted back apparently to prepare children and young people for the workplace of the Industrial Revolution.

Of course, there may also be a more obvious reason for the prevalence of conservative school curricula and this concerns the astronomic expense of introducing ICT into classrooms. Even within the triad states politicians have developed a fear of increasing state expenditure on education derived from the belief that any government which increased direct taxation would never be re-elected. Unfortunately for this view, in order for schools to participate in and prepare pupils for the knowledge economy, they would need to have the kind of provision now emerging in many universities:

- local area networks with fast web access;
- specialist teaching rooms with computers, printers, software and peripherals available for every student;
- generic classrooms with several computers and with facilities for computer projection and/or interactive whiteboards for presentation;

- all teaching staff skilled in generic ICT skills;
- specialist staff skilled in the applications of ICT to their particular subject;
- technical staff to maintain and update the network.

The costs here are fearsome, despite the falling prices for ICT hardware which have characterized the last two decades. The electrical cabling, security, safety and software costs exceed those of the hardware. In addition, there would be the need to skill up an entire generation of teachers and technicians. Not only that, but as the technology is changing so rapidly, politicians could be just about sure that any investment they made would not be future proof but would need to be renewed every three years. The narrow, unchallenging and inexpensive certainties of the nationalist curriculum are in this financial context all the more politically attractive. The rich suburbs of American cities have long been an exception to this generalization and others are beginning to emerge. Nevertheless, if schools in the main are to be anything more than marginal institutions to the knowledge economy, then their curricular systems will need to be radically addressed. Leaving school immediately at the end of compulsory schooling will thus be cumulatively disadvantageous for life chances in the knowledge economy, since it excludes young people from the more relevant curriculum available in some universities. Needless to say, there are social class and, in many states, 'race' and language characteristics of those who leave school early.

It is the nature of the teaching profession, its remuneration and access to relevant training which forms the second set of reasons for the inability of schools in the triad states to come to terms with the knowledge economy. In many states of Europe, such as Germany, the Netherlands, the UK and Greece, there is a different preparation for primary teachers than for secondary. In general terms, the former are educated in new universities or *hogeschools*, while the latter are educated in old universities. Within Europe there are great differences in the duration and rigour of teacher education. In France, where primary and secondary arrangements are parallel, students must first have a degree which is likely to take at least four years to obtain; then they must attend an IUFM (postgraduate teacher education school) to take either the CAPES (diploma of primary education) or CAPEP (diploma of secondary education). In either case, the Certificate takes two years to complete and the failure rate between year one and two can be as high as 50 per cent. In the UK, by contrast, a primary teacher can be prepared by a three-year Bachelor of Education course and a secondary teacher can go straight into school after the first three-year degree, and qualify as a teacher while actually working in school. Not surprisingly, the status of the teaching force and their perceived job satisfaction, though interestingly not their remuneration, is higher in France than in the UK. With regard to remuneration, with the exception of Switzerland (Rafferty, 1998) and some rich suburbs of the USA (Knapp and Woolverton, 1995), teachers' salaries have been perceived to be falling relative to other professional workers for the last two decades. There is a possible connection here with the introduction and maintenance of centralized school curricula. Teachers have no part in determining or shaping the knowledge they teach. Increasingly their task is being seen as a technical matter of 'delivery'. The deskilling as well as the feminization of the teaching workforce may be connected to falling relative levels of payment and prestige.

Associated with this deskilling in many states has been a concentration on the training, evaluation, control, surveillance, discipline and regimentation of the teaching force (Foucault, 1979). The associated policies include:

- strict state control over the institutions and curricula of initial teacher education (sometimes revealingly referred to as training) even where this is conducted in a university (Ward, 1998);
- a similar state involvement in in-service education, often focused on the perceived immediate needs of the classroom at the expense of, say, Master's level study;
- regular and arduous inspections of schools by state agencies, often with publicly available reports and sometimes resulting in political and journalistic criticism or indeed pillorying ('naming and shaming');
- national curriculum systems with associated national testing in subjects deemed to be core, sometimes leading to the compilation of national or regional league tables on the basis of results;
- a lack of trust in teacher and headteacher professionalism manifested through the increased involvement of politicians and business people in the governance of schools and through the increased number of directives and 'initiatives' from central government;
- attempts to devise mechanisms for dismissing teachers and heads perceived to be ineffective;
- pay rises either below inflation or phased and frequently linked to deterioration in working conditions and autonomy;
- attempts to link teachers' salaries to their performance on inspections or to their pupils' performance on national tests, often via the introduction of appraisal arrangements;
- a climate of criticism of schools and teachers amounting sometimes to undisguised hostility in the statements of politicians and journalists of both left- and right-wing persuasions.

Obviously, England and Wales provide the case example here, where all the above elements can be found. Many can also be readily identified, however, in states as various as France, the Netherlands and Greece (Thomas, 2002).

There are at least two consequences of these policies for the capacity of states to bring their school curricula closer to the needs of the knowledge economy. First, in the USA, the UK, the Netherlands and Russia, though not in France or Greece, teaching is ceasing to be an attractive profession. Especially when the economy is booming, pupils with high school-leaving qualifications or students with good degrees will be attracted into better paid, less regulated and less stigmatized professions. In the long term this will result in a poorer qualified teaching force, lower morale and teacher shortages. Graduates and school leavers with high-level ICT skills are precisely the ones who will most readily obtain employment in the knowledge economy and not be attracted to working in schools. Even draconian state interventions in teacher education, such as that in England and Wales, may be insufficient to remedy the ICT skills shortage among teachers when they take place against the background of the other policies just described which prove aversive to entry into the profession. Second, these policies result in an existing teaching force, demoralized by stigmatization and poor pay, overburdened with the work requirements of regular inspections and national assessment schemes, and bemused and fatigued by successive waves of government education 'reform'. There is a danger that such a teaching force has lost the professional freedom and capacity to behave proactively in curriculum matters. The consequence of state policies with regard to the profession itself means that governments cannot look to teachers to rescue them from the short-sightedness of their centralized school curriculum initiatives. In many states globalization and the knowledge economy on the one hand and national curricular systems and the nature of the school teaching workforce on the other appear to be moving in opposite directions.

References

Bash, L. and Green, A. (eds) (1995) *World Yearbook of Education 1995: Youth, Education and Work*. Series edited by D. Coulby and C. Jones. London: Kogan Page.

Bash, L., Coulby, D. and Jones, C. (1985) *Urban Schooling: Theory and Practice*. London: Cassell.

Blunkett, D. (1999) *Challenge to Invest in Human Capital*. London: Department for Education and Employment.

Burton-Jones, A. (1999) *Knowledge Capitalism: Business, Work and Learning in the New Economy*. Oxford and New York: Oxford University Press.

Castells, M. (1989) *The Informational City: Information Technology, Economic Restructuring and the Urban-Regional Process*. Oxford: Blackwell.

Castells, M. (1996) *The Information Age: Economy, Society and Culture. Volume 1: The Rise of the Network Society*. Oxford: Blackwell.

Castells, M. (1997) *The Information Age: Economy, Society and Culture. Volume 2: The Power of Identity*. Oxford: Blackwell.

Castells, M. (1998) *The Information Age: Economy, Society and Culture. Volume 3: End of Millennium*. Oxford: Blackwell.

Coulby, D. (2000) *Beyond The National Curriculum: Curricular Centralism and Cultural Diversity in Europe and the USA*. London and New York: Routledge-Falmer.

Coulby, D. (2002) The Knowledge Economy, the European Union and Universities. *Panepistemio*, 4: 3–20.

Cowen, R. (ed.) (1996) *The World Yearbook of Education 1996: The Evaluation of Systems of Higher Education*. Series edited by D. Coulby and C. Jones. London: Kogan Page.

Department for Education and Employment (1997) *Raising Standards for All: The Government's Legislative Plans*. London: Department for Education and Employment.

Department for Education and Skills (2002a) *14–19: Extending Opportunities, Raising Standards (Summary of DfES Consultation)*. London: DfES.

Department for Education and Skills (2002b) *Raising Standards. The 14–19 Green Paper*. London: Department for Education and Skills.

Etzkovitz, H. and Leydesdorff, L. (eds) (2001) *Universities and the Global Knowledge Economy: A Triple Helix of University–Industry–Government Relations*. London and New York: Continuum.

European Commission (1996) *Teaching and Learning: Towards the Learning Society*. Brussels: European Commission.

European Commission (2002) *A New Impetus for European Youth. White Paper*. Luxembourg: Office for Official Publications of the European Communities.

European Commission Directorate-General for Education and Culture (2002) *Education and Training in Europe: Diverse Systems, Shared Goals for 2010*. Luxembourg: Office for Official Publications of the European Communities.

Fazackerley, A. (2003) Science Dies Out in English 'Deserts'. *Times Higher Educational Supplement*, 11 July, p. 56.

Foucault, M. (1979) *Discipline and Punish: The Birth of the Prison*. Harmondsworth: Penguin.

Karabel, J. and Halsey, A. H. (1977) *Power and Ideology in Education*. New York: Oxford University Press.

Knapp, M. S. and Woolverton, S. (1995) Social Class and Schooling, in J. A. Banks and C. A. M. Banks (eds) *Handbook of Research on Multicultural Education*. Macmillan: New York.

Lash, S. and Urry, J. (1994) *Economies of Signs and Space*. London: Sage.

Marsden, D. and Ryan, P. (1995) Work, Labour Markets and Vocational Preparation: Anglo German Comparisons of Training in Intermediate Skills, in L. Bash and A. Green (eds) *The World Yearbook of Education 1995*. Kogan Page: London.

Neef, D. (ed.) (1998) *The Knowledge Economy*. Boston, MA: Butterworth-Heinemann.

Phillips, R. (1998) *History Teaching, Nationhood and the State: A Study in Educational Politics*. London: Cassell.

Rafferty, F. (1998) Small Classes, No Computers. *Times Educational Supplement*, July, p. 22.

Stewart, T. A. (1997) *Intellectual Capital: The New Wealth of Organisations*. London: Nicholas Brearley Publishing.

Suroor, H. and Behal, S. (1998) Nationalist Curriculum Prompts Walk-outs. *Times Educational Supplement*, November, p. 18.

Tawakkul, D. (1999) *A Study of Chinese Policy Towards National Minorities with Reference to Higher Education: A Case Study of the Central University for Nationalities*. Ph.D. dissertation, London Institute of Education.

Thomas, E. (ed.) (2002) *The World Yearbook of Education 2002. Teacher Education: Dilemmas and Prospects*. Series edited by D. Coulby and C. Jones. London: Kogan Page.

Thurow, L. (1999) *Creating Wealth: New Rules for Individuals, Companies and Countries in a Knowledge-based Economy*. London: Nicholas Brearley Publishing.

Ward, S. (1998) Intercultural Education and Teacher Education in the United Kingdom: A Case of Reversible Decline. *European Journal of Intercultural Studies*, 9(1): 41–52.

Witchit Srisa-an (2000) Universities and the International Knowledge Enterprise, in G. Neave (ed.) *The Universities' Responsibilities to Society: International Perspectives*. Pergamon: Oxford, pp. 141–9.

Zukin, S. (1988) *Loft Living: Culture and Capital in Urban Change*. London: Radius.

Zukin, S. (1991) *Landscapes of Power: From Detroit to Disney World*. Berkeley, CA: University of California Press.

Zukin, S. (1995) *The Cultures of Cities*. Oxford: Blackwell.

Part II
Tradition and modernity

3   The survival of nationalism in a globalized system

Evie Zambeta

Introduction

This chapter examines the nature of globalization and discusses the extent to which this is compatible with nationalism. As has been previously discussed in this volume (Introduction and Chapters 1 and 2), no matter whether an old or a new phenomenon, globalization is happening and exercises manifold economic, political, social and cultural impacts. In this chapter it will be argued that, though globalization is challenging the power of the state, the state continues to be a major mechanism through which globalization processes are accomplished and take place. Moreover, in many cases, it is the state that acts as the mediating agent in the intervention of global processes into local communities, or, in other words, the state mediates the global and the local. It will be further argued that globalization does not lead to homogenization between different societies, it enhances pre-existing economic and social inequalities. In the context of a monopolar polity that has developed after the fall of the Berlin Wall, globalization is fundamentally an aspect of the political hegemony of the one world power. However, while on the one hand political and cultural imperialism is not a process that meets with no resistance, on the other hand, nationalism is a persisting phenomenon in contemporary societies. Loyalties to traditional ideas and institutions related to religion, distorted images of a glorified past, ideologies of cultural supremacism or xenophobic discourses on fragile identities tend to fuel nationalist movements.

Education systems will be the institutional sites on which the analysis draws. It will be argued that education is in many ways the state institution that facilitates both globalization and nationalism. This chapter therefore consists of two sections. The first section discusses the nature of globalization and its impact on social change and examines the extent to which globalization and nationalism are actually opposing forces. The second section of the chapter explores both the implications of globalization and the manifestations of nationalism on state education systems and concludes by discussing the extent to which nationalism can survive in a globalized system.

Globalization and nationalism

Globalization and nationalism could be perceived as being parallel forces in conflict. While globalization is usually associated with the increasing 'interconnectedness' between the economies and societies which transcends the territoriality of states (Held *et al.*, 2000), nationalism, as a political project which aims to link states to nations, tends to underline difference, distinctiveness, segregation and separatism. However, the processes of globalization and nationalism are not mutually exclusive, despite their apparently contradictory character. The intersection of these two forces is negotiated at the level of the state and has led to, as a consequence, a dramatic change in the dynamics of power relations, both within and among states.

Globalization and socio-political change

The formation of a global market is considered as the most striking development under globalization. It is worth questioning, however, the extent to which the phenomenon of global economic and political interdependence is qualitatively distinct and new. The Industrial Revolution, for example, could be perceived as a similar process that presupposed a powerful economy facilitated by a hegemonic colonial state. Hobsbawm notes that 'conquering markets by war and colonization required not merely an economy capable of exploiting those markets, but also a government willing to wage war and colonize for the benefit of British manufacturers' (1999, p. 27). The government that offered protection to the British producers against Indian textile imports in the 1700s was the one that opened the way to the Lancashire cotton industry in India, when in 1813 the East India Company was deprived of its monopoly there. Interestingly, none of these developments that gave rise to English industrialism and wealth necessitated a state education system or compulsory education for all.

Globalization has been defined as a new phase of capitalism which is based on intensification of capital accumulation, while technology has been the fundamental facilitating agent in the globalizing process. Although any attempt to conceptualize globalization unavoidably follows a scheme which explores the various manifestations of it in the economic, political, social and cultural fields, in fact this sort of taxonomy mainly reflects the analytical approach of the academic towards a complex and manifold social process. The above taxonomy provides for a necessary methodology serving analytical purposes and should not be perceived in ontological terms. What is significantly important is the fact that globalization affects dramatically all these fields at the same time and, even more importantly, the transitions that occur in any of these fields have tremendously rich impact on all the others. This in turn means that it is almost impossible to understand, for example, the political implications of globalization without taking into account the role of transnational corporations (TNCs) – some of them indeed more powerful than many states – in controlling global food, industry or services (Gabel and Bruner, 2003). Moreover the proceedings in the stock markets in Tokyo, London and New York have a tremendous impact in shaping global and regional economies. The internet and satellite television play a vital role in the transmission of information, ideas and perceptions of the world, as well as in the dissemination of cultural products, symbols and meanings.

As early as in 1989 David Harvey wrote:

> I want to suggest that we have been experiencing . . . an intense phase of time-space compression that has had a disorienting and disruptive impact upon political-economic practices, the balance of class power, as well as upon cultural and social life . . . the transition [from Fordism] to flexible accumulation was in part accomplished through the rapid deployment of new organizational forms and new technologies in production. Accelerating turnover time in production entails parallel accelerations in exchange and consumption. Improved systems of communication and information flow, coupled with rationalizations in techniques of distribution made it possible to circulate commodities through the market systems with greater speed.
>
> (1989, p. 284)

Harvey's account actually describes the situation that is now defined as the knowledge economy: the economy that is able to maximize profit by accelerating turnover time. In the context of the knowledge economy the maximization of profit is accomplished by the incorporation of new knowledge in the mode of production (e.g. microchip technology, robotics). This economy is not only characterized by a major shift from the production and consumption of goods into the production and consumption of services. It is also genuinely transformed into a quaternary economy (see Chapters 1 and 2). This dramatic shift is largely attributed to the knowledge base of the economy. As Castells has defined it, a country's competitiveness in the global economy and its position in the international division of labour and wealth are predominantly dependent on the capacity of its economy to articulate science, technology, management and production (Castells, 1996).

In circumstances of accelerating globalization, the power of the state and traditionally perceived state sovereignty are dramatically challenged.

The post-1648 Westphalia era, which has resulted in the steady concentration of power in the hands of the state, is considered by the exponents of globalization as coming to an end. As it has been argued, the so-called nation-state has become 'too small for the big problems of life, and too big for the small problems of life' (Giddens, 1990, p. 63). Many of the most important of today's problems bring to the surface the tension between the fixed geography of the state and the non-territorial nature of the issues that are at stake. Environmental policy towards problems such as the global warming, or poverty in the less economically developed countries (LEDCs) cannot be anticipated by the sole action of any individual state. Globalization is considered as being the cause of major political change. It is to this political change that the next two paragraphs turn.

First, globalization causes change in the distribution of power among the supranational, the regional, the state and the sub-national or local level. State sovereignty is seen as being genuinely diminished by the rise of international organizations which develop certain constraints on the ability of the state to control its internal affairs. The political capacity of national and supranational organizations, such as the Organization of Economic Cooperation and Development (OECD), the International Monetary Fund (IMF) or the World Trade Organisation (WTO), to control the economy and the growth strategies of the states or regions that fall under their jurisdiction acts as one of the major determinants of the global power relations (Rosenau, 2002; Wilkinson and Hughes, 2002). At the same time some political entities below the central state emerge as powerful stakeholders in the international arena. Most of the states of the USA have official standing at the WTO. In the European Union (EU) many local authorities have official representation in Brussels. The Lyon region, in collaboration with Geneva and Turin, maintains its own diplomatic offices abroad as representatives of the regional economy. Furthermore, decision-making in regional organizations, particularly in the EU, usually involves lobbying on the part of local, corporate and state bodies within and among member states, a fact which in many cases cuts across state power and questions dramatically the internal bonds of states. Recent times have been characterized as the age of a power shift to non-state actors (Mathews, 1998). The information and communication technology (ICT) explosion has broken governmental monopolies on the collection and management of large amounts of information and disrupts traditional hierarchies, while it develops new ones based on economic, cultural or social capital. On the other hand, the vast increase in the numbers of TNCs and international non-governmental organizations (NGOs) indicates the development of economic and social networks that transcend the state borders and mediate in global governance. In some cases NGOs, often related to business, influence decision-making and provide expertise that governments or international organizations lack. In this respect, the power of the state could be perceived as being hollowed out by the forces of globalization. At the same time, however, the state remains the main mediator in the regulation of the global economic and political transaction. Indeed, some states have the power either to initiate global policies or to resist them. The USA, for instance, has played a key role in the establishment of the WTO, while it determines not to abide by the Kyoto Protocol and to join a list of states that do not ratify international treaties, such as the Law of the Sea Treaty, the Convention on the Elimination of All Forms of Discrimination Against Women and the Convention on the Rights of the Child (Lal, 2002).

Second, globalization causes changes not only in the modes of public administration and public policy in general, but in the collective behaviour and political culture as well. Central state bureaucracies are rejected for being ineffective in the resolution of many regional and local problems. New forms of governance emerge which involve more sophisticated systems of regulation and state steering through devolution of power to new agents of both a public and private character (Held and McGrew, 2002a, 2002b). Decentralization, deregulation of public services and privatization are some of the most usual measures adopted by many states in the past two decades (Callaghan, 2000). This is a process that has been related to the neoliberal attack on the welfare state as it was known till the 1970s. The central state has been accused of corruption, managerial incompetence and lack of accountability, democratic deficit and glorification of corporate interests. In many states the shift in political culture from social welfare to neoliberalism has been presented as an inevitable imperative for the country's modernization, competitiveness and integration into the global economy. In this context the discourse on the renewal of social democracy and the development of the 'Third Way' ideology (Giddens, 1998) depicts the retreat of social democracy through its redefinition.

Though globalization is used as an all-encompassing concept, it is far from being a homogenizing process. It is rather a manifestation of the unequal international division of labour, power and wealth which is intensified and facilitated by technology. However, the hierarchical relations between regions and states are not shaped or static, but they are rather contested and transformable. Some states, such as Finland, manage to change their place in the international competition by transforming their economies into knowledge economies. Other states, particularly the USA, which produce and control the internationally most powerful means of warfare, are in the position to impose new forms of colonialism and generate dominant views regarding 'political values', 'human rights', 'terrorism', knowledge and culture (Lal, 2002). On the other hand, in a context of a knowledge economy, intellectual property is considered as the major advantage which will determine a state's place in the international competitive economy. Today, the USA as the only superpower controls not only the most powerful means of warfare but also dominates global advertising, marketing, the entertainment industry and culture (Lehman, 1998). Therefore globalization is generating uneven development, and political and cultural domination. In fact it sharpens social and cultural hierarchies in international terms.

Arguably, globalization is a process that has been facilitated by colonialism. The dissemination of English throughout the globe had been initiated by colonialism and has provided a basic tool for global-ization, a tool which has equipped institutions varying from Microsoft, CNN and MTV to museums, periodicals or academic conferences. How-ever, decolonization did not lead to an era of equally free and powerful states. Globalization is an uneven and an unequal process. Castells (1996) argues that the global economy is characterized by interdependence and asymmetry, increasing diversification within each region, selective inclusiveness and exclusionary segmentation, which as a result leads to a variable geometry that tends to change the historical economic geog-raphy. As Doreen Massey has put it, globalization develops a new social geography of difference since 'some initiate flows and movement, others don't; some are more at the receiving end of it than others; some are effectively imprisoned by it' (Massey, 1993, as cited in Robins, 2000, p. 198). ICTs are key components of the network society but at the same time they are polarising the world into the connected and the isolated. In the United Nations (UN) words:

- *Geography divides.* Thailand has more cellular phones than Africa. South Asia, home to 23 per cent of the world's population, has less than 1 per cent of Internet users.
- *Education is a ticket to the network high society.* Globally, 30 per cent of Internet users had at least one university degree.
- *Income buys access.* To purchase a computer would cost the average Bangladeshi more than eight years' income, the average American, just one month's wage.
- *Men and youth dominate.* Women make up just 17 per cent of the Internet users in Japan, only 7 per cent in China. Most users in China and the United Kingdom are under 30.
- *English talks.* English prevails in almost 80 per cent of all websites. Yet less than one in 10 people worldwide speaks it.

(UNDP, 1999, p. 346)

Globalization, as the widening, deepening and speeding up of global interconnectedness (Held *et al.*, 2000), changes dramatically the order of power relations across the world. People feel the implications of the exercise of power which is located in key sites, no matter how remote these sites are from them. Space is diminished through technology and time acceleration. Transcontinental or interregional flows of capital, goods, services, people, symbols and meanings exercise an unprecedented impact on the formation of local economies and societies, influencing the everyday experience of people. Therefore identity formation is mediation between the global and the local. When Baghdad is under siege and its citizens are in shelters to avoid the smart bombs, satellite TV offers a spectacular version of it to people in Athens, London or New York. The same spectacle, though, reaches people in smaller or remote rural areas worldwide. State news broadcasting can hardly prevent the influence that the big satellite channels exercise in shaping public opinion.

In the field of culture and ideas, deeper questions of meaning and interpretation arise. The transitions that took place in the societies of Eastern Europe have exercised a considerable impact not only on the geopolitical order as such, but also on the revision of political ideologies throughout the globe (Derrida, 1996). Furthermore the partition of many states into smaller political units and the development of separatist movements, in many cases, have been accompanied by the emergence of new nationalisms. If, as Giddens (1990) suggests, modernity is inherently globalizing while at the same time tradition is an integral part of modernity, it follows that tradition and globalization are not necessarily conflicting or mutually exclusive processes. Although modernity is a social process which revolutionizes the modes of production and the social relationships, at the same time certain aspects of tradition are internalized and negotiated within the modernity project. Though globalization is associated with revolutionary innovations and developments in every field of economy, politics and culture, there is no evidence that globalization is incompatible with tradition. The revival of interest in religion among young people in many parts of the world (Angvik and Von Borries, 1997; Kepel, 1993), and the return to basic institutions such as the family and the community, indicate that tradition may be able to reinterpret and reproduce itself in new social contexts. The development of hybrid identities (Bhabha, 1996; Hall and Du Gay, 1996) could be perceived as a negotiation between the powerful and the marginal or between the past and the present. Hybridity can be understood both as the dynamics of an identity that resists assimilation by developing new creative forms of self-expression (as happens with diasporic identities (Ritzvi, 2000)), and as a recontextualization of tradition.

Nationalism in global times

Nation-building is fundamentally a process through which a dominant culture tends to become a hegemonic culture, a proselytizing culture and a culture of conversion and assimilation that claims a universalistic effect. Dominant religions become 'national religions', while dominant idioms become 'national languages'. In fact, this nation-building process pre-supposes political leadership and control and it is accomplished by states. The culture of the powerful elite becomes the dominant culture of the state that asserts universal approval among its citizenry. Even stronger is the claim that the national culture is the unifying culture that all the citizens of any particular state share in common, the hard core of the nationalism argument. The nationalist project, summed up in the principle of identification of the territoriality of the state with that of the nation, has led to the demand of statehood and to the develop-ment of modern states. This demand of statehood is based on the claim that cultural distinctiveness can only be ensured and preserved through political self-determination. There are many versions of nationalism, however, varying from the early modern period growth of monarchical power to the dissolution of the big empires and the formation of the nation-states, the overthrow of the colonial yoke during the twentieth century and the development of separatism within the late modern states. In twentieth-century Europe in particular, states have either repre-sented themselves as nation-states, or, in the case of the USSR, have internalized the nationality principle into their structures (Breuilly, 1993). Globalization on the other hand could be seen as an opposing force to the fundamental principles of nationalist ideology since it jeopardizes cultural distinctiveness and disrupts political self-determination. Even if this is the case, however, it should not lead to the conclusion that nation-alism does not survive in times of globalization.

In 1990 Bauman predicted that one of the possible forthcoming changes may be the 'denationalization of the state'. This would presup-pose that a major change would take place, which would entail the separation between the nation and the state in a process similar to the one of the separation between the church and the state (Bauman, 1990). The extent to which secularization has actually happened in Western societies is discussed in more detail later in this chapter. The above statement implies, however, that globalization encourages the gradual privatization of culture and the resurgence of ethnicity as against the allegedly homogeneous national identity. Bauman says that state-endorsed nationhood is increasingly contested as the principal frame of cultural identity. Smaller-scale allegiances are developed, and are em-bedded with social meaning, which is forged at the community level (Bauman, 1995). In the global era the state cannot embrace, let alone integrate, the multitude of cultures and identities of its citizens or inhabitants. For that reason the state cannot control culture in the way it was thought that it could in the past. To the extent that this is a correct assumption, the case might be that the reproduction of the state today presupposes a negotiation of its power in the global, national and local levels that leads to the constant bargaining and redefinition of domains of sovereignty. Privatization of culture and post-national citizenship identity (Delanty, 2000; Turner, 2000) might be a strategy for the state to maintain its own power. This strategic management though, and especially the denationalization of citizenship policy, is not an attribute of every state. In fact it is a tendency that meets with strong resistance in most states, either on the part of ruling elites or from traditionally conservative social groups. The way the state negotiates with ethnicity and treats diversity depicts the extent to which nationalism and tradition continue to be the key parameters for the reproduction of power in each particular state.

At the same time the tendency towards the traditional form of state nationalism still persists. States continue to reproduce national narratives through, for example, history teaching in schools or the definition of friends and enemies in foreign policy. Seeking political unity, states tend to construct fortresses, as in the case of citizenship and immigration policy. Indeed, immigration policy and the policy towards refugees and asylum seekers, especially the one adopted in most of the EU member states, are perceived as part of security policy. The TREVI (Terrorisme, Radicalisme, Extremisme, Violence Internationale) group, for example, which consists of the EU Ministers of Justice and Internal Affairs, as well as top executives from security and intelligence services, interprets regulations regarding immigration as part of a European legal order that perceives immigration flows and international crime as potentially inter-related trends (Pimbli, 2001). Only recently in Greece, for instance, immigration has been treated as an issue to be dealt with by the Ministry of Internal Affairs rather than by the Ministry of Public Security (Katsivardakou, 2004). The continuing attachment of citizenship policy to national identity rather than habitation is a condition that undermines any concept of European citizenship and reveals a substantial deficit in the institutionalization of civic, political, social and cultural rights (Bottomore, 1995; Habermas, 1994). Even European enlargement has been substantially undermined since the citizens of the new member states are subjected to restrictions regarding freedom of movement. Countries such as Greece and Sweden were the first to declare restrictions in accepting a labour force from the accession countries, fearing that the large waves of Poles and other Eastern Europeans would develop instability in their labour market and social insurance and welfare systems. Only the UK, among the EU states, has raised no barriers to the acceptance of the new member states' citizens, implying that the country's economy needs skilled and rather cheap labour. However, the Euro-barometer statistics show that xenophobia is growing in the EU countries, while Islamophobia has tended to become a public hysteria in the USA, as is indicated by the fact that New York airports have become a difficult destination for any person coming from an Islamic country.

Globalization is associated with the concept of increasing intercon-nectedness and interstate diffusion of capital, goods, cultures, symbols

and meanings. This, however, does not mean that globalization is a force
which enhances homogenization of societies and cultures and, as a consequence, eliminates particularism. Though globalization is apparently in
conflict with nationalism, new nationalisms and separatism are in many
ways facilitated by the context of globalization. Separatist movements
coming from 'clever regions' that become more competitive in the global
economy (for example, Basques in Spain, the League of the North in
Italy) or oppressed ethnicity that achieves awareness and new effective
modes of political expression (for example, Kurds in Turkey), are both
forms of contemporary nationalism facilitated by globalization processes.
Scottish, Basque or Québécois nationalisms, however, indicate the fact
that national integration has never been achieved in these multinational
states. On the other hand, public awareness regarding the political
oppression or systematic ethnic cleansing in many parts of the world,
as, for example, in Kosovo under the Milosevic regime, became possible
– at least in Europe and North America – partly through the internet.
The same applies with regard to women's oppression under the Taliban
regime in Afghanistan. The new ICTs facilitate both states' oppressive
strategies and manipulation of public opinion, as well as social resistance
and activist groups worldwide. Mathews says:

> within hours after the Chiapas rebellion in Southern Mexico in
> January 1994, the Internet swarmed with messages from human
> rights activists. The worldwide media attention they and their
> groups focused on Chiapas, along with the influx of rights activists
> to the area, sharply limited the Mexican government's response.
> What in other times would have been a bloody insurgency turned
> out to be a largely nonviolent conflict. 'The shots lasted ten days'
> Jose Angel Gurria, Mexico's foreign minister, later remarked, 'and
> ever since, the war has been . . . a war on the Internet'.
> (Mathews, 1998, p. 96)

The resurgence of ethnicity is one of the major factors of contemporary new nationalism that has led to the breaking up of some states.
Berger says that 'what to one will appear as a profound loss will be
seen by another as the prelude to liberation' (Berger, 1970, as cited in
Bauman, 1995, p. 148). The process which transforms ethnic identity
and tension into nationalism is quite interesting though. The case of
Eastern Europe for instance indicates the fact that indeed ethnicity and
cultural identity matter. This is particularly the case in contexts of
increasing urbanization and diffusion of literacy, parameters which allow
ethnic groups to develop their own intelligentsias. On the other hand,
existing social inequalities and cultural hierarchies within the former
communist regimes have deprived the non-dominant ethnic groups of
access to power. Language policies, for example, have advantaged

certain language groups against others. Additionally, the transition from the bureaucratic single-party and corrupt political regimes to the multi-party system in some cases, as in the former USSR, developed a power vacuum which left ethnicity as the only remaining coherent element (Breuilly, 1993).

In certain social and political contexts religion is constructed as an integral part of identity that gives rise to nationalism. Religion is a social construct. The collective meaning embedded in religion constitutes a crucial element of tradition that is bequeathed from one generation to its descendants. The social meaning of religion, however, does not remain static, but it is recontextualized, reinterpreted and reinvented with regard to the present. This is the power of religion. All three major sociologists, Marx, Durkheim and Weber, thought the significance of religion would decrease in modern times. It seems, however, that in certain social settings religion continues to represent a strong part of collective identity despite social growth or progress in the fields of science and technology. Although secularism has been considered as a characteristic of modern states, especially in Europe and North America, in many states there is no clear separation between the church and the state. The Queen is the official leader of the Church of England, while the King of Denmark has to be a member of the Evangelical Lutheran Church, perhaps the only two persons in Europe who do not enjoy freedom of religious conscience. What is called 'blasphemy' is a crime in Germany, Greece, Ireland, Italy and the UK. Church weddings enjoy equal standing with civil marriage in Denmark, Spain, Greece, Ireland, Italy and Portugal. The justification of divorce legislation only became possible in 1970 in Italy, in 1977 in Portugal, in 1981 in Spain and in 1995 in Ireland, due to tempestuous opposition on the part of the Catholic Church (Foundethakis, 2000). On the other hand, the explosion of religious fundamentalism puts the social roots of secularism under question in the USA. In secular France the treatment of religious symbols at schools seems to become more severe when those symbols do not refer to Christianity. The rise of new nationalisms, which in some cases relate to religious diversity, and the development of religious fundamentalism, not only in Europe but in various areas throughout the globe, represent the use of religion as a resurgent element of historical conflict. In this respect, religion is not incompatible with modernity. Religion in many cases coexists with, if not fuels, the modernity project.

Religious diversity has given rise to hatred, conflict and warfare in the past, especially in Europe. The conceptualization of current geopolitical conflict in terms of religious difference and cultural borders has its origins in the work of Samuel Huntington (1999) which has been popular and influential in USA, while it has developed many descendants (Scruton, 2002). It should be noted here that Huntington's reduction of identity to language and religion is a static and problematic way of

viewing the complexity of culture. Religion, however, is not by definition a social phenomenon which unavoidably leads to fundamentalism.
Religious identity is not always the reason that explains ethnic conflict.
The turbulent period that has led to the dismemberment of the former
Yugoslavia has been understood as a resurgence of religious fundamentalism that has fuelled ethnic conflict (Carter and Norris, 1996). It is
noted, for example, that:

> in spite of the fact that language is by far the most salient factor in
> the formation of Albanian national consciousness, the fact that
> the great majority of Albanians are Muslims has become one of the
> principal features focusing hostility on them in both Serbia and
> Macedonia.
>
> (Allcock, 1996, p. 69)

A relatively different approach, however, is adopted by Todorova (1997),
who suggests that the image of the violent Balkan identity is merely an
invention and construction of Western orientalism. In many cases the
Western powers have fostered ethnic conflict in the area in order to
manage it afterwards (Glenny, 2000). Recent phenomena such as ethnic
cleansing in Bosnia or Kosovo, condemnable as they are, can be understood neither as a peculiarity of the Balkan temperament (for example,
Thessalonica has not been deprived of its Jewish population due to
nationalist aggression among the people living in this region), nor as a
violent conflict between religiously diverse ethnic groups. This said, the
recent genocides that took place in the area could never be legitimated
through historical comparisons or relativism. What is argued here is that
ethnic conflict in the Balkans cannot be understood through reduction to
religious conflict. Certainly there are substantial social and economic
aspects in the type of nationalism that has flourished in the area, related
to the role of elitist groups who have developed non-transparent and
unaccountable political regimes. Moreover, communism had by no
means obliterated ethnic identity and national consciousness. While the
nation-building process in the Balkans is far more recent and compressed
than in other parts of Europe (Mazower, 2001), the democratic deficit in
the post-communist countries, coupled with economic recession, has
generated a deep social crisis (Hroch, 1996). In the case of the Balkan
ethnic conflicts religion has been used by powerful elites as a symbolic-
ally significant component of identity that fuelled current nationalist
ideologies.

   If the nation and the state have been one another's project (Appadurai,
1990), the project is by no means completed. In times of globalization,
despite the wide diffusion of ideological and cultural meanings, as
Anthony Smith (1990) points out, it is hard to envisage the absorption of
ethno-national cultures. In this process the state is an integral part of the

emergence of globalization rather than an impediment to it. The state has been, and continues to be, the main political entity that supports both globalization and nationalism. This, however, is an asymmetrical process. Some states initiate global flows, while some others are merely victims of them.

Education systems as the battleground of globalization and nationalism

Education is in many ways a battleground of both globalization and nationalism. Education systems have been key institutions in state formation (Green, 1990) and nation-building and they have facilitated nationalist projects promoted by states (see also Chapter 11). National systems of education present a striking similarity. State intervention for the introduction of compulsory schooling is a phenomenon that took place in Europe, the USA and Japan between the mid-eighteenth and late nineteenth century. Institutionalization and discipline of the student, state control of the overall structure and school knowledge, generalization of the official language and the history thesis of the respective state, classification and framing of knowledge are some of the enduring characteristics of mass schooling. While educational systems share many institutional characteristics, at the same time they predominantly contribute to the national, political and cultural differentiation of their attendants. Political socialization and citizenship formation is thus one of the main functions of state schooling across the world.

It has been argued that there is a substantial difference between schools and universities. While compulsory schooling is associated with national curricular systems and the mere reproduction of tradition and nationalism, universities tend to be more open to cosmopolitanism and reflection (Coulby, 2000). To the extent that this is the case, the consequence might be that there is a stratification of society within the terms of nationalism/globalization. Those social groups that tend to leave school at an early age, such as the poor or the marginalized minorities, are more likely to be exposed to predominantly nationalist curricula than the groups who have the chance to attend education for a longer time. The resistance towards schooling on the part of working classes or minorities, such as Roma families (Hancock, 2002; Liegeois, 1999; McDonald, 1999), could be partly explained in view of the fact that the school is actually hostile to the culture and social practices of these groups. Those groups who are able to cope with the selection procedures of the educational system (usually the social elites) enjoy the privileges of university attendance. The traditional academic freedom and autonomy, although in recent times under siege due to managerial scrutiny (Cowen, 2000), has had the effect of distancing university knowledge from state control and nationalism. In this respect, the universities are much closer to what has been described as cosmopolitan virtue, while the schools could be perceived as being at the very opposite end of the scale. The basic components of cosmopolitan virtue are those of:

- scepticism towards grand narratives;
- awareness and care for other cultures;
- distancing from one's own context and reflexivity;
- acceptance of hybridization, post-emotionalism and 'presentism' as against nostalgic images of the past;
- secularity and irony, both as a method and as a mentality (Turner, 2000).

These contingent identities of cosmopolitanism have been an attribute of the bourgeoisie which is now accentuated by globalization. It is hard to be post-emotional, though, in Palestine or when your child is faced with the Aids terror or famine in sub-Saharan Africa. Though the above distinction between schools and universities seems striking, since universities have also been key institutions in constructing and reproducing national narratives and the official history thesis of the state (see also Chapter 11), it is true, with variable differences, that universities leave more space for reflection and critical inquiry compared to schools.

Features of globalization in education

It is argued that globalization impacts dramatically upon the state–education relationship. Burbules and Torres (2000) suggest that there is a distinct political agenda that derives from the globalizing process and in particular the neoliberal version of it. A variety of multilateral and international organizations, such as the IMF, the OECD, the World Bank and the EU, develop, implement and justify specific educational policies which are transferred, or even directly imposed, at the state level. These policies have a predominantly economic rationale and they perceive education as an instrumental element of economic and labour market policy. The effect of these policies is the growing standardization of education which is performed through internationally diffused benchmarking tools, evaluation and assessment techniques. These new modes of education governance tend to relate education finance to performance indicators and standards, while they transform the overall structure of education systems worldwide. Globalization does not only impact on state education policy in general but it influences dramatically the type of knowledge that is considered as valuable in each society. Education reforms are financially driven and, as Martin Carnoy (2000) notes, tend to redistribute access to schooling away from lower-income students. Following are some of the most significant features of globalization in education.

Education and training as an instrumental part of economic policy

Since the formation of state education systems, in the nineteenth century, and especially after the Second World War, education has been considered as an integral part of social policy with redistributive effects (Marshall, 1995). Education has been considered as a key part of citizenship that not only facilitates participation in the labour market, but also widens access to a common economic, political and cultural heritage that enhances social cohesion. Equality of opportunities and compensatory education has been among the proclaimed goals of welfare state education policy in the post-war period. Today, however, education is increasingly perceived as part of economic and labour market policy. This is related to the peculiar integration of the knowledge economy principles into a public policy which is genuinely neoliberal. Education (especially universities) is perceived as a central institution in the knowledge economy which not only develops human resources but which directly raises the competitiveness of the economy. Nevertheless, the outcome of this recognition has hardly been the increased investment in public education and the attempt towards a wide and equal distribution of educational goods. On the contrary, during the last decade, a generalized and systematic attack on public education provision has taken place in many states, especially in Europe and the USA. Many of these trends are related to the attempt towards reintegrating education into a national and at the same time global economic agenda (Apple, 2000). Public education has been accused of being socially unaccountable, managerially bureaucratic, academically underperforming, economically inefficient and, for all these reasons, incapable of responding to the needs of the highly demanding knowledge economy. From this perspective education should directly serve the needs of the economy and the labour market by raising 'employability' and producing new skills and knowledge. The goal of equality of opportunities seems to have been abandoned in favour of competitiveness and entrepreneurship within the current global educational agenda.

In the context of the EU, as particular documents such as the *White Paper on Education and Training* (European Commission, 1995) make absolutely clear at the outset, education is perceived as a labour market policy and as a critical agent in the international economic competition between Europe, Japan and the USA. The Lisbon strategy for *Education and Training 2010* concludes that 'the Union must become the most competitive and dynamic knowledge-based economy in the world capable of sustainable economic growth with more and better jobs and greater social cohesion' (Europa 2010). In order for this goal to be achieved, social welfare and education systems are to be modernized. However, the prevailing concept of social welfare and education is defined though market-driven directives.

Education as a marketable commodity and the commodification of knowledge

In the year 2000, global public expenditure in the broad education sector exceeded one thousand billion dollars. This covers more than 50 million teachers, a billion students and hundreds of thousands of educational establishments. Some see this immense bloc as a dream market for future investment (Education International & Public Services International, 2000). Today, education is increasingly becoming a marketable commodity, either within state boundaries or in the global market. This is particularly the case for countries like the USA, the UK and Australia that treat education, universities in particular, as one of their major export industries. Of course, by exporting education they are exporting language and culture at the same time. In 1995 the international trade in higher education was estimated at 27 billion dollars. Higher education is the fifth exporting service in the USA, directed mainly to Asia (Japan, China, Taiwan, Malaysia, India, Indonesia and Korea). In the last General Agreement on Tariffs and Trade (GATT) round, the Uruguay round, the General Agreement for Trade in Services (GATS) agreement was agreed, which allowed the WTO to set the rules and regulate the international trade in the services sector. It was the first time that services, including intellectual property and education, were treated as part of global trade regulations. This agreement actually sets the rules of international competition in services and facilitates the establishment of an international market in education. These regulations have substantial consequences for the future of public education in general since they open up national education systems to the global education market. One of the first impacts of this agreement has been the pressure towards internationally recognized accreditation of educational institutions. The Bologna process in Europe could be seen as part of the same trend towards facilitating an international market of higher education. By this process, knowledge becomes standardized, classified and modified in exchangeable modules that comprise parts of undergraduate courses and full-time or part-time Masters' programmes (see also Chapter 1). These programmes are advertised in an international market aiming to attract students and parents who are willing to spend large amounts of money for a degree. Marketization of education is certainly related to the increasing international student mobility of the social elites. The so-called 'international education market', though, is not truly international. There is no balance in this market. It is an industry largely initiated by the universities of the West, and especially by English-speaking institutions, and it is exported to the rest of the world. Therefore, setting the rules of competition and homogenizing accreditation mechanisms does not entail either the rationalization of the rules of the game or that the game becomes more fair and transparent. It rather means that the infiltration of American and

English universities will be even further facilitated since their education model will become 'global'.

The growth of scrutiny institutions and the homogenization of testing at an international level

The intensification of evaluation and assessment is a process related to the commodification of education mentioned in the last section and more generally to the neoliberal agenda in education. This agenda leads to the attack against school and teacher autonomy. Evaluation and testing have been presented in neoliberal policy as means for accentuating accountability and raising standards in education (Zambeta, 1993). Regular inspections in schools and universities by a variety of specialized and ad hoc bodies and agents have had as a consequence the increased scrutiny in educational institutions for both teachers and students. The adoption of league tables in the UK, which place schools and universities in a hierarchical order according to their performance assessment, is part of education marketing and the outcome of a policy which now has become a transferable prototype. The introduction of the 'new public management' principles in education had as a consequence the explosion of testing. Furthermore, educational measurement promoted by international organizations, such as the International Association for the Evaluation of Educational Achievement (IEA), the OECD and the World Bank, and often adopted by states, represents a highly quantitative view of progress and finance-driven reforms rather than an attempt towards school improvement (Carnoy, 2000). In 2002, the EU Commission, in a mission to 'monitor progress', set up a Standing Group on Indicators and Benchmarks, which develops benchmarking tools and statistical indicators in order to assess European education systems. Such trends have as a consequence the increased homogenization of testing at an international level. This by no means implies that there is a growing convergence in terms of 'quality' between different educational settings. The intensification of evaluation and assessment mechanisms leads to the standardization and consolidation of internal hierarchies and the social stratification of educational institutions.

Dominance of the English language

English is increasingly becoming a compulsory subject in curricular systems worldwide. Families all over the world invest large amounts of money to ensure that their children will acquire competence in English. English is not only the ticket to the network society, but also a prerequisite for a high-status job or a condition for being part of what is 'modern culture', be it music, cinema, fashion or journalism. The

language the workers have to use in offices in many transnational corporations, no matter whether these offices are in Berlin or Athens, is
English. The language of instruction at Khazar University, in Azerbaijan,
is English and the most popular subjects are business, English and
management (Rust, 2000). An increasing number of Turkish universities
offer courses in English. Access to postgraduate programmes in Greek
universities presupposes an accredited qualification in the English language. On the other hand, the teaching, for instance, of East Asian
languages in Australia might be seen as relativizing the global dominance of English. A more pessimistic view, however, might be that
this indicates the contribution of education in economic and cultural
infiltration.

English teaching is not just a linguistic activity, it is also an accultur-
ation process (Coulby, 2000). The dominance of English has of course
been facilitated by colonialism and it is not a recent outcome of globalization (see also Chapters 12 and 14). Globalization, however, generates
and consolidates the colonizing effect of English domination. When
people are working on their computers or on the internet they spend
their day thinking and operating in English. When they attend international meetings or conferences they are doing the same. The domination of English hinders non-native speakers from having a powerful
impact on the dominant discourse in any domain. Scientific and academic languages are to a large extent English discourses, since most of
the academic journals are published in English. Competence in English
is ranking the world. This fact has an effect which goes far beyond the
stratification within academic communities. It dramatically impacts on
the type of knowledge produced. If the international academic discourse
is colonized by the English language, this has multiplier effects in
the reproduction of knowledge and culture. It diminishes intellectual
inquiry in other languages and impoverishes the potential variety of
interpretations of the world.

Curriculum reform and 'valuable knowledge'

During the last decade there has been a growing tendency towards
curriculum reform that makes education systems more responsive to
globalization trends. English language, computer literacy, science, technology, economics and management tend to be the subjects that are
gaining more importance within school and university curricula.
It should be noted, however, that school systems are much more rigid
in realizing and integrating shifts in knowledge than universities
(Coulby, 2000; see also Chapters 1 and 2). However, integration of social
change is an uneven process across and within educational systems.
Some universities, or more accurately some university departments and

laboratories, are key institutions in the knowledge economy, developing new knowledge. Some others are much more likely to stick to knowledge reproduction. Some school systems are more likely to prefer tradition and resistance towards modernization than others. This differentiation between institutions and educational systems might help explain the extent to which a country can be a competitive player in the knowledge economy. While education is an important factor, parameters such as the attraction of off-shore companies' investment and a flexible banking system are more crucial prerequisites for a country's shift to the knowledge economy.

Globalization, however, affects the conceptualization of valuable knowledge in each society. Even more importantly, the powerful discourses on the part of the agents of globalization (OECD, WTO, EU, World Bank, satellite TV channels) transmit the construction of social subjects at the local level and inscribe perceptions of what is worthy knowledge or culture, what should be learned at schools and what could be dropped and silenced (Gough, 2000; Lindblad and Popkewitz, 2001; Odora Hoppers, 2000). In these terms, globalization is a governing force of curriculum formation, education policy, practice and research worldwide.

The introduction of entrepreneurial culture in school and universities

Globalization is used by governments and decision-makers as a prescribing factor on domestic policy for transforming education into an instrument for raising the country's competitiveness in the global arena. In other words, education is increasingly perceived as a means of increasing wealth. The introduction of an entrepreneurial culture in school and universities is a policy promoted by agents of globalization and adopted by many states. The EU in particular has integrated the goal of promoting entrepreneurship into its basic strategies and relates its accomplishment to education policy (Zambeta, 2002). The 'European Community Support Frameworks', as well as the *Education and Training 2010* Lisbon strategy (Europa 2010), set entrepreneurialism as a principal goal of education. The restrictions in public education funding and the encouragement of schools and universities to seek additional sources in the private sector is another factor which leads to the encouragement of entrepreneurialism in education. On the other hand, the implementation of the 'new public management' principles in education systems is not only transferring the private sector mentality to the educational domain, but it develops a competitive environment and market conditions in educational institutions. The emergence of the competitive school, teacher, student, curriculum or university should lead to the emergence of the entrepreneurial self.

Devolution of power and increasing decentralization in education institutions

Devolution of power and decentralization tend to be global trends in education and a new form of governance that has affected even core examples of welfare education systems, such as that of Sweden (Lindblad *et al.*, 2002). Devolution of education power to various agents, usually involving public–private partnership, or even of a strictly private character, tends to redefine the relationship between education, the state and the market (Lindblad and Popkewitz, 2001; Whitty, 1998). On the other hand, states such as Germany could be seen as an opposite example to this. Devolution of power to new agents of scrutiny and control is actually a new form of state steering rather than a policy which leads to actual decentralization. Centralization, rather than decentralization, has been the main right-wing policy in countries such as the UK during the neo-conservative government. Decentralization is often a form of restructuring, which, although it could have positive effects, in most cases does not. This is due to the fact that it is accompanied by an 'anti-public spending ideology' and a disengagement of public commitment to education provision and quality. Various schemes of privatization, such as the voucher scheme, have been introduced in countries such as the USA, New Zealand, Chile and, even briefly, in UK nurseries. At the same time, globalization is considered as a force which increases the demand for schooling, since a more highly skilled labour force is needed more than before – due to technological change – and is better paid in the labour market (Carnoy, 2000, p. 55). This, however, does not always entail an increase of public investment in education, a fact which leads to further discrepancies and enhances social inequality, since access to high-quality education and higher-status occupations will be increasingly dependent on socio-economic background.

Universities and research are becoming increasingly important

In the context of the knowledge economy, universities and research are becoming central institutions for the development and competitiveness of the economy. Some universities are key components of the network society in that they not only produce the know-how but also the high-technology product as such (see Chapter 2). Universities thus become key sites for new technology production and consumption. The former, however, is only true for some elitist institutions in the high-GDP states. It tends to be less so in less developed educational systems and poorer economies. In fact the university becomes more diversified than it used to be in the past. The pressure for further expansion of higher education and training systems on the one hand and the fiscal crisis of education and welfare systems on the other have as a consequence the rapid development of a tertiary education sector which is less focused on research and more focused on teaching vocationally oriented or operational knowledge. This sector offers higher education at a substantially lower cost. Some sceptics, though, argue that the role of the university in the context of globalization becomes more instrumental with regard to the production of skills, the fulfilment of performance indicators or the attraction of funded research and less devoted to intellectual inquiry (Cowen, 2000; Readings, 1996). The question whether societies still need an institution for critical reflection and to what extent the university will continue to be this institution remains open.

Features of nationalism in education

Globalization is not a force that meets with no resistance. Moreover, it is not just a one-way process. Policies and cultural products are globally diffused, but locally appropriated. Even if imposed by agencies of power they nevertheless have more dialectic outcomes. Terms such as Harvey's 'global village', the concept of the 'glocal' developed by social geographers or Appadurai's 'vernacular globalisation' indicate the mediation between the global and the local and perhaps the specific reconfigurations of globalization at the local level. This is a process that in certain cases allows the restoration of tradition despite the forces of globalization. While, for instance, English language and American culture are considered as dominant aspects of globalization, it seems that they are also affected by the forces of globalization. In the USA, Michael Apple observes an attempt towards a reinstallation of tradition that takes the form of a selective vision of a common culture: an emphasis on the 'Western tradition', on religion and on the English language. This is interpreted as a cultural fear in respect of Latin America, Africa or Asia (Apple, 2000).

Education systems, and especially schooling, have been key sites for the reproduction of tradition in modern societies. The social construction of nationhood through the amalgamation of a shared vision of the past, the generalization and imposition of the dominant language, religion and culture and the consolidation of social hierarchies has been the basic mission of education systems. This function of educational systems is now challenged by globalization. Nonetheless, despite the dramatic impact of globalization, tradition and nationalism persist in educational systems. The survival or revival of religious indoctrination and the persistence of nationalist history teaching are some indicative evidence of that.

Religious indoctrination

Education systems are a construct of modernity, while at the same time they represent the contradictions of the modernity project (Coulby and

Jones, 1995). State intervention in education and the development of education systems could be perceived as a process of rationalization and expansion of social rights to literacy and knowledge. The institutionalization of free and compulsory education for all, from the mid-eighteenth to the early twentieth century throughout Europe, corresponds to the massive expansion of educational institutions and to the gradual displacement of the church in educational provision (Green, 1990; Vaughan and Archer, 1971). While pre-modern, church-controlled education would serve to mould the faithful, state education systems would aim to educate the citizen. It could be argued that the epistemological request of the Enlightenment, for rationality as the principle for knowledge acquisition and the clear distinction between 'reason' and 'faith' (Psychopaedis, 1996; Tsinorema, 1996), finds its institutional expression in state education. However, modern education has not stopped being uneven and socially selective, while rationality is not always the basis of school knowledge. Education, as a manifestation of the modernity project, represents at the same time both an emancipatory demand related to Enlightenment ideas and one of the main state mechanisms of social control. While inherent in the idea of modernity is a contrast with tradition, in fact many combinations of the modern and the traditional are to be found in contemporary societies (Giddens, 1990). Religion constitutes a survival of tradition within the context of modernity, which presents an impressive resistance and a capacity of readjustment to new social conditions. As tradition reinterprets itself with regard to new social contexts and is reinvented, so does religion. Religion is not necessarily incompatible with modernity. The power of religion in shaping collective identities has been immense over time and this continues to be the case in certain social settings. Education systems, as representative institutions of the modernity project for control over political socialization, provide an illustrative example of the symbiotic relationship between religion and modernity.

European educational systems, in particular, as manifestations of modernity have not all distanced themselves from religion. Religious teaching, with all its variations, remains compulsory and catechist in the main in countries such as Denmark, Greece or England. Although secularization processes have taken place in many European states, most of the European education systems have not abolished their links to the churches. The way church–state relations are defined in the constitution of each country does not always indicate the place of religion or the nature of religious teaching in schools (Zambeta, 2003). The churches, even in cases where they have stopped enjoying the status of the established state church, manage to maintain their influence on education through many direct or indirect ways. Even in cases of clear separation between the church and the state, as in France, the par excellence secular state in Europe, or Belgium, the churches have not been deprived of their right to establish schools, under the form of private schooling. The reinstatement of religious teaching in the post-communist countries, as for instance in Poland (where the subject of religion is optional but rather influential) or Romania (where religion is taught as a compulsory subject at schools), depicts the dynamic restoration of religion in these countries as part of the uprooting of Marxist orthodoxy. In Serbia the reintroduction of religious education is a debated issue today (Vukomanovic, 2002). In Turkey, although secularism has been a fundamental part of the Kemalist definition of the modern state, religious classes have become obligatory since 1981. Religious identity is presented in school textbooks as drawing the borderline between the national self and the external others (Copeaux, 2002).

Furthermore, in many education systems, the influence of religion is evident not only in the subject of religion per se, but in many other subject areas of the school curriculum, history textbooks in particular. Education practices such as acts of collective worship, the morning prayer or various school festivals represent the crucial place of religion in many European education systems and its influence on the culture of schooling. In the case of Greece, the construction of Orthodoxy as an integral part of Greek national identity is reproduced partly through the educational system. This social and educational practice ignores the existing religious diversity and cultural complexity in contemporary societies. Greek education is an extreme case of religious catechism among the EU countries (Sotirelis, 1998; Zambeta, 2003).

It should be noted, however, that in most of the EU member states there is a tendency towards an alleviation of the catechist character of religious teaching in favour of a relatively pluralistic model. The fact of existing religious diversity and the possibility of religious education according to one's own faith has become an issue even in countries where religious teaching is of a catechist mode. However, in countries such as Italy, Spain, Portugal or the Netherlands the subject of religious education is not compulsory for the students. Even in Ireland, despite the dominance of religion in shaping national identity and in the historical construction of the educational system, religious teaching is not, officially, compulsory. However, the model of a secular subject on religion (what is called 'study of religions') remains weak throughout European education. At the moment this model corresponds to the paradigm of religious education followed in the Netherlands, but there is a tendency towards a transition to this model in other countries also.

Nationalist history and discourses on cultural supremacy

Education systems have been key institutions in nation-building. This inherent function of education is the most powerful fundamental element of it that resists change. Nationalism persists in school curricular systems. Nationalist narratives make claims for a national culture's 'distinctiveness', originality, nobility and supremacy. Dominant discourses on the cultural supremacy of the nation, underlining the distinctiveness, continuity, nobility, originality and purity of its legacy to the world, constitute common features of school curricula (Coulby, 2000). In so doing, these nationalist discourses link themselves to racism. Cultural distinctiveness, originality and purity presuppose the uncontaminated cultural existence in a protected territory, an imaginary cage that prohibited cultural exchange through time. An alleged 'culture of origin' is a culture that claims to have preserved its distinct nature and characteristics without negotiation or interaction with other cultures. Moreover, even if there has been interaction, as for instance in the case of occupation by asymmetrically armed forces, a culture of origin has often proved to be resistant to the foreign influence and has managed to keep its authenticity. This, however, indicates the irresistible enchantment and superiority of this particular culture. Perhaps this discourse has never been expressed more vividly than by this multicoated phrase of Horace regarding the Greek–Roman cultural osmosis: '*Graecia capta ferum victorum cepit et artes intulit agresti Latio*' ('Captured Greece captured its fierce conqueror and brought the arts to the agrarian Latio') (Horace, *Epistulae*, 2, 1, 156–7). At the same time, however, the argument of cultural originality claims that authenticity relies on the lack of interference or borrowing from other cultures. In so doing, it implies the racial purity and cleanliness of a nation's culture. The systematic oblivion to cultural interaction as well as social imaginaries of cultural supremacy are intrinsic parts of the narratives embedded in national historiographies. State-endorsed visions of the past are often inscribed by arguments that derive from those nationalist ideologies (see also Chapter 11).

Historiography has been a crucial part of nation-building. The consolidation of nationhood in modern states has been largely based on the construction of the history of the specific state and its diffusion and generalization through the educational system. The production of proof regarding the nation's continuity through space and time is a mission of critical importance accomplished by the organic intellectuals of modern states. In the case of Greece, for instance, the construction of the official history thesis is the product of nineteenth-century romantic historiography that has been transferred to school textbooks and remains largely unchanged since then (Koulouri, 1988; Skopetea, 1994). This thesis was aimed at the restoration of the continuity between Greek classical antiquity and the modern state, an argument that presupposed the recognition of the genuinely Hellenic identity of Byzantium. The ahistorical use of the concepts of 'nation' and 'time' is the main feature of Greek history textbooks in their attempt to construct the historical continuity of the Greek nation (Avdela, 1997; Frangoudaki and Dragonas, 1997). The battle over the authentic and pure form of the Greek language, as the official language of the modern Greek state, was an exemplification of the nationalist ideology that dominated for about a century (Frangoudaki, 2001). The construction of the Turkish history thesis has also been a political project to demonstrate a historical continuity dissociated from the Ottoman legacy, something which was then considered as a necessary precondition for the formation of the modern Turkish nation-state. While in the multi-ethnic Ottoman Empire religious affiliation was the main social category, the history thesis of the modern Turkish state attempted to reformulate the Turkic identity by linking it to language. This attempt was encouraged by the Turkish nationalism of the 1930s and was accomplished through the collaboration of the intellectuals of the newly formed state: poets, linguists and academics. The Turkish nationalist narrative of that period claimed the common and purely Arian origins of the Anatolian Turks, which were presented as an ancient civilization that influenced all the notable cultures of the world (Ersanli-Behar, 1998). Later on, in the 1970s, the history thesis which was established by Kemalism and imposed secularism in the country was to be broadened by the 'Turkish–Islamic synthesis' in order to incorporate Islam in the definition of Turkish national identity.

In the context of the new Balkans, Marxist historiography was abandoned and the 'old' official history was replaced by new narratives. The vision of the past was revised and old myths were replaced either by new ones, or by even older ones that derive from the period of the formation of the Balkan national states (Koulouri, 2002). Antiquity is used in the new history textbooks as the documentary evidence of the nations' continuity and an important element in new nation-building (Vouri, 2000). Mutually contested territorial claims correspond to contrasted views regarding the spatial continuity of different nations. The worship of memory and at the same time the healing effect of eclectic oblivion and the mythology of the past, have become the political project of the new history textbooks. Ethnocentrism is a prominent characteristic of history teaching that, in a context of competing states, feeds xenophobia and nationalism.

National narratives are contrasting views of the past which usually form opposing pairs of interpretations (Koulouri, 2002). In the former Yugoslavia, for instance, the common history that was taught until 1990 consisted of separate sections on general history and on what was then considered national history and the history of the 'other Yugoslav nations'. After the breakdown of Yugoslavia, this history was replaced by rival ethnic historiographies. Interethnic violence is presented in many textbooks in strongly emotional ways, while shared history has been silenced. A large majority of recent textbooks cultivate an image of a great past related to the territory of the specific state, such as an image of a Great Slovenia, Great Serbia or Great Croatia (Koren, 2002). At the same time the first Yugoslavia (of 1918) is treated as 'the prison for nations', where every nation sees itself as the victim of the others. Croatia and Slovenia see themselves as economically exploited and politically oppressed by the 'Great Serbian hegemony'. Serbia sees itself as the victim of 'Croatian separatism', Macedonia sees itself as denationalized and assimilated and Bosnia and Montenegro are seen as underdeveloped and impoverished. The second (Communist) Yugoslavia, though it is more positively evaluated, is also criticized for injustice to each one of the nations involved. The most conflicting accounts of the past refer to the Second World War, the assessment of Socialist Yugoslavia and its collapse, and the wars of 1991–5. Serbian textbooks present the Serbs as the most active resistance towards the Axis forces, whereas this is doubted in the Croatian textbooks.

The rewriting of history in the Balkan states forms mutually exclusive national histories that share the same structure in epistemological terms. They are all normative discourses and dogmatic interpretations of history which ignore the views of the other and present themselves as uncontested truths (Koulouri, 2002, p. 47). Once again, education and history teaching is a vehicle of nationalist projects.

Conclusion

Neither globalization nor Europeanization seem to be challenging nationalism. While English and computer literacy tend to be some of the shared school subjects throughout the globe, they are often accompanied by nationalist history and distorted images and perceptions of the world. Education systems, the school in particular, are some of the most conservative social institutions where tradition prevails. Schools present immense resistance to change.

States still matter (Held and McGrew, 2002a, 2002b) in issues wider than education. But they certainly continue to control schooling. This does not mean that they continue to control socialization in the way they used to do in the past. The flows of cultures, symbols and meanings in a globalized system are genuinely uncontrollable by any traditional ideological mechanism of the state, such as education. Though education systems, schools in particular, continue to be perhaps the most effective mechanism available to contemporary societies for dissemination of literacy and knowledge, it is quite possible that their relative power is being gradually diminished. Global media, fast food, fashion or music may be more influential factors in shaping young peoples' identities than the school curriculum. Tradition and nationalism may be challenged in a globalized system. But they are still there developing new hybrids.

References

Allcock, J. B. (1996) Borders, States, Citizenship: Unscrambling Yugoslavia, in F. W. Carter and H. T. Norris (eds) *The Changing Shape of the Balkans*. London: UCL Press, pp. 63–79.

Angvik, M. and Von Borries, B. (eds) (1997) *Youth and History: A Comparative European Survey on Historical Consciousness and Political Attitudes among Adolescents*. Hamburg: Korber-Stiftung.

Appadurai, A. (1990) Disjuncture and Difference in the Global Cultural Economy, in M. Featherstone (ed.) *Global Culture: Nationalism, Globalisation and Modernity*. London: Sage, pp. 295–310.

Apple, M. (2000) Between Neoliberalism and Neoconservativism: Education and Conservativism in a Global Context, in N. Burbules and C. A. Torres (eds) *Globalisation and Education: Critical Perspectives*. New York: Routledge.

Avdela, E. (1997) Time, History and Identity in Greek School, in A. Frangoudaki and T. Dragonas (eds) *'What's Our Country?' Ethnocentricity in Education*. Athens: Alexandria, pp. 49–71.

Bauman, Z. (1990) Modernity and Ambivalence, in M. Featherstone (ed.) *Global Culture*. London: Sage, pp. 143–69.

Bauman, Z. (1995) Searching for a Centre that Holds, in M. Featherstone, S. Lash and R. Robertson (eds) *Global Modernities*. London: Sage, pp. 140–54.

Bhabha, H. K. (1996) Culture's In-Between, in S. Hall and P. Du Gay (eds) *Cultural Identity*. London: Sage, pp. 53–60.

Bottomore, T. (1995) Citizenship and Social Class: Forty Years Afterwards (Introduction and translation: Olga Stasinopoulou), in T. H. Marshall and T. Bottomore (eds) *Citizenship and Social Class*. Athens: Gutenberg, pp. 125–94.

Breuilly, J. (1993) *Nationalism and the State*. Manchester: Manchester University Press.

Burbules, N. C. and Torres, C. A. (eds) (2000) *Globalisation and Education: Critical Perspectives*. New York and London: Routledge.

Callaghan, J. (2000) *The Retreat of Social Democracy*. Manchester: Manchester University Press.

Carnoy, M. (2000) Globalisation and Educational Reform, in N. P. Stromquist and K. Monkman (eds) *Globalisation and Education: Integration and Contestation Across Cultures*. Lanham, MD: Rowman & Littlefield, pp. 43–62.

Carter, F. W. and Norris, H. T. (eds) (1996) *The Changing Shape of the Balkans*. London: UCL Press.

Castells, M. (1996) *The Information Age: Economy, Society and Culture. Volume 1: The Rise of the Network Society*. Oxford: Blackwell.

Copeaux, E. (2002) Religious Identities in Turkish Textbooks, in C. Koulouri (ed.) *Clio in the Balkans: The Politics of History Education*. Thessaloniki: CDRSE.

Coulby, D. (2000) *Beyond The National Curriculum: Curricular Centralism and Cultural Diversity in Europe and the USA*. London and New York: Routledge-Falmer.

Coulby, D. and Jones, C. (1995) *Postmodernity and European Education Systems: Centralist Knowledge and Cultural Diversity*. Stoke on Trent: Trentham.

Cowen, R. (2000) Academic Freedom, Universities and the Knowledge Economies. *Panepistemio*, 2: 3–23.

Delanty, G. (2000) *Citizenship in a Global Age*. Buckingham: Open University Press.

Derrida, J. (1996) *Specters of Marx: The State of the Debt, the Work of Mourning, and the New International*. New York and London: Routledge.

Education International & Public Services International (2000) The WTO and the Millenium Round. What is at Stake for Public Education? Common Concerns for Workers in Education and the Public Sector. *Panepistimio*, 2: 59–98.

Ersanli-Behar, B. (1998) The Role of Language in Turkish Historiography, in R. Larsson, J. Hjarpe and L. Wallenius (eds) *Boundaries of Europe*. Uppsala: FRN, pp. 102–12.

Europa 2010 *Education and Training 2010: Diverse Systems, Shared Goals*. Available at: http://europa.eu.int/comm/education/policies/2010/et_2010_en.html.

European Commission (1995) *White Paper on Education and Training. Teaching and Learning: Towards the Learning Society*, COM (95)590. Brussels: European Commission.

Foundethakis, P. (2000) Religion and Constitutional Culture in Europe. *Revue Hellenique De Droit International*, 53: 227–75.

Frangoudaki, A. (2001) *The Language and the Nation 1880–1980: One Hundred Years of Struggle for the Authentic Greek Language*. Athens: Alexandria.

Frangoudaki, A. and Dragonas, T. (1997) *'What's Our Country?' Ethnocentricity in Education*. Athens: Alexandria.

Gabel, M. and Bruner, H. (2003) *Globalinc: An Atlas of the Multinational Corporation*. New York: The New Press.

Giddens, A. (1990) *The Consequences of Modernity*. Cambridge: Polity Press.

Giddens, A. (1998) *The Third Way: The Renewal of Social Democracy*. London: Polity Press.

Glenny, M. (2000) *The Balkans, 1804–1999: Nationalism, War and the Great Powers*. London: Granta Books.

Gough, N. (2000) Globalisation and Curriculum Inquiry: Locating, Representing and Performing a Transnational Imaginary, in N. P. Stromquist and K. Monkman (eds) *Globalisation and Education: Integration and Contestation Across Cultures*. Lanham, MD: Rowman & Littlefield, pp. 77–98.

Green, A. (1990) *Education and State Formation: The Rise of Education Systems in England, France and the USA*. New York: St Martin's Press.

Habermas, J. (1994) Citizenship and National Identity: Some Reflections on the Future of Europe, in B. Turner and P. Hamilton (eds) *Citizenship: Critical Concepts*. London: RKP, pp. 341–58.

Hall, S. and Du Gay, P. (eds) (1996) *Cultural Identity*. London: Sage.

Hancock, I. (2002) *We Are the Romani People*. Hatfield: Centre de Recherche Tsiganes, University of Hertfordshire Press.

Harvey, D. (1989) *The Condition of Postmodernity*. Oxford: Blackwell.

Held, D. *et al.* (2000) Rethinking Globalisation, in D. Held and A. McGrew (eds) *The Global Transformations Reader*. London: Polity Press, pp. 54–60.

Held, D. and McGrew, A. (2002a) *Globalisation/Anti-Globalisation*. Cambridge: Polity Press.

Held, D. and McGrew, A. (eds) (2002b) *Governing Globalisation*. London: Polity Press.

Hobsbawm, E. (1999) *Industry and Empire*. London: Penguin.

Hroch, M. (1996) *From National Movement to the Fully-formed Nation*. Athens: Themelio.

Huntington, S. (1999) *The Clash of Civilizations and the Remaking of the World Order.* Athens: Terzo Books.

Katsivardakou, D. (2004) *Legalization of Economic Immigrants and Human Rights: Institutional Framework and Public Administration Practices in Greece.* Unpublished MA thesis, Department of Early Childhood Education, University of Athens.

Kepel, G. (1993) *The Revenge of God: The Resurgence of Islam, Christianity and Judaism in the Modern World.* London: Polity Press.

Koren, S. (2002) Yugoslavia: A Look in the Broken Mirror. Who is the 'Other'?, in C. Koulouri (ed.) *Clio in the Balkans: The Politics of History Education.* Thessaloniki: CDRSE, pp. 193–202.

Koulouri, C. (1988) *History and Geography in Greek Schools (1834–1914).* Athens: Historical Record of Greek Youth, GSY.

Koulouri, C. (ed.) (2002) *Clio in the Balkans: The Politics of History Education.* Thessaloniki: CDRSE.

Lal, V. (2002) *Empire of Knowledge: Culture and Plurality in the Global Economy.* London: Pluto Press.

Lehman, B. A. (1998) Intellectual Property: America's Competitive Advantage in the Twenty-first Century, in D. Neef, A. Siesfeld and J. Cefola (eds) *The Economic Impact of Knowledge.* Boston, MA: Butterworth Heinemann, pp. 77–92.

Liegeois, J.-P. (1999) School Provision for Roma Children: A European Perspective. *EJIS*, 10(2): 137–50.

Lindblad, S. and Popkewitz, T. (2001) Education Governance and Social Integration and Exclusion: Studies in the Powers of Reason and the Reasons of Power. Uppsala Reports on Education 39. Uppsala: EGSIE.

Lindblad, S., Ozga, J. and Zambeta, E. (2002) Changing Forms of Educational Governance in Europe. *European Educational Research Journal*, special issue, 1(4).

McDonald, C. (1999) Roma in the Romanian Educational System: Barriers and Leaps of Faith. *EJIS*, 10(2): 183–200.

Marshall, T. H. (1995) Citizenship and Social Class, in T. H. Marshall and T. Bottomore (eds) *Citizenship and Social Class*, trans. and intro. O. Stasinopoulou. Athens: Gutenberg.

Mathews, J. T. (1998) Power Shift: The Age of Non-State Actors, in D. Neef, A. Siesfeld and J. Cefola (eds) *The Economic Impact of Knowledge.* Boston, MA: Butterworth Heinemann, pp. 93–105.

Mazower, M. (2001) *The Balkans: From the End of Byzantium to the Present Day.* London: Phoenix Press.

Odora Hoppers, C. A. (2000) Globalisation and the Social Construction of Reality: Affirming or Unmasking the 'Inevitable'?, in N. P. Stromquist and K. Monkman (eds) *Globalisation and Education: Integration and Contestation Across Cultures.* Lanham: Rowman & Littlefield, pp. 99–119.

Pimbli, R. M. (2001) *The Concept of Europe and European Citizenship.* Unpublished MA thesis, Department of Early Childhood Education, University of Athens.

Psychopaedis, K. (1996) Towards a Theory of Modernity, in Greek Civilisation and General Education Studies Association (ed.) *Modernity: Time for its Assessment.* Athens: Greek Civilisation and General Education Studies Association, pp. 9–28.

Readings, B. (1996) *The University in Ruins.* Cambridge, MA: Harvard University Press.

Ritzvi, F. (ed.) (2000) *International Education and the Production of Global Imagination*. New York: Routledge.

Robins, K. (2000) Encountering Globalisation, in D. Held and A. McGrew (eds) *The Global Transformations Reader*. London: Polity Press, pp. 195–201.

Rosenau, J. (2002) Governance in a New Global Order, in D. Held and A. McGrew (eds) *Governing Globalisation*. London: Polity Press, pp. 70–86.

Rust, V. D. (2000) Educational Reform: Who Are the Radicals?, in N. P. Stromquist and K. Monkman (eds) *Globalisation and Education: Integration and Contestation Across Cultures*. Lanham, MD: Rowman & Littlefield, pp. 63–76.

Scruton, R. (2002) *The West and the Rest: Globalisation and the Terrorist Threat*. London: Continuum.

Skopetea, E. (1994) Balkan National Histories, in Society of Modern Greek Studies and General Paideia (ed.) *Nation – State – Nationalism*. Athens: Moraitis School, pp. 305–17.

Smith, A. D. (1990) Towards a Global Culture?, in M. Featherstone (ed.) *Global Culture: Nationalism, Globalisation and Modernity*. London: Sage, pp. 171–92.

Sotirelis, G. (1998) *Religion and Education: The Constitution and the European Convention. From Catechism to Pluralism*. Athens: Sakoulas.

Todorova, M. (1997) *Imagining the Balkans*. New York: Oxford University Press.

Tsinorema, S. (1996) Rationalism and Relativism: Modernity or Postmodernity?, in Greek Civilisation and General Education Studies Association (ed.) *Modernity: Time for its Assessment*. Athens: Greek Civilisation and General Education Studies Association, pp. 29–57.

Turner, B. S. (2000) Cosmopolitan Virtue, in E. Isin (ed.) *Democracy, Citizenship and the Global City*. London: Routledge, pp. 129–47.

UNDP (1999) Globalisation with a Human Face, in D. Held and A. McGrew (eds) *The Global Transformations Reader*. London: Polity Press, pp. 341–7.

Vaughan, M. and Archer, M. S. (1971) *Social Conflict and Educational Change in England and France 1789–1848*. Cambridge: Cambridge University Press.

Vouri, S. (2000) Antiquity as Source of National Trace in the Balkan History Textbooks (1991–6), in A. Kapsalis, K. Bonidis and A. Sipitanou (eds) *The Image of the 'Other'/Neighbour in the Balkan States History Textbooks*. Athens: Typothito-Dardanos, pp. 101–15.

Vukomanovic, M. (2002) Religious Education in Serbia, in C. Koulouri (ed.) *Clio in the Balkans: The Politics of History Education*. Thessaloniki: CDRSE, pp. 313–19.

Whitty, G. (1998) *Devolution and Choice in Education: The School, the State and the Market*. Buckingham: Open University Press.

Wilkinson, R. and Hughes, S. (eds) (2002) *Global Governance: Critical Perspectives*. London: Routledge.

Zambeta, E. (1993) Education as Social Policy, in P. Getimis and D. Gravaris (eds) *Welfare State and Social Policies*. Athens: Themelio, pp. 223–52.

Zambeta, E. (2002) Europeanisation and the Emergence of Entrepreneurial Culture in Greek Education: Reflections from Education Policy. *Education and Social Justice*, 4(2): 15–23.

Zambeta, E. (2003) *School and Religion*. Athens: Themelio.

4 Education, national identity and religion in Japan in an age of globalization

Masako Shibata

Introduction

Much of the contemporary analysis of educational change begins from the concept of globalization, especially economic globalization. How the economic pressures of globalization and international competition are working out in education is not a simple linearity. Older cultural beliefs, remembered pasts and new political movements prevent such linearities. While economic and political boundaries are blurring, the intensification of globalization has stimulated the rise of nationalism and the search for national identity (Robertson and White, 2003, p. 24). After the Cold War, religion as an institution has come back on to the agenda for the redefinition of nationhood (Juergensmeyer, 1995; Kepel, 1992; Robertson, 1992).

In this age of globalization, the Japanese government has been nonetheless unsuccessful in its struggle to link – again – religion and national identity in the minds of schoolchildren. This is largely because, as will be demonstrated in this chapter, religion as a whole has not been prominent in educational discussions and has been a delicate topic, especially in terms of nationhood. The major aim of this chapter is to explain this politically and educationally sensitive treatment of religion in the country. It is traceable, as will be argued, back to the formation of the quasi-religious Emperor State in the last third of the nineteenth century and its defeat in the Second World War. In particular, the way in which the Emperor State collapsed and its theocratic footing vanished in the war had a decisive impact on the substantial reduction of the role of religion as a political institution in post-war Japan.

In addition, this chapter aims to explore two consequences of the detachment of religion from the state and from national ideology in present-day Japan. Paradoxically, both consequences led to nationalistic claims. First, there emerged arguments that the absence of religious education had brought about a dangerous religious *naïveté*, especially among young people, and thus that traditional moral and spiritual education should be re-emphasized. Second, while arguments for and against the reinforcement of national identity focus on the resurgence of the politico-religious ideology, new notions of Japanese national identity have been burgeoning among the young. Apart from the governmental efforts, and despite anti-nationalist advocacy by educators, new notions of national identity are noticeable in a sense of 'national pride' in popular cultures, along with the growing interaction between people and cultures on a global scale.

To begin with, before concentrating on Japan, the chapter clarifies its general approach to the social and educational positioning of religion, particularly in the age of globalization. The second section illustrates how religion as a basis of national identity was constructed and deconstructed in the processes of Japan's state formation. The third section discusses the struggle of the post-war government to restore Japanese identity within the theme of spiritual heritage. The following two sections explore other consequences of the detachment of religion from the public institutions: discussions on problems which arose from the treatment of religion in post-war Japan in the fourth section; and the development of a new sense of national pride witnessed in recent Japanese sub-cultures in the fifth section.

The social and educational positioning of religion in an age of globalization

Looking back at the history of the modern era, it is evident that the identification of nations depended on elusive political ideologies. Nations are not the invention, though possibly are a device, of political ideologies. Except for some 40 years during the Cold War, wars were not waged against different political ideologies, but to claim territories, ethnic supremacy, cultural autonomy or religious orthodoxy (Castells, 1997; Gray, 1998). These elements are now becoming the key to the redefinition of a 'self' of nationhood.

Although what creates and maintains national identity is complex, local and particular cultures remain eloquent of a collective identity. In a global age, localism and particularism still carry great weight and a communal unity largely rests on the shared value of common cultural heritages. Those who share this value identify themselves as the members of a societal community, a nation. Above all, religion lays a basic foundation for such national identity:

> No more arresting emblems of the modern culture of nationalism exist than cenotaphs and tombs of Unknown Soldiers. ... The cultural significance of such monuments becomes even clearer if one tries to imagine, say, a Tomb of the Unknown Marxist or a cenotaph for fallen Liberals. Is a sense of absurdity avoidable? The reason is that neither Marxism nor Liberalism are much concerned with death

and immortality. If the nationalist imagining is so concerned, this suggests a strong affinity with religious imaginings. As this affinity is by no means fortuitous, it may be useful to begin a consideration of the cultural roots of nationalism with death, as the last of a whole gamut of fatalities.

(Anderson, 1991, pp. 9–10)

Anthony Smith (2001) goes further by arguing that nationalism is a form of religion per se as it represents the essence of public culture. Religions explicitly demonstrate the symbolic values of the cultural autonomy of nations, and are therefore useful political devices for defining the notions of nationhood.

In an age of globalization, religious identity has increasingly been understood as a core notion in nationhood and as a vital political instrument for national cohesion. In fact, some states identify their 'authentic citizens' in terms of their religious faith. This is particularly overt in some new states. It is noteworthy that the governments of most former communist states have been trying to form new notions of national identity within religious frameworks. To the disappointment of some of the former communist elite, these governments are preoccupied with the old political premise that the people should share the long-established values of religious morality (Kepel, 1992; Ramet, 1984). The Polish identity as Catholic had long survived, first, oppression by Prussian Protestantism and the Russian Orthodox Church and, further, the 40 years of communist rule. After the demise of the Soviet Union and of its control over Poland, this identity now provides an important spiritual basis for the reconstruction of the Polish state. By the same token, Belarus publicized a parliamentary confirmation in October 2002 of the dominant role of the Russian Orthodox Church in the public domain.

In education too, religion in public schooling is a subject of serious concern. In European Christendom, religious education has powerfully been acting as political education (Coulby and Jones, 1996). While belief in Christianity is declining in Europe, the political demand for Christian education is now growing. In the name of secularism, 'Islamophobia' has been gaining ground. In united Germany, President Johannes Rau's argument against the ban on Muslim women's headscarves in the public schools was not accepted by some German states, which now consider ruling out such religious clothing. Drawing the major attention of the European media, the French President Jacques Chirac endorsed the policy of forbidding conspicuous religious insignia, notably the *hijab*, in public institutions. A southern French municipality decided to stop providing pork-free lunch for Muslims, who now have a school meal only on Friday, the Christian fish day. Berlusconi's coalition government warned that the economic functions of mosques in Italian society would be subject to closer control than before. Without doubt, religious concerns now powerfully affect the political behaviour of states. In the coming age of globalization, the blurring of political borders will not jeopardize the role of the national education system but will change its modalities.

As seen in these political decisions, it is not a central question whether the state takes a secular or non-secular approach to the institutional setting of public education. Even in some Western societies where secularism officially prevails, religious motifs have been drawn on as the basis of nationhood and collective identity (Smith, 2001). Therefore the social and educational positioning of religion is not understood in terms of the dichotomy between secularism and non-secularism as legal systems. There are diverse modifications of the theory and praxis of secularism. Moreover, although it is essentially a legal system, secular education as such is not a neutral one, but implies political preference and cultural bias (Gundara, 1997). Peter Berger explained what is central to secularism in practice:

> The decisive variable for secularization does not seem to be institu-tionalization of particular property relations, nor the specifics of different constitutional systems, but rather the process of rational-ization that is the prerequisite for any industrial society of the modern type.
>
> (Berger, 1967, pp. 136–7)

The secularization of education is a distinctive feature of modernity and the idea of Western Christendom (Beyer, 1994). In its civilization, secularism has developed over a long lapse of time. As Max Weber observed in European societies, the long-term consequences of secular-ization are a plurality of values as well as a threat to the conventional meaning of social order. Yet, in Western Christendom, if secularization moves on as the relocation of religion from the public to the private sphere, the values of the faith still hold their social functionality, and continue to prescribe overall societal values (Beyer, 1990). Despite the shift of the social positioning of religion, the moral and spiritual norms of the faith still exert strong influence on public life.

In short, regardless of the institutional link of the faith to the state, reli-gion commits itself to safeguarding communal morals and cohesion under secularism. An often-cited example is Christianity in the US, where the religion has little influence upon the laws, but has directed the customs of the community and regulates the state (Bellah *et al.*, 1992, 1996; de Tocqueville, 1994). On the other hand, the French have devel-oped an idea of secularism which has in principle sought an equilib-rium between the ecclesiastical power of the church and the laic rights of civil society. The reassertion of religious education in the *Grundgesetz* (Basic Law) of 1949 in West Germany is explicable as seeking such an equilibrium. This act in Germany can be interpreted as the rebalancing of the clerical and secular power by reinforcing the first, which had been oppressed by the rule of National-Socialist laity.

However, the secular education system of post-Second World War Japan reflects none of the American, French or German assumptions about the relationship between the state and religion. In the next section, I will show how this happened. In the first part, I will illustrate the political use of indigenous religion, known as *Shinto*, by the state in its building process in the nineteenth century. The next part deals with the collapse of the state, and demonstrates the rationale of secularization which was given under the US Military Occupation after Japan's defeat in the Second World War. The immediate aftermath of this secularization is briefly examined in the rest of the section.

Religion and national identity: a problematic theme in the history of the modern Japanese state

The period of state formation: the Meiji era (1868–1912)

Shinto, as a religion, can be characterized as an ancient Japanese belief or way of perception of the world based on a mixture of nature- and ancestor-worship (Eliade, 1987). The word, Shinto, as such is generally defined as the way of *kami*, gods or supernatural forces. Although Shinto teaches no dogma or no absolute truth of a single god or a church, the belief has permeated Japanese thinking through the religious practices of the people and a worldview based on their concept of *kami*. Along with Buddhism, this polytheistic religion has formed the religious consciousness of most Japanese people since the sixth century. The syncretism of these beliefs laid the lasting foundation of the moral staunchness of the Japanese people.

However, in the process of the formation of the modern Japanese state, the Meiji government politicized Shinto as state Shinto by instilling the deification of the throne of the Emperor. In the crisis of the Western threat to national sovereignty, the new notions of Japanese identity were abruptly invented for the particular *raisons d'état* of Meiji Japan (Shibata, 2004). 'Revering the Emperor and expelling the barbarians' by 'enriching the country and strengthening the military' became the national aspiration. The Emperor assumed divine right as a direct descendant in the unbroken imperial lineage of the Sun Goddess. To systematize Shinto mysticism as a political device, the government embedded the neo-Confucian moral code into Shinto. By identifying State Shinto as a political idea, the government shielded it from other religions, which were outlawed in educational practices and suffered from the government's coercion. Now Shinto was transformed as the de facto state religion of monotheism. The Japanese religious syncretism of a millennium was broken within the political institution of the modern Japanese state. Religion as defined by the state began to take a key part in a whole range of the modernization projects of the modern state. This is a specific aspect of Japan's modernization project within which the national government did not ensure its political power by reducing its religious claim as in the West. The Meiji government urgently devised a politico-cultural scenario for the 'family state' headed by the Emperor. What Anthony Smith calls 'modernizing nationalism' was formed in Meiji Japan by this notion of ethnic national identity. In it, the Japanese saw themselves as 'ethnic citizens', a racial group which emphasized the role of myths of descent, historical memories and religion (Brody, 2002; Smith, 1991). The political ideology of State Shinto culminated in the ultra-nationalism which flourished until Japan's defeat in the Second World War.

The period of the US Military Occupation after the Second World War (1945–52)

The Japanese state, headed by the God Emperor, collapsed as a result of his acceptance of the Allies' Potsdam Agreement in August 1945. The victorious powers in the Second World War designed a scheme for the reconstruction of the Axis countries. It was decided that not only the military but also the spiritual basis of their atrocious acts should be eradicated. In the quadripartite Occupation of Germany (1945–9), the Allies' measures centred on 'denazification'. In preparing plans for the spiritual recovery of the German people, the Allies had agreed with the policy of non-interference with internal ecclesiastical affairs from the wartime period. The US Occupation Authorities were particularly careful not to interfere with religion in Germany, despite the disputed relationship between wartime anti-Semitism and the Christian churches or even Christianity, despite some conflict with the other Allies (Shibata, 2003b; see also Cornwell, 1999; Rubenstein, 1996; Wyman, 1984). General Lucius Clay, the Military Governor, noted:

> Military government has never interfered in the internal affairs of the Church. Religious institutions have been recognized, however, as a significant element in the social structure of Germany and have been given commensurate consideration in the program of re-education and reorientation conducted for the building of a peaceful and democratic Germany.
>
> ('Statement of Lucius Clay', 13 April 1949,
> OMGUS File No. Z45 F 5/340–3/10)

Japan's departure from militarism and ultra-nationalism was marked by the demystification of the Emperor and the elimination of the politico-religious ideology of State Shinto (Shibata, 2003a). The paradox of the Japanese modern state depending on a theocratic footing was resolved. In terms of Western civilization, the secularization of education is the premise of a modern state. In December 1945, the Supreme Commander for the Allied Powers (SCAP) issued a military order, the so-called Shinto Directive, which prohibited the 'sponsorship, support, perpetuation, control, and dissemination of Shinto by the Japanese national, pre-fectural, and local governments, or by public officials, subordinates, and employees acting in their official capacity'. Thus secularism was established in Japan.

The American preoccupation with religion was also marked by their speedy accusation of militarism among Japanese Christians. This was done even earlier than banning Shinto. On 24 October 1945, SCAP ordered the Japanese government to purge those Christians by stating that:

> The attention of this headquarters has been directed to certain acts on the part of officials of educational institutions, founded and supported by Christians of foreign nations, which represent inexcusable and unjustifiable subversion of such institutions to militaristic and ultra-nationalistic ends.

This order was delivered to about one hundred Christian educational institutions throughout the nation, and over 80 institutions were screened within a few days after the enactment of the order (Rikkyo Gakuin, 1996, p. 489).

The problem of the treatment of the Emperor was more complex than that of religion as such for the US. The State-War-Navy Coordinating Subcommittee for the Far East received a piece of advice from Edwin Reischauer, a Harvard scholar of Japanese studies who served the US State Department during the war. He suggested that 'Any attempt to persuade the emperor to participate in his own "debunking" should be made in such a manner as to be unknown to the Japanese people and should be handled with such diplomacy as to give no suggestion of compulsion' (Appendix in 'Treatment of the Institution of the Emperor' of the State-War-Navy Coordinating Subcommittee for the Far East, 11 December 1945, Notter File (Post World War II Foreign Policy Planning: State Department Records of Harley A. Notter), No. 1520 H-128 in the Japanese National Diet Library). On New Year's Day in 1946, Emperor Hirohito offered his statement, prepared by SCAP, which declared that '[People] are not predicated on the false conception that the Emperor is divine, and that the Japanese people are superior to other races and destined to rule the world' ('Imperial Rescript on Reconstruction of 1 January 1946' (GHQ SCAP, 1948, pp. 77–8)).

The 'humanised' Emperor was exempted from indictment as a war criminal and became 'the symbol of the State and the unity of the people' (Article 1) under the Constitution of 1946, drafted by SCAP. Now the US could avoid creating favourable conditions for Japanese communists, who had already shown their wish for the Emperor's abdication. State Shinto and any other potential use of religion for politico-religious ideologies were swept away by Article 20: 'The State and its organs shall refrain from religious education or any other religious activity'. The Fundamental Law of Education (FLE) of 1947, the post-war Japanese educational canon, also maintains that 'The schools established by the state and local public bodies shall refrain from religious education or activities for a specified religion' (Article 9). 'Today', said William Bunce, a major drafter of the Shinto Directive, 'the separation of religion and state in Japan is as complete as in any country in the world' (Bunce, 1948, p. 171).

The demystification of the Emperor and the separation of state and religion were the best available compromise for the American Christian ideal, democratic principles and political interest. General Douglas McArthur, the Allied Supreme Commander in occupied Japan, stated that 'I could make the emperor and seventy million people Christian overnight, if I wanted to use the power I have' (cited in Nishi, 1983, p. 42). William Woodard, SCAP's religious officer in the Civil Information & Education Section, retrospectively noted that:

> The concern of the American military with Japanese religions was definitely out of the ordinary. Respect for local customs, including religion, as a basic principle of military government and involvement, not to say interference, in the religious affairs of an occupied country is clearly ruled out by army regulations. [Nevertheless] . . . the impact of Occupation-sponsored reforms on the religious institutions and the religious life of the Japanese people was far-reaching and in some respects revolutionary. The religions of Japan will never again be what they were on September 2, 1945, the day the Terms of Surrender were signed aboard the battleship Missouri in Tokyo Bay.
>
> (Woodard, 1972, p. xi)

Defeat in the Second World War deprived the Japanese modern state of its mystique and the basis of Japanese identity in *political* terms was shaken (Smith, 1991).

In the FLE, the purpose of education was also stated afresh. It was no longer to rear dutiful subjects of the state, but to educate people who shall 'contribute to the peace of the world and welfare of humanity by building a democratic and cultural state' (Preamble) and 'who shall love truth and justice, esteem individual value, respect labor . . .' (Article 1). Judicially and philosophically, the FLE is based on the Constitution and forms the nucleus of post-war Japanese educational principles, which were followed in other educational statutes.

Along with the ban concerning religion, in December 1945 SCAP suspended the subject of *shushin*, moral education largely based on Confucian ethics. It was never reinstalled in the school curriculum, unlike the other barred but later revived lessons, such as Japanese history and geography, judo and kendo (Japanese fencing). Within the process of restating the whole purpose of education, the aspects of religious and moral education – which had been central to the notions of national identity and national cohesion – were eliminated from public schooling.

The early post-Second World War period

After the end of the Occupation, educational issues were discussed in conflict between two blocs: the Japan Teachers' Union (JTU) versus the government and the Ministry of Education. The JTU was founded in 1947 with the support of the US Occupation Authorities, as part of their policy for the democratization of Japanese education. Ironically, the JTU soon became solid political factions of either the Japanese socialist or communist parties. In 1952, the Union declared that school teachers were workers, and abandoned the role models as reverent educators which had been imposed by the pre-war state.

On the other hand, the government pursued a policy along American capitalist lines. The post-war Japanese government has predominantly been led by the conservative Liberal Democratic Party (LDP) since 1955. The US and the Japanese governments had entered into a close alliance from the second half of the Occupation period. Robert Ward explained the policy shift: 'Only Japan, our recently defeated and still mistrusted enemy, possessed the sort of developmental potential that we needed in a local ally. So the embarrassing decision was made upon a 180-degree shift' (1966, p. 31). Now America's 'most dangerous enemy' became the 'most important ally' in Asia. When the Korean War broke out in 1950, the US permitted the Japanese government to form the Police Reserve Force, a quasi-army, by breaching the Japanese Constitution drafted by its own hand. The JTU countered with a slogan: 'Never send our students to battlefields'.

Conflict between the two blocs was particularly severe when moral and spiritual education was concerned. The government had felt uneasiness about neglecting to teach traditional ethical values in the schools due to the abolition of *shushin* and the practical absence of religious education. The Ministry of Education had already tried to reinstall a new version of moral education (*dotoku*) in 1958. In 1966, the Central Council for Education (CCE), a governmental permanent advisory panel, also tried to reinforce the ideal mentalities of Japanese citizens by instilling religious sentiments into students.

Reacting against these governmental acts, the JTU passed strictures on the government. The Union called the governmental attempt a 'reverse course' and criticized it as a clear sign of an attempt to revive *shushin*, which could potentially lead to thought oppression as before 1945. Feeling deep remorse for the past ultra-nationalism and the consequent war, school teachers in the post-war period articulated their public responsibility for dispelling nationalism and fought for the separation of state and religion.

Because of a fear of the reinstatement of ultra-nationalism, sensitivity to religion in general, and above all to Shinto, has been a major feature of educational discourse in post-war Japan. Neither governmental policy nor school practices have been anti-religious, but secularism in post-war Japan has been functioning through the active affirmation of a deliberate detachment of public institutions from religion at large. Although the FLE prohibits education only 'for a specified religion', the actual experience of the publicly funded schools in Japan shows that religious education as a whole has been quarantined from instruction, not to mention from the official school curriculum, throughout the post-war period. Assertions on the value of religious education, let alone the revival of it, have been considered akin to reactionary acts, as the principle of the separation of state and religion symbolizes a core of the notions of democracy in post-war Japan. From the 1950s through the 1970s, anti-nationalists and leftists were also powerful. Their voice received appreciation from the liberal public for their political and educational roles in deterring reactionary rule.

The recovery of 'national confidence' in the age of global capitalism

However, a conservative scenario began to take hold. From around the 1980s, the government as well as industry and the public in Japan have been regaining their 'national confidence' in international affairs, and *inter alia*, in the economy. After the dismal struggle to expand their overseas operations in the 1950s and 1960s, Japanese industries have grown on capitalist lines. Japan's economic achievement was, as Ward foresaw, 'The Legacy of the Occupation'. The consequences of Japan's recovery were more than the Americans had expected. In the 1980s, while the US leaders were feeling their 'Nation at Risk', Japan began to achieve a major position in the world economy. In terms of manufacturing capacity, while productivity in the US began to fall in 1979, that in Japan grew at an annual rate of 7.1 per cent between 1976 and 1981 (Reich, 1983, p. 118). Eventually, the Japanese economy became the second largest, after that of the US. In the automobile industry alone, the production in Japan (9.4 million) exceeded that of all North America (7.0 million) in 1992 (Kaplinsky and Posthuma, 1994, pp. 3–4).

Japan's economic presence was particularly strong in Asia. Japan-based transnational corporations built up a solid network of raw-material supplies, production and labour in the region. In due course, Japan established a stable trading and production bloc in Asia, such as the pre-war Japanese military regime had dreamt of, though unjustly, but failed to realize. Ironically, Japan's wartime dream of building the 'Great East-Asian Co-Prosperity Sphere' virtually came true after, and arguably because of, her defeat in the Second World War. Hofheinz and Kent illustrated that, 'since World War II, Japan has essentially achieved its goals of growth to world power status and of dominance of western Pacific markets without firing a shot' (1982, p. 11; see also Hatch and Yamamura, 1996). Japanese methods of business management were widely diffused as models not only in Asia but also to developing countries in other regions. Western nations were challenged by so-called *Easternization* in the international business world (Kaplinsky and Posthuma, 1994).

Given Japan's rise in the world economy, there was also a growing desire and demand that the country should take an active role in the international community. But this time, unlike in the pre-war period, the government's nationalist policy went hand-in-hand with its awareness that Japan should stand on a friendly footing in the international community. For the purpose of renewing the country, Prime Minister Yasuhiro Nakasone (1982–7) advocated a large-scale educational reform. The government regarded the reform of this time as the 'Third Educational Reform', after the first one in the early Meiji era and the second one during the US Occupation after the Second World War.

To put forward this reform, Nakasone formed the Ad-hoc Education Reform Council (AHERC), (1984–7). The reform had three major aims: to liberate the education system from ministerial control and restrictions, to diversify learning content and to internationalize education and Japanese young people. Officially, the government showed its particular enthusiasm about the third one. In principle, moreover, educational internationalization received relatively broad acceptance in educational circles. In 1983, the Ministry of Education set forth a 'Plan to Accept 100,000 Foreign Students', to internationalize Japanese universities. Moreover, in accordance with the 'Ron-Yasu' alliance, Nakasone promised US President Ronald Reagan to invite young Americans to Japan. This was the beginning of the Japan Exchange & Teaching (JET) Programme, one of the largest educational exchange programmes in the world. From the start of this programme in 1987, about 90 per cent of the JET participants were dispatched to schools throughout the country and taught English as Assistant Language Teachers (ALTs).

The results of these internationalization programmes have not been positive, at least not recognizably so. The growing influx of foreign students has merely led to the absorption of Japanese education by foreigners, rather than exposing the Japanese to an international academe

(Ebuchi, 1997). There has been no substantial improvement in the English proficiency of Japanese students either. In international English tests, the Japanese still rank almost the lowest in Asia. The reported effects of the JET programmes were even harmful. Especially in its early phase, friction between Japanese teachers and the foreign assistants was said to have caused emotional and psychological strain for the ALTs. In analysing this conflict, Eric Cazdyn probably overrates the JTU's ideological strength in the late 1980s by stating that, 'For the mostly socialist and communist oriented members of the teachers' union, the liberal, procapitalist ideology that almost all of the ALTs bring with them is a risk to their own political agenda' (Cazdyn, 2003, pp. 238–9). Instead, research by David McConnell shows a more realistic view; the conflict was 'cultural' rather than political. The ALTs had problems with the school and classroom culture in Japan. In practice, Japanese classrooms are teacher-centred and heavily based on Confucian values from the point of view of Western liberalism (McConnell, 2000). The anguish felt by the ALTs was captured by the media: 'Teacher Torture' (*Tokyo Journal*) or 'Japan Pulls up Welcome Mat with Racial Insensitivity' (*The Japan Times*).

Regardless of the immediate outcome, a policy of educational internationalization was pursued for the benefit of national interest. The long-term purpose of the JET programme was to enable young Japanese people to function worldwide in at least passable English without feeling a sense of cultural inferiority. The proficiency in English of the Japanese was also said to be important for clearing up foreigners' 'misunderstandings' about Japanese insularity and parochialism. Moreover, the government tried to ensure that Japanese culture was understood by the young foreigners. The degree of ALTs' understanding about Japanese culture is judged by the host schools, and is an important criterion for the Ministry's evaluation of the success of the JET programme. Cazdyn gives a cogent analysis of this behaviour of the Japanese government as *self-Orientalization*: 'there are those in Japan who promote an ideology whereby Japan comes to terms with Japan based on the West's terms' (Cazdyn, 2003, p. 234).

The tide of the 1980s was running in favour of the government's nationalist policy. The gradual decline of the Soviet economy and its ideologies was in full view. Radical socialist and communist ideals seemed to be inopportune in Japanese educational debates, and the membership of the JTU was shrinking. Moreover, witnessing Japan's economic ascendancy, other Asian countries tried to achieve similar success by following the Japanese policy of promoting strong nationalist sentiments and 'traditional' culture. Political leaders in Asia were drawn to the so-called Look East Policy, instead of aiming to catch up with the West. Outside politics too, the value of the 'Japanese mentality' was publicized and appreciated abroad. NHK (Japan Broadcasting Corporation), the country's sole public broadcaster, distributed a highly popular Japanese soap opera, *Oshin*, outside the country. The drama was about a girl who was born in a poor peasant family in pre-war Japan and had overcome various sufferings with patience, determination and hard work throughout her life. This TV programme, started in 1983 in Japan, was sent out to Singapore the next year and has later been broadcast in around 60 foreign countries. In some places, the programme recorded high viewer ratings – 82 per cent in Iran, 81.6 per cent in Thailand, 75.9 per cent in China and 70 per cent in Poland. 'Asian Values' were broadly appreciated: authoritarianism, nepotism and corruption were often illegitimately justified as a political means to maintain repressive rules and social order (Anderson, 2001; see also Morris-Suzuki, 1998).

New conservative scenarios gained firm hold. The visit by Nakasone to the Yasukuni Shrine, the Shinto tombs of the war dead, was a clear manifestation of the policy for Japanese identity formation. Anderson's assertion about the bond between 'nationalist imaginings' and 'religious imaginings' makes sense. Nakasone's visit stirred up the so-called Yasukuni controversy; it was alleged to be wrong – legally, because it violated the principle of separating state and religion, and morally, because the war dead included those who were condemned as top-ranking war criminals by the Allies' International Military Tribunal for the Far East or the Tokyo Judgement (1946–8). The Prime Minister's visits to the shrine as such started during the US Occupation, and most of the subsequent post-war Premiers, including a Christian, followed suit. But Nakasone's visit in 1985 invited international and domestic rage of a tempestuous kind, as he went to the shrine as Prime Minister in an official vehicle and, causing additional conflict, offered public money for prayers on 15 August, the anniversary of the end of the Second World War for the Japanese. Since Nakasone's visit, it has become a kind of a 'loyalty test' for a new Premier how he worships in the shrine or if he does so at all.

For the Nakasone cabinet, the recapturing of a Japanese national identity by the citizens was part and parcel of Japanese education for a new global era. The AHERC suggested that the government should provide moral and behavioural standards for future Japanese citizens, so that they could contribute to the international community with their consciousness as Japanese. Nakasone and the other LDP members wanted to revise the FLE, especially the Preamble and Article 1, whose ideas were, for them, too abstract and general and not specifically applicable to Japanese people. They often alleged that the FLE was designed in the midst of the deconstruction of Japan by the Americans, whose ultimate purpose was to mutilate the Japanese spiritually. The AHERC advocated adding statements about the values of traditional culture, the importance of national identity and a sense of patriotism to the FLE. But discussions on the revision of the FLE led to no visible result at that time.

Nonetheless, the groundwork for further debate was laid down. Prime Minister Keizo Obuchi (1998–2000) and the Education Minister Hirofumi Nakasone (1999–2000, Premier Nakasone's son) designed more concrete institutional changes to reignite debates on the revision of the FLE. One of the important changes was to legalize *Hinomaru* and *Kimigayo* as the national flag and the national anthem respectively. Before 1945, these two national symbols had exhaustively been used by the military regime to instil nationalism into the Japanese, and in 1945 SCAP imposed restrictions on their use. In 1958 the restrictions were removed. Since then, the Course of Study prepared by the Ministry of Education has encouraged the use of *Hinomaru* and *Kimigayo* in school ceremonies, without identifying the legal status of the two items. The government had long struggled with opposition from the JTU, which rejected the use of these 'symbols of Japanese aggression'. In some school ceremonies, mainly in the 1970s and the 1980s, teachers persuaded students to turn their back on *Hinomaru*, and to remain seated during the playing of *Kimigayo* or even to leave the auditorium. The dispute over *Hinomaru–Kimigayo* flared up in 1999, when the government produced a plan to enact a law which would endorse the flag and the anthem as the official national symbols. Before the enactment, there was even a suicide of a high school principal in Hiroshima, who was torn between the order of the local board of education and the refusal to follow it by the school teachers. Discussions for and against respect for the national symbols are no longer a matter of individuals' devotion or virtues but of a political conflict between the two factions. In August 1999, the National Diet passed the law, with the support of 76 per cent of the Diet members.

Outside officialdom too, a conservative movement became visible in education. In 1996, a number of academics and thinkers established the Japanese Society for History Textbook Reform, and argued that major post-war textbooks described modern Japanese history as 'an age of Japanese aggression' and 'a succession of Japan's criminal acts' in Asia. The Society also urged the correction of the 'left-wing historicity', which had allegedly dominated Japanese intellectual circles. According to the Society, such Marxist views of Japanese history were formulated by historical accounts based on the Tokyo Judgement.

The Ministry of Education seemed to be gathering momentum for rewriting the purpose of Japanese education as enshrined in the FLE. The reform scheme of Obuchi and Nakasone was succeeded by the National Commission on Educational Reform (NCER) (2000–1). In December 2000, the NCER compiled its Final Report, '17 Proposals for Changing

Education'. It argued that in a new age of globalization the Japanese people needed to develop and give a great deal of respect to their traditions and culture from the viewpoint of contributing generally to humanity while possessing an awareness and an identity as a Japanese person.

Apparently, the tone of the NCER was not decisive. No single person in the Commission proposed the recovery of religious education in public institutions, but suggested a minor rewriting or reinterpretation of Article 9 of the FLE. Without doubt, the proposed revision of the FLE received disapproval from, for example, the JTU, a number of academic societies, and the communist and socialist parties. The Council itself found it too difficult and politically too sensitive to take further steps for highlighting the significance of religious education in the official statements. It was noted that teaching religious sentiments in general terms without attaching them to any religious affiliation is difficult or impossible. But a concern about the lack of religious education remained strong. It became even acute after Japanese people became aware that religion as a belief could be a violent outlet for disillusioned people, especially the young and the elite.

The problematic of religion and education in contemporary Japanese society

Indeed, the terrorist attack in the Tokyo Underground disclosed the religious *naïveté* of the young Japanese. The massacre with sarin gas in 1995 was conducted by *Aum Shinrikyo*, a newly-risen cult. The *Aum* phenomena questioned not only the religious knowledge of the young, but the positioning of religion in post-Second World War Japanese education and society as a whole.

Most of the cult leaders, excluding the head, were among the best-educated people in the country. They were natural scientists, doctors and lawyers who graduated from the most renowned universities. Almost half the *Aum* members were in their twenties. The members promoted terror, aiming to overthrow the existing state and to establish a holy kingdom of their own and a 'civilization'. In its utopia, *Aum* would create a new type of human kind who could levitate and communicate through meditation and physical–spiritual training, completed by yoga, a kind of Tibetan Buddhism and an electronic headgear powered by six volts. This 'Creation', as well as the weapons of mass destruction, was necessary for *Aum* to save the world from the calamity of wars, which would purportedly soon be breaking out between American imperialists and Japan-based multinational corporations.

Not only most Japanese, but also other governments and people outside the country were shocked. Some educators and thinkers sought answers to questions such as: 'How could such acts be possible in one of the wealthiest, least unequal, safest, most ethnically homogeneous and most culturally integrated societies in the world?' (Castells, 1997, p. 98). Explicit in *Aum*'s alert was strong antagonism against the new world order of global capitalism. What was clear to many eyes was that the *Aum* phenomenon was not to be dealt with as a mere 'collective madness'.

Some authors attributed the atrocities to the lack of 'Japaneseness' in the minds of the *Aum* members, and potentially of many other young Japanese. These thinkers saw the apocalyptic violence as a sign of the decay or collapse of traditional Japanese society. The period of a religious quasi-vacuum in post-war Japan brought about, it was said, the irretrievable consequences that little attention was given to religious movements by the state and the people. This resulted in the uncontrollable burgeoning of various religious sects and, as demonstrated by *Aum*, the abuse of religious freedom by them in post-war Japan (Inoue, 1995; Noda, 1995). Furthermore, because of their lack of knowledge of religion and of any metaphysical account of the world, the young Japanese fell into the confusion of occultism (Inoue, 1997; Shimada, 2001; Yamazaki, 1992). The *Aum* phenomena promoted an intangible awareness of the danger of the religious *naïveté* of the young. Public schooling was condemned for quarantining moral, spiritual education from the children. It was also suggested that the post-war 'religion-free' educational system had created negative feelings about religion, in particular among the young. Religion has indeed been treated with particular sensitivity in the public institutions. There were occasions when teachers called on principals to prevent students from praying in Shinto shrines during school excursions. Students joining their hands in prayer prior to the school lunch were said to be performing a forced religious ritual. Some authors regard such precautions against Shinto-nationalism as excessive. Overall, many Japanese inside and outside the educational arena pointed out that there might be a 'fatal defect' in the post-war education system of the country.

So too did the Japanese government and its adherents. For conservative policy makers, the resources for moral commitments have been lost, as the result of the Allied confusion of State Shinto as a political ideology with Shinto as religion per se and Japan's erroneous translation of secularism into a quasi-taboo on religious education in the post-war period. Thus, they further argue that Japanese schools need to reinvigorate indigenous morals with a religious basis, since Western people can still draw on spiritual disciplines from the Christian code of conduct (Nakasone, 2000a, 2000b).

Clearly, this argument does not hold. This is apparent if one glances at the obsolescence of '*Ruhe und Ordnung*' in the German classroom, let alone the atrocious shootings and recurrent violence in many schools in European Christendom. Yet, if the decline of the conventional meaning of social order is a consequence of secularization, the struggle of the Japanese government to counteract the overall moral decline among the citizens might be part of a global phenomenon in secular societies.

Other thinkers recognize the conditions of the burgeoning of the cult specifically in Japanese society. It was suggested that the gas attack was a violent manifestation of the culturally desperate young Japanese, who were alienated in, and felt dissatisfaction with, the 'high-tech yet culturally-dormant, authoritarian and extremely patriarchal society' of Japan (Castells, 1997, pp. 102–4). *Aum*'s worldview was also said to resemble the political traits of the pre-war Japanese Emperor State (Lifton, 2000). After interviewing a number of perpetrators and victims of the underground terrorism, Japanese novelist Haruki Murakami goes further by noting that the ideal of *Aum*'s utopia and that of pre-1945 Manchuria overlap each other. In both cases, Murakami sees great disappointment at Japanese society felt by the young elite, who otherwise would have taken constructive advantage of their society and their talent. Though only from the ideological point of view, his depiction of the pre-war elite rings true also about the cult leaders:

> the best and brightest – the cutting-edge technocrats, technicians, and scholars – gave up the lives promised them in Japan and went off to the continent they saw as so full of possibilities. . . . As long as they stayed in the Japanese State with its coercive structure, they believed it was impossible to find an effective outlet for all their energy.
>
> (Murakami, 1997, pp. 306–7)

Manuel Castells and many others find socio-cultural despair in the cult's violence against the society. They were also searching painfully for social norms and spiritual authority in which they could have faith, and which they could identify with their commitment to society. What is common in the above-mentioned arguments is the view that the cult members were disillusioned by, and were lost in, Japanese society. *Aum*'s plot to overthrow the existing state was a rebellion against established socio-cultural norms in the guise of a perverted religious conspiracy.

Overall, the *Aum* phenomenon raised a serious question about the social and educational positioning of religion in modern Japanese history. Because of the fear of the resurrection of ethnocentric nationalism, Japanese people have been preoccupied with the blame for its core on religion. This also left in post-war Japan, as Robert Kisala and Ian Buruma suggest, an unanswered question about responsibility, apart from that of 'ideology' and 'institution', for the rise and growth of violent pre-war ultra-nationalism. Kisala implies his scepticism about the role of religious institutions in post-war Japan in heightening people's consciousness about peace, and suggests that 'romantic pacifism' in post-war Japan has demonstrated an aspect of 'the inability [of the Japanese] to deal in any realistic way with their own actions in the war' (Kisala, 1999, p. 179). Buruma states that post-war Japan has been unable to establish a broadly accepted understanding about the responsibility of the Japanese for the war. Unlike in West Germany, the leadership in Japan both on the Right and the Left has failed to deliver the statement of 'Japanese conscience' about war guilt, which would convince the Japanese people, regardless of their political stance, social standing or educational background (Buruma, 1994).

Identity formation beyond the state: some scenes in contemporary popular cultures

Japan's pattern of secularization brought about the demise of ultra-nationalism shaped by Shinto mysticism. The impact of secularism was also decisive on the weakening of the state-formulated notions of national identity. During the last half of the twentieth century, the nationalist tenets of imperial times steadily lost popularity among Japanese people. Premier Mori's claim that Japan is the gods' country caused embarrassment to the people, if they paid much attention to it at all. Such an account of nationhood no longer gained popular acknowledgement. The textbook written by the Japanese Society for History Textbook Reform received fierce criticisms both domestic and international. The long narratives of Shinto myths and apparent advocacy of reverence for the imperial lineage were part of the problems in the textbook. According to the request of the Ministry of Education, a number of descriptions were rewritten, and the textbook finally passed the Ministry's examination in 2001. But, in the end, only a few local educational boards throughout the country adopted the textbook.

The manifestation of Japanese cultural identity and a sense of national pride are now articulated in the private sphere, taking different approaches and bearing different cultural messages. The sense of national pride is explicit in popular sub-culture, particularly among the younger generations. Through the expansion of mass media, the use of advanced technology and the growth of the worldwide interaction between people and information, we notice the expressions of pride and narcissism about culture which has developed in Japan. In this phenomenon too, we witness a search by youth for a vent for their frustrated sentiment. That which was greatly discouraged in the schools, such as *Kimigayo*, *Hinomaru*, the beauty of Japanese polytheism and even the justification of Japan's conduct of the war, began to be supported crudely by current Japanese youth. This phenomenon is seen as an upsurge of so-called '*petite* nationalism' (Kayama, 2002). It can be called 'petite', not only because its actors are young, but also because nationalist feeling has been shown naively, without the strong consciousness of its ideological basis.

A frequently quoted example is the waving of *Hinomaru* by the young audience in the FIFA World Cup matches in 2002. The supporters of the Japanese national team were open in showing their feeling of affection for the team which represented the nation and a sense of their identification as Japanese. While teachers encourage students not to face *Hinomaru* standing or to sing *Kimigayo* at school ceremonies, young Japanese did not hesitate to hoist the national flag or to listen to pop idols singing the national anthem at the football stadiums.

In literature too, emphasis on excellence in Japanese cultural heritages is noticeable. Sales of books on the beauty of the Japanese language are also booming (Komori, 2002). But the large sales of some *manga* (Japanese comic books) also show strong interest in indigenous culture among young readers. *Vagabond* is the *manga* version of *Miyamoto Musashi*, a celebrated novel, written in the mid-1930s about a paragon of the *samurai* spirit. The 18-volume *Vagabond* has sold a total of over 20 million copies and continues to sell, while conventional *samurai* dramas on TV keep on losing their audiences. It is true that *Vagabond* attracted particularly young people partly because of the fashionable drawing, which is unconventional for warrior stories. In the *manga* version, the seventieth-century solitary swordsman, Musashi, appears to be a gorgeous young man with a slender body, silky hair and bright eyes. However, it is also said that young people are fascinated by the theme of an integrated view of life and death. This theme seems to be fresh to the young and to be needed in the face of frequent violence in life in general and in the schools (Ogura, 2001).

The more controversial best-selling series of 'nationalistic *manga*' is probably *Gomanizumu Sengen*. The title of the series means literally a 'declaration of arrogance or pride'. The message of the cartoonist, Yoshinori Kobayashi, is that 'I do not hesitate to be called arrogant for stating sound arguments', which have been alleged to be unsound in post-war Japanese society. Initially, he wrote on overall social issues from his conservative viewpoint; such as moral hypocrisy about civic movements, impartiality of journalism, gender equality and individualism (Kobayashi, 1993). Kobayashi eventually attacked post-war Japanese intellectuals for instilling in the Japanese a sense of self-hate which derived from the account of Japan's conduct in the Second World War given by the Tokyo Judgement. By intellectuals, Kobayashi earlier meant left-wing Marxists, but recently he means right-wing conservatives who increasingly take a subservient political attitude to the Americans (Kobayashi, 2001). In the *Gomanizumu* series, Kobayashi justifies Japan's invasion into Asian countries during the war, and refutes claims about the Nanjin Massacre and the military comfort women. He also states that the atomic bombing on Hiroshima and Nagasaki had a strong nuance of racism held by the Americans, who are therefore entitled to discuss Japan's war guilt only after abandoning their nuclear weapons. As of 1995, *Gomanizumu* had sold over 1.2 million copies in the first six issues (Kure, 1995, p. 3), and the series printed almost a further score of volumes by 2003. While finding Kobayashi's position 'distasteful', Kisala agrees with his argument about the failure of post-war Japanese leaders in dealing with the responsibility for the war. On the other hand, it is suggested that *Gomanizumu* has been effective as a kind of psychotherapy for the post-war Japanese, who have been suffering from the burden of sin or guilt for being Japanese (Abe, 2001). At any rate, the *Gomanizumu* series caught attention globally. The widespread popularity of *Gomanizumu* and its potential influence on the public are an eloquent example of the power of the media in instilling nationalism into a large audience beyond the authority of the state and school textbooks.

Hayao Miyazaki's subtle but long-lasting effort to treasure the values of an indigenous worldview has also increasingly been appreciated by the Japanese audience. His recent movie, *Sen to Chihiro no Kami-kakushi* (*Spirited Away*) marked the record for box-office profit in Japanese cinema history (over 30 billion yen) by capturing more than 23 million people in Japan alone. In this animation movie, Miyazaki screened explicitly more than ever the wonder and fascination of Japanese animism and polytheism. Another message that he continues to deliver is his harsh criticism of Hollywood and Disney. His work gives the lie to the ideologies of commercialism and 'American democracy', which instil the oversimplified formula of 'good against evil' into children and neglect to teach various contradictions in the human world.

As seen in Miyazaki's work, the products of Japanese popular culture are now spread abroad without concealing their Japanese or Asian flavour. This was different earlier. While *manga* in the early 1980s, for example, sold nearly 1.7 billion copies a year inside Japan, this 'Asian sub-culture' was by no means popular in the West. Foreigners were puzzled at Japanese men and women, children and adults who were gazing at *manga* practically anywhere, even in the commuter train or in the café sitting with friends. Among foreign critics, *manga* were notorious for being full of violence and sex. Although *manga* were already available in Europe in the 1970s, the themes of their stories at that time were distinctively of the West. But the recent *manga*, such as the *Dragon Ball* series and *Akira*, openly disclose the character of Japanese culture both in the narrative and the drawing style. From the 1990s, *manga* have become part of popular youth culture abroad. From the mid-1990s in Germany, for instance, the sales of Japanese *manga* exceeded those of 'classic' Western comics. Even in South Korea, where the import of Japanese popular cultures was officially permitted only after 1998, *manga* have been widely read both before and after the lifting of censorship. A number of public museums inside and outside Japan have begun to treat *manga* as part of Japanese 'aesthetic' culture instead of a mere sub-culture (Berndt, 2002b). It is true, as Sharon Kinsella suggests, that Japanese government agencies contributed to promoting the *manga* culture in the West. The Ministry of Education and the Japan Foundation were involved in *manga* exhibitions in Paris, London, Berlin and other major European cities. But the massive purchase of *manga* worldwide by children and those who normally do not enjoy access to museums and official exhibitions shows that the persistent and ever growing popularity of *manga* was beyond the effort of Japanese officials. After the Japanese people lost their self-assurance as a result of the burst of the economic bubble, the increasing appreciation of *manga* by foreign readers helped the Japanese regain confidence about their 'national culture' (Berndt, 2002a). The new Japanese cultures carry the powerful messages of the public and have been distributed outside the country as part of 'global culture', whether intellectuals in Japan and abroad like it or not.

Conclusion

In the context of globalization, the institutional role of religion has increasingly received political attention. Religion is gaining a prominent position in discussions on public education in many places in the world. In the Japanese context, however, the government has been struggling to reinforce the religious notions of national identity among the citizens. State and local administrators and even teachers with no union affiliation mostly considered religious education to be politically too sensitive to be present in Japanese education.

The way in which secularism was introduced in Japanese education left a lasting influence. The theocratic footing of the Japanese modern state, the basis of the state of the God Emperor, was resolved after its defeat in the war. Secular education was the premise of a modern state in Western terms. The impact of the defeat of the Emperor State and the following US military occupation was massive and, as Woodard predicted, decisive for the political role of religion in Japanese public life. A consequence was, to put it bluntly, that religion as an institution has lost its position in Japanese society and education. Apparently in the publicly funded schools in post-war Japan, there has been an absence of religious education and a lack of occasions for students to deal with the metaphysical account of life and death. The Emperor State and its Shintoistic ideology have been the major targets for the principles of post-war Japanese democracy to overcome. Being haunted by the fear of ultra-nationalism, the Japanese have been preoccupied with its potential resurrection through the state political ideology, in particular within a religious framework. But scepticism about the educational role, even a constructive one, of religion has remained overwhelming. Religion as a whole has been isolated from a prominent position in educational discussions, especially in terms of the notion of national identity.

Another result of the preoccupation with the resurgence of politico-religious nationalism was the uncovering of the sentiments of national identity and national pride by the young generations. Such nationalist sentiments are openly expressed in popular culture. The expressions seem to be naive and ingenuous, but can be regarded as an alternative outlet for what has been circumvented in post-war education.

It is possible to suggest that the notions of Japanese identity shown in the dynamics of popular culture can be a preference not only for the young, but can be an operational institution for Japan to identify a 'self' in this global era. In the history of the modern Japanese state, the government regarded the formation of Japanese national identity as vital for national development. The Meiji government aimed at it through military force. Having experienced the awful result of this in the Second World War, the post-war government aimed to develop the country economically. After a brief period of the achievement and the burst of the bubble economy, Japan's economy has exhibited a downward trend. After all the trial and failure, the Japanese now seem to be reworking the notions of national identity in their sentiment of pride in 'indigenous culture'. The Japanese people's strong interest in what can be called a phenomenon of 'glocalism' in Japan shows that the tensions of nationalism are high, if not monolithic as before 1945.

The aspirations of the state to supersede the West and to gain ascendancy over other states are less prominent than hitherto. The ambition of the state and the people for economic advancement, which was a driving force of educational development in the construction and reconstruction of the modern Japanese state, is now cooling down. Now, the tensions of nationalism seem to be growing in the public sphere. A question remains: what should the national education system and individual institutions and educators do for the social good? As a potential for social and educational change, Japan needs to develop a climate of acceptance of the involvement of the cultural 'others' within the gates, lest the internationalization of education or global education remains as merely the mantra of the state and educators.

References

Abe, K. (2001) *Samayoeru Nationalism: Orientalism, Japan, Globalisation*, Kyoto: Sekaisisosha.

Anderson, B. (1991) *Imagined Communities: Reflections on the Origin and Spread of Nationalism*, London: Verso.

Anderson, B. (2001) Western Nationalism and Eastern Nationalism: Is There a Difference that Matters?, *New Left Review*, 9: 31–42.

Bellah, R., R. Madsen, W. Sullivan, A. Swindler and S. Tipton (1992) *The Good Society*, New York: Alfred A. Knopf.

Bellah, R., R. Madsen, W. Sullivan, A. Swindler and S. Tipton (1996) *Habits of the Heart: Individualism and Commitment in American Life*, Berkeley, CA: University of California Press.

Berger, P. (1967) *The Social Reality of Religion*, Harmondsworth: Penguin Books.

Berndt, J. (2002a) 'Nippon' kara nogareru manga, in *Nippon wa omoshiroi ka*, ed. Sensho Metier editors, Tokyo: Kodansha.

Berndt, J. (2002b) Tenji sareru manga: bijutukan ni okeru manga no 'bigaku', in *Manbiken: Manga no bi, gaku-teki na jigen heno sekkin (Towards an Aesthetics of Comics)*, ed. J. Berndt, Tokyo: Daigo Shobo.

Beyer, P. (1990) Privatization and the Public Influence of Religion in Global Society, in *Global Culture: Nationalism, Globalization and Modernity. A Theory, Culture & Society Special Issue*, ed. M. Featherstone, London: Sage Publications.

Beyer, P. (1994) *Religion and Globalization*, London: Sage Publications.

Brody, B. (2002) *Opening the Door: Immigration, Ethnicity, and Globalization in Japan*, New York: Routledge.

Bunce, W. (ed.) (1948) *Religions in Japan: Buddhism, Shinto, Christianity. From the Report prepared by the Religions and Cultural Resources Division, Civil Information and Education Section, General Headquarters of the Supreme Commander for the Allied Powers, Tokyo, March 1948*, Rutland: Charles E. Tuttle Company.

Buruma, I. (1994) *The Wages of Guilt: Memories of War in Germany and Japan*, London: Cape.

Castells, M. (1997) *The Information Age: Economy, Society and Culture, Vol. II: The Power of Identity*, Oxford: Blackwell.

Cazdyn, E. (2003) Uses and Abuses of the Nation: Toward a Theory of the Transnational Cultural Exchange Industry, in *Globalization: Critical Concepts in Sociology – Culture and Identity*, ed. R. Robertson and K. White, London: Routledge.

Cornwell, J. (1999) *Hitler's Pope*, New York: Viking.

Coulby, D. and C. Jones (1996) Post-modernity, Education and European Identities, *Comparative Education*, 32(2): 171–84.

de Tocqueville, A. (1994 [1831]) *Democracy in America*, London: David Campbell Publishers.

Ebuchi, K. (1997) *Daigaku kokusai-ka no kenkyu*, Tokyo: Tamagawa Daigaku Shuppanbu.

Eliade, M. (1987) *The Encyclopedia of Religion, Vol. 13*, New York: Macmillan Publishing Company.

General Headquarters, Supreme Commander for the Allied Powers, Civil Information Education Section, Education Division (GHQ SCAP) (1948) *Education in the New Japan, Vol. 1*, Tokyo: GHQ SCAP.

Gray, J. (1998) *False Dawn*, London: Granta Publications.

Gundara, J. (1997) Religion, Secularism and Values Education, in *World Yearbook of Education 1997: Intercultural Education*, ed. D. Coulby, J. Gundara and C. Jones, London: Kogan Page.

Hatch, W. and K. Yamamura (1996) *Asia in Japan's Embrace: Building a Regional Production Alliance*, Cambridge: Cambridge University Press.

Hofheinz, R. and C. Kent (1982) *The Eastasia Edge*, New York: Basic Books.

Inoue, N. (1995) Gendai shakai no 'yamai' to 'shin-shukyo' toshiteno Aum Shinrikyo, *Shukan Asahi*, 30 May: 35–8.

Inoue, N. (1997) *Shukyo to kyoiku: Nihon no shukyo-kyoiku no rekishi to genjo*, Tokyo: Kobundo.

Juergensmeyer, M. (1995) *Nationalism no sezoku-sei to shukyo-sei*, Tokyo: Tamagawa Daigaku Shuppanbu. (Translation from the English: (1993) *The New Cold War? Religious Nationalism Confronts the Secular State*, Berkeley, CA: University of California Press.)

Kaplinsky, R. and A. Posthuma (1994) *Easternisation: The Spread of Japanese Management Techniques to Developing Countries*, Ilford: Frank Cass and Company Limited.

Kayama, R. (2002) *Petite-Nationalism shokogun: Wakamono tachi no Nippon-shugi*, Tokyo: Chuokoronsha.

Kepel, G. (1992) *Shukyo no fukushu*, Tokyo: Shobunsha. (Translation from the French: (1991) *La Revanche de Dieu*, Paris: Seuil.)

Kisala, R. (1999) *Prophets of Peace: Pacifism and Cultural Identity in Japan's New Religions*, Honolulu, HI: University of Hawaii Press.

Kobayashi, Y. (1993) *Gomanizumu Sengen 1*, Tokyo: Fusosha.

Kobayashi, Y. (2001) Katsuji-ban Gomanizumu Sengen: Taiwan wa shinjirarenai kuni nanoka?, *Seiron*, March: 52–67.

Komori, Y. (2002) Japanese Language Booms and Nationalism, *Japanese Book News*, 40 (Winter): 1–2.

Kure, T. (1995) *Kobayashi-Yoshinori-ron josetsu: Gomanizumu towa nani-ka!*, Tokyo: Shuppanshinsha.

Lifton, R. (2000) *Shumatsu to kyusai no genso: Aum Shinrikyo toha nanika*, Tokyo: Iwanami Shoten. (Translation from the English: (1999) *Destroying the World to Save It: Aum Shinrikyo, Apocalyptic Violence, and the New Global Terrorism*, New York: Metropolitan Books.)

McConnell, D. (2000) *Importing Diversity: Inside Japan's JET program*, Berkeley, CA: University of California Press.

Morris-Suzuki, T. (1998) *Re-inventing Japan: Time, Space, Nation*, Armonk, NY: M. E. Sharpe.

Murakami, H. (1997) *Underground: The Tokyo Gas Attack and the Japanese Psyche*, London: The Harvill Press.

Nakasone, Y. (2000a) Niju-seiki no bunmei to tetsugaku soshite tetsugaku wo kataru, *Nihon Kyoiku Shinbun*, 7 January.

Nakasone, Y. (2000b) Start shita kenpo chosa-kai: Nakasone moto shusho ni kiku, *Sankei Shimbun*, 19 February.

Nishi, T. (1983) *MacArthur no 'hanzai': Hiroku Nihon senryo*, Tokyo: Nihon Kogyo Shimbunsha.

Noda, N. (1995) *Bunmei shototsu jidai no seiji to shukyo*, Tokyo: PHP.

Ogura, O. (2001) *'Vagabond' to Miyamoto Musashi no nazo*, Tokyo: Koala Books.

Ramet, P. (1984) Conclusion, in *Religion and Nationalism in Soviet and East European Politics*, ed. P. Ramet, Durham, NC: Duke University Press.

Reich, R. (1983) *The Next American Frontier: A Provocative Program for Economic Renewal*, New York: Penguin Books.

Rikkyo Gakuin Hayku-niju-go-nen-shi Henshu-iinkai (ed.) (1996) *Rikkyo Gakuin hyaku-niju-go-nen-shi, 1*, Tokyo: Dainippon Insatsu.

Robertson, R. (1992) *Globalization: Social Theory and Global Culture*, London: Sage Publications.

Robertson, R. and K. White (2003) Globalization: An Overview, in *Globalization: Critical Concepts in Sociology – Analytical Perspectives*, ed. R. Robertson and K. White, London: Routledge.

Rubenstein, R. (1996) Holocaust and Holy War, *The Annals of the American Academy of Political and Social Science*, 548 (November): 23–44.

Shibata, M. (2003a) Destruction and Reconstruction: A Comparative Analysis of Education Reform in Japan and Germany under the US Military Occupation after World War Two, in *Can the Japanese Change Their Education System?*, ed. R. Goodman and D. Phillips, Oxford: Symposium Books.

Shibata, M. (2003b) Doitsu 'sai-kyoiku' to shukyo-kyoiku: 1933 Reich-seikyo-joyaku mondai wo meguru America no tai-doku senryo-seisaku, *Sengo Kyoiku-shi Kenkyu*, 17: 37–49.

Shibata, M. (2004) Controlling National Identity and Reshaping the Role of Education: The Vision of State Formation in Meiji Japan and the German *Kaiserreich*, *History of Education*, 33(1): 75–85.

Shimada, H. (2001) *AUM: Naze shukyo wa terrorism wo undanoka*, Tokyo: Transview.

Smith, A. (1991) *National Identity*, New York: Penguin Books.

Smith, A. (2001) *Nationalism*, Cambridge: Polity Press.

Ward, R. (1966) The Legacy of the Occupation, in *The United States and Japan*, ed. H. Passin, Englewood Cliffs, NJ: Prentice-Hall.

Woodard, W. (1972) *The Allied Occupation of Japan 1945–1952 and Japanese Religions*, Leiden: E. J. Brill.

Wyman, D. (1984) *The Abandonment of the Jews: America and the Holocaust, 1941–1945*, New York: Pantheon Books.

Yamazaki, M. (1992) The Intellectual Community of the Showa Era, in *Showa: The Japan of Hirohito*, ed. C. Gluck and S. Graubard, New York: W. W. Norton.

Part III

Globalization and education policy

5 Travelling and embedded policy

The case of post-devolution Scotland within the UK

Jenny Ozga

Introduction: explaining education policy

This chapter looks at a particular form of devolution – that is, political devolution within the UK – and assesses its significance for education policy within the context of globalization. The chapter attempts to use the case of devolved education policy making in Scotland as a vehicle for the exploration of more general themes that confront policy sociologists attempting to explain education policy; for example:

- the need to locate change in education within a broad framework of enquiry, that takes account of exogenous, macro-social change;
- the need to draw on resources from across the social sciences that enable understanding of that change;
- the need for reflexivity in research that enables identification of the assumptions about the source, scope and pattern of education policy that are implicit in research on education (Dale, 1986; Ozga, 1987, 2000).

These themes lead to a focus on policy-making and politics. They enable a view of education policy that recognizes its framing by globalization and trends to trans- and supra-national policy-making. Within the framework of policy sociology, there is an emergent strand of theorizing and investigation that seeks to respond to the problem of interpreting the translation of globalization into education policy. Such work includes Taylor *et al.* (1997), who discuss global policy transfer, and Ball's characterization of a 'small' world with 'big' policies (1998). This chapter connects to these arguments. It accepts that, at the very least, globalization offers a significant challenge to the nation-state's capacity to design and support previously established patterns of welfare provision, including, for example, the key roles of national systems in socializing citizens and allocating their labour market positions. Put simply, using globalization as a framing device means that there is appropriate acknowledgement of rapid social, political and economic change as well as recognition of the importance of context (Held *et al.*, 1999). As Giddens puts it in his well-known definition:

> Globalisation can thus be defined as the intensification of world-wide social relations which link distant localities in such a way that local happenings are shaped by events occurring many miles away and vice-versa. This is a dialectical process because such local happenings may move in an obverse direction from the very distanciated relations that shape them. Local transformation is as much a part of globalisation as the lateral extension of social connections across time and space.
>
> (Giddens, 1990, p. 64)

From this perspective, as Appadurai argues, it is possible to identify 'vernacular globalisation' in which there is change and reconfiguration in global, national and local interrelationships but which is mediated by local and national history and politics (Appadurai, 1996). Old notions of 'centre' and 'periphery' are collapsed in communities that are overlapping, complex and disjunctive. Disorganized capitalism creates fundamental disjunctures between the economy, culture and politics (Appadurai, 1990). Globalization produces rebalancing of national and global functions. Thus the nation-state faces stresses that arise from the need to compete globally to ensure a share in the rapid accumulation and transfer of wealth; from the deepening of inequalities and from the growth of insecurity and uncertainty. From this general position I draw two conclusions about education policy:

1   that at international level there has emerged a coherent set of policy themes and processes through which policy makers (at national, international and transnational levels) are reshaping education systems;
2   that these policy agendas and processes interact with traditions, ideologies, institutions and politics that have developed on national terrains.

Furthermore, as Alexiadou and Jones (2001) argue, the relationship between points (1) and (2) indicates growing embeddedness of 'travelling policy' within national policy elites, and differing degrees of local 'policy inflection' in which various forces (local policy communities, trade unions, social movements) have forced adaptation of global agendas, or in which local policy elites have integrated travelling policy with national agendas (Alexiadou and Jones, 2001, p. 2). There is, of course, a good deal of debate about how the conduits of travelling policy operate and a need for further enquiry into exactly how the design and delivery of national policy agendas respond to pressure from supra-national organizations and agencies (Lingard, 2000). Alexiadou and Jones' (2001) discussion of *travelling* and *embedded* policy takes travelling policy to refer to supra- and transnational agency activity, as well as to common agendas (for example for the reshaping of educational purposes to develop human capital for the information age). Embedded policy is to be found in 'local' spaces (which may be national, regional or local), where global policy agendas come up against existing priorities and practices. This perspective allows for recognition that, while policy options may be narrowing, national and local assumptions and practices remain significant and mediate or translate global policy in distinctive ways.

Political devolution within the UK

Seen within this framework, political devolution within the UK becomes a site for the exploration of the relationship between 'travelling' and 'embedded' policy. It offers opportunities to explore the mediating influence of what the 'Education Governance, Social Integration and Exclusion' project (EGSIE) called the 'collective narrative' (Lindblad and Popkewitz, 2000b, 2002; Lindblad *et al.*, 2002). I discuss this concept further on pp. 122–5, but for now it may be defined briefly as the relationship between policy and cultural identities in different national systems (Popkewitz *et al.*, 1999). I argue that the UK offers a particularly interesting site because of its government's strong engagement with convergent or 'travelling' policy that tightens the bond between the economy and education, and because of its related project of 'modernization' that seeks to decontextualize policy-making and reconfigure it as highly rational and pragmatic. Yet, at the same time, policy is being re-contextualized and 'local transformation' is taking place that provides enhanced recognition of 'embedded' distinctiveness. England, Wales and Scotland have different, though interdependent, education systems for which there has been progressive devolution of responsibility during the last two decades (Raffe *et al.*, 1999). Ideologies, priorities and policy implementation have differed and continue to differ and there are signs that post-devolution the systems are tending towards increased divergence. UK policy agendas are developed in pursuit of modernization and to meet the challenge of globalization. The UK government defines these agendas in relation to competitiveness and the discourse of the market, but they may be received and inflected rather differently in England, Scotland and Wales (Ozga, 2003).

Devolution established a new set of policy relationships within the UK following the creation of separate assemblies with devolved powers in Wales and Northern Ireland, and a separate parliament in Scotland. The Scottish parliament, based in Edinburgh, has responsibility for all matters not 'reserved' by the UK government at Westminster. Most of the 'reserved' matters relate to the common UK market, but they also include international relations, defence and provisions for dealing with terrorism, immigration and nationality, national security, employment and equality legislation, nuclear safety and research councils. Education and training are devolved matters, as are health, the environment, agriculture, forestry and fisheries, sport and the arts, local government, social work, housing and planning, economic development, the law and home affairs, including criminal justice. Devolution in the UK, according to Keating, is not like the Spanish experience: it builds on existing administrative devolution in which each of the UK territories had distinctive ways of making policy and delivering services (Keating, 2001, p. 2). Indeed, Paterson argues that Scotland's social welfare policy had a Scottish character for a long period pre-devolution, which was, perhaps, intensified during the Conservative administrations led by Margaret Thatcher. He explains the significance of this in the following terms:

> The welfare state in Scotland was Scottish in the implementation of large areas of policy. In certain crucial topics it was also Scottish in the devising of policy – for example, education, law, social work and the arts. These were crucial in the sense that they shaped the character of society more profoundly than many of the topics that were not administered in Scotland – matters such as macro-economic policy . . . Scottish institutions were held to constitute Scottish identity. They were taken to be the embodiment of a putative tradition of popular sovereignty which was believed to be older and more legitimate than the sovereignty of the parliament at Westminster.
>
> (Paterson, 1998, pp. 62–3)

During the years of Conservative government Scottish policy-making in education resisted the UK government's pressure for local management of schools and for deregulation, and was largely hostile to demands to introduce competition as the guiding principle for improvement of performance. There was a considerable mismatch between Thatcher's drive for market-oriented and culturally conservative educational reform and the Scottish context. Reforms did not take or were substantially modified. In this period modification of UK initiatives protected key characteristics of Scottish provision, while at the same time the Conservative government's pressure on this key social institution (and others) produced popular support for political devolution in order to protect Scottish welfare policies and practices from trends towards privatization, competition and individualism. It is unclear if the New Labour UK government elected in 1997 understood that background to devolution, or, indeed, if it envisaged devolution as anything more than a managerial solution to party political problems. There seems to be a potential mismatch between the 'travelling policy' of the modernization project as pursued by the UK government and the playing out of devolution as a form of representation of difference, or 'embedded' policy.

Modernization

Given these tensions, it seems likely that devolution will accentuate differences in education policy. This may create problems for the UK modernization project in education. Modernization in education policy has tied education firmly to the economy (DfEE, 1997) and thus underplayed its role in social and cultural formation. Furthermore, modernization in governance involves a shift towards what Perri 6 (1998) has described as 'implied consent' by the public to government's problem-solving initiatives. This in turn removes 'old politics' from the framework of system design. The modernization project thus goes beyond system redesign to embrace a re-imagining of politics (Ozga, 2003), linked to the decline of representational politics and their replacement by what Castells (1998) calls 'informational' politics. This re-imagining includes the development of forms of governance that encourage citizens' self-reliance and self-management, and that persuade people to change the way they behave:

> This means forging new systems of co-operation, innovation and learning in every sector. Democracy in practice must mean the chance to shape our own lives, through systems which allow us to meet collective goals in a more diverse, fluid and individualised society.
>
> (Bentley, 2001, p. 1)

The UK modernization project has certain key elements: the mirroring of an idealized version of business; the creation of networks through which government and business may promote cultural change, and the fostering of responsible self-government. In all of these spheres education is important and education policy is at the forefront in the encouragement of private sector involvement in what was public sector activity. Education is the favoured site for the development of self-regulation and responsibility. Managerialism carries the modernization agenda forward through its reinforcement of policy-making as technical and pragmatic, driven by a calculus of economy and efficiency (Clarke *et al.*, 2000). Thus modernization and managerialism operate in a landscape that is, effectively, globalized (Fergusson, 2000).

Collective narratives and embedded policy

These new forms of governance must map against, overlap or conflict with existing policy patterns and processes: the 'assumptive worlds' and institutional contexts of policy makers in education. In England, educational administration post-1944 was sustained by deep assumptions about culture, ability and difference, and was practiced by an elite shaped by these assumptions (Gewirtz and Ozga, 1990). More recent work (Jones, 1999) suggests that the current modernization project in England is no less mythically informed. In Scotland, the assumptive worlds of policy makers, and the shaping myths on which they drew, pointed to a policy community (McPherson and Raab, 1988) rather than a policy elite.

This theme was explored in the EGSIE project through analysis of the significance of what was called the *collective narrative*, which relates policy to cultural identities in different national systems (Popkewitz *et al.*, 1999). That collective narrative, whatever its complex cultural and social origins, was most coherently articulated by national and local policy makers, who used it to moderate and mediate travelling policy. The EGSIE project research on Scotland and England produced some evidence of different 'collective narratives' from policy makers. This seemed to have effects in terms of the ways in which policy was made (for example, it helped to explain differences in the role and influence of business interests, differences in the consultation process in relation to social inclusion/exclusion policy development) and hence for the policies themselves (Alexiadou and Ozga, 2002; Ozga, 1999). Most significantly in relation to differences between Scotland and England within the shared policy framework of the UK, there seemed to be differences in welfare redesign. This was perhaps most apparent in policy for social inclusion. In England government appeared to offer social inclusion to its citizens on the basis of *exchange* (i.e. evidence of good citizenship through responsible self-management and engagement in waged work). However, in Scotland, social inclusion was offered on the basis of *entitlement* (inclusion as a citizenship right) (Ozga, 2003). At issue here, as I have argued above, is understanding the playing out of the encounter between the shared features of 'travelling' policy and the existing policy formations with their established relations and institutional contexts.

Scotland: the changing context of governance

The Scottish parliament is operating in a situation in which there may be rather contradictory pressures in relation to changing governance. On the one hand, there is the UK government's modernizing agenda, which is attempting to change the nature of government and politics throughout the UK. On the other hand, as I have said, there are distinctive patterns of practice within the Scottish policy community that have existed for a considerable time. Research for the EGSIE project with policy actors in Scotland and England suggested that the modernization project in Scotland is not as advanced as in England. By this I mean that the discourse of governance in Scotland remains concerned to promote a revived partnership that does not include dominant business interests. There is still considerable reliance on a 'collective narrative' that gives status to the expert voice of teachers and local authority officers and not much indication of adapting governance to reflect private sector interests and behaviours.

The capacity to get things done still seems to lie mainly with government (albeit in a new form and place), the civil service and the professional partners, operating as a policy community. Our informants raise some of these issues in response to questions about changes in governance, with particular reference to the balance of power between Whitehall and Edinburgh:

> Policy at the moment is still determined by Whitehall, I do not think the Scottish parliament has yet got to grips with this issue because I think one reason for that is that its independence of Whitehall is still in the process of being mapped out. The party links between the ruling group in Whitehall and the ruling group in Scotland are still strong enough to provide a uniform approach on these kind of issues. So although the Scottish Parliament has introduced policies of social inclusion, as indeed has Whitehall, they have not simultaneously dropped those aspects of the market which in effect have defeated their policies of social inclusion.
>
> (Ozga *et al.*, 2001, p. 461)

Another possible source of tension reflects responses to pressure on local (i.e. Scottish) autonomy and responsiveness in education policy by steering mechanisms that allow little local latitude. Target-setting and specific funding are significant here. There is disagreement with the tight steering of policy and our respondents in Scotland emphasize differences in practices and relationships, even if a similar policy goal is being pursued. The following quotation from another informant highlights differences in which performance measurement and target-setting are implemented in the two systems:

> we have got an agenda about the raising of attainment and the tools in the setting of targets which is significantly different in the way it is frequently portrayed, particularly in the South [i.e. England] as the league tables illustrate. The targets which schools are asked to set are not targets against some arbitrary fixed point in the

examination structure. They are targets set against the contexts of that particular school's environment and the needs of the children within the school. There is no question about arbitrary targets being set across these schools being measured simply one against another without regard to background.

(Ozga et al., 2001, p. 470)

As stated earlier, devolution needs to be seen not as creating an entirely new situation, but as building on existing administrative devolution where policies could be adapted for 'local' contexts. In addition, among the powerful pressures for policy convergence is the current reasonably close party political alliance between the UK Labour government and the Labour–Liberal coalition governments of the Scottish parliament to date. However, Scottish policy has diverged in relation to higher education support and long-term care for the elderly. The significance of this divergence is not yet clear. It may signal the emergence of substantial differences about the nature of the welfare state informed by different 'collective narratives'. It may reflect deepening differences in the nature of a revised social contract between government and citizens in the two nations: a contract based on exchange in England and entitlement in Scotland. On the other hand, the modernization project has strong UK-wide effects. Keating argues that the modern, integrated welfare state provides the context for UK devolution, and adds that 'there are questions about how much divergence is possible in these conditions' (Keating, 2001, p. 13). However, this reading, while drawing attention to powerful forces for convergence, may underplay the influence of 'collective narratives' and neglect the part played by embedded policy in the context of vernacular globalization.

Conclusion

The modernization of governance is a key policy project for the UK government. Education is a priority area of policy and a central element in the drive to make the UK an effective competitor in a globalized economy. However, education, as I have suggested, is also strongly embedded in national cultures, including those of the constituent nations of the UK. This means that it is not always amenable to modernization, and there may be considerable tensions between practices and forms of governance understood as 'national' and the agenda of modernization, which is refracted through these forms and practices. This tension between education's centrality as a policy site for the Westminster (UK) government, and its simultaneous status as a location of cultural and political identity and practice in the devolved polities (but perhaps especially Scotland) may become more evident. Changing governance in the UK takes place against a background both of long-established patterns of internal variation and of new institutional arrangements and actors who are not uniformly compliant with the direction of change. The modernization process may, indeed, produce self-conscious revisiting of models and myths of governance (collective narratives) that appear threatened by the modernizing radicalism of the UK centre. It could be argued that it is in the definition of civil society that a new post-devolution, post-welfarist 'collective narrative' may be constructed, to provide energy to 'embedding' policy. Here the attempts of the Scottish parliament to generate public debate and to promote consultation should be noted, and Keating (2004, p. 1) points to 'the continued social democratic tradition in Scotland and the more consultative policy style'. Allan (2003) also stresses the extent to which new forms of policy-making, notably the committee-based inquiry process, provides new space for political influence on policy-making.

The account given here is intended, at least partly, to reiterate the importance of the local in responding to, and mediating, globalizing pressures and travelling policies. I have attempted to argue that policies get re-contextualized and remodelled according to local and national histories, traditions and social relations. One of the fundamental characteristics of globalization is that it can revitalize local institutions and formations. Faced with homogenizing travelling policy, particular groups or societies can be encouraged to revisit and reconstruct the value basis of their organization, and may generate new energy in its production within social and cultural institutions. Such agendas may need to be written against what seem to me to be some of the more insidious forms of travelling policy: for example those that demand waged work as the price of inclusion, or require evidence of responsible, forward-thinking self-investment from people who have little social or financial capital with which to trade. In doing this work of defining and developing civil society there is, perhaps, the possibility of greater divergence between Scotland and England, given the extent to which emergent definitions of 'the public' in England seem to concern a space that has been sucked into the market. Resisting that definition may be enabled by judicious use of existing 'collective narratives' that re-engage with some of the older Scottish traditions of civil society. Some accounts of the Scottish Enlightenment tradition envisage civil society as a foundation for reciprocity, mutuality and cooperation. This 'collective narrative' could provide resources for a construction of civil society that redefines the public as not distinct from the state or the market but mediating and shaping the relationship between them. As McCrone puts it:

> In short, people think of themselves as Scots – and they do, in increasing numbers, over being British – because they have been educated, governed and embedded in a Scottish way. It is a matter of governance, not of sentiment; or, if anything, the latter derives

from the former. This 'governance' is a social system, but, especially in Scotland since 1999, a 'political' i.e. a constitutional one. A law-making parliament both embodies as well as transforms and determines that social will.

(2004, p. 4)

References

Alexiadou, N. and Jones, K. (2001) 'Travelling Policy/Local Spaces', paper presented at the Congrès Marx International 111, Paris, September.

Alexiadou, N. and Ozga, J. (2002) 'Modernising Education Governance in England and Scotland: Devolution and Control', *European Educational Research Journal*, 1(4): 676–91.

Allan, J. (2003) 'Daring to Think Otherwise: Educational Policy Making in the Scottish Parliament', *Journal of Education Policy*, 18(3): 289–301.

Appadurai, A. (1990) 'Disjuncture and Difference in the Global Cultural Economy', in M. Featherstone (ed.) *Global Culture: Nationalism, Globalisation and Modernity*, London: Sage.

Appadurai, A. (1996) *Modernity at Large: Cultural Dimensions of Globalisation*, Minneapolis, MN: University of Minnesota Press.

Ball, S. J. (1998) 'Educational Studies, Policy Entrepreneurship and Social Theory', in R. Slee, G. Weiner and S. Tomlinson (eds) *School Improvement for Whom?*, London: Falmer Press.

Bentley, T. (2001) *It's Democracy, Stupid: An Agenda for Self-government*, London: Demos.

Castells, M. (1998) *The Information Age: Economy, Society and Culture. Vol. 3: End of Millennium*, Oxford: Blackwell.

Clarke, J., Gewirtz, S. and McLaughlin, E. (eds) (2000) *New Managerialism, New Welfare?*, London: Sage.

Dale, R. (1986) *Perspectives on Education Policy* (Unit 1 of Open University Course Policy-making in Education), Milton Keynes: The Open University.

Department for Education and Employment (DfEE) (1997) *Excellence in Schools*, Cm 3681 (July), London: Stationery Office.

Fergusson, R. (2000) 'Modernising Managerialism in Education', in J. Clarke, S. Gewirtz and E. McLaughlin (eds) *New Managerialism, New Welfare?*, London: Sage.

Gewirtz, S. and Ozga, J. (1990) 'Partnership, Pluralism and Education Policy: A Reassessment', *Journal of Education Policy*, 5(1): 37–48.

Giddens, A. (1990) *The Consequences of Modernity*, Oxford: Polity Press.

Held, D., McGrew, A., Goldblatt, D. and Perraton, J. (1999) *Global Transformations: Politics, Economics and Culture*, Cambridge: Polity Press.

Jones, K. (1999) Education en Grande-Bretagne de 1979 à 1998: la revolution des conservateurs et ses prolongements, *Syndicalisme et Societe*, 2(1): 59–84.

Keating, M. (2001) 'Devolution and Public Policy in the UK: Divergence or Convergence?'. Available at: www.devolution.ac.uk/Keatingpaper2.htm.

Keating, M. (2004) 'How Distinctive is Holyrood? An Analysis of Legislation in the First Scottish Parliament'. Available at: www.devolution.ac.uk/Keating paper3.htm.

Lingard, B. (2000) 'It Is and It Isn't: Vernacular Globalisation, Education Policy and Restructuring', in N. Burbules and C. Torres (eds) *Globalisation and Education: Critical Perspectives*, New York: Routledge, pp. 79–108.

Lindblad, S. and Popkewitz, T. S. (2000a) 'Educational Governance and Social Inclusion and Exclusion: Some Conceptual Difficulties and Problematics in Policy and Research', *Discourse: Studies in the Cultural Politics of Education*, 21(1): 5–45.

Lindblad, S. and Popkewitz, T. S. (eds) (2000b) *Public Discourses on Education Governance and Social Integration and Exclusion*, Uppsala Reports on Education 36, Uppsala: Universitetstryckeriet.

Lindblad, S. and Popkewitz, T. S. (eds) (2002) *Education Governance and Social Integration and Exclusion: Studies in the Power of Reason and the Reasons of Power*, Uppsala Reports on Education 39, Uppsala: Universitetstryckeriet.

Lindblad, S., Ozga, J. and Zambeta, E. (2002) (eds) 'Changing Forms of Educational Governance in Europe', *European Educational Research Journal* (special issue), 1(4).

McCrone, D. (2004) 'Cultural Capital in an Understated Nation: The Case of Scotland', paper presented at the Symposium on Cultural Capital and Social Exclusion, St Hugh's College, University of Oxford, 8–9 January. Available at: www.institute-of-governance.org/onlinepub/mccrone/culturalcapital.html.

McPherson, A. and Raab, C. (1988) *Governing Education: A Sociology of Policy since 1945*, Edinburgh: Edinburgh University Press.

Ozga, J. (1987) 'Studying Education Policy Through the Lives of the Policy-Makers: An Attempt to Bridge the Micro-Macro Gap', in L. Barton and S. Walker (eds) *Policy, Teachers and Education*, Buckingham: Open University Press.

Ozga, J. (1999) 'Two Nations? Education Policy and Social Inclusion and Exclusion in England and Scotland', *Education and Social Justice*, 2(1): 44–51.

Ozga, J. (2000) 'Education: New Labour, New Teachers?', in J. Clarke, S. Gewirtz and E. McLaughlin (eds) *New Managerialism, New Welfare?*, London: Sage.

Ozga, J. (2003) 'Two Nations? Education Policy and Social Inclusion/Exclusion in the UK', paper presented at the Symposium on Education Policy in the UK, British Educational Research Association Annual Conference Edinburgh, September.

Ozga, J., Shain, F., Stead, J. and Munn, P. (2001) 'Education Governance and Social Exclusion/Inclusion: A Report on the Interviews with Scottish System Actors', in S. Lindblad and T. S. Popkewitz (eds) *Listening to Education Actors on Governance and Social Integration and Exclusion*, Uppsala Reports on Education 37, Uppsala: Universitetstryckeriet, pp. 459–74.

Paterson, L. (1998) 'Scottish Civil Society and the Scottish Parliament', *Études Écossaises* 5, Grenôble: Université Stendhal.

Perri 6 (1998) *On the Right Lines: The Next Centre-right in the British Isles*, London: Demos.

Popkewitz, T. S., Lindblad, S. and Strandberg, J. (1999) *Review of Research on Education Governance and Social Integration and Exclusion*, Uppsala Reports on Education 35, Uppsala: Universitetstryckeriet.

Raffe, D., Brannen, K., Croxford, L. and Martin, C. (1999) 'Comparing England, Scotland, Wales and Northern Ireland: The Case for "Home Internationals" in Comparative Research', *Comparative Education*, 35: 9–25.

Taylor, S., Rizvi, F., Lingard, B. and Henry, M. (1997) *Educational Policy and the Politics of Change*, London, Routledge.

6 Europeanization and education policy

Nafsika Alexiadou

Globalization and Europe

This chapter will discuss the emergence of a closer than ever European Union (EU) as part of an economic, political and cultural 'globalizing process' with effects on education policy and practice. Discussing the impact of the EU on education policy in a volume about globalization is relevant when we consider globalization as a reconstitution of the power, functions and authority of national governments (Held *et al.*, 1999). Within the sphere of the EU, the traditionally understood sovereignty of nation states is partially replaced by 'complex transnational networks' (p. 9). This process, which the EU member states themselves initiated and negotiated, has led to the creation of a network of states that have invited and accepted an additional political authority within their national sovereign borders. This authority, residing in Brussels, impinges not only on economic, but also on political and cultural aspects of state organization and functions, such as that of educating citizens.

The term 'Europeanization' can be discussed in terms of the specific institutional impact of the European integration process on the domestic institutions of the governments of member states, as well as their politics and policies (Bulmer and Burch, 2000). This definition is useful when one looks at institutions of particular sectors of education, and refers to the process as one of convergence of 'policy norms' rather than whole systems (Radaelli, 1999). But the term can also be seen in broader terms as a 'light' form of internationalization whereby the European space is 'characterised by a common and shared history and culture, and as an economic, political and cultural alliance vis-à-vis the rest of the world' (Kehm, 2003, p. 110). The defensive nature of this definition suggests the emergence of the EU as a counterbalance to globalization and to forms of regional economic and political alliances elsewhere in the world (Hay, 2002). The purpose of such counterbalance would be to protect existing economic powers, institutions, traditions and cultural identities, although it could also be seen as a form of 'transcendence and overcoming of the nation state and its historically evident dangers' (Amos *et al.*, 2002, p. 204).

The voluntarily entered strategic relations of cooperation among European member states often set legal parameters that, once accepted, enabled particular forms of action and restricted or limited others. However, in both the above definitions of 'Europeanization', the nation state is still the most significant actor in selecting which relationships it will enter, and how these will be interpreted and implemented. Member states do not only receive and implement policies designed at the EU level, but they are actively engaged in the construction of these policies, even though with varying degrees of power to shape direction and outcome. Sassen (1998) and Ross (1998) attack the rhetoric of governments that the state is only able to respond to external, 'global' or international constraints in one way. Their argument concerns the widespread introduction of neo-liberal policies and, even though referring to economic globalization, is equally relevant to issues of Europeanization. They argue that political choice and agency should be brought forward in the analysis of state responses to both neo-liberal policies and processes of economic convergence:

> deregulation and other policies furthering economic globalisation cannot simply be considered as an instance of a declining significance of the state. Deregulation is a vehicle through which a growing number of states are furthering economic globalisation and guaranteeing the rights of global capital, an essential ingredient of the former. Deregulation and kindred policies constitute the elements of a new legal regime dependent on consensus among states to further globalisation.
>
> (Sassen, 1998, p. 200)

Hay (2002) emphasizes the same point, i.e. that the structural constraints many governments claim to be a result of globalization or Europeanization are exaggerated, and do not of themselves determine the particular direction of policy for national governments. The distinction is made here between globalization as a set of processes and/or outcomes that reflect a 'real', 'material' impact and structural change, and a 'discourse of globalization' (or Europeanization) used by governments in order to justify unpalatable domestic reforms (usually of the public sector and welfare). The significance of this distinction lies in the implications of accepting the former or the latter with regard to possibilities for political action and state power or powerlessness, and for 'restoring notions of political responsibility and accountability to contemporary political and economic dynamics' (Hay and Rosamond, 2002, p. 150).

In line with the earlier defensive definition of Europeanization, Europe for many analysts seems to be offering an alternative model to the (perceived by many) threatening Anglo-American dominance in economic and cultural terms, but also to the erosion of traditional functions of the welfare state and its displacement by the market. The project of European integration is seen, especially by those in the left-of-centre politics of EU countries, as based on a more strongly social democratic politic, and as offering a model of modernization in which social partnership is important. It is hoped that Europeanization will further preserve the distinct European model of social politics where neo-liberal discourses are interpreted in ways that take into account social projects, against the threats of an unregulated globalization. As Oskar Lafontaine argues:

> A downward race between countries is ... by no means an inevitable consequence of globalisation. It is the result of a misconstrued policy and can be corrected. . . . To avoid the further erosion of our economic, social and cultural foundations, we must rethink current economic policy ... The political foundation of the European Union is an economy based on social and ecological responsibility. This market economy could operate as a useful model for a regulatory framework of the new global economy.
>
> (Cited in Hay and Rosamond, 2002, p. 57)

The contrast between globalization as an economic imperative and a social market model of European integration casts European left-of-centre policies against forces that promote policies of neo-liberalism as the desirable response to a positively regarded project of globalization, mainly promoted by New Labour in Britain. Of course, this should be taken with caution, on two main counts. First, in a number of European contexts, 'it is the process of European integration which is invoked as the proximate cause of often painful social and economic reforms elsewhere legitimated in terms of globalisation' (Hay and Rosamond, 2002, p. 157). Second, we should not overestimate the extent to which Europe represents a political, social and cultural unity (Held *et al.*, 1999).

Here there seem to be two readings of the process of European integration and social policy, both of which are relevant for education. Wolfgang Streeck (1999) and Fritz Scharpf (2001) are typical proponents of the pessimistic view that sees the European Monetary Union (EMU) project as driven by the political right and a strong business agenda that promotes reduced social protection, further deregulation of labour markets, wage differentiation and other supply-side strategies that seem to be the only political options freely available among the countries of the single market. National governments are seen as weaker or unwilling to influence economic growth and employment in their territories due largely to European legal constraints (Scharpf, 2001). The effect of such policy direction on issues of social justice and education is that member states are focusing on 'investment in collective means of production, that is, infrastructures of all sorts' and particularly on investing in human capital, through education, as a 'productive asset of the community' (Streeck, 1999, p. 5). The drive within the EU to deregulate labour markets even further will result in (or indeed require) an unequal educational and social pool, and in that case concerns with 'social exclusion' of individuals, groups and whole regions across Europe will become even sharper.

Not all commentators on European social policy agree with the above interpretation of a hegemonic driving neo-liberal force behind the developments of the last decade. Jane Jenson and Philippe Pochet (2002) argue instead that the pro-business bias and neo-liberalism of the EMU project was 'corrected' by new political alliances across Europe that sought to render it sensitive to the advantages of treating employment and social protection as productive forces in supply-side management, rather than a simple drain on competitiveness. As these two commentators argue, retrenchment has not been the result of the first decade of Europe post-Maastricht, despite the initial strong drive from various business groups, which might support the argument that globalization is driven largely by national states' political choice and commitment.

Ross (1998) invites us to consider the Single European Market and EMU as contributory factors to globalization and not just as a result of it. He argues that European governments have actively decided to create structural constraints upon what they can do and sacrificed many of their 'capacities to shape market flows, monetary policy and budgets' (p. 180). The future will show the extent to which the 'social market model' promoted across Europe with its basis on humane welfare and corporate political settlements is viable. But, as I have argued elsewhere (Alexiadou, 2005), European education policy seems to be adopting a form of Anglo-American 'Third Way' character.

The following section deals with the formation of education policy within the framework of the EU, and examines a number of themes that relate to the changing purposes but also loci of control of education in the context of Europeanization.

Education policy and the EU

One of the main functions of education systems has for a long time been the construction of nation states and national identities. Hobsbawm (1990) reviews the role of education in building national traditions, selectively transmitting official national cultures, and establishing national language as a core value in the construction of a national identity. These traditional roles of education systems are fairly recent (eighteenth to twentieth centuries in Europe), and have been linked to our modern understanding of 'sovereignty' of nation states. More recently, however, and particularly from the 1980s onwards, we see across Europe the emergence of educational projects and initiatives that promote educational goals framed against an international context. Jones and Alexiadou (2001) have used the idea of 'travelling' education policies, referring to two sets of ideas. The first concerns the work of intergovernmental organizations that have developed sets of policy themes seeking to reshape national schooling systems and cultures. Such organizations include the World Bank, the OECD and the EU. Their policy agendas interact with existing traditions, ideologies and forms of national organization, but do intend to change the conceptualizations of educational purpose in particular directions. Kenway (1994) and others have extensively discussed the idea of the 'economising of education' as part of an international drive to prioritize the economic functions of education in developing human capital, and in effectively creating the identities of consumers and flexible workers in competitive capitalist economies. The social role of education in the creation of citizenship and social cohesion is frequently mentioned in the discourse of these agenda-setting international organizations, but this role is not the main driver of policy. The second kind of 'travelling policy' is one which crosses boundaries between different disciplines and social practices and, particularly, arguments from management theory and economic policy as they are deployed in the field of education. The kinds of education policy agenda that have crossed national frontiers characteristically embody managerial and economic themes. Ball lists neo-liberalism, performativity, public choice theory and a 'new managerialism' as border-crossing elements of globalized discourse (in Jones and Alexiadou, 2001). Alongside the development of policy themes and statements of purpose, these international organizations have established a range of activities that define education policy, such as established norms of performance based on international collections of data and the creation of league tables. As we shall see later, in the case of the EU, this norm-setting activity is becoming an increasingly powerful tool to shape the direction and outcome of national education policy-making.

Next to these 'travelling themes' of education policy, the EU provides a very specific and regulated space within which we can consider education. Questions about the economic, civic and nation-building functions of education are all addressed in specific terms. So, in EU law, education policy is governed by the principle of 'subsidiarity', which sets limits to the competence of the EU to intervene in the content or organization of education systems of individual member states. According to this principle, the Community may only take action in education if the proposed objectives cannot be achieved by the member states internally or in cooperation. The Treaty of the European Union signed in Maastricht in 1992 confirmed the contribution of the Community to education as one of 'ensuring quality', 'encouraging cooperation', 'supporting and supplementing national action', and 'respecting the responsibility' of member states for their education systems (now Article 149, EC Treaty; see also Article 16 of the Draft Treaty Establishing a Constitution for Europe). Despite an early interest in education and training at the European level, concerns raised from the mid-1980s onwards about the level and quality of skills of the European workforce brought education and training to the attention of policy makers as key conditions for the creation of a competitive economy. The link between education, training and the economy was firmly established, and the value of qualifications and their recognition were increasingly part of the political agenda of the Union.

Education policy has been discussed primarily in relation to its contribution to economic growth (Brine, 2002). This has been reaffirmed in the commitment of the Lisbon (2000) and Stockholm European Council (2001) meetings to make the EU the most competitive knowledge economy in the world, highlighting the role of education and training in achieving this goal. The Maastricht Treaty of the European Union constituted European citizenship, and saw the beginnings of a social-side response to monetary union (Falkner, 1999). Still, the emphasis in the definition of 'citizenship' is on the 'market liberties of the economic citizen' (Leidfried, 2000, p. 45), which reflects and reinforces 'the continuing prioritisation of economic rights in the European Union' (Douglas-Scott, 2002, p. 491). The political aspect of citizenship is widely acknowledged to be fairly underdeveloped, while 'social citizenship' is vaguely defined and seems to be all-encompassing. Defining social citizenship in more specific terms is likely to have implications for national sovereignty in matters of welfare and in definitions of national identity. But, even though the main activities of the Community were driven by concerns with economic integration, the construction of a 'European identity' was emphasized as essential as far back as 1973 and the Copenhagen summit. Since then, the themes of 'European identity' and 'citizenship' have been recurrent and formalized in the latest Treaties of Maastricht and Amsterdam. Lewicka-Grisdale and McLaughlin (2002) describe the key events in the development of these themes, one of which was the 1988 Resolution on the European dimension in education of the Council of Ministers and the Ministers of Education. The Resolution, based on a report called 'Enhanced treatment of the European dimension in education', recognized that: 'the Community's economic policies would be effective only if they were accompanied by appropriate policies in the field of education', which would support 'a European model of culture correlating with European integration', conceived 'economically, socially, politically and culturally' (p. 55).

This aspect of EU programmatic statements and policies with regard to key functions of education is similar to that of nation state-building and the techniques used to forge a sense of a national identity. Article 126 of the third chapter of the Maastricht Treaty considerably expands the competence of the EU in actions that develop the 'European dimension' in education, mainly through the teaching of languages and the exchange of education participants (Tulasiewicz and Brock, 2000). Even though the new Treaty does not allow harmonization of regulations or laws across the EU, it may 'give a legal basis for protection against Community action which is harmful to the identity and language of a certain culture', preserving the principle of 'diversity' of education of individual member states (p. 24). Karlsen (2002) summarised the goals for Community action on education into three central aims, all of which feed into both the economic mobility and 'identity'-related functions of education. These are: (1) promoting mobility, exchange and cooperation in education and training through student and teacher exchange programmes, (2) developing a European dimension as part of a wider attempt to create a European identity, and (3) encouraging academic recognition of qualifications and study and exchange of information. The creation of a European identity, of course, has also been linked to the issue of the 'imagination of Europe as a policy space', and the 'discursive construction of Europe', a process that goes beyond merely aggregating particular features of the member states' economies (Rosamund, in Dale, 2005, p. 9).

The changing relationship between the redesigned sovereignty of EU states and education brings forth a number of important questions that education analysts should consider:

- If the emphasis of the emerging EU policies on education is primarily on preparing people for a competitive labour market and a 'knowledge economy', what does this mean for the role of education in redressing questions of social inequalities and opportunities?

The Irish Presidency of the Council of the European Union (during 2004) reiterated the 2000 'Lisbon strategy' to make Europe 'the most dynamic and competitive knowledge based economy in the world by 2010'. Education and training are seen to make a key contribution to this aim. Noel Dempsey (2004), the Irish Minister for Education and Culture, adopted this aim as the goal for Ireland's presidency with respect to education, summarized under the theme of *Building an Inclusive and Competitive Europe*. The economic emphasis on education's role is stronger compared to that of other functions of education:

> Clearly, the role of Education and Youth policies in supporting the development of a knowledge based economy is central. The EU also recognises the diverse nature of culture between Member States

and between regions of the EU, while also emphasising the common cultural heritage of the EU Member States.

(Dempsey, 2004)

Extracts such as this leave unanswered a number of questions about the role of education in a more integrated European policy context, such as the following:

- Within the EU, what happens to the civic functions of education systems, and to those functions that have been connected to the construction of national identities and nation states? How do questions of citizenship (national and European) feature in the new Europe?
- How is education going to be governed at the EU level?

In the rest of the chapter I will address these questions through a brief discussion of two issues. The first refers to a new governance tool, the Open Method of Coordination (OMC), recently introduced to deal with 'sensitive' areas of social policy. The second concerns the internationalization of higher education at the European level, and the introduction of the 'Bologna Process'.

The open method of coordination

This section draws on collaborative work with Bettina Lange, which has been further elaborated in Alexiadou and Lange (2003). The EU's lack of legal capacity to interfere in the structure, organization and content of education of national member states led to the recent use of a new governance tool in the sphere of education: the Open Method of Coordination (OMC). This chapter's brief review of the OMC does not aim to exhaust the literature on the subject, but rather to make the connections between the idea of 'travelling policy' from the EU to national education systems, and the issue of governability of a sensitive area of social policy that is protected by the principle of subsidiarity.

The OMC was first introduced at the Lisbon summit in 2000, at a Premiers' meeting of the EU member states. It is a new 'light-touch' regulatory tool which aims to 'achieve progress in politically sensitive areas' (de la Porte, 2002, p. 38), and is employed in order to achieve greater convergence among EU member states. It works through benchmarking, which involves the definition of indicators for measuring progress in education policy and the setting of EU, national and regional targets, as well as through the exchange of 'best practice' and regular monitoring (de la Porte, 2002, p. 38). Since the OMC is a new governance tool its contents and form are still evolving, but it is clear that it aims to depart from traditional EU legal prescriptions. It is a more 'diffuse national adaptation to a wide array of transnational norms' (Chalmers and Lodge, 2003, p. 1). Hence, the OMC involves new forms of 'soft law', which will allow for greater influence of the EU Commission in comparison to the EU Council in the law-making process (Trubek and Mosher, 2001, p. 4).

The OMC was first developed in the context of the EU's employment, pensions and social inclusion policies, intending to be an 'appropriate tool for an integrated approach towards achieving economic and social renewal' (Regent, 2003, p. 190). It is now, however, also utilized in the policy field of education. The OMC should help to meet the EU Concrete Future Objectives for Education Systems. Its benchmarking system aims to contribute to the realization of these objectives across the EU at the local level (COM, 2001; Dale, 2003).

The OMC aims to respect national differences in the organization, values and political arrangements for education (i.e. the principle of subsidiarity), while at the same time achieving common EU objectives and coordinating activity across the EU. It is clear that the OMC will impact on policies at higher education level, through further encourage-ment of university students and staff mobility, as well as through increasing the transferability of higher education qualifications to all of the EU labour markets. The commitment to create a 'Europe of know-ledge' is to be achieved by the OMC and by parallel efforts to create a European Research Area by 2010. At primary and secondary levels, however, its potential impact remains unclear. The OMC will radically challenge how education policy is governed in the EU and will have a significant impact on policy-making, since member states no longer enjoy exclusive sovereignty over education policy. Furthermore, the OMC's emphasis on the local implementation of a benchmarking system opens up interesting questions about its application in devolved and highly decentralized education systems. These issues raise a number of questions, which concern:

- the ways in which the OMC tries to harmonize education policy across the EU through the use of norm-setting (benchmarking and performance indicators);
- the relation of the OMC practices to ideas of equality of opportunity in education, social justice and social cohesion;
- the relations of education governance and distribution of power between the supranational, national and regional/local policy makers and actors; and
- the compatibility of the OMC methods and targets with existing education policy in the various EU members.

It is most likely that EU education policy will give rise to a complex system of multi-level governance. The term 'governance' includes changing relationships between states and markets in education policy, and relationships between public political actors, such as the EU, nation states and regional and local government (Lawn and Lingard, 2002), but also the ways in which governments coordinate activities and actors rather than directly performing these activities themselves (Jessop, 2003). Multi-level governance in EU education policy is based on strong symbolic political ideas, such as visions of EU integration and devolution in national political systems (Falkner, 1999). It also works through specific governance practices, such as the centralization of education policies at national level through the setting of centrally defined standards for education services and products, accompanied by greater influence of market principles and practices, such as encouraging consumer choice and competition between education service providers for 'customers' and resources (Lawn, 2001). Multi-level governance exists already in some EU member states, such as the UK. England and Scotland, for instance, have been interpreting the UK government's education policies in very different ways since devolution (Alexiadou and Ozga, 2002). It is still too early to evaluate the ways in which existing education systems will manage to accommodate the EU regimes. It is likely that there will be areas of conflict and areas of convergence between the EU and member states in the sphere of education policy. But the multi-level forms of education governance and the development of education policy in the EU increasingly through 'networks' (Novoa and Lawn, 2002) are opening possibilities for instruments such as the OMC to operate in powerful ways and without necessarily infringing upon the principle of subsidiarity.

Education policies and practices offer a significant site for the generation of cultural norms and visions, and for the creation of identities, as well as for linking education and persons to the world of work in particular ways. The operation of instruments such as the OMC will bring particular understandings of these through the 'travelling' managerialist practices of benchmarking, the development of indicators for education performance and the monitoring of compliance. This is of course a very 'top-down' statement. The ways in which member states, regional and local education actors will respond to these are likely to include a wide range of strategies of accommodation, resistance or redefinition of terms of reference to suit national or local practices (see, for example, Green, 2002; Edwards and Boreham, 2003).

The following section looks at higher education in the context of European integration, and touches upon some of the questions raised already with respect to education governance, issues of convergence of policy norms and the question of 'travelling' policy themes that impact on higher education changes in Europe.

Higher education in Europe

Higher education (HE) offers an interesting case as a field of policy that falls in the intersection between Europeanization, wider global trends, and national traditions. Both the governance of HE in the integrated Europe, and its changing functions, character and the role of academics, are issues that will be concerning analysts of the sector for a long time to come. In this section I give a brief overview of some of the key developments in HE, across Europe and within the EU.

As the sector that has always enjoyed more autonomy in the various national contexts in Europe than any other education sector, HE has always been more open to areas of international cooperation and innovative experimentation. But, at the same time, HE institutions have, since the nineteenth century, been closely associated with the nation state, through the formation of the administrative elites, scientists, the intelligentsia and trained personnel for the welfare state, but also as symbols of 'cultural recognition' (Paterson, 2001, p. 139). The recent creation across Europe of a mass system of HE that enrols 15–50 per cent of young people, has led to a redefinition of the relationships between HE and the state, one that has been even further changed by the process of Europeanization. We can observe across European states a move towards decentralizing responsibility for HE, through the introduction of enhanced institutional autonomy (with regard to finances) and accountability (to consumers, the economy, the government), managerial practices of evaluation, intrusive management into and increasing regulation of the work of academics, and ideas of entrepreneurialism (Neave, 1998). The older forms of centralized steering of HE institutions on the part of the central government was perceived to be inadequate to achieve the intended (increasingly complex) outcomes required from HE. Similar wide-ranging reforms of HE across Europe were introduced under the umbrella concept of 'self-regulation' of HE institutions, which, since the 1980s, became very popular with governments (Maasen and Stensaker, 2003). As a result, Sporn (2003) argues that we see in European HE a strengthening of the 'middle' level of institutional management and leadership, at the expense of the top level (state) or the bottom level (academic units and faculty). But, as Maasen and Stensaker (2003) point out, we should pay more attention to the symbolic and normative aspects of 'self-regulation' rather than assume a consistent or coherent approach to the restructuring that took place. They argue that in practice the efforts of many governments to introduce 'self-regulation' in their HE systems often resulted in divergent and frequently contradictory governance arrangements. Universities opted to emphasize elements of 'trust' in their relationship with the state, whereas the states seemed to be driven in their actions by an agenda based on 'lack of control' or distrust of the institutions (Maasen and Stensaker, 2003).

We can summarize such common trends of HE developments across Europe under the themes of: (1) massification of HE in most countries of the EU, (2) a gradual withdrawal of the central state from the steering of the governance of institutions, (3) a policy of self-regulation or institutional autonomy, and (4) increasingly, the rise of what Paterson (2001) calls the 'region building' role of HE. The expected contributions of HE to the regional economy and culture, and the equalization of educational and employment opportunities, are all seen to have particular implications in an EU that sees an increasing number of countries devolving political power to their regions (for example, Belgium, Spain, the UK), but also itself emphasizes a process of regionalization and regional/local implementation of policies (for example, through the OMC or the Committee of the Regions).

The EU has from early on considered universities as a potentially important institution in the process of European integration. The (failed) idea of setting up a European University in 1955 was followed by the creation of a number of successful HE programmes, such as the Erasmus programme in 1987, and later those of Tempus, Lingua, Comett, etc. (Corbett, 2003a). The success of these programmes led to a clear reference to education policy in the Community within the Maastricht Treaty, although with respect to the distinction between 'general' and 'vocational' education, and always firmly placed within the subsidiarity framework. There is a certain ambiguity in so far as HE is concerned, since it falls between 'general' and 'vocational' education (Garrido, 2002), but since 1992 the Community has a legal structure to deal with issues of HE. National sovereignty over education has always been a paramount concern within the EU, but gradually questions of convergence of HE structures, types of institutions, accreditation and courses began being considered. What was developing was a set of initiatives and policies that would lead to a tendency for 'harmonization' of HE across Europe.

The most obvious example of that is the 1998 initiative taken by France, Germany, Italy and the UK to launch the development of what is known as the European Higher Education Area (EHEA) by 2010. Interestingly, the initiative of these four countries was taken outside the institutional framework of the Union. This initiative developed into the 'Bologna Process', sometimes referred to also as the 'Sorbonne–Bologna–Prague Process', after the location of the meetings from the inception of the initiative (Fredriksson, 2003). It is based on the 1999 'Bologna Declaration', which aimed at the convergence of national policies and the creation of the EHEA. By the end of 2003, there were 38 signatories to the Process. The detailed aims of the Bologna Process (and the EHEA) are to further encourage mobility of staff and students, comparability of degrees, a transferable system of credits, the promotion of cooperation in quality assurance and the promotion of a European dimension in HE.

Two years after the signing of the Declaration, discussions and/or reforms of HE structures were taking place across many European countries (Haug and Tauch, 2001). The adoption of a structure of HE on the basis of two main cycles (three years of a Bachelor's degree followed by two years of a Master's degree), and the establishment of common frameworks of quality assurance and accreditation, means the radical reorganization of studies in many European countries, something that is on the HE agenda of all signatory countries.

The Commission was not the source of the initiative but provided support and expertise. So, a few months later, the Lisbon European Council included education and training among the policy areas where the OMC could be used (Pierini, 2001). The EU has committed to a parallel strategy to create a European Research Area by 2010, and took a number of initiatives that aim to contribute to the 'Lisbon strategy' and the creation of the competitive 'Europe of knowledge' (European Commission, 2001). The Commission has given full support to the Bologna action lines, and to the twin goals of 'fostering the attractiveness of European higher education on a global scale', and forging cooperation across Europe in matters of HE. It also acknowledges that 'higher education systems and institutions are less and less "protected" behind national borders and increasingly open to competition and pressures from beyond them' (COM, 2003, 2004). In Prague (2001) and Berlin (2003), European Higher Education Ministers attempted to identify further action points, and to define concrete targets in order to make the EHEA a reality, while the European Council adopted in 2001 the report entitled *The Concrete Future Objectives of Education and Training Systems*. The Berlin Conference of Ministers attempted to translate the ambitious goals of the Bologna Process and the Lisbon strategy into a series of common objectives, and also set up the evaluation of progress in reaching those objectives against 'European Benchmarks' (European Commission, 2003).

The Bologna Process, and the set of initiatives and reforms that it has sparked since 1999, highlight the tensions between the usually conflicting EU goals of 'competitiveness' within a globalized 'war of knowledge', and 'cooperation'. But it is also interesting for what it implies about:

- its implications for HE governance across Europe;
- the balance between the principle of 'respect for diversity' of national systems while at the same time encouraging convergence;
- the role of academics in this fast-changing landscape of European HE.

The OMC is likely to be the instrument adopted by the Commission in dealing with the first two issues, while the discussion around the role and 'voice' of academics in this process varies greatly across the signatory countries and is only recently beginning to emerge. The recent emphasis on the economic and regional functions of HE, and the strengthening of the 'middle' level of institutional management, would suggest that academics might have less of a voice in the restructuring of their institutions. On the other hand, the political and symbolic emphasis on 'self-regulation', devolution of powers and institutional autonomy could open spaces for the definition of HE purpose in a new and larger Europe that draws on less economically driven and managerial agendas. The Bologna Process could, as Corbett (2003b) argues, be seen as 'an opportunity to be taken up or spurned': 'Academics could surely only gain – intellectually, culturally and as interest groups – in being associated with the Bologna process and being part of the groups which helped to shape policy in a way consistent with core academic values' (p. 9).

Some final remarks

The process of European integration has opened up a number of challenges to education policy and practice across Europe. Some of these challenges are only discussed at the level of policy makers and do not seem to affect directly the daily lives of educational practitioners (for instance, questions of governance), while others promise a more direct impact on practice (such as the implementation of the Bologna Process). This chapter has reviewed selected policy issues that touch upon the economic, political, governance and cultural aspects of education policy within the context of Europeanization. Many of these reveal the tensions between national practices and entrenched political cultures on one hand, and developments in the EU institutional frameworks that aim to converge or even harmonize policies on the other. This tension, of course, is the reason why education is covered by the principle of subsidiarity, which aims to respect national diversity. But the multiple functions of education and educational institutions open up spaces where the 'national' is being overridden by the transnational, and the convergence of policy norms becomes inevitable. In this respect, European integration is a form of globalization that employs a series of powerful techniques for the setting up and steering of specific educational goals and objectives. Whether we see this process as a counterbalance to other 'global' powers or as a contributor to globalization itself is interesting in terms of the politics of globalization, but less significant in terms of the impact of these processes on education. What is more important is that the nationally defined roles and functions of education are changing in directions that seem to be dictated by the necessities of a globalized economy. The commitment of the EU to become one of the major players of such an economy underpins most of the issues that have been reviewed in this chapter. Where the process of Europeanization might be seen as distinctly different from that of globalization is in the explicit recognition and respect of the 'national' in matters of education, but also in the attempts to deal with issues of social protection and cohesion.

So, education is expected to play a key economic role in the construction of the 'Europe of knowledge', and, given the integrated nature of policy within the EU, education is also linked to employment policy and to initiatives pursuing social justice. But, of course, one of the major challenges that EU policy makers will face is to identify the features of the 'knowledge economy' and how this can be actually implemented given the limitations of subsidiarity. The open method of coordination intends to achieve this, but identifying the 'right' objectives and targets for measuring progress runs the risk of either becoming too vague to be of any real significance in the attempt to 'fit all', or becoming too prescriptive and imposing on education practice. Similarly, the centrality of universities in developing mobility of people, transferability and comparability of qualifications and credits and a European identity among the EU citizens can be seen as a 'threat to the heterogeneous vitality of the continent's culture but it could offer a source of liberation from dominant nationalistic knowledge systems' (Coulby and Jones, 1995, p. 139).

In view of the enlargement of the EU, and the further diversity of economies, cultures, political systems, languages and educational practices that are already part of the new EU, there will be even more emphasis on 'diversity within unity', rather than a homogenization of education policies. With regard to the governance of education, instruments such as the OMC are more likely to constitute the main ways in which education policy is 'made', while the developments in the sphere of HE would suggest that member states are keen to sign up to initiatives that are seen to move European education policy closer. The extent to which convergence will apply to areas beyond the structures of systems and frameworks is something that we can explore in the future. But, without underestimating the power of 'indicators' and 'benchmarks' (especially when tied to sources of funding) in shaping policy direction and even formally defined outcomes, I would suggest that the complexity of education and the cultural wealth that underpins it are such that we can afford to be optimistic about the process of further European integration.

I want to close, however, with a note of caution that refers to two issues: the first concerns the survival of 'marginal' or 'peripheral' languages in Europe (not explored in this chapter), which are likely to be threatened by many of the educational and other developments that take place as part of further integration; the second is the danger of subsuming the key functions of education under the development of 'human capital' as part of the drive to create a competitive economy. The threats identified here with the process of globalization are equally applicable to Europeanization in so far as the growth of the economy is the only or primary driver for education policy. The creation across the EU of a fiercely competitive and hierarchical system of HE on the basis of institutional prestige, wealth, language of operation and international appeal is a futuristic scenario that seems rather possible. In terms of social justice, of course, such a scenario would bring a major overhaul to the feasibility of policies and practices around social equality. The recent discourse on the convergence of HE, for example, is drawing largely on the language of 'global competitiveness', but it also highlights European HE as a sphere of cooperation, and exchange of ideas, people and practices. Despite the restrictions (legal and other) that are placed around HE practice by the process of convergence, I would argue that academics can play a significant role in the shaping of direction of institutional practice in order to avoid the danger of limiting the roles and functions of education to those of the economy.

References

Alexiadou, N. (2005) Social exclusion, and educational opportunity: the case of British education policies within a European Union context, *Globalisation, Societies and Education Journal*, Vol. 3, No. 1 (forthcoming).

Alexiadou, N. and Lange, B. (2003) The Open Method of Coordination: a new form of EU governance in education policy, Research Proposal submitted to the Nuffield Foundation for Social Science Research (unpublished).

Alexiadou, N. and Ozga, J. (2002) Modernising education governance in England and Scotland: devolution and control, *European Educational Research Journal*, Vol. 1, No. 4: 676–91.

Amos, K. S., Keiner, E., Proske, M. and Radtke, F. (2002) Globalisation: autonomy of education under siege? Shifting boundaries between politics, economy and education, *European Educational Research Journal*, Vol. 1, No. 2: 193–213.

Brine, J. (2002) *The European Social Fund and the EU: Flexibility, Growth, Stability*, Contemporary European Studies 11, London: Continuum.

Bulmer, S. and Burch, M. (2000) Coming to terms with Europe: Europeanisation, Whitehall and the challenge of devolution, Queen's Papers on Europeanisation No. 9/2000.

Chalmers, D. and Lodge, M. (2003) The Open Method of Co-ordination and the European welfare state, in ESRC Centre for Analysis of Risk and Regulation, *Discussion Paper* No. 11, pp. 1–24.

COM (2001) 59 final, Concrete future objectives of education systems, published in the *Official Journal*. Available at: wysiwyg://19/http://europa.eu.int/scad-plus/leg/en/cha/c11049.htm.

COM (2003) 58 final, The role of universities in the Europe of Knowledge, *Communication from the Commission*.

COM (2004) 156 final, The new generation of community education and training programmes after 2006, *Communication from the Commission*.

Corbett, A. (2003a) Ideas, institutions and policy entrepreneurs: towards a new history of higher education in the European Community, *European Journal of Education*, Vol. 38, No. 3: 315–30.

Corbett, A. (2003b) Europe: a threat or an opportunity for national systems of higher education?, paper presented at the Society for Research in Higher Education Seminar on *The White Paper and the Bologna Agreement: Are They Compatible?*, 1 July.

Coulby, D. and Jones, C. (1995) *Postmodernity and European Education System*, Stoke-on-Trent: Trentham Books.

Dale, R. (2003) The Lisbon Declaration, the reconceptualisation of governance and the reconfiguration of European educational space, paper presented at the RAPPE Seminar on *Governance, Regulation and Equity in European Education Systems*, Institute of Education, University of London, 20 March.

Dale, R. (2005) Forms of governance, governmentality and the EU's Open Method of Coordination, in W. Larner and W. Walters (eds) *Global Governmentality*, London: Routledge.

de la Porte, C. (2002) Is the Open Method of Coordination appropriate for organising activities at European level in sensitive policy areas?, *European Law Journal*, Vol. 8, No. 1: 38–58.

Dempsey, N. (2004) *Building an Inclusive and Competitive Europe*. Available at: www.ue2004.ie/templates/standard.asp?sNavlocator=4,25.

Douglas-Scott, S. (2002) *Constitutional Law of the European Union*, Harlow: Pearsons Education.

Edwards, R. and Boreham, N. (2003) The centre cannot hold: complexity and difference in European Union policy towards a learning society, *Journal of Education Policy*, Vol. 18, No. 4: 407–21.

European Commission (2001) *The Concrete Future Objectives of Education and Training Systems*, Report from the Education Council to the European Council, Press Release, No. 5980/01, Brussels, 14 February.

European Commission (2003) Realising the European Higher Education Area, Contribution of the European Commission to the Berlin Conference of European Higher Education Ministers, Berlin, 18/19 September.

European Council (2001) *Presidency Conclusions*, Stockholm European Council, No. 100/1/01. Available at: http://europa.eu.int/council/off/conclu/index. htm.

Falkner, G. (1999) European social policy: towards multi-level and multi-actor governance, in B. Kohler-Koch and R. Eising (eds) *The Transformation of Governance in the European Union*, London: Routledge.

Fredriksson, U. (2003) Changes of education policies within the European Union in the light of globalisation, *European Educational Research Journal*, Vol. 2, No. 4: 522–46.

Garrido, J. L. G. (2002) The European university looks ahead towards the future, in J. A. Ibanez-Martin and G. Jover (eds) *Education in Europe: Policies and Politics*, Dordrecht: Kluwer Academic Publishers.

Green, A. (2002) The many faces of lifelong learning: recent education policy trends in Europe, *Journal of Education Policy*, Vol. 17, No. 6: 611–26.

Haug, G. and Tauch, C. (2001) *Trends in Learning Structures in higher education (II)*, Follow-up Report to the Bologna Declaration prepared for the Salamanca and Prague Conferences, March/May.

Hay, C. (2002) Globalisation, 'EU-isation' and the space for social democratic alternatives: pessimism of the intellect: a reply to Coates, *British Journal of Politics and International Relations*, Vol. 4, No. 3: 452–64.

Hay, C. and Rosamond, B. (2002) Globalisation, European integration and the discursive construction of economic imperatives, *Journal of European Public Policy*, Vol. 9, No. 2: 147–67.

Held, D., McGrew, A., Goldblatt, D. and Perraton, J. (1999) *Global Transformations: Politics, Economics and Culture*, Cambridge: Polity Press.

Hobsbawm, E. (1990) *Nations and Nationalism since 1780*, Cambridge: Cambridge University Press.

Ibanez-Martin, J. A. and Jover, G. (eds) (2002) *Education in Europe: Policies and Politics*, Dordrecht: Kluwer Academic Publishers.

Jenson, J. and Pochet, P. (2002) Employment and social policy since Maastricht: standing up to the European Monetary Union, paper presented at *The Year of the Euro*, Nanovic Institute for European Studies, University of Notre Dame, Indiana, 5–8 December.

Jessop, B. (2003) The future of the state in an era of globalisation, *Internationale Politik und Gesellschaft (International Politics and Society)*, Vol. 3. Available at: http://fesportal.fes.de/pls/portal30/docs/FOLDER/IPG/IPG3_2003/ARTJE SSOP.HTM.

Jones, K. and Alexiadou, N. (2001) The global and the national: reflections on the experience of 3 European states, paper presented at the annual European Conference on Educational Research, The European Educational Research Association, Université Charles de Gaulle, Lille, France, 5–8 September.

Karlsen, G. E. (2002) Educational policy and educational programmes in the European Union, in J. A. Ibanez-Martin and G. Jover (eds) *Education in Europe: Policies and Politics*, Dordrecht: Kluwer Academic Publishers.

Kehm, B. M. (2003) Internationalisation in higher education: From regional to global, in R. Begg (ed.) *The Dialogue between Higher Education Research and Practice*, Dordrecht: Kluwer Academic Publishers.

Kenway, J. (ed.) (1994) *Economising Education: The Post Fordist Directions*, Deakin, Australia: Deakin University Press.

Lawn, M. (2001) Borderless education: imagining a European education space in a time of brands and networks, *Discourse*, Vol. 22, No. 2: 173–84.

Lawn, M. and Lingard, B. (2002) Constructing a European policy space in educational governance: the role of transnational policy actors, *European Educational Research Journal*, Vol. 1, No. 2: 290–307.

Leidfried, S. (2000) National welfare states, European integration and globalisation: a perspective for the next century, *Social Policy and Administration*, Vol. 34, No. 1: 44–63.

Lewicka-Grisdale, K. and McLaughlin, T. (2002) Education for European identity and European citizenship, in J. A. Ibanez-Martin and G. Jover (eds) *Education in Europe: Policies and Politics*, Dordrecht: Kluwer Academic Publishers.

Maasen, P. and Stensaker, B. (2003) Interpretations of self-regulation: the changing state–higher education relationship in Europe, in R. Begg (ed.) *The Dialogue Between Higher Education Research and Practice*, Dordrecht: Kluwer Academic Publishers.

Neave, G. (1998) The evaluative state re-considered, *European Journal of Education*, Vol. 33, No. 3: 265–84.

Novoa, A. and Lawn, M. (eds) (2002) *Fabricating Europe: The Formation of an Education Space*, Dordrecht: Kluwer Academic Publishers.

Paterson, L. (2001) Higher education and European regionalism, *Pedagogy, Culture and Society*, Vol. 9, No. 2: 133–60.

Radaelli, C. (1999) *Technocracy in the European Union*, New York: Longman.

Ross, G. (1998) European integration and globalisation, in R. Axtman (ed.) *Globalisation and Europe: Theoretical and Empirical Investigations*, London: Pinter.

Sassen, S. (1998) *Globalisation and its Discontents*, New York: The New Press.

Scharpf, F. (2001) European governance: common concerns vs the challenges of diversity, Jean Monnet Working Paper No. 6/01, New York University. Available at: www.jeanmonnetprogram.org/papers/01/010701.rtf.

Sporn, B. (2003) Management in higher education: current trends and future perspectives in European colleges and universities, in R. Begg (ed.) *The Dialogue Between Higher Education Research and Practice*, Dordrecht: Kluwer Academic Publishers.

Streeck, W. (1999) Competitive solidarity: rethinking the 'European Social Model', Presidential address to the Conference *Globalisation and the Good Society*, the Society for the Advancement of Socio-Economics (SASE), Madison, Wisconsin, 8–11 July. Available at: www.sase.org/conf1999/streeck.html.

Trubek, D. M. and Mosher, J. S. (2001) New governance, EU employment policy, and the European social model, Jean Monnet Working Paper No. 6/01, New York University. Available at: www.jeanmonnetprogram.org/papers/01/011501.html.

Tulasiewicz, W. and Brock, C. (2000) Introduction: the place of education in a united Europe, in C. Brock and W. Tulasiewicz (eds) (2000) *Education in a Single Europe*, London: Routledge.

7   Swedish, European, global

Lisbeth Lundahl

Introduction

For the better part of the twentieth century, Sweden has successfully combined capitalism and a strong social democratic welfare state. Swedish trade politics have traditionally been open and anti-protectionist.
Sweden has been pragmatic and efficient in importing and making use
of technical innovations and new cultural trends, not least from the
USA. Swedes, however, have been much more wary of international
influences which could challenge the existing welfare-state model. This
may explain the hesitancy towards the project of the European Union.
When Sweden entered the EU in 1995, the nation was clearly divided and
in a referendum in September 2003 a majority of the Swedes voted
against entering the European Monetary Union.

   The aim of this chapter is to analyse how Swedish education politics
respond to and act towards globalization and Europeanization in the
late twentieth and early twenty-first centuries. Several researchers have
pointed to the need for scientifically investigating how globalization of
education is realized in the specific national and local contexts (Ball, 1998;
Jones, 1998; Lingard and Rizvi, 1998; Henry *et al.*, 2001). Hence Henry
et al. (2001) conclude:

> In education, we have witnessed the emergence of global flows of
> educational ideas around issues of educational governance and
> purposes. But how these ideas become embedded within the policy
> agendas of nation states is neither well researched nor well
> described.
>
> (p. 3)

Sweden is regarded as an example of a capitalist and social democratic
welfare state that has undergone a rapid and radical transformation
during the last three decades. The change follows a pattern which is
similar to that in many other nations, but its meaning and concretization
have to be understood in relation to the specific nature of Swedish
modern history and politics. A central question is thus how Sweden

opens and/or closes itself to new spaces and ideas of education policy and governance – the European and global ones.

Globalization may primarily be referred to as a process through which national economies become increasingly open to supranational influence. However, globalization is also to a great extent a political and ideological phenomenon (Mishra, 1999). Both increased global competition and mobility of capital, and the far-reaching impact of neo-liberal ideology and market thinking have thus framed and transformed politics at the national and local levels in the last three decades (Ben-Elia, 1996; Bogason, 1996; Mishra, 1999). Globalization is not a completely new phenomenon emerging in the twentieth and early twenty-first centuries. Its speed, range and impact, however, have reached new levels during this period. Europeanization may be understood both as the direct impact of EU policies and, more broadly, as the impact of European integration on national education policies and debate (Ollikainen, 1999). In practice, however, it is often difficult to distinguish between effects of such policies and a more general impact of structural factors that enforce or stimulate similar developments in different countries, more or less regardless of European integration policies.

In the following section, the Swedish post-war model of welfare and economic policy is briefly outlined, in order to understand the particular historical and cultural context of educational change in Sweden. The main part of the chapter is devoted to an analysis and discussion of how global and European influences have changed and been translated into the Swedish political context.

Combined aspirations for economic growth and social welfare

The Swedish model (1930s–70s)

The Swedish labour movement has been uniquely powerful from an international perspective. The Social Democratic party has been in office since 1932 except for two periods, 1976–82 and 1991–4. Consequently, Sweden has been regarded as one of the primary examples of the social democratic, welfare-state regimes, as contrasted to the liberal welfare states (e.g. the USA, the UK and Australia), and conservative regimes (e.g. France, Austria, Italy and Germany). Social Democratic welfare regimes are characterized by universalism: the party's policies are not only targeting the most needy, but include the whole population through high economic transfers and social insurance (Esping-Andersen, 1996). However, it would be misleading to emphasize only the strength of the Swedish labour movement in an analysis of the Swedish case; rather the strength and organized relations between economic and political actors more generally must be recognized.

In the 1930s, after a long period of class-based unrest and conflicts, Sweden entered an era of organized relations between capital and politics. The influential Main Agreement in 1938 between the Swedish Employers' Confederation and the Swedish Confederation of Trade Unions meant a clear division of labour in the economic sphere between the parties of the labour market and the state. The trade union movement could contribute to moderate wage demands and industrial peace because of the worker-friendly welfare policies of the Social Democratic government. The employers accepted such welfare policies in exchange for industrial peace and the absence of State interventions in the economy (Weir and Scocpol, 1985; Heclo and Madsen, 1987; Fulcher, 1991). Supported by the trade unions, Swedish industry underwent intensive structural rationalization and transformation in the following decades, moving from production based on raw materials to high-technology production. The Social Democratic welfare policies helped reduce the negative effects of this restructuring. Both 'the Swedish model' of cooperation and division of labour between the State and social partners, and the fact that Swedish infrastructure and industry were not destroyed during the Second World War contributed to the steady economic growth and rise of living standards in Sweden in the post-war period (1945–70).

A combination of growth and welfare aspirations has been a crucial feature of Swedish post-war labour policies. In Esping-Andersen's words:

> The Swedish labour movement has had the unique capability to create a synthesis of equality and gain strivings, and of welfare and efficiency, which has been favourable to all parties. Every phase of the welfare state development has been equally characterised by its attitude to the problems of efficiency and those of power.
>
> (Esping-Andersen, 1994, p. 77; my translation)

This thinking is well illustrated by the Social Democratic education ideology, which, albeit not uncontested, dominated Swedish education policy for a considerable part of the post-war period (Lundahl, 1990). Good elementary education and equal access to secondary and higher education were regarded both as a matter of social justice, and as an important precondition for economic growth and prosperity, necessary for further welfare reforms. The gradual introduction of nine-year comprehensive education in the 1950s, confirmed by a final Parliament decision in 1962, built on such motives. The subsequent reforms of upper secondary education in the 1960s and higher and adult education in the 1970s rested on similar ideas for promoting social equality as well as economic growth. The resulting educational system had several distinctive features from an international perspective. The idea of comprehensive education was thus realized at an early stage. Even in the early 1970s, upper-secondary education included more than three-quarters of all 16–19-year-olds. For many years, Swedish vocational education was regarded as a rather extreme example of school-based vocational education and training (VET) (Jallade, 1989). The reforms of adult education in the early 1970s were far-reaching in international comparison. Also, the proportion of GDP invested in education has been and still is high (Ministry of Education, 2004).

The Swedish model restructured or dismantled? (1970s)

For the better part of the 1970s, economic and political instability and growing conflicts dominated the political agenda. The Social Democratic initiatives in the field of labour legislation in the first half of the 1970s were seen as harmful by industry and as a break from the traditional division of responsibilities between the State and the parties of the labour market. Similar to its sister organization in Western Germany, the Swedish Employers' Confederation (Svenska Arbetsgivareföreningen, SAF) launched an offensive to recapture the initiative of problem formulation and restore public confidence in enterprise and the market. The first non-socialist government since the 1930s came to power in 1976. Back in office in 1982, the right wing of the Social Democrats influenced governmental policies to a large extent. Now the efforts of the SAF and the Conservative party to launch 'the market project' and their critique of the welfare state were increasingly successful; ideas of deregulation and cuts in the public sector were not only voiced from the right, but were also supported by powerful actors within the Social Democratic administration. Swedish export corporations, central to the Swedish economy, increasingly invested abroad, and threatened to leave the country if the high level of taxation was not lowered. As a result, several radical tax reforms were decided in the 1980s and 1990s, reducing state taxation. During the deep recession at the beginning of the 1990s, unemployment rose from under 2 per cent to almost 10 per cent in a short time, and has remained high since then. Mishra (1999) argues that the beginning of chronic high employment and changes in the structure of taxation are the most obvious results of globalization of the Swedish welfare state. At the same time, the welfare state has not been rolled back to any substantial degree. Mishra correctly concludes:

> That this has happened only to a limited extent is due to a number of factors, chiefly political in nature. The fragmentation of the political Right, continuing support for social programmes in the country and a large and well-organized union movement are some of these. Besides, a time factor is also involved.
>
> (Mishra, 1999, p. 79)

In the early 2000s, Sweden is certainly a part of economic globalization. Swedish multinational companies thus account for 25 per cent of employment in Sweden, 50 per cent of its exports and 90 per cent of Swedish industrial R&D investments. In relation to its size, Sweden was the world's largest foreign investor in the 1990s. In the early 1990s, this development was hampered for a time, but gained impetus again and took new forms. For example, nearly 50 of the offices of the biggest multinational companies moved out of Sweden between 1997 and 2000. International investments and acquisitions of Swedish companies accelerated, and in 1999 such investments accounted for 25 per cent of Swedish GDP (Tson Söderström, 2001). In the same period, foreign ownership of shares in Swedish corporations quoted in the Swedish market place increased considerably, and amounted to over 40 per cent in 2000. After that, there has been some decline, but still one-third of the shares had foreign holders in 2003 (Statistics Sweden, 2004).

It may seem as if Sweden no longer serves as a good example of the Social Democratic welfare state, and has moved in the direction of a liberal welfare regime. More generally this would fit well with a hypothesis of welfare regime convergence (Esping-Andersen, 1996; Kautto *et al.*, 2001). In their study of social and gender policies of the Nordic countries, Kautto *et al.* (2001), however, conclude that a distinct 'Nordic model' in welfare or living conditions still seems to exist. In their study of welfare policies in the EU countries, Vogel *et al.* (2003) come to similar conclusions.

Linking education more closely with the economy: education politics in the 1970s and early 2000s

As was shown above, Swedish education has generally been supposed to serve economic as well as social purposes, and this is also true of the last decades. However, economy and market ideas have pervaded education to an extent unthinkable 30 years ago. In Sweden, as in numerous other countries, efficiency and reduction of State costs, quasi-markets, accountability, comparability and increased local autonomy have been keywords of education government and reform. Education is modelled on the market and the enterprise (Carter and O'Neill, 1995; Ball, 1998; Whitty *et al.*, 1998; Daun, 2002). Even in Sweden, neo-liberalism, performativity and new managerialism have been important underlying ideas of this change (Ball, 1998).

First steps of decentralization and deregulation (1975–90)

The Swedish education reforms in the 1950s and 1960s were accompanied by detailed State steering, which was regarded as essential to realize the overriding aim of equality of education. Schools and teaching were regulated and controlled through national curricula and syllabi, by specially destined State subsidies and by a vast number of other regulations concerning resources, organization, staff and daily work. In the 1970s, the public sector was repeatedly criticized from different directions, and education was often chosen as an important example of what had gone wrong with the Swedish welfare system. While people of the left argued that education did not reach its equality goals, the right maintained that Swedish education was expensive, inefficient and rigid, and did not provide young people with any alternatives. Local actors' lack of influence over education was a common theme. The Conservative party (*Moderaterna*), the Swedish Employers' Confederation, and other industrial and trade organizations, now putting education high on their agenda, played an important role in introducing a new thinking and vocabulary of education: alternatives and competition, individual choice and responsibility, competence and excellence (Lundahl, 1990, 1997). During the latter half of the 1970s and in the 1980s, several steps were taken towards decentralization and increased local political control, but still the principle of a relatively strong State government was maintained in order to protect equality of education. In 1989 the employment responsibilities for school personnel were transferred from the State to the municipalities. In 1990 a new allocation system of state funding was introduced, putting an end to detailed economic steering from the state. But, on the whole, central State governance remained strong. The changes in the 1970s and 1980s did not lack explicit economic motives, and the need to reform education in order to improve Sweden's international competitiveness was sometimes expressed. But international economic comparisons were hardly put forward as a main argument; rather the stress was on the failings of the old welfare system and the educational needs of modern Sweden (Lundahl, 2002a).

The 1990s: neo-liberal turn?

In September 1991, the second non-socialist government came into office since the 1930s, and in 1991–4 championed a successful neo-liberal policy, explicitly described as a part of a global system shift, 'Because it is about a genuinely radical change. A system shift more extensive than many participants of the Swedish debate seem to be aware of' (speech by Conservative Prime Minister Carl Bildt, 13 October 1993). Choice and market reforms were carried out and vouchers and generous conditions for establishing independent schools were introduced by the Conservative Minister of Education. A new funding system meant that specified subsidies from the State to the municipalities were replaced by lump sums for all responsibilities: education, care of old people and refuse collection. By now the State had relinquished practically all its earlier economic steering tools in education, and a quasi-market system had been introduced. Within a few years, Sweden went from having one of the most centralized to one of the most decentralized education systems in the Western world (OECD, 2001). When the Social Democrats returned in 1994, their government politics focused on the reduction of an enormous State budget deficit, rather than on proactive welfare reforms, and few efforts were made to alter the non-socialist decisions previously taken.

However, the Swedish story is not an entirely neo-liberal one. New forms of state control over education were introduced in the 1990s, such as national tests, a new grading system and quality audits. As in other countries, proactive State regulation was replaced by retroactive surveillance (Daun, 2002). Also, some education reforms of the 1990s had an explicitly inclusive character. In spring 1991, the Parliament decided to reorganize upper-secondary education into 16 national three-year programmes with a common curriculum in certain core subjects. The vocational programmes were prolonged by a third year, and their academic contents were strengthened. The reform, opposed by the non-socialist parties, was motivated by both welfare and economic/labour market factors, and thus followed a traditional Social Democratic reform formula. It was supposed to increase individual flexibility and employ-ability as well as individual security by reducing the divisions within upper-secondary education and ensuring that all national and special programmes did qualify for higher studies (Lundahl, 1998). Also, a large adult education reform ('the Rise of Knowledge') was implemented to raise the education level of people with limited schooling, and to reduce unemployment. Thus, even in the 1990s, Swedish education policy included comprehensive measures following the more traditional welfare model, as well as clearly neo-liberal reforms and decisions that weakened State governance, while emphasizing responsibility and self-regulation at local and individual level (Lundahl, 2002a).

The situation at the turn of the century

In the late 1990s, the effects of the policy of economic austerity in schools were clearly visible and became important in shaping the political agenda. In many respects, social inequalities and segregation had increased in Sweden in the 1990s. Young people, immigrants, poorly educated people and single parents were hit hard by unemployment and a deterioration in living standards. A growing number of adolescents left compulsory and upper-secondary school without complete grades. Also, differences in school achievements related to gender and to social, geographical and ethnic backgrounds tended to grow. When state finances improved at the end of the 1990s and allowed for social reforms once more, special funding was directed to the municipalities in order to replenish education, health care and social care. Central economic steering was thus reintroduced to some extent. At the same time, further steps were taken towards decentralization and management by objectives. A five-year period of trials, meaning the abolition of the national timetables in compulsory schooling in one-third of the municipalities, started in 2000. Quality audits and school inspections were introduced as means of governance and control (Lundahl, 2002a).

Finally, curricular reforms and State-supported school development reflect the increased needs of communication and information across nations during the last decades. Being a small country, language education has always had a prominent place in Swedish compulsory and upper-secondary education. Swedish children are now taught English from primary level through upper-secondary education, in academic as well as vocational programmes. A majority of pupils study a second foreign language in compulsory education, mostly German, French or Spanish. In the 1990s, considerable political efforts were made to improve the ICT infrastructure and competence in schools. In 1999–2000 1.7 billion Swedish crowns (approximately 170 million Euros) was invested in the largest of these projects (the IT in schools project), including competence development of 60,000 teachers (Ministry of Education, 2004).

The world reflected in contemporary Swedish education politics

To what extent and how international influence and demands are reflected in contemporary Swedish education politics will now be discussed, in terms of the following aspects:

- to what extent recent Swedish education politics follow a neo-liberal, 'global' model;
- to what extent educational change *is presented and discussed* in terms of globalization/Europeanization or not;
- if international influence is presented as self-evident and inevitable;
- if international policies and/or policies of other countries are regarded as important as models for national action or not;
- to what extent the international dimension of education is a source of conflict and argument.

Global and neo-liberal – or not?

As was discussed on pp. 152–3, the links between the economy and Swedish education have been strengthened during the last decades. This has been accomplished in at least three ways:

- increased importance is attached to education as infrastructural investment, supporting economic growth;

- 'the market' and 'enterprise' serve as models for education and schools;
- education is privatized or marketed.

Ball (1998) distinguishes two related policy agendas: one aiming at closer connections between education and national economy, while the other subordinates education under a market or business logic and redefines it from a public to a competitive private good. In the first case, the grip of the State over education is still strong, but, in the second case, this grip is loosening.

Education as a factor of economic growth

As was pointed out earlier, Swedish education politics has traditionally been characterized by both motives of growth and democracy and social welfare and justice. However, the balance between them has shifted from time to time, and, in particular, the non-socialist government of 1991–4 stressed human capital and competition strongly (also see p. 153). The reforms of pre-school, compulsory and upper-secondary education do not represent any major breaks with the earlier thinking. For example, the upper-secondary education reforms of both 1991 and 2004 have aimed at providing academic and vocational education within rather few programmes, giving broad knowledge and skills, and allowing for flexibility. This is supposed to be mutually beneficial to working life and the individual. Altogether, the State holds an indisputable central position when it comes to human capital investment.

Research and higher education politics have been increasingly pervaded by ideas of economic utility; such education and research are essential if Sweden is to assert itself internationally, and they also contribute to local and regional development. Today, universities cooperate with industry, municipalities and counties to a much higher extent than was the case 10 or 20 years ago. International exchange and competition have been central features of higher education and research for a long time, but such aspects have gradually become stronger, Sweden's membership of the EU being one, but not the sole, contributing factor.

The market and business serve as models

Adopting market and business models perhaps constitutes the most striking change of education during the last decades. As was previously pointed out, Swedish compulsory schools have become the most autonomous among the OECD countries in a short period of time. Efficiency and quality are supposed to be enhanced by local actors, who will use resources, creativity and knowledge better if they are not regulated in detail by the state. Schools should act as small enterprises, competing for pupils by good results and interesting profiles. But it should be remembered that a democratic motive has been important when schools were given more autonomy. Teachers, pupils and parents obtaining more influence over school work has been and remains a crucial idea behind decentralization and deregulation of education at the local level. Local bargaining and individual wage-setting was introduced in the 1990s and led to increased competition over and between teachers. Benchmarking has become increasingly influential as average grades and test scores of schools and municipalities are made public and are compared in the media. No general system directly linking school budgets to such results and comparisons has, however, been established. In conclusion, there are many examples of how education governance and thinking about schools has changed. The idea of 'the strong society' has largely been replaced by a market and business model. But this thinking still takes place within a system where the State decides on national objectives and controls results and quality of education, and where the local political level, the municipality, has a decisive power over resources and substantial possibilities to influence education in other respects.

Education as a part of the market

The non-socialist government (1991–4) launched several successful offensives to break the State monopoly over education and put education in a market situation. Earlier, practically all schools were publicly run; now generous rules for establishing so-called independent schools were introduced, and vouchers and possibilities of inviting tenders in certain subjects were introduced. Independent schools may be run by a number of actors: parents, teachers, private companies, religious and other organizations. Even though the number of independent schools rapidly multiplied in the 1990s and continues to increase, they only account for about 5 per cent of all primary and secondary schools. Independent schools are tax funded and essentially have to follow the national curriculum guide. This is nothing unique to Sweden; almost no recognized private schools in Europe are run without some form of subsidy (Daun, 2002; Fredriksson, 2003). For a long time, vocational education had been school-based and part of public upper-secondary and tertiary education. As opposed to most other countries, a vast majority of Swedish pre-schools are public. In principle, all compulsory education, school meals and school books included, is free of charge. Increasingly, however, supplementary services such as school cafeterias, cleaning and certain expert support are privatized, and a limited private sponsoring has also been introduced in some schools. In conclusion, the major part of Swedish education still comprises 'pure public' services, and the share of 'free market' services is only marginal. But the trend goes clearly in the direction of increasing numbers of independent schools run by private companies and organizations, increasing shares of private supplementary services and a higher degree of cooperation between public education, industry and other parts of society.

The international perspective has been largely absent

By and large, Swedish education policy has tended to be treated as a Swedish matter. With the exception of higher education, the international perspective has been absent to a high degree, even after the entrance into the EU in 1995. For example, when interviewed about the most important changes of education governance in the last 10 to 15 years, leading Swedish education politicians and officials did not bring up global or European factors. When explicitly asked if international factors had been influential in the change of the 1980s and 1990s, some politicians and officials, however, argued that the OECD reports had had a certain impact.

A study of policy documents and education debates in the early 2000s leads to almost the same conclusion. Swedish education is still seldom explicitly analysed and discussed in relation to international conditions or actors. Some examples of the silences are given below. One important exception, however, is the recent interest from the Ministry of Education in the reform of higher education in accordance with the Bologna process, which received little attention in Swedish education politics and debate until 2004. This year, adjustments of the structure and grading system of higher education in accordance with the Bologna process were proposed in public reports from the official committee on postgraduate studies and the Ministry of Education (SOU, 2004, p. 27). For the first time, the creation of a European Higher Education Area (Conference of Ministers, 2003) was discussed more widely in Sweden.

Every second year since 1994, the Swedish government has presented a developmental plan for the pre-school, primary and secondary school system and for adult education. Even if the number of international references in the plans has increased, such passages are still marginal and mainly concern the position of Swedish schools in the OECD evaluations. In the developmental plan from May 2002, it is characteristically argued: 'Swedish education has accomplished a lot and is a (good) international example'. It is added, 'In spite of the fact that Swedish education asserts itself, the aim must be set higher' (Government Paper, 2001/2, p. 188). Similar conclusions have been drawn by the Minister of Education elsewhere (Ministry of Education, 2003; Östros 2003), but without further discussion of education in an international perspective. In its report, *Education in Europe: A Report on Education in Sweden and*

Common European Goals (2004), the Ministry of Education, however, explicitly relates the state of Swedish education to the three strategic educational goals formulated by the Ministers of Education in the EU in 2001. Once again, the conclusion is mainly positive: 'Sweden has got a good educational system and good prerequisites. Nevertheless, hard and persistent efforts are required – in all member countries and among all actors in our country – to reach the goals put forward' (Ministry of Education, 2004, p. 6).

The teacher education reform in 2000 and the preparations for a reform of upper-secondary education during the first years of the 2000s hardly referred to an international or EU dimension at all. When discussing Swedish upper-secondary education and VET more generally, the need to foster flexible and well-educated citizens to cope with rapid economic and technological development and changing working life has been stressed repeatedly, but as a rule without bringing up the global dimension of such processes. And in spite of VET being a central interest in youth and employment policies of the EU, explicit references have seldom been made in Sweden to European policies in this respect. The fact that career development and counselling have been put high on the agenda by OECD, the World Bank and the European Commission (Watts and Sultana, 2003; Watts, 2004) has hitherto received little attention by the Swedish authorities.

An inevitable change

The Swedish development of the 1980s and 1990s, with decentralization, deregulation, increased efficiency and market thinking as key elements, shows striking similarities with the so-called new orthodoxy of education politics in the USA, the UK, New Zealand and Australia (Carter and O'Neill, 1995; Ball, 1998). However, neither the international parallels nor common underlying mechanisms of educational change are pointed out and debated very often in the Swedish policy context. Instead, a rather anonymous, general image is recurrently given – that of a rapid transition from an industrial society to knowledge or information society, resulting in new demands on schools and education. The state neither can nor should regulate education in detail any longer (Lindblad *et al.*, 2002; Lundahl, 2002b). The range and possibilities of political action seem to be limited in this discourse. Politics tend to become reactive rather than proactive.

No explicit references to international models

Sweden has historically been fast to pick up new ideas and innovations from abroad. This is also the case for recent education politics. A broad range of neo-liberal and new managerial ideas and concepts have been imported in the last 20 years from the USA, the UK and New Zealand: enterprise, competition, choice and vouchers, school autonomy and school management, modern apprenticeship training, benchmarking, quality audits and control, excellence and individual responsibility. The list could be prolonged almost endlessly. In this respect, Sweden may be regarded a good example of policy borrowing. However, and this is the point, such borrowing is almost never explicit, and it is not used to legitimate policy decisions (Halpin and Troyna, 1995). The most recent example is the gradual introduction of a national system of quality audit and control in Sweden, which has taken place with few references to its many international predecessors (Lundahl, 2004).

Similar versus conflicting images

On the whole, the fast restructuring of Swedish education politics in the 1980s and 1990s created far less conflict and debate than might be expected. The changes of governance were formulated and elaborated both by socialist and non-socialist governments, but with somewhat different sets of arguments. Also, there have been no conflicting opinions regarding the crucial role of competence and knowledge if Sweden is going to assert itself in global economic competition. But this theme was brought up more frequently, and with more emphasis by the non-socialist government in 1991–4 than by its Social Democratic predecessors and successors. The Bildt government thus coined a motto that Swedish education should become the best in Europe. In its analysis of future education, *Agenda 2000: Knowledge and Competence for the Next Century*, the Ministry of Education established that the Swedish economy and education had been overtaken by a number of OECD countries since 1970. Now strong measures had to be taken in order to turn Sweden into a first-order knowledge-based nation (Ds, 1994, p. 35). Some years later, the former Conservative Minister of Education, Mr Unckel, developed these ideas in a book in which international perspectives and comparisons were at the forefront. He concluded:

> Make knowledge development a central task for Sweden … Formulate the aim that our country somewhat further on in the 2000s will be one of the world's foremost knowledge and cultural nations – and see to it that this aim is attained.
>
> (Unckel, 1998, p. 167)

While the achievements of Swedish education in international comparisons are described rather positively in Social Democratic policy documents, OECD statistics are used to underpin non-socialist critiques against socialist economic and education policy, and to legitimate radical action.

Something borrowed and something new? Some final remarks

The modern Swedish economy has always been highly dependent on international competition and exchange, and increasing economic globalization is a central feature of Sweden's economic development of the last decades. To a growing extent, education is regarded as a crucial factor in enhancing international competitiveness and growth. Also, the rapid educational restructuring that has taken place in Sweden in the last decades has followed similar paths to that in many other countries. I have concluded that Swedish education politics and debate often have been surprisingly silent about the international aspect. Next I will discuss this seeming paradox.

Brown and Lauder (1996) discuss education in the global economy in terms of neo-Fordist and post-Fordist routes to economic development. The first, clearly neo-liberal, route is characterized by the weakening of the power of the State and trade unions, and the celebration of privatization and competitive individualism. The post-Fordist alternative, where the State still has a crucial role in investing in strategic economic sectors, and providing the labour market with multi-skilled, highly qualified workers, comes closer to the Swedish case. In this latter sense there has not been a radical break with earlier Swedish education and economic policies. Ball (1998) distinguishes two related policy agendas: 'The first involves reaffirmation of the state functions of education as "public good", while the second subjects education to the disciplines of the market and the methods and values of business and redefines it as a competitive private good' (Ball, 1998, p. 123). Even if the balance has shifted between the two agendas under Social Democratic and non-socialist rule, Swedish education politics has consequently sought to combine them, and in ways that are perceived as legitimate in the Swedish context. It is obvious that explicit policy borrowing (Halpin and Troyna, 1995) has not been a favoured strategy; a whole range of concepts and ideas have been imported and reterritorialized, but without spelling it out. The conclusion of Steiner-Khamsi (2002) seems correct even in the Swedish case: 'It is important to point out that externalization functions as the last source of authority and tends to be activated once self-referentiality falls short of argumentation. In most instances, self-referentiality prevails and internal references are sufficient' (2002, p. 70). One may add: internal references seem to have been not only sufficient, but necessary, in order to convince Swedes that education reforms are legitimate. References to education policies of the Reagan, Thatcher or even Blair administrations would hardly have gained major popularity in Sweden, where a majority of the population supports the traditional welfare model (Svallfors, 1999). This may also be a part of the explanation of the silence about global and European aspects of education and education politics.

However, the silence regarding EU policies and agreements needs some further analysis. Ollikainen (1999) discusses some reasons behind the success of EU programmes in Finland in the education policy field:

- A correspondence and lack of ideological conflicts between basic objectives of Finnish education policy and EU objectives. Most objectives of EU programmes have corresponded to national ones; others have been reinterpreted to match them.
- The practical conditions of EU programmes have fitted the needs of Finnish education policy well. At a time of reduced state funding of education, the EU programmes provided channels of funding.
- Finnish institutions have actively participated and succeeded well in the competition set up by the EU programmes . . . getting a fair amount of projects accepted became almost a matter of national pride.
- The EU programmes are perceived as bringing in something new, they . . . were regarded as filling an existing void in the field of educational cooperation.

In Sweden, there has been a greater reluctance or hesitation towards the EU than was the case in Finland. This may have affected the initial willingness to adopt EU policies and recommendations in the field of education too readily. In the field of education, decision-makers may furthermore, wrongly or rightly, have felt that Sweden already had reached some of the basic objectives put forward by the EU. For example, Sweden at a rather early stage had a high ratio of young people who had completed upper-secondary education and well-developed school-based VET. However, such relative advantages may disappear rapidly – and to a certain extent they already have. It is quite apparent that Sweden must relate itself more consciously and systematically to the global and European context, regardless to whether one wishes to be Swedish, European or global – or all of them.

References

Ball, S. (1998) Big Policies/Small World: An Introduction to International Perspectives in Education Policy. *Comparative Education*, 34: 119–30.

Ben-Elia, N. (ed.) (1996) *Strategic Changes and Organizational Reorientations in Local Government: A Cross-National Perspective*. London: Macmillan Press.

Bogason, P. (ed.) (1996) *New Modes of Local Political Organizing: Local Government Fragmentation in Scandinavia*. Commack, New York: Nova Sciences Publishers.

Brown, P. and Lauder, H. (1996) Education, Globalization, and Economic Development. *Journal of Education Policy*, 11: 1–24.

Carter, D. S. G. and O'Neill, M. H. (1995) *International Perspectives on Educational Reform and Policy Implementation*. London: The Falmer Press.

Conference of Ministers (2003) *Realising the European Higher Education Area*, Communiqué of the Conference of Ministers responsible for Higher Education in Berlin, 19 September. Available at www.bologna-berlin2003.de/pdf/Communique1.pdf.

Daun, H. (ed.) (2002) *Educational Restructuring in the Context of Globalisation and National Policy*. London: RoutledgeFalmer.

Ds (1994) *Agenda 2000: Kunskap och kompetens för nästa århundrade (Agenda 2000: Knowledge and Competence for the Next Century)*. Stockholm: Ministry of Education (in Swedish).

Esping-Andersen, G. (1994) Jämlikhet, effektivitet och makt (Equality, Efficiency and Power), in P. Thullberg and K. Östberg (eds) *Den svenska modellen*. Lund: Studentlitteratur, pp. 75–105 (in Swedish).

Esping-Andersen, G. (1996) *The Three Worlds of Welfare Capitalism*. Cambridge: Polity Press.

Fredriksson, U. (2003) GATS, Education and Teacher Union Policies. Paper presented at the European Conference of Educational Research, Hamburg, 17–20 September.

Fulcher, J. (1991) *Labour Movements, Employers and the State: Conflict and Cooperation in Britain and Sweden*. Oxford: Clarendon Press.

Government Paper (2001/2) *Utbildning för kunskap och jämlikhet: regeringens utvecklingsplan för kvalitetsarbetet i förskola, skola och vuxenutbildning (Education for Knowledge and Equality: Government Development Plan concerning Quality Work in Preschool, Primary, Secondary, and Adult Education)*. Stockholm: Ministry of Education (in Swedish).

Halpin, D. and Troyna, B. (1995) The Politics of Education Policy Borrowing. *Comparative Education*, 31: 303–10.

Heclo, H. and Madsen, H. (1987) *Policy and Politics in Sweden: Principled Pragmatism*. Philadelphia, PA: Temple University Press.

Henry, M., Lingard, B., Rizvi, F. and Taylor, S. (2001) *The OECD, Globalisation and Education Policy*. Oxford: Pergamon/IAU Press.

Jallade, J.-P. (1989) Recent Trends in Vocational Education and Training: An Overview. *European Journal of Education*, 24 (2): 103–25.

Jones, P. W. (1998) Globalisation and Internationalism: Democratic Prospects for World Education. *Comparative Education*, 34 (2): 143–55.

Kautto, M., Fritzell, J., Hvinden, B., Kvist, J. and Uusitalo, H. (eds) (2001) *Nordic Welfare States in the European Context*. London: Routledge.

Lindblad, S., Lundahl, L., Lindgren, J. and Zackari, G. (2002) Educating for the New Sweden?, *Scandinavian Journal of Educational Research*, 46: 283–303.

Lingard, B. and Rizvi, F. (1998) Globalisation and the Fear of Homogenisation in Education. *Transformations in Education*, 1: 62–71.

Lundahl, L. (1990) New Variations on Old Themes: The Swedish Conservative Party and the Battle over Comprehensive Education 1900–1985. *Journal of Education Policy*, 5: 157–66.

Lundahl, L. (1997) A Common Denominator? Swedish Employers, Trade Unions and Vocational Education in the Postwar Years. *International Journal of Training and Development*, 1: 91–102.

Lundahl, L. (1998) Still the Stepchild of Swedish Educational Politics? Vocational Education and Training in Sweden in the 1990s. *TNTEE Publications*, 1: 39–53. Available at http://tntee.umu.se/publications.

Lundahl, L. (2002a) From Centralisation to Decentralisation: Governance of Education in Sweden. *European Educational Research Journal*, 1 (4): 625–36.

Lundahl, L. (2002b) Sweden: Decentralization, Deregulation, Quasi-Markets – And Then What? *Journal of Education Policy*, 17: 687–97.

Lundahl, L. (2004) Styrning med kvalitet (Governing With Quality), in K. Holmlund (ed.) *Vad har kvalitet med skolan att göra? (What Has Quality Got to Do With Education?)*. Lund: Studentlitteratur (in press) (in Swedish).

Ministry of Education (2003) *Alla skolor ska vara bra skolor: regeringens kvalitets-program för skolan (All Schools Should Be Good Schools: The Government's School Development Program)*. Stockholm: Regeringskansliet (in Swedish).

Ministry of Education (2004) *Utbildningen i Europa: en rapport om utbildningen i Sverige och de gemensamma europeiska målen (Education in Europe: A Report on Education in Sweden and the Common European Goals)*. Utbildningsdeparte-mentets skriftserie, rapport 6. Stockholm: Regeringskansliet (in Swedish).

Mishra, R. (1999) *Globalization and the Welfare State*. Cheltenham: Edward Elgar.

OECD (2001) *Education at a Glance: OECD Indicators 2001*. Paris: OECD/CERI.

Ollikainen, A. (1999) *The Single Market for Education and National Educational Policy: Europeanisation of Finnish Education Discourses 1987–1997*. Åbo: Åbo Universitet, Research Unit for the Sociology of Education.

Östros, T. (2003) Lika rätt till kunskap är förutsättningar för jämlikhet (Equal Right to Knowledge is a Prerequisite of Equality), in *Skolboken. En skrift om skolans roll och om socialdemokratisk skolpolitik. (Book of Education. A publication on the Role of Education and Social Democratic Education Policy)*. Stockholm: Tankesmedjan Idé och tendens (in Swedish).

SOU (2004) *En Ny Doktorsutbildning: kraftsamling för excellens och tillväxt. Betänkande av forskarutbildningsutredningen (New Postgraduate Education: Efforts to Promote Excellence and Growth. Report from the Committee on Postgraduate Education)*. Stockholm: Regeringskansliet (in Swedish).

Statistics Sweden (2004) *Ägandet av aktier i bolag noterade på svensk marknadsplats 1983–2003 (Holdings of Shares in Corporations Quoted on Swedish Marketplaces 1983–2003)*. Statistics Sweden. Available at www.scb.se/templates (in Swedish).

Steiner-Khamsi, G. (2002) Reterritorializing Educational Import: Explorations into the Politics of Educational Borrowing, in A. Nóvoa and M. Lawn (eds) *Fabricating Europe: The Formation of an Education Space*. Dordrecht: Kluwer Academic Publishers.

Svallfors, S. (1999) The Middle Class and Welfare State Retrenchment: Attitudes to Swedish Welfare Policies, in S. Svallfors and P. Taylor-Gooby, *The End of the Welfare State? Responses to State Retrenchment*. London: Routledge/ESA Studies in European Society, pp. 34–51.

Tson Söderström, H. (ed.) (2001) *kluster.se. Sverige i den nya ekonomiska geografin (kluster.se. Sweden in the New Economic Geography of Europe)*. Ekonomirådets rapport. Stockholm: SNS Förlag (in Swedish).

Unckel, P. (1998) *Kunskap som egen investering (Knowledge as Personal Investment)*. Stockholm: Timbro (in Swedish).

Vogel, J., Svallfors, S., Theorell, T., Noll, H.-H. and Christoph, B. (2003) *European Welfare Production: Institutional Configuration and Distributional Outcome*. Dordrecht: Kluwer Academic Publishers.

Watts, A. G. (2004) Bridging Policy and Practice in Career Development: An International Perspective. Keynote address delivered at the National Consultation on Career Development (Natcon) in Ottawa, Canada, 26 January.

Watts, A. G. and Sultana, R. G. (2003) Career Guidance Policies in 36 Countries: Contrasts and Common Themes. Paper commissioned by CEDEFOP for the Career Guidance and Public Policy: Bridging the Gap Conference, OECD and the Canadian Government in collaboration with the European Commission, the World Bank and the International Association for Educational and Vocational Guidance, Toronto, Canada, 6–8 October.

Weir, M. and Scocpol, T. (1985) State Structures and the Possibilities for 'Keynesian' Responses to the Great Depression in Sweden, Britain, and the United States, in P. E. Evans, D. Reuschmeyer and T. Scocpol (eds) *Bringing the State Back In*. Cambridge: Cambridge University Press.

Whitty, G., Power, S. and Halperin, D. (1998) *Devolution & Choice in Education: The School, the State and the Market*. Buckingham: Open University Press.

8 Globalizing differences

Special educational needs, inclusion and the market place

Philip Garner, Christopher Blake and Suchitra Narayan

In this chapter we assess the lives of children and young people who experience learning difficulties against the prevailing economic and social conditions obtaining in the world. At the outset we make a number of general and context-setting remarks concerning the impact of globalization on children and young people experiencing special educational needs (SEN) or learning difficulties. Then we expand on these themes with particular reference to concerns which impact negatively on this group of children and young people.

For the purposes of illustration throughout this chapter, we draw particularly from one area of special education which is now a major issue of concern in many countries: the case of children and young people who experience emotional and/or behavioural difficulties (EBD), and the consistent failure of education systems to attend to their learning and social needs. Our use of this grouping is strategic. They constitute what is viewed as a marginalized population who are regularly perceived to be less deserving of professional attention or input. Moreover, these are the children and young people who are elegantly described by O'Brien (1999) as 'hard cases', whenever discussion regarding educational inclusion unfolds. They are a grouping who pose the utmost challenge to both developed or emerging educational inclusivity. And, in laying down the gauntlet, they expose both the frailty of logic and the diligent opportunism of politicians and planners in their adoption of 'inclusion' as a panacea for the world-wide dilemmas in education.

Each of the themes we introduce is closely related, such are the global synergies between inclusion, learning difficulties, their national and regional resourcing and the distribution of wealth which results in an unequal access to those resources. It is worth commenting in this respect that the sharp division between regions on a global scale is paralleled on a more local scale. In England, for example, which has, over the last 25 years or so, refined its system of educational provision using a set of officially recognized indicators of inclusivity, there remain areas (local education authorities) within large cities which have little resource-capacity to meet the needs of an expanding number of children with

SEN. This contrasts sharply with other locations, which not only have fewer identified cases of SEN, but also significantly more capability to attend to them.

Education as a global corporation

Recent changes and reorientations prior to the publication of the *World Yearbook of Education 1999* (Daniels and Garner, 1999) brought the issue of globalization into sharp focus. At the point of writing an introduction to that volume, it was apparent that much was in the melting pot: moreover, considerable challenges still remained and, while some of these were country-specific, others assumed a global dimension. It is on these that our attention has been concentrated in the construction of this chapter, and they should be seen as the general backdrop against which many of our more specific observations are made.

Subsequently, four notable challenges for the new millennium were identified; each appeared to be a hallmark of an increasingly globalized response to the educational inclusion of children and young people experiencing learning difficulties. Thus, the demands of the knowledge society, the need for conceptual (as opposed to skills) preparedness, the tensions inherent in market-led education systems and the challenge of new pedagogy were seen as features of education systems that were attempting to address real or apparent paradoxes (Daniels and Garner, 2000). All four remain, moderated only partially by local actions.

The globalization of difference, as expressed by disability or SEN, has resulted in further marginalization of these groups and the commodification of 'need'. The rise of the market has been accompanied by consumer-based appropriations of freedom and choice. In England, for example, 'choice' in education is only readily accessible to those who have the benefit of the social and cultural capital by which preferences are determined. Parents or carers of children experiencing SEN regularly encounter difficulty in enrolling their child(ren) in a school of their choice. Those who present 'learning difficulties' are viewed negatively (Cooper, 1993), because their 'difference' runs contrary to the process of commodification, with its need to standardize 'products' or 'services' in order to secure economies of scale and to deliver 'profit' through measurement in officially sanctioned school league tables. Schools which are towards the bottom of such league tables often have a greater proportion of pupils with SEN. It is these schools that attract fewer pupils and, in consequence, a lower funding level to meet an increasingly wide and complex range of needs (Kumar, 1993).

The impact of (lack of) choice in these circumstances also results in a perverse, negative and local manifestation of globalization. As schools become selective about who they will or will not accept on roll, so too their catchments become enlarged. Many secondary schools in England, for example, no longer have a discrete local function as an educational and social gathering point. Neighbourhoods, as a result, become fractured, and social relationships start to become impaired. In such circumstances, where the 'hard-to-place' child with learning difficulties is an educational itinerant, their sense of belonging and inclusion is tenuous – even non-existent.

Similar situations occur on an international scale, and when aligned with a further characteristic of globalization in special education – the 'privatization of 'need' – there are signals of meltdown for marginalized communities and individuals. The privatization of education in an increasing number of countries has turned education into big business. Again, we can cite England as an example of this trend. In Southwark, a borough of London, the education service was contracted out to a private company. Elsewhere, Kenway and Bullen (2001) have noted similar trends in the marketization of Australian schooling. The quantification of 'success' in such circumstances is narrow, and serves the needs of the corporation and the country, rather than those of individual children and young people. Those with SEN are expensive to cater for, difficult to assess in terms of performance and are seen to reflect negatively on the reputation of individual schools or their sponsoring commercial partners.

The rapid corporatization of education has also failed to attend to the differential learning needs of children and young people with SEN. The attendant rise of managerialism in many education systems is a particular feature of this. Those in authority are encouraged and trained as 'managers', and in functioning as such are charged with 'delivering' the 'right' outcomes. These are invariably sets of targets which are unreachable (or contested) by many with SEN. Partly as a result of this, SEN and inclusion are now dominated by procedures and processes which are determined from the centre (a case in point being the Code of Practice in England, which regulates via a restricted set of routines, rather than encouraging teachers to respond creatively to individual learners). The widespread adoption of managerial hierarchies, each with gate-keeping functions, ensures that children are sifted into groups according to narrow versions of cognitive ability, creativity or physical capacity. Moreover, these mechanisms are used to measure the performance of children (and schools), with the net result that those who underperform are further demonized.

Globalizing difficulty: the quest for uniformity

The first of our themes comprises the nature and prevalence of 'learning difficulties' within school-age populations. Here we briefly explore the problems of establishing definitive data with regard to this group, a difficulty which is exacerbated by cultural and societal norms, by financial considerations, and by individual and global estimates of the number of children and young people who experience learning difficulties or disabilities. A variety of factors obfuscate a clear picture of the current situation. Definitions of what constitutes a 'learning difficulty' vary between individual countries, and even regionally or institutionally within them. Moreover, it is likely that the numbers of children experiencing SEN are probably much higher than formal estimates (Jonsson and Wiman, 2001) as a result of the under-identification of children whose SEN is 'non-observable'.

Traditional special educational provision has long struggled with the problem of terminology. Even within what have been termed 'mature' systems of education (Daniels and Garner, 1999), controversy has been never far below the surface, especially as, in the most recent period, certain categories or groupings of 'need' have regularly secured greater resource allocations than others. Thus, education professionals and parents/carers have seen it as their duty to ensure that an officially recognized 'label' is secured in order that the funds to address the 'need' will follow. What is noticeable is that the desire to refine such ascertainment takes precedence over the imperative to change the systems of belief and the organizational structures which result in exclusion.

Virtually every country has, at some stage or another, encountered what Hobbs (1975) inferred to be a definitional minefield. Such a state of affairs is as apparent in developed systems of provision (Howie, 2000; Kavale *et al.*, 1996; Thomas and Loxley, 2001) as it is in countries or regions which are less advantaged by educational tradition or location (Okyere, 1994; Satawi and Smadi, 1995). Even within individual countries, there are discrepancies and contradictions. But the current situation is that there is no universally accepted criterion for assessing and identifying learning disabled students: 'Recent controversies on the use of diagnostic instruments having questionable validity, and the conflicting definitions of learning disabilities, have made the identification process more difficult and less dependable' (Kibria, 1995, p. 67).

The need to identify the scale of the problem is one of the most unfortunate aspects of the rapid globalization of learning difficulties for two reasons. First, it reinforces the focus upon the child or young person, while deflecting attention from the below-surface challenge of ingrained prejudice and systemic professionalization of resources. Instead of leading to refinements in the way that 'difficulty' or 'difference' is perceived, it simply reinstates old stereotypes and lionizes inertia. Countries in the northern hemisphere, more usually and ostensibly well developed in respect of their inclusive approaches, have done much to set the agenda here. Proponents of so-called full inclusion have shown little engagement with practical matters of provision in regions and countries that are struggling to secure even basic conditions of health-care, welfare and education. The transmission of an approach deemed to be sustainable in one, advantaged national setting reveals a desire to colonize special education.

Second, the steadfast belief by international support and development agencies, as well as national governments, that uniformity in assessment and identification is efficacious and relevant to individual cases seems disingenuous. These moves seem to be informed more by the real global policy catalyst at work here: the need for individuals and whole countries to be economically sustainable. Such an intention is seen as central to the education of children and young people with disabilities. The case for inclusive education of children with disabilities is often framed in terms of human rights or justice. Yet the economic argument for educating children with disabilities is also strong. Lack of adequate education remains the key risk factor for poverty and exclusion of all children, both disabled and non-disabled. For children with disabilities, however, the risk of poverty due to lack of education may be even higher than for children without disabilities. Children who are excluded from education are virtually certain to be long-term poor. They almost inevitably become an economic burden on society and on their families.

Elsewhere, there is much made of the cost-effectiveness of inclusive systems by organizations such as the World Bank. This highlights reductions in social welfare costs, increased productivity and wealth creation, increased government revenue from taxes paid, reduced transportation costs and so on as being among the benefits of inclusive education. Little mention is made, beyond a bland acceptance of 'right', of the learner's own individual requirements. Jonsson and Wiman (2001) further confirm that the 'emphasis should be placed on mainstreaming disabled people into regular schools'. We do not doubt that these are overall net benefits; but our contention is that these should be accrued as incidental to locally-owned approaches which empower individuals for their own sake.

The relationship between funding and educational provision

In this section we consider some of the ways in which educational ideas, and the practices which are informed by them, mirror the distribution of cultural and economic capital. Our contention is that the ideas which are hot-housed in more economically developed countries (MEDCs), in economic and social conditions that are (for many people) advantageous, are hardly transferable to other, less economically developed countries (LEDCs). The educational inequalities that arise from these resource discrepancies appear to us to represent a perversity, such is the largely negative impact on school-age populations.

Disability, and the capacity of education systems to respond to its challenges, is closely related to poverty. The United Nations, for instance, has regarded disability as a socio-economic indicator (UN, 1990). The poor are more likely to be disabled or to experience a learning difficulty (Brock, 1999); individuals within these groupings are disadvantaged throughout their lives. On a global basis it is estimated that approximately one family in every four has a family member with a significant disability (Elwan, 2002). So the vast numbers involved ensure that the issue is a significant development issue.

The demographics of disability are revealing. By 2005 it is estimated that there will be over 100 million adolescents with a disability living in LEDCs, to which can be added a further 30 million from MEDCs. When these numbers are compared with the cumulative GDPs of both sets of countries, an alarming imbalance is apparent. The chances of a disabled young person securing an appropriate, inclusive education in Namibia are significantly less than that of a similar individual in Norway. Commenting on this situation, Alur (2003) suggests that disabled people are 'amongst the weakest and poorest and are powerless in effecting a change' (p. 3) and that dependence on charities, non-governmental organizations or grant-in-aid has resulted in 'the limited and fast dwindling capacity to raise funds' (p. 3). The product of this 'institutional embrace' is that, for example, in India over 90 per cent of the disabled population falls outside State supervision. A perverse, local parallel of this imbalance and dependency is that within national boundaries the distribution of resources and capital is equally problematic and reveals sharp differences in capacity to access any benefits of industrial or commercial development. These internal inconsistencies are as visible in MEDCs as in LEDCs.

ADHD: global branding in action

Finally, our gaze turns to a specific policy thrust which has swept global policy-making in special education. The drive for educational inclusion has gathered both ideological and practical momentum. It is not our intention to comment on the conceptual or organizational features of this here (see Daniels and Garner, 1999, for a recent account). Rather, we make specific reference to the most challenging issue facing teachers, educational planners and others at the current time: that of children and young people who present behaviour perceived to be unacceptable in school, resulting in them being excluded, or at risk of exclusion (see, for example, Kniveton, 2004). By doing this we point to the contradiction, or deceit, in the notion of universal 'inclusion': that those most in need of social or educational inclusion are often scapegoated by exclusion on account of their perceived differences.

The work of national governments, global alliances, development agencies and charities in policy formulation in special education has largely been directed towards securing a standardized 'education for all', predicated on the demand of resource costs. This has been manifest on an international scale by the so-called inclusion movement. Earlier in this chapter we have remarked on the often partial application of the underlying principles of inclusion, dependent largely upon the differential view taken (whether within individual countries or between one country and another) of the 'need'. Nowhere is this better explicated than in the case of children and young people who present challenging behaviour – a term so diffuse and contested that its application to one child and not another verges on whim or perversity. As a nominal categorical grouping it is nonsense. This is especially so in the case of so-called 'attention deficit and/or hyperactivity disorder' (ADHD).

The term ADHD is now widely accepted, and is becoming increasingly used internationally. Indicative of the rapid grip it has assumed is the spread of ADHD in the UK. Lloyd (2003), for example, points out that:

> Somehow, in just over a decade, it has gone from being an obscure term from an American psychiatric lexicon, not used by professionals in Britain, to part of every day discourse and a label that can be used by teachers to describe a child.

> (p. 105)

Meanwhile, ADHD 'experts' (many of whom also provide specialist consultancies and private clinics to deal with the 'problems' they have identified) have claimed that ADHD is internationally recognized (Kewley, 1999). Opponents of such within-child, medicalized views of SEN have argued that there are no reliable scientific criteria for making an ADHD diagnosis (Baldwin and Cooper, 2000). Such opposing standpoints, played out clinically, academically or in terms of local, ground-level impacts, neatly illustrate the negative effects of global approaches in SEN.

ADHD has particular relevance as an illustration of fragmentation in SEN, of the impact of global commercial markets on educational provision, and of the extent to which the term 'educational inclusion' has variable meaning dependent on cultural or national location. We will now briefly illustrate each of these.

The international profile given to ADHD has developed relatively recently. However, it is noticeable that much of the literature in respect of both identification and aetiology has emerged from North America, the UK and Australia. This has sought to secure a workable diagnosis and a distinctive 'category' of need, receiving the accolade by the culturally dominant American Psychiatric Association *Diagnostic and Statistical Manual IV*. A number of questions arise from this, for which there are no straightforward answers. What are the factors behind the rapid rise in diagnosis (*sic*)? Why is ADHD a phenomenon in MEDCs but not in LEDCs? One simple, unqualified response to such questions is that in LEDCs the emphasis is upon meeting basic needs rather than the superimposition of a values-led system of sorting and categorization. This is not to say, of course, that the identification of individual learning requirements is wholly a negative process, but rather that any applica-tion of the principles of so-called inclusive education have to be considered in a much broader context. It is iniquitous that MEDCs remain as the pivot for promotion of inclusive ideologies, influenced largely by a resource ability to deliver on principles that are divorced from the real lives of those who are most affected by the negative fall-outs of globalization.

Concluding observations

Monkman and Baird (2002) have observed that 'Like beauty, the signifi-cance of globalisation is in the eye of the beholder', arguing that 'Those on the political Left criticise globalisation as Western hegemony and imperialism and seek alternatives, while those on the Right praise global-isation as the triumph of Western civilisation and liberal democracy' (pp. 497–8). For special education this has been especially true. The notion is contested in respect of the benefits it has brought to those individuals and communities who are marginalized on account of their (real or perceived) learning difficulties. In this chapter we have sought to illus-trate the playing out of these tensions by focusing on particular features of a globalized version of special education. We believe that the influ-ence of inclusive ideology has, in the initial stages of policy-formulation, led to a dangerous monoculturism which has at times approached a fundamentalist stance in some settings, global reference groups and individual nation states. The benefits of including children and young people in mainstream settings based solely upon a moral prerogative are open to debate.

The net benefits of inclusive education are unevenly spread across populations and across spaces. The principal reason for this uneven access to positive outcomes is the substantive link between resources and educational progress. The studied indifference of policy makers and academics, plying their trade within inclusion plc, to the real needs of large sections of the global population movement is an acknowledge-ment that money and the market place are now more than ever the determinants of social justice within education. Educational inclusion, in this respect, has assumed the role of camouflage, in effectively disguising how little structural change has taken place, on a global canvas, in changing the educational experiences of the most at-risk groupings of children and young people in our societies.

References

Alur, M. (2003) 'A situational analysis: the dilemma of what to do with the education of disabled children', in NRCI, *The North South Dialogue II on Inclusive Education*. Mumbai: NRCI.

Baldwin, S. and Cooper, P. (2000) 'How should ADHD be treated? Head to head', *The Psychologist*, 13 (12): 598–602.

Brock, K. (1999) 'A review of participatory work on poverty and illbeing: consultations with the poor', Global Synthesis Workshop, Poverty Group, PREM. Washington, DC: The World Bank.

Cooper, P. (1993) *Effective Schools for Disaffected Students*. London: Routledge.

Daniels, H. and Garner, P. (1999) *The World Yearbook of Education 1999: Inclusive Education*. London: Kogan Page.

Daniels, H. and Garner, P. (2000) *Inclusive Education Supporting Inclusion in Education Systems*. London: Kogan Page.

Elwan, A. (2002) *Poverty and Disability: A Survey of the Literature*. Washington, DC: The World Bank, Social Protection Unit, Human Development Network.

Hobbs, N. (1975) *The Futures of Children*. San Francisco, CA: Jossey-Bass.

Howie, D. (2000) 'Key issues in special educational needs in New Zealand', in C. Brock and R. Griffin (eds) (1999) *International Perspectives on Special Educational Needs*. Saxmundham: John Catt Educational.

Jonsson, T. and Wiman, R. (2001) *Education, Poverty and Disability in Developing Countries: Thematic Group on Disability Issues*. Helsinki: Finland.

Kavale, K., Forness, S. and Duncan, B. (1996) 'Defining emotional or behavioral disorders: divergence and convergence', in T. Scruggs and M. Mastropieri (eds) *Advances in Learning and Behavioral Disabilities*. London: JAI Press.

Kenway, J. and Bullen, E. (2001) *Consuming Children: Education, Entertainment, Advertising*. Philadelphia, PA: Open University Press.

Kewley, G. (1999) *Attention Deficit Hyperactivity Disorder: Recognition, Reality and Resolution*. London: David Fulton Publishers.

Kibria, G. (1995) 'Learning problems among school children in the developing countries: a perspective of a hidden agenda', *International Journal of Special Education*, 10 (2): 63–71.

Kniveton, B. (2004) 'A study of the perceptions that significant others hold of the inclusion of children with difficulties in mainstream classes', *Educational Studies*, 30 (3): 331–42.

Kumar, V. (1993) *Poverty and Inequality in the UK: The Effects on Children*. London: National Children's Bureau.

Lloyd, G. (2003) 'Inclusion and problem groups: the story of ADHD', in J. Allan (ed.) *Inclusion, Participation and Democracy: What Is the Purpose?* Dordrecht: Kluwer Academic Publishers.

Monkman, K. and Baird, M. (2002) 'Educational change in the context of globalisation', *Comparative Education Review*, 46 (4): 497–508.

O'Brien, T. (1999) *Positive Approaches to Behaviour*. London: David Fulton Publishers.

Okyere, B. (1994) 'Special education in Ghana: problems and prospects', *International Journal of Special Education*, 9 (1): 13–18.

Satawi, A. and Smadi, A. (1995) 'Constructing a scale for handicapped problems in the United Arab Emirates', *International Journal of Special Education*, 11 (1): 66–72.

Thomas, G. and Loxley, A. (2001) *Deconstructing Special Education and Constructing Inclusion.* Buckingham: Open University Press.

United Nations (1990) *Disability Statistics Compendium: Statistics on Special Population Groups,* Series Y, No. 4. New York: UN Department of International Economic and Social Affairs, Statistical Office.

9 Teaching and the globalization of knowledge

Leslie Bash

Introduction

The focus of Western states upon education policy in the late twentieth and early twenty-first centuries has signalled its assumed primacy in national development together with an unparalleled quest for increased global competitiveness. As such, it presents a specific corollary: the presumed existence of a permanent, global demand for teachers. In popular discourse it is taken for granted that learning and the acquisition of knowledge are contingent upon the actions of teachers and that effective teaching is the key to effective education. Yet, at the same time, some kind of constructivist paradigm has gained hold of the popular imagination, reinforced by late modern technology and moving beyond assumptions regarding teacher intervention and readiness for new learning. Children are increasingly seen as possessing the capacity to be self-taught and therefore questions are inevitably raised about the possibility of according legitimation to sources of educational knowledge beyond the classroom. In the broader context of knowledge sources, this places current and future education firmly within a globalized context characterized by ubiquitous electronic, digitalized information. In short, it can be argued that there has been a fundamental infrastructural change requiring an equally fundamental change in the conceptualization of the role and function of teachers.

This chapter therefore poses an alternative perspective and a possible counter argument to the continued acceptance and promotion of conventional pedagogical relationships. The globalization of knowledge increasingly places teaching at the margins of the learning process and may eventually question the necessity for teachers in a digitally redefined educational future. Teaching is at a moment of crisis, its occupational culture remaining relatively unchanged for centuries. Moreover, the globalization of knowledge challenges the legitimacy and *raison d'être* of *national* education systems per se. Yet, such an argument may possibly be seen as counter-intuitive: without teaching, learning is unstructured, haphazard and may not happen at all (reinforced by the common-sense equation of education with – compulsory – schooling). Moreover, national education systems are required to guarantee the survival and development of nation-states, the taken-for-granted units of macro political and economic action.

Education in the West is experiencing a legitimation crisis. Schools and universities as sites of knowledge production and reproduction appear increasingly anachronistic as their functions are rapidly replaced by constantly moving webs and networks of ideas, data and applications. By the same token, the more general socialization and social control functions of schools are placed in relief, while the higher education sector across the world expands to provide little more than a symbolic recognition of credential inflation and the postponement of employment. Habermas (1980) put the point succinctly in identifying a crisis of legitimation as the credibility gap between the reproduction of cultural traditions and changed socio-economic circumstances. The rupturing of a vital link in part identifies the 'changed circumstances' of the last 20 years or so. That link is between educational institutions as the repository of valued *knowledge* on the one hand, and the sites of *wealth production* on the other. The rupture has occurred precisely because *knowledge itself* 'has replaced industrial organisation and production as the major source of productivity' (Evers, 2000, p. 5). Knowledge *production*, rather than simply the *application* of knowledge, is often now located within the research and development departments of large corporations, whether they are concerned with drug manufacture, aerospace engineering or software production. The research fortunes of universities are increasingly shaped and determined by the quality of collaborative arrangements with industry.

At the same time, the conventional modalities of teaching appear to be relatively fixed. The traditions of teaching, while varying to a degree among societies, are generally locked into a didactic framework, premised upon a model of the teacher as the major, if not sole, source of legitimate educational knowledge. Despite the now somewhat unfashionable ideology of child-centredness and the introduction of technologies that promise new modalities of learning, the traditional teacher–learner nexus remains largely unchallenged. A glance through time and space might suggest the essentially unchanging and uniform character of school classrooms along with a common ritualistic dimension to the teacher–learner dynamic.

For most children, it is the social dimension of teaching and learning that is of prime significance and it is this, the conventional core of the formal educational process, which provides much of the subject matter for critique in this chapter. This is taken to be problematic both at the micro level of educational practice and at the macro level of educational policy. More specifically, the task is to question taken-for-granted knowledge about teaching that reinforces a conservative view of the teacher and of the teaching process. This is juxtaposed with a discourse at the level of the central state that has focused upon the increasingly globalized nature of the economy and the professed need for a more flexible labour force educated in a flexible manner. However, this also stands, ironically, in contrast with a discourse, equally put forward by the state, which centres upon the promotion of narrow, relatively static, content-driven curricular considerations based upon conventional educational practices.

The focus on *teaching and the globalization of knowledge* has arisen partly out of an earlier, critical concern for the current state of teacher education (now teacher *training* in England). It should be noted that this concern is echoed in a number of countries where the drive for regulation and accountability in education has been subjected to critique against the background of not dissimilar macro socio-economic changes. Recognition of the significance of global forces has contributed to the shaping of discourse according to the values of the market, while education policy has rapidly confined itself to the achievement of a set of utilitarian outcomes. Government ministers urge universities to place education at the service of the economy, while apparently considering the pursuit of non-utilitarian knowledge to be less worthy of public funding.

This essentially ideological stance readily locks into a radically changing Western economic system where industrial manufacturing as the traditional basis of capitalism since the mid-nineteenth century is giving way to what is popularly known as the knowledge economy. Microsoft's manufacture of computer applications for commercial and domestic use rather than Ford's production of cars and trucks is now at the commanding heights of an internationalized economy. Knowledge, nonetheless, is a highly diversified commodity: on the one hand, much of it constitutes big business bounded by a confusing array of intellectual property law and regulation, while, on the other, a good deal is freely accessed, without cost, but all of it increasingly within a context of globalization.

Globalization: a word for all seasons

'Globalization', with its late capitalist resonance, accompanied by a high degree of ambiguity, has swiftly descended into cliché. As such, it can be positioned in relation to a variety of phenomena and, at the same time, carry with it diverse ideological orientations. Globalization implies a fundamental technological, economic and socio-cultural transformation on a more or less world-wide basis. Yet even a superficial analysis would yield difficulties in giving a precise identification to this transformation, let alone in sustaining uncontested theoretical positions regarding its consequences.

Globalization assumes at least a world economic system comprised of a 'multiplicity of linkages and interconnections between states and societies' (McGrew, 1992, p. 23). Yet the concept of globalization might denote little more than the inevitable progress of capitalism. Indeed, as a world-wide phenomenon, something of the sort was envisaged by Karl Marx, who noted that the mid-nineteenth-century capitalist class had:

> through its exploitation of the world market given a cosmopolitan character to production and consumption in every country. ... In place of the old local and national seclusion and self-sufficiency, we have intercourse in every direction, universal interdependence of nations.
>
> (Quoted in Bottomore and Rubel, 1963, pp. 145–6)

Globalization has indeed been perceived as such by 'anti-capitalist' political activists, capturing media attention at high-profile meetings of world political/economic elite representatives (G7, WTO). The perceived social consequences of globalization vis-à-vis inequalities and the environment have provided the impetus for a new, cross-national, left political agenda, though to what extent this will gain more success than the social democratic ideologies of the twentieth century remains to be seen. Even so, while perceived primarily in economic terms, globalization is generally acknowledged to have technological, social and cultural dimensions that embody complexity, diversity and contradiction.

Thus, globalization confounds conventional conceptions of social and economic advancement, challenging the positivistic view of universal progress, and incorporates phenomena as diverse as 'McDonaldization', the Internet and cultural convergence. Others might wish to add, as a corollary, the generally unwanted rise of unbounded international terror, even though its apologists might wish to perceive it as an understandable response, and a mode of resistance to the very phenomenon of (Western) globalization. Indeed, there are those who would challenge the reality of globalization as a truly *international* capitalist phenomenon bringing the fruits of economic growth to every part of the world. Notably, there is the persistence of regionally structured poverty, the exclusion of many countries and cities from the 'global network' and the stubborn persistence of belief systems and collective sentiments which either run counter to, or offer alternatives to, multinational capitalism. These latter range from the multiplicity of ethnicisms and nationalisms through to world-wide religious orientations of an absolutist character. These 'alternatives', as matters of individual and collective *identity* appear to provide some kind of counterweight to globalization, but also contribute to the weakening of national economic and political borders.

It may be possible to speak of more than one single globalization process. The apparent hegemony of neo-liberal globalization, seen in terms of the concentration of power in the market economy into a small number of multinational corporations (Comeliau, 2002, p. 97), with its attendant consumerist behaviour, is paralleled by, and overlaps with, non-Western globalization networks and their cultural correlates. Islamic networking may exemplify one such alternative globalization process, rooted in traditional cultural and socio-economic relations, but utilizing state-of-the-art communications technologies to sustain the international dynamic. Moreover, in this sense, globalizing operations, employing traditional forms of social relations in the service of modernizing activity, are not new (as seen for example in the case of the financial operations of the Rothschild kinship network of 200 years ago).

In addition may be added the expanding communications technology-based outsourcing of work to where employees are paid considerably less but, arguably, are better qualified (call centres located in India). Here then is a developing international economic order based upon low labour costs, avoidance of state regulation and the establishment of oligopolistic, or even monopolistic, positions on a global plane. Moreover, it could be argued that the process of globalization is hardly multinational but, rather, it masks a largely US-led economic expansionism seeking to maximize profits and minimize costs. This view is further reinforced by Schiller (1999), who points out that globalization is increasingly underpinned and driven by electronic networking, with its origins in the neo-liberalism of the United States, correlated with the decline of state-led welfarism.

Globalization and teachers' professionalism

Globalization has, and will have in the future, significant ramifications for the world of education in general and for the organization of the teaching and learning process in particular. In addressing the latter point, it is accepted that there has been a tendency to view the impact of late capitalism and globalization on the social relations of production, as characterized by Marx, as alienating or anomic. In the context of education, Braverman's (1973) thesis on deskilling and 'proletarianisation' has been applied to teaching and is ever more relevant in the wake of increased state regulation of teaching and learning. In England, the Office for Standards in Education (Ofsted) and the National Curriculum with its attendant system of national testing and assessment have been the most concrete manifestations of the drive towards centralized control as the state focuses upon international competitiveness.

Professional educators in Western societies have been seen as increasingly beset by alienation. Thus, everywhere, 'teaching is being remade by global economic forces which have little to do with the relational world of teaching and learning inhabited by children and teachers' (Smyth and Shacklock, 1998, pp. 201–2). After decades of struggle towards professionalization the status of the teacher is challenged as a consequence of structural socio-economic change posed by globalization. In addition, the chronic problems characterized by states' accelerating demands on the public purse have manifested themselves in the pursuit of significant policy change. Thus, in the context of the English school system, the rationalization of fiscal crisis is played out as schools hire increasing numbers of 'para-professionals' (see p. 183–4), whose presence may question the very identity of the teacher.

At the level of popular discourse, the act of teaching is often held to be a near-universal attribute. Religious leaders having traditionally undertaken a teaching role, parents almost by definition are perceived to have a primary teaching function, and it is evident that children teach each other on a continual basis. Teaching, as with a view of power 'rooted deep in the social nexus' (Foucault, 1982, p. 208), may be said to pervade interpersonal relationships: it is a fundamental dimension of human interaction but it is mostly part of taken-for-granted behaviour and often unintentional. There is little consciousness of social and moral responsibility other than that which characterizes conventional inter-personal relations. On the other hand, the traditional view of parents as significant educators also suggests they are to be held accountable to society at large for the actions of their children. This is on the assumption that they have a duty to equip them with a set of moral standards, basic knowledge of acceptable social behaviour and so on. As a consequence, should parents fail to meet these obligations there may be legal sanctions invoked against them. At the same time, a large degree of autonomy would seem to be built into the Western model of parenthood. Parents are apparently able to exercise their role in respect of their children in an individualistic – if not idiosyncratic – manner, as long as this is not held to result in harm or neglect.

Having said that, in both ancient and modern societies, teaching is commonly identified as a specific, intentional act, with the individual performing such acts on a regular basis receiving the title of *teacher*. Moreover, the teacher has been traditionally assumed to possess special attributes, the most prominent of which are *knowledge* and *authority*. In historical perspective, it would appear that the label of teacher has been attached to individuals of renown in diverse cultural settings following noted acts of knowledge transmission (Moses, Jesus, Mohammed, Gandhi). In these cases, the legitimation of the teacher's status would appear to accord with Weber's (1978, pp. 1121–3) ideal type approach to authority: from an initial charismatic basis which is subsequently routinized through tradition. In the modern era, when considering the basis of the authority of those who have occupied formal positions as teachers, tradition has held fast. Charisma, enshrined in the popular notion of the inspirational teacher, might be seen as no more than an additional characteristic.

In suggesting that prevailing models of teaching conform to some kind of ideal type it is not surprising that such types rapidly assume a mythological character. Yet, these mythologized ideal types are juxtaposed with a model of knowledge dissemination and mediation assumed as the outcome of the interplay of the following:

- a *globalized* structure of socio-economic relations;
- a *digitalized* international network of communications;
- a *bureaucratized*, regulated structure of professional activity.

However, the persistence of these educational myths against the imperatives of globalization requires some elaboration. Functionalist sociology would suggest that there are consequences, whether intended or unintended, which serve to integrate and maintain structures of social relations. As such, myths serve well-understood functions that bind individuals together in the pursuit of the good and in the identification of the bad, and in so doing support and legitimize the prevailing social order. Self-defined national and religious groups are prominent in this regard and their associated myths frequently possess robustness and longevity.

Among the more enduring myths are those that surround the problem of knowledge. Western tradition has continually invoked the biblical story of the creation, which focuses, among other things, upon the problem of knowledge: eating the fruit of the tree of knowledge transforms men and women from purely biological to moral beings where 'you shall be gods knowing good and evil' (Genesis 2). Knowledge is held to be dangerous and the destroyer of innocence; yet it endows those who know with power. Belief systems rooted in Judaeo-Christian traditions might suggest that knowledge is not necessarily available on a universal basis. Before the Gutenberg revolution, knowledge derived from literary sources could be retained by the elect and transmitted, mediated and interpreted at a time and pace dictated by priests and other gatekeepers. It was with the mass reproduction of the scriptures through the printing press, in the vernacular – and the onset of the Reformation with the possibility of direct access to God without the mediation of the priest – that the knowledge revolution exploded. The last decades of the twentieth century saw yet another information revolution – perhaps even more transformational than that of Gutenberg's – where the Internet above all represents a distinct modality of knowledge production and dissemination and one whose ramifications for education have yet to be fully understood and analysed. However, the pace of the current information revolution should not be overestimated. As with the change to print from manuscript media, the transformation is not that of a clean break with a previous technology. Nor can it be seen in predictive terms or as politically neutral as far as concomitant behaviour is concerned (Landow, 1992, pp. 30–2). The central point concerns the locus of control, and, in the context of a global, digitalized modality of knowledge transmission, control may be all.

Changes in the teaching profession

Regarding the institutional contexts of teaching and learning, it is apparent in hindsight that in the early universities knowledge possessed a somewhat narrow character. It was not merely that there was less to 'know', but rather that the function of universities was vocational, in the sense that they aided the fulfilment of a 'calling', since they were closely linked with the preparation of priests. In addition, however, they also served the more modern idea of vocation, inasmuch as they trained lawyers and government administrators. In both cases, universities functioned as the preserve of a small, privileged social group and what counted as knowledge was likewise preserved.

However, with time, the control of knowledge became more problematic. The growth of mass elementary schooling merely emphasized the problem rather than creating it. At the same time, though, it shifted the issue of the control of knowledge to the new arena of teacher training. Nineteenth-century Western Europe with its ever increasing industrial working class on the one hand, and its rising professional and commercial middle class on the other, required a controlled environment to ensure an appropriate but limited education for the former and to preserve and institutionalize the gains of the latter through a system of elite schooling. The role of teacher training was clear: to provide the labour to run the elementary schools, mainly through recruitment from the literate and numerate members of the working class. Likewise, the middle class were served by university graduates who were recruited to the elite secondary schools, with the possession of a degree alone demonstrating their fitness for the task. Thus, by the late nineteenth century, teaching itself was seen in no uncertain terms as a microcosm of a class-divided society, with an English elementary school teacher having rather less in common with a teacher in an English public school than the ledger clerk had with a City banker.

It is against this background that the question might be raised concerning what currently constitutes appropriate professional knowledge in the institutionalized context of teaching and learning. It should be noted that this is not relevant merely for those who are designated as teachers since it is possible to identify other sources for children's learning. It is clear that teacher educators/trainers were for some considerable time permitted to define professional knowledge in relation to teachers, at least in many Western European nations and North America

(Turner and Bash, 1999). On the other hand, the final two decades of the twentieth century witnessed the changing role of the state vis-à-vis public education and challenges to the professed autonomy of universities and other higher education institutions involved with the initial, professional education of teachers. The liberal democratic legacy that from time to time has been in the ascendant in American politics, together with post-war European social democracy, has been driven to the margins in the pursuit of the market and the perceived need for accountability.

As global competitiveness became the dominant concern, with the focus on targets and measurable achievement, it became almost inevitable that the role of teachers and teacher *trainers* (rather than *educators*) should become more circumscribed. The role of the teacher has become little more than a delivery system for externally prescribed curriculum outcomes. At the same time, the teacher trainer is little more than a functionary to enable universities to produce cloned classroom practitioners. If this is the case, then what is regarded as appropriate professional knowledge for teachers can be addressed: it is whatever can aid the process which will enable school students to reach prescribed educational targets and obtain appropriate qualifications. Teachers' performance is then measurable, accountability is reinforced, and autonomy is significantly curtailed.

Within a globalized context of macro political-economic goals, fiscal constraints and an insufficient supply of qualified teachers, the imperatives for states to pursue efficiencies become paramount. Consequently, in the case of publicly funded English primary schools innovative policies were required to secure the achievement of externally prescribed learning outcomes for the vast majority of children. The perceived solution was that, while primary school teachers were required to deliver appropriate elements of the National Curriculum to meet this provision (Bash and Coulby, 1989), their role was to be supplemented by the presence in the classroom of para-professionals who do not have qualified teacher status. Their lower status meant that they could be paid at a significantly lower rate than teachers, while in practice performing a not dissimilar function in the classroom.

Given the historical position of teaching assistants, traditionally the fillers of paint pots and sharpeners of pencils, together with diverse motives for their employment, their exact function and purpose has been subject to considerable discussion and exposition (Moyles, 1997; ATL/ NLA, 2000; Lee, 2002). Meanwhile, central government has been able to construct its own pedagogical agenda and has progressively formalized the place of teaching assistants in the primary classroom (Great Britain, 2000, 2003). Furthermore, though not mandatory, teaching assistants are now able to obtain qualifications, on a part-time basis, in aspects of teaching and learning. Indeed, unconstrained by the demands of centrally regulated teacher training programmes, teaching assistants have had the opportunity of addressing issues, often sociological and philosophical in character, denied to initial teacher trainees. The unintended (or intended?) consequence of this possible changed status of the teaching assistant is the emergence of the para-professional as a challenge to the current role and status of the classroom teacher and the locus of legitimate pedagogical knowledge.

A further change is that there has been a distinct move away from a teacher-led discourse, embedded in the traditional sites of educational professionalism – the classroom, staff room and union – to a management-led discourse shaped by politically defined demands: targets, efficiency, accountability and the market (Smyth and Shacklock, 1998, pp. 104–6). This has led to additional, more fundamental questions concerning the relationship between schooling as conventionally defined, with the focus on the classroom and the teacher, and education, a process which extends beyond the classroom and its institutional constraints. Paradoxically, knowledge has broadened increasingly and the teacher in the classroom is relatively less significant as a source of information. While governments continually attempt to recruit increasing numbers of teachers in the face of chronic shortages, the challenging question is whether teachers are needed at all. And, if they are needed, then what kind of professional knowledge is going to be required in a future shaped by the radical changes projected for the twenty-first century? And, finally, has the time been reached when, as far as the advanced industrial world is concerned, schools and those who operate them are outmoded?

Towards an alternative model

The assumption of a distinction between the institutionalized processes of *schooling* and normative conceptions of *education* provides the basis for an alternative view of current and future frameworks for knowledge acquisition. In brief, the locus for learning is increasingly to be found beyond the teacher-led classroom, with access to non-traditional modes of learning support and to diverse, frequently electronically based, sources of knowledge. In respect of the latter, this distinction is addressed in diverse contributions to the *World Yearbook of Education 2004* (Brown and Davis, 2004).

One possible response to a situation where schools, as commonly understood, are out of step with the realities of the twenty-first century is the abolition of these institutions. Schools as physical and organizational structures have changed little since the inception of mass compulsory education in Western societies. While the organizational structures of big business have undergone significant transformation in the wake of globalization, schools remain wedded to nineteenth-century conceptions of hierarchy and knowledge transmission. However, given the dominance of parochial perspectives, such a radical move is unlikely to gain popularity either with the teaching profession or with the electorate. On the other hand, not to undergo change might result in the increasing marginalization of schools in the entire learning process.

An alternative scenario presents itself, characterized by a somewhat different approach to the conventional institutional modality of teaching and learning. Such an approach looks to avoid some of the issues of autonomy, accountability and control which have hitherto circumscribed debates about teaching and might be seen as relevant to all levels of formal education: from the primary level through to the university. This alternative approach draws upon recent theoretical studies premised on the notion of the *network society* as suggested by Castells (2000). It seeks to challenge some of the more fundamental assumptions concerning the structural and institutional contexts of formal education. This, in turn, assumes that the twenty-first century is characterized by 'a truly multi-cultural, interdependent world, which can only be understood, and changed, from a plural perspective that brings together cultural identity, global networking, and multidimensional politics' (Castells 2000, p. 27).

Classical sociological theory, whether right or left leaning, assumed stable institutional structures existing either in the past/present or projected into the future following evolutionary or radical/revolutionary social change. The recent work of Castells, however, may suggest the following. Partly as a consequence of radical technological advances, the complex relationships, and thus the flows of communication which typify the late capitalism of the early twenty-first century, can no longer be assumed to be enclosed within firmly bounded structures and institutions. This has also been accompanied by the demise of the hegemony of communist/social democratic, statist ideologies and the promotion of cultural/religious identity to the forefront of the political arena. Together with the imperatives of information and communication technologies, we have witnessed the growth of more provisional, flexible, and possibly volatile, forms of social and economic organization.

The key notion is the network, a looser, constantly changing set-up, but one which is potentially more responsive to contemporary social, political and economic demands. The Internet, by definition, exemplifies the network society, supplemented by organizational intranets and smaller computer networks. It is of course a transnational network that, through email and other means of online communication, is able to breach the boundaries of the state as well as the walls surrounding traditional religious and cultural communities. The virtual communities/networks created in the wake of the informational revolution have the potential to transcend and subvert taken-for-granted institutional arrangements – or they may herald new institutional modalities alto-gether. Castells speaks of the abandonment of the Fordist – assembly line – mode of mass production in the last decades of the twentieth century, with its replacement by more flexible arrangements (Toyotism and just-in-time), where production location, based on networked flexibility, can be just about anywhere. At the same time, the almost instantaneous communication of stock market movements around the world can ensure a single global financial response to perceived economic phenomena.

A focus on the events surrounding the Iraq War serves as an inter-esting illustration of knowledge production and dissemination in the context of a global network and instantaneous communication. The social and technological changes of the late twentieth century suggest a signi-ficant distance from William Russell's pioneering journalism of the Crimean War, the school history textbook or even the graphic film record of the war in Vietnam. Children no longer receive their knowledge of war solely mediated by teachers and supplemented by books, news-papers or the newsreel. There is now the ability to log in to a variety of sources of information: the press, radio, television and the Internet. It may be somewhat premature for the production of meaningful research findings regarding young people's engagement with informa-tion concerning the Iraq War. On the other hand, anecdotal evidence concerning teenage children and their reporting of discussions with their friends suggests that they do find themselves within face-to-face relations with peers and adults as well as mediating information via the electronic media.

Castells (2000) remarks that educational institutions are possibly the least affected by 'the virtual logic embedded in information technology' (p. 428). Schools remain as much child-care facilities as they are institu-tions for knowledge acquisition, while universities retain their customary provision for face-to-face engagement with lecturers and professors (despite the existence of distance-based learning in both open and tradi-tional universities in a number of countries). More significantly, as far as higher education is concerned, the future system will, according to Castells, be characterized by 'networks between nodes of information, classrooms' sites, and students' individual locations' (p. 428).

What may be the form taken by higher education in the future might also be applicable to the sites of compulsory education. Although teachers are still reluctant to change from a pedagogical model that is essentially didactic towards one that is more facilitative, the reality is that they are already encountering the era of networked education. It exists where the teacher is positioned in a set of relationships that might include the following: teachers, teaching assistants, other adults, con-ventional school-based resources and electronic media (located within schools and outside). Such networks have greater flexibility than the classroom-based context of teaching and learning. Moreover, networked-education merely reflects a reality that has probably always existed, highlighting the social basis of learning where children move in and out of informational contexts.

If we take, for example, information and communication technology (ICT), which is now a taken-for-granted dimension of the primary class-room (Griffin and Bash, 1995), it would be reasonable to suggest that, despite its apparent currency for young people, it has become merely another dimension of the curriculum. Not surprisingly, primary school-children make few links between ICT at school and their own experience of engagement with information technology through computer games. The question remains as to the extent to which children learn more about ICT in school or in using a games console (such as the PlayStation 2). In approaching teaching and learning from a different angle, our response might be that we need to locate learners within a broader network of 'teaching' relationships – and home computers (and even games consoles) should not be placed at the margin. Indeed, what may be perceived as unstructured data-accessing and digital recreational activity on the part of children in fact equips them with confidence, skills and an entire technological culture crucial to 'the control and transfer of global information and communication' (Downes, 2004, p. 127).

Conclusion

Globalization challenges the credibility of the tightly bounded character of conventional teaching. In an era of greater ease of access to information and the products of late capitalist culture throughout the world, particularism collides with universalism. Almost everywhere, despite counter hegemonic measures by traditional political elites, the locals encounter the cosmopolitans, if only partially and superficially. It does mean that the function and professional identity of the teacher may need to be significantly questioned, whether the transmitter of traditional wisdom or catalyst for child-centred activity. The teacher is no longer the sole legitimate dispenser of information (if that ever was the case) and therefore there may be a need to re-examine what constitutes appropriate professional knowledge for teachers.

If teachers are to retain (or regain) any kind of control and auton-omy – and if they are to be able to deal effectively with demands for accountability – then there is a requirement to be more realistic about the contexts of learning in the twenty-first century. In so doing it is possible that a challenging but exciting future awaits the next genera-tion of educational professionals as knowledge becomes increasingly globalized.

However, it is quite possible that the practice of teaching will fail to meet the challenge of its own limitations in the face of the knowledge-driven, globalized society. Unreconstructed, teaching will become increasingly a technicist activity allied to the purveyance of commodified, assessment-driven schooling shaped by contradictory macro educational policies in the alleged pursuit of international competitive advantage. It is also possible that the state will cease to be the supreme actor in a structure of social and economic relations which is global in character. In the face of these circumstances, even this rather more limited identity of the teacher as the delivery system for national educational prescription is threatened. If the challenge is not met, teachers may yet be relegated to a position focused more on the care and control of children and young people than with the preparation for the global society of the twenty-first century and beyond.

Note

This chapter draws upon a paper originally presented at Brunel University, UK, in March 2003. I should like to express my gratitude to Dr Suzanne Greenwald of the Cambridge-MIT Institute for her helpful advice regarding the final draft of this chapter.

References

ATL/NLA (2000) *A Class Act: The Role of Learning Support Assistants in Primary and Secondary Schools*, London: Association of Teachers and Lecturers/National Literacy Association.

Bash, L. and Coulby, D. (1989) *The Education Reform Act*, London: Cassell.

Bottomore, T. and Rubel, M. (eds) (1963) *Karl Marx: Selected Writings in Sociology and Social Philosophy*, Harmondsworth: Penguin.

Braverman, H. (1973) *Labor and Monopoly Capital*, New York: Monthly Review Press.

Brown, A. and Davis, N. (2004) *World Yearbook of Education 2004: Digital Technology, Communities and Education*, London/New York: RoutledgeFalmer.

Castells, M. (2000) *The Rise of the Network Society*, Oxford: Blackwell.

Comeliau, C. (2002) *The Impasse of Modernity*, London/New York: Sed Books.

Downes, T. (2004) 'Playing and learning with digital technologies', in A. Brown and N. Davis (eds) *World Yearbook of Education 2004: Digital Technology, Communities and Education*, London/New York: RoutledgeFalmer.

Dunning, J. (ed.) (2002) *Regions, Globalisation, and the Knowledge-Based Economy*, Oxford: Oxford University Press.

Evers, H.-D. (2000) *Epistemic Cultures: Towards a New Sociology of Education*, Sociology of Development Research Centre Working Paper 330, Bielefeld: University of Bielefeld.

Foucault, M. (1982) 'The subject and power', in M. Foucault *Beyond Structuralism and Hermeneutics*, Chicago, IL: University of Chicago Press.

Great Britain (2002) *Teaching Assistants in Primary Schools: An Evaluation*, London: Office for Standards in Education.

Great Britain (2003) *Standards for Higher Level Teaching Assistants*, London: Department for Education and Skills.

Griffin, J. and Bash, L. (eds) (1995) *Computers in the Primary School*, London: Cassell.

Habermas, J. (1980) *Legitimation Crisis*, London: Heinemann.

Landow, G. (1992) *Hypertext and Critical Theory*, Baltimore, MD: Johns Hopkins University Press.

Lee, B. (2002) *Teaching Assistants in Schools: The Current State of Play*, Slough: The National Foundation for Educational Research.

McGrew, A. (1992) 'Conceptualising Global Politics', in A. McGrew and P. Lewis, *Global Politics: Globalisation and the Nation-State*, Cambridge: Polity Press.

Moyles, J. (1997) *Final Report on Research Entitled 'Jills of All Trades? ...': An Investigation into the Working Roles and Relationships of KS1 Teachers and Classroom Assistants*, London: Association of Teachers and Lecturers.

Schiller, D. (1999) *Digital Capitalism*, Cambridge, MA: MIT Press.

Smyth, J. and Shacklock, G. (1998) *Re-making Teaching*, London/New York: Routledge.

Turner, M. and Bash, L. (1999) *Sharing Expertise in Teacher Education*, London: Cassell.

Weber, M. (1978) *Economy and Society*, Berkeley, CA: University of California Press.

Part IV

Globalization and nationalism

Post-colonial perspectives

10 Globalization and the narrative of civilization

Classical Greece as curricular construct

David Coulby

Westernization as civilization: globalization and school and university knowledge

This chapter and the subsequent one concentrate on a specific aspect of globalization: the tendency towards the homogenization and Westernization of culture which has been identified in the earlier chapters of this volume. In particular they are concerned with the extent to which the concept and exemplification of civilization is becoming westernized. This is of overwhelming significance to schools and universities since what a given state perceives to be civilization will strongly influence large areas of the curriculum. If the notion of civilization is tending to converge between states, and if that notion is one which originates in the USA and the EU, then it is possible that the range of civilizations open to investigation in the classrooms of Europe and America and indeed of other areas of the world may actually become restricted.

The starting place is that there have been many forms of human civilization in different places and different periods (radically stated in Fernandez-Armesto, 2001). Of course, even this statement is highly contested by those people who believe that their civilization, their religion, their literature, their technology, their mode of government and their cuisine are superior to all the others that have ever existed. To recap the argument, this chapter is based on the case made for cultural relativism in Chapter 14. Writing and mathematics, to take two significant achievements of civilization, were not discovered and developed only in one place and then transmitted gradually outwards. Many civilizations developed forms of recording and both mathematics and writing were developed in China before there is any evidence of contact with non-Asian civilizations (Fairbank and Goldman, 1998). The Maya people of the Yucatan peninsula and what is now Guatemala had developed advanced forms of recording and mathematics more than a thousand years before the Spanish conquest (Hamnett, 1999). The civilizations of the eastern Mediterranean in the Bronze Age and subsequently the Iron Age, by contrast, did develop through contact between the civilizations of Africa (Egypt), Asia (the Tigris–Euphrates area, Hittites in Anatolia, subsequently Phoenicians) and Europe (Minoan Crete and later Hellenic Greece). In a globalized world in which a technical development or cultural product made in one continent can spread rapidly to all others, it is difficult to imagine self-contained civilizations developing for centuries, even millennia, without any contact with each other. However, it is important to stress the significance and duration of these self-contained civilizations, because otherwise that of the eastern Mediterranean Bronze Age is in danger of obliterating others from the memory of educational institutions.

In 'the West' (a rather broad concept at this point of the argument and meaning from Luxor to Los Angeles but soon to be narrowed down), as civilization has developed, so simultaneously has emerged a narrative of civilization, the discursive strategy of cultural imperialism. It is this Western narrative of civilization and its tremendous impact on school and university curricula that these two chapters attempt to identify and deconstruct. Although these chapters subject this narrative of civilization to question and even parody it should be recognized that it is exceptionally widely and unquestionably held, not least by those working in educational institutions. To give a brief first statement of this narrative of civilization: it is that civilization first emerged in Classical Greece; it was developed by the Roman Republic and Empire; there then followed a Dark Age in which civilization was all but lost; with the Renaissance, Europe, first in the Italian city states, rediscovered the civilization of Greece and Rome; this was then spread across the continent and developed during the Enlightenment; the age of imperialism spread this civilization to the rest of the world; modern Europe and the USA thus see themselves as the 'heirs' of Classical Greece (Hale, 1993).

In this narrative of civilization there are at least three major flaws. First, that within it Classical Greece has, for anyone acquainted with the arguments of cultural relativism, an astonishing prevalence and priority. It is perceived to be a (if not the) superior civilization and the one which came first and influenced all others. Second, other civilizations, those originating in Yucatan, say, or the Yangtze Valley, are not recognized as equivalent to that of Classical Greece. Third, the civilization of Classical Greece itself is not perceived to have been influenced by the preceding civilizations of the eastern Mediterranean Bronze Age. The arguments here might be seen to be the recondite concerns of scholars of archaeology, and so, in a way, they are. But with the globalization and Westernization of culture there is a possibility that this narrative of civilization will also be paraded for global acceptance. Already it has a surprising amount of credence in school and university curricula in Europe and North America. The narrative of human civilization itself may be in the process of being globalized, and educational institutions are the agents of this process.

Because of the pre-eminence of Classical Greece within this narrative of civilization, this is the central concern of these two chapters. This chapter considers the version of Classical Greece that is commodified in curricular systems, examining the nature of the Athenian achievement and the extent to which it is accurately reflected in curricular systems in a wide range of subjects. In particular, the chapter discusses philosophy, politics, drama, mathematics, science and architecture. It then considers the arguments of Bernal's *Black Athena* (1987, 1991) and the extent to which studies of Classical Greece have been inscribed by racist scholarship. At stake here is the issue that the narrative of civilization being propagated by the curricula of many educational institutions is critically flawed. What is being globalized may be not only not international but actually anti-international. The point at issue is the extent to which teaching about Classical Greece in schools and universities tends to reproduce Eurocentrism and xenophobia. Finally, this chapter focuses briefly, by way of exemplification, on the National Curriculum in England.

Classical Greece in curricular systems

The teaching of the classical Greek language is by no means as prevalent in elite education in Europe and North America now as it was in the nineteenth century. Nevertheless, it is still available in, for instance, fee-paying schools in the UK, gymnasia in Germany, elite curricular tracks in the Netherlands and prestigious universities in many states. Furthermore, although the language may be gradually disappearing, the influence of Classical Greece on curricula remains strong. As an element of classics, classical history, European civilization or straight history courses, Greece remains a current and important theme. In wider curricular areas as varied as mathematics and architecture Classical Greece remains a key point of reference. This chapter considers the version of Classical Greece that is commodified in curricular systems as the globalization of a particular narrative of civilization.

Greek civilization is a wide topic: from the buildings, frescos and jewellery of Minoan Crete to the poetry of Cavafy and Seferis. Obviously this chapter is not attempting to cover this vast and varied richness. What is meant by Greece or Classical Greece (sometimes formulated as 'Ancient Greece' as in the English National Curriculum described in the final section) in the narrative of civilization and its associated curricular systems is actually the product of a much narrower historical period, generally that on either side of the Peloponnesian War (431–404 BCE). The period before and during this war is frequently referred to as the fifth century (that is before the Common Era). It is a period of immense cultural, political and scientific richness, particularly in the city-state of Athens (see next section, pp. 197–8) (Cartledge, 1993). It is this civilization that the narrative and the curricular systems so frequently refer to as Greece.

The Greek states had achieved a fragile unity in holding back invasion by the Persian Empire earlier in the fifth century (Herodotus, 1972). Athens' quasi-imperial ambitions, based on commercial and naval strength, then clashed with the military state of Sparta (Thucydides, 1972). Out of this clash a third city, Thebes, briefly emerged to prominence. Although Athens appeared soon to recover from her defeat in the Peloponnesian War, in the event neither Athens nor Thebes nor Sparta could resist the rise of Macedonia. Alexander conquered Athens and destroyed Thebes before he made his crossing of the Bosphorus. The independence, the democracy and the cultural richness of the fifth century were not to be recovered.

There is a danger of assuming the cultural supremacy of the contemporary when considering the presentation of civilizations within curricular systems (Braudel, 1989, 1990). It is anachronistic to judge previous societies by the postmodern political correctness of contemporary Europe or North America. Indeed this might be a temptation of an alternative, postmodern but equally hegemonic narrative of civilization (Coulby and Jones, 1995; Usher and Edwards, 1994). Thus, because Athens was indisputably a slave society, this does not inevitably mean that nothing the city achieved was of any value. Indeed it is erroneous to equate slaves in fifth-century Athens with the eighteenth-century European slave trade or the plantation system of the West Indies and the southern states of the USA (Colley, 2003). But the culture and civilization of Athens were constrained by slavery and this is evident within both the extent and limitation of the achievement. Without some understanding of the role of slaves in a self-professed democracy the nature of that society cannot be understood. Similarly, the role of women in Athens was quite different from that within modern, Western societies. Again it would be anachronistic to ask Athens to fulfil contemporary expectations with regard to gender equality. It is nevertheless necessary to recognize the constraints on Athenian notions of liberty, democracy and participation constituted by the place of women in that society. *Inter alia* and by contrast, Athens does better than many contemporary states in its lack of homophobic prejudice.

As well as the roles of slaves and women there is a further contextualization necessary for fifth-century Athens. It was a state in a position of almost permanent warfare. Against Persia, Sparta, Syracuse and unwilling Ionian and Aegean satellites, the male, non-slave citizens of Athens were being continually called upon for active service in either the army or the navy. Athens was embattled and, at both the beginning and end of the fifth century, conquered. Athens is not the only perceived great civilization to be generated in a time of war: other ready examples include the Renaissance periods in Florence, Venice, Holland and England. Nevertheless, warfare provides the background to the culture of this city-state and its products can rarely be fully understood without this contextualization. A case has been made (Coulby and Jones, 2001) that warfare itself has been an important element of curricular systems in European schools and universities. Part of the attraction of Classical Greece is an unquestioning reproduction of narrow notions of heroism.

'Even if the whole world submits to slavery': why Classical Greece is important but not quite so universally important

Philosophy

The successive generations of Socrates, Plato and Aristotle belong to this period. The former left no writings of his own but is known through that of his disciples, especially Plato. Aristotle was for a time the tutor of Alexander of Macedon. The dialogues of the reactionary, mystical and anti-democratic Plato have been highly influential in a wide diversity of historical contexts, from the decline of imperial Rome through Renaissance Florence and seventeenth-century Cambridge to the Romantic movement in England and Germany. In many cases the writings of the neo-Platonists seem radically disarticulated from their inspiration.

Aristotle's attempt to systemize both the procedures and the products of human thought have been if anything even more influential. The procedures and aspirations of Enlightenment science are embedded in his attempts to open the physical and human world to scrutiny. Aristotelian science is considered briefly on pp. 200–1. Certainly there is much in common between both the nature of his curiosity and his mode of enquiry and the subsequent methods of Bacon and discoveries of Galileo.

In Plato's portrayal of Socrates some of the enduring features of European idealism are encapsulated. Socrates' stress on the good, the true and the beautiful and of the vital links between them is echoed throughout elite European culture. Christian scholars, especially in the medieval period, did their best to link this idealism to the harsher messages of the Bible. In some ways Plato's account of Socrates' death prefigures the biblical account of the crucifixion. Similarly, Socrates' attempts to obtain the truth by dialogue, openness and criticism, in a context in which the wisest are they who know that they know nothing, exemplifies the best traditions of openness and scrutiny within European philosophy. That said, they provide a fragile ethics for pluralistic, transitional and warfare societies and they have certainly been used, along with Christianity, to denigrate the knowledge systems of non-European societies.

Plato's adventures in Sicily and Aristotle's in Macedonia place the limits on their political philosophies. Syracuse, Sparta, Athens and Macedon were states in a struggle for survival and dominion. Plato's *Republic* or Xenophon's perverse flirtation with the Laws of Lycurgus were essays in escapism which have carried little conviction beyond the academy. Indeed the continuing popularity of this former text in university courses in North America, Europe and beyond is a significant example of the restrictive and regressive impact of this narrative of civilization on global knowledge.

Politics

Athens, like many other city-states (Argos as well as Thebes and Corinth), was, at various points in the fifth and fourth centuries, a democracy. At other times it was an oligarchic government more acceptable to the Spartans. There are limitations to the democratic achievement. Certainly, any attempt to link the politics of Athens with those of Washington, DC, is misplaced. But the Athenians not only developed democracy as a system, they also developed the ethics and the politics that made them appreciate this form of government. They developed the values of liberty and democracy and they vigorously celebrated and publicized these values. The speeches of Pericles and Demosthenes (as well as Thucydides' portrayal of Pericles) encapsulate these better than the dialogues of the oligarchic Plato. When it was all virtually over, when Macedonia was almost literally at the gates, Demosthenes addressed the Athenian citizens in these terms:

> While we are still ourselves preserved, while we still possess a great city with enormous resources and the highest honour, what action are we to take? Perhaps this is a question many in this audience have long wanted to ask. I will answer it, and add a proposal which you can further if you like it. You must make your own defence, take your own measures. I mean this in terms of ships, money and men. Even if the whole world submits to slavery, Athens must fight for freedom.
>
> (Phillipic III, in Saunders, 1970, p. 282)

Athens and, in other political contexts, Sparta, have been held up as ideals of civic government and organization. The former has been claimed to be the progenitor of North American and subsequent European democracy. While these claims may operate well at the level of rhetoric or the invention of tradition, they have little to do with the circumstances within which the Greek states operated. While the slaves of Athens might have enjoyed better material circumstances than the Spartan helots, they were without human as well as civil rights. The condition of female citizens was little better. This was an Iron Age society after all. Athens oscillated between demagogic democracy and elitist oligarchy; Sparta was stable in its militarist totalitarianism. Both cities were predicated on warfare, exploitation and conquest. They rose by war and by war they fell. Some of the political ideals now prevalent in Western states and beyond received an early and appealing statement in Athens. These ideas have been differentially influential in a variety of states across the succeeding two and a half millennia. Other ideals, of Montaigne, Locke, Voltaire, Jefferson and many others – themselves perhaps equally questionable in other of their values – have come to supplement them. Athens has been influential on the development of democratic thought. It is neither the one true source of such, nor the fountainhead of one pure, uninterrupted stream of Western democracy.

Drama

The Athenian period is one of the richest eras of European drama: Aristophanes' comedies as well as the tragedies of Aeschylus, Sophocles and Euripedes are widely performed in the contemporary period far beyond the boundaries of Greece or Europe. These writings were influential on Roman dramatists and, directly as well as through them, on wide tranches of European drama and opera since the Renaissance. In terms of dramaturgy they represent the transition from ritual to verisimilitude which, in the case of the tragedies, gives them the passion of both. Their themes of destiny, vengeance and redemption have retained their power. The themes of the *Oedipus Trilogy*, for instance, refracted perhaps through *Hamlet*, have made their twentieth-century impact via Freud, Anouilh, Stravinsky and Pasolini.

The combination of drama with verse and rhetoric of the highest passion and intensity dealing with the deepest human passions – love, envy, ambition, loss – retains its ability to move readers or audiences. This combination has typified the richest products of European tragedy from the Elizabethan and Jacobean writers, through Racine, Corneille and Goethe to Lorca, or from Monteverdi, through Purcell, Handel and Gluck to Verdi, Wagner, Puccini and Britten.

The drama of the Greek period is likely to be misunderstood without some knowledge of its religious, social and political context. The religious significance and the social festivals in which these dramas were performed are paramount. Their political content is also significant. Euripedes' play *The Women of Troy* is readily read as a commentary on the recent Athenian massacre at Melos as well as on the invasion of

Sicily. Allies of Sparta, the Melians were attacked by Athenian forces; the male population was slaughtered, the women were sold into slavery, and the island was then colonized by Athenians. In the play the chorus of Trojan women lament:

> And I never again
> Shall sway to the shuttle's song
> Weaving wool spun from a home-bred fleece!
> Instead one last, last look at the faces of my dead sons,
> Then go to meet yet worse –
> Forced, maybe, to the bed of some lustful Greek . . .
> By day servile and meek,
> Carrying water from the well.
> . . . This is my first prayer,
> To go to famous Athens, where
> The streets are golden, so they tell.
> (Euripedes, 1972, p. 96)

Needless to say, the reference to Athens is characteristic Euripedean irony. In studying Euripedes, the tendency is to concentrate on the great-work-of-European-literature. The danger is that, in celebrating the decontextualized genius of the Athenian playwright, the reader is oblivious of the Athenian massacre that he had set out to condemn. Perhaps, indeed, these texts become all the more acceptable to the aesthetic consciousness the greater the extent to which historical significance is removed. Part of the majesty of Athens' achievement in drama is actually to place limits on the extent to which this civilization can be idealized.

Science and mathematics

The importance of Aristotle to scientific enquiry has been mentioned above. In addition, the Greek period included Democritus, Pythagoras and Euclid. While claims that the former was the first atomic theorist may be far-fetched, it is difficult to locate writings within any other pre-Renaissance tradition which concentrate so clearly and imaginatively on the nature of matter.

The builders of the pyramids at Giza or, for that matter, at Chichen Itza, or the New Kingdom tombs at Thebes (Luxor) were not without geometrical and astronomical knowledge. In terms of predicting astronomical events and especially the Nile floods the Egyptians had this knowledge in written form by the end of the Old Kingdom. What Euclid does is to offer geometrical knowledge as a mode of intellectual enquiry and activity apparently for its own sake. So influential was

Euclid's approach that his text was studied in mathematics in English schools and universities into the nineteenth century.

It is not, then, that Classical Greece's achievements in science and maths were insignificant: it is that, first, they were not the only achievements and, second, these are not the only versions of science and mathematics. Modern mathematics is a multicultural product. It came to the Europeans via Islam, in which the Arabs had maintained and developed the knowledge of antiquity (Joseph, 1992). More importantly, the programme of science that the Enlightenment saw itself as inheriting from Classical Greece is a particular version of scientific method, codification and purpose. It is concerned with the systematic understanding and classification of humanity and nature (Coulby, 2000b). Its methods are experimental and invasive, and its purposes all too often to understand in order to control or exploit. Other versions of science, not derived from Greece or from Europe at all, envisage more harmonious relationships between humanity and the environment. Despite the crisis of Western science, these versions are all too easily neglected in European schools and universities (Hicks and Slaughter, 1998; Orr, 1992). But if Classical Greece cannot be credited with the successes of the Enlightenment it must not be blamed for its failures either. The danger is that narrative of civilization which is only prepared to acknowledge one form of maths and science which it perceives as being derived from Classical Greece.

It is access to international knowledge which is important; also, the ability to contextualize that which comes from one's own tradition within frameworks derived from others; and the capacity to recognize the weaknesses of one's own knowledge system and to engage in the search for alternatives. It is knowing that Classical Greece is not important, or at least not the only civilization that was important, which is ultimately of the most profound epistemological significance. As Socrates might have pointed out.

Architecture

The Acropolis has become the symbol of Hellenism. Mass tourism and photography as well as architectural emulation from Rome through to the twentieth century have made the Parthenon an icon of Athenian civilization.

Pericles was not the first leader to construct buildings the grandeur of which was intended to embody human ideals. Reference could be made to Babylon or Ur of the Chaldes, but the best known examples are those of Egypt. The Pyramid mortuary complex of the Old Kingdom is not only a statement of greatness and monumentality but also of human power, divinity and eternity. The complex planning and iconography of New Kingdom temples such as Karnak again attempt to build the fragile relations between human and divine power, between the temporal and the eternal (Rice, 1997).

But fifth-century architecture, surviving in Corinth, Delphi, Paestrum and Agrigento as well as on the Athenian Acropolis, does something rather different. Despite the looming presence of the Parthenon on its rock over the city, this is an architecture of human scale. Certainly it is religious, celebratory, even perhaps triumphalistic, but it is to be entered and walked on by men and women. It is designed to awaken wonder, delight and affection, not merely awe and humility. Its Renaissance imitators were to stress its harmony, between lightness and mass, between artifice and spontaneity, and between humanity and divinity (Hale, 1993).

The Acropolis broods over the smog of the vast modern city. Ever present, monumental and white, it is a reproach as well as an exhortation. The blue and white flag of modern Greece flies beside the Parthenon, expressing the state's aspiration to ownership and continuity. It is difficult to reconcile this with the crowded bustle created by Pericles. To repeat the obvious: it was coloured not white; it was covered in statues most of which are now dispersed; and it was part of a living city not a tourist site. There is also the fact that what the modern gaze so reveres is actually stripped of its religious purpose. To see the Parthenon without the gods is to see something different from the original construction: Athens without Athena.

The triangular pediment supported by ribbed columns has become a global lexicon for prestige and civilization. From New York to St Petersburg this is the style adopted by palaces, museums, courts, banks, stock exchanges and elite shops, residences and leisure facilities. The commonplace, almost vernacular use of this style has done so much to establish Greece, and fifth-century Athens in particular, as the foundation of European civilization. To visit the Acropolis is not to find oneself in touch with the mystery and bloodshed of the fifth century but rather to encounter a monumental and reassuring reminder of the diurnal European urban experience. The narrative of civilization has provided a set of conventions for public building (Hall, 1998; Mumford, 1966). It has also made it more difficult to understand the source of its own inspiration. The built form of the Western city itself manifests this strategy of civilizational continuity and prestige.

After the fall of Greece in 1942, Mussolini visited the Acropolis. He mentioned the visit in his correspondence with Hitler:

> Hitler's response was enlightening. Writing from his HQ in the East, he envied Mussolini his visit to the Acropolis: 'I perhaps better than anyone else can share your feelings with regard to a place where all that we today call human culture found its beginning.'
>
> (Mazower, 2001b, p. 67)

Creating the heirs of Athens

Through the evolution of the narrative of civilization, Athens has long been and remains today a ready symbol for those wishing to claim renowned antiquity for their particular version of culture, science or democracy. It is worth stressing the particularism of this historical hostage-taking. Europeans have not tried to kidnap the Hittites, the Medes or the Babylonians after all and have shown an obdurate reluctance to claim any descent from Egypt. In the context of the American-led invasion of Iraq, the links between that country and Ancient Babylon are studiously ignored. The achievement outlined in this chapter is one with which Europeans do wish to be associated. It is not too difficult to re-codify it as the birthplace of art, science and democracy. It is readily exemplified in a preserved and astonishingly widely translated literature, philosophy and history. It is embodied in the shining marble radiance of the Parthenon.

It was also a civilization that was fortunate – at least in terms of its continuity – in the moment of its decline. Conquering Athens and the whole of Greece as a preliminary, the armies of Alexander swept a version of Hellas across Asia and into Egypt. Although Alexander himself may have been Medised and Athenian notions of politics and science were soon travestied in imperial conquest and post-imperial warfare, an ideal had been spread throughout the Greek-speaking world and beyond. The forces of republican and imperial Rome were soon to spread this ideal even wider and more enduringly.

It is worth examining the discourses and practices of some of the prominent periods and states that have claimed to be Athens reborn or that have given it a particular pre-eminence. In this way it may be possible to identify the characteristics of the European narrative of civilization as it emerges. These periods of interest include:

- Rome;
- the Renaissance;
- Pax Britannica and Modern Classicism;
- the modern Greek state;
- mass tourism and its taken-for-granted European culture.

These periods are briefly examined in turn.

The story of the relationship between Greece and Rome is well known: Rome, the conqueror, was herself conquered. Roman martial power was able to subdue the squabbling city-states long before the beginning of the imperial period. The Romans were sensitive to the legacy of Classical Greece in scientific and cultural terms. Combining this with their own formidable expertise in military, engineering, organizational and legal matters, they were able to establish the first (and arguably last) system of European (not only) civilization. The Romans, like Alexander, were Hellenophiles. They not only enjoyed and continued Greek culture and science, they also adopted, with significant differences, their pantheon and theology. They taught their elite boys Greek both in order to give them access to the cultural and learned texts and also as a mark of social distinction. Greeks were employed across the imperial period as artificers and craftsmen as well as teachers. Those Romans who themselves were to be highly influential on the nature of European education and civilization were deeply suffused with Greek learning. Cicero, to take a prominent example, and one with a significant presence in school and university curricula, makes reference to Greek history, philosophy and oratory throughout his writing and was himself a translator of Plato's *Protagoras* and *Timaeus*. Via copies of buildings and sculptures, via literary and dramatic emulation as well as through translations of texts, it was the Roman version of Classical Greece that was to pass into European history and commonplace understanding.

The most remarkable and explicit attempt at a 'return' to Greek (and Roman) civilization was that of the Renaissance. Greece is the new element here: Byzantium, although Greek speaking, was a continuation of the Roman Empire; Carolingia, again, explicitly espoused Rome rather than Greece; Muscovy, after the fall of Constantinople, established itself as the third Rome. The archaeological, exegetical and polemicist energies of the Renaissance, however, were very much focused on Greece as well as Rome. The language of classical Greek was re-established in the homes and academies of wealthy Florentines. Greek texts began to be published, first in Venice and then across Western Europe. Ideals of beauty perceived to have derived from Classical Greece were followed in painting as well as sculpture. Palladio espoused the building styles of Vitruvius and his progenitors. Even the majority of those intellectuals and artists who did not read Greek still claimed to be part of its rebirth. Interestingly this did not cause them to be interested in the final death throes of Byzantium (Norwich, 1982). It is worth noting too that, at this point, there was little geographical interest in the sites of Classical Greece, occupied as they were mainly by the Ottomans.

The nineteenth-century UK never claimed such an explicit ancestry to Classical Greece. Nevertheless, from Byron, Keats and Shelley onwards, it adopted an explicit Hellenism. The appropriation of the Parthenon marbles within the neo-Athenian façade of the British Museum aptly symbolizes the attempt to embody a successor state in terms of civilization and democracy. In *Culture and Anarchy* Arnold offers Greek civilization as an alternative to perceived contemporary philistinism (Arnold, 1960). For Arnold, as for some Enlightenment philosophers, Greek clarity is opposed to religious, especially Catholic, obscurantism. Indeed, at all stages from the Renaissance on Greece is used overtly or covertly to counter Christianity. This, of course, without any attempt to rediscover, let alone revive, the actual religious beliefs and practices of the Greeks themselves. There were, however, more clearly imperial aspirations within the UK that made Rome also an attractive progenitor. At the end of the imperial period E. M. Forster's novels and short stories present one of the most highly idealized visions of Greek civilization and how it has impacted on England.

The highly centralized modern Greek state is held together by language and Greek Orthodoxy (Koliopoulos and Veremis, 2002; Mazower, 2001a). The Classical Greek legacy, although revered and commodified, is not the central component of its identity. Nevertheless, it has proved an antecedent which the state has found it impossible not to adopt (see Chapter 11). Although Athens was not originally the capital of the newly independent state, the government did soon move there. The small Turkish town was soon graced with its beautiful nineteenth-century neo-classical buildings. The Acropolis was adopted as a national trophy and status symbol. Ancient Greek language, history and culture became cornerstones of the school and university curriculum. The narrative of civilization is inevitably particularly poignant in Greece as contemporary intellectuals agonize over how the people who created the civilization of Europe are now relegated to such a marginal role (Persianis, 1998; Psomiades and Thomadaki, 1993). In 2004 Athens (not Olympia) hosted the Olympic Games.

Greece is now a venue for mass tourism from the whole of Europe and beyond. Millions of visitors a year come from, in particular, Scandinavia, Germany, Benelux, Japan and the UK. As well as sun and sea, archaeology forms a significant element in these visits (Diaz-Andreu and Champion, 1996). Not only the Acropolis and the Archaeological Museum, but also Delos, Delphi, Knossos and Heraklion, are significant sites for these pilgrimages. By visiting these and other sites and museums, tourists from the north of Europe identity themselves as admirers of and descendants from the civilization of Classical Greece. There is an assumption behind this not always well-informed tourism that these sites represent the foundation of Europe, of civilization-as-we-know-it. The narrative of civilization is renewed within the facile lexicon of mass tourism.

The colour of the goddess: *Black Athena* and the narrative of civilization

In his provocatively titled volumes Bernal (1987, 1991) raises two questions over the origins of Classical Greek civilization. The first concerns the influence of other Bronze Age societies on the civilization of Classical Greece. The second concerns the settlement of Greece by people from Egypt.

At the time of the Peloponnesian War, there were in the eastern Mediterranean other major civilizations. There was of course Persia, with which the Greek states were periodically at war before and after the fatal internal conflict. In addition, there was the vastly old New Kingdom of Egypt, and also the Phoenicians. Bernal's claim is that the language, religion, culture and society of Greece were influenced by these external forces; that Greek civilization did not spring up spontaneously but was rather a part of its historical and geographic context. He pays particular attention to the influence of the Phoenicians and especially the Egyptians. His contention is that Greek language, religion, society and culture were highly influenced by the long-established civilization of Egypt. Europe, then, did not create its own civilization in an autonomous vacuum; rather, it was influenced by one of the oldest and greatest of the Bronze Age civilizations, that originating in Africa.

The second, more contentious claim, is that there is evidence of Egyptian colonies on the Greek mainland, especially around Thebes. If this were to have been the case then the influence of Egypt is due to the actual presence of highly skilled and civilized Egyptian settlers who helped the development of the Bronze Age in Greece. If this is accepted – and it certainly is not in present day Greece – then it follows that Athenian civilization is itself a creation, at least in the first place, of the Egyptians; that the founding civilization of Europe was actually African; that Athena was black.

This chapter follows the analysis of post-colonial discourse theory mentioned in earlier chapters (Said, 1995; Young, 1990, 1994, 1995). This theory has examined the cultural and intellectual phenomenon of the colonial period and indeed of the contemporary period. The examination is concerned with the way in which imperialism shaped people's thinking and values as well as conquering and subjecting countries and peoples. In particular it focuses on the way in which people in the imperial states saw the people who were being colonized and saw themselves. It is concerned with the way in which Europeans saw non-Europeans and how they saw themselves. It is, to use a Greek word, concerned with the barbarity that considers one part of the world to be civilized and another part to be barbarians. The processes of globalization have been connected with cultural and other forms of neo-imperialism. The narrative of Classical Greek civilization is in many places the curricular manifestation of this imperialism.

The strength of Bernal's argument does not rest exclusively on these two claims, the second of which at least would be difficult to prove either way, but rather in his analysis of the development of classical studies in Europe in the eighteenth and especially nineteenth centuries. Contrasting the Aryan model of the classicists with the ancient model of Herodotus and the Greeks themselves, he demonstrates the ways in which Phoenician and Egyptian influences were systematically written out of the narrative of Athens. Bernal's argument is that the racism and anti-Semitism, so prevalent in European society during the period of imperialism, made it difficult to accept African and Jewish influence on what was seen to be the founding civilization of Europe. The classicists systematically rewrote their narrative to exclude these influences and in place created a Greece that created itself without external assistance and which, to their views, was thus satisfactorily white (Young, 1994).

In taking on the theme of Athens into their curricular systems there is a risk that states are uncritically accepting the views of these classicists. If this were the case then the version of Athens which is taught in schools and universities would not only be a severe distortion of the facts but would also be a component of racist and anti-Semitic knowledge. As well as the importance of Athenian civilization being exaggerated in such a way as to devalue the contributions of other (especially non-European) epochs, the nature of this civilization is being deracinated from its origins. The influences of Asia and Africa on these origins are being deliberately and systematically excluded. The result is a form of European (and North American) triumphalism where civilization is seen as being created and handed down within the confines of one continent. It is important to stress that Greece itself was not involved in this process, though the question remains the extent to which the modern state actually reimported from northern Europe a decontextualized version of the fifth century (Zambeta, 2000). The final section of this chapter examines the latest version of the National Curriculum for England in order to understand the extent to which these distortions actually occur in one European state.

'The influence of their civilization on the world today': Athens in the National Curriculum for England

The National Curriculum for England went into effectively its third version in December 1999 (Department for Education and Employment and Qualifications and Curriculum Authority 1999a, 1999b). Originally a creation of Margaret Thatcher's administration, it remains a profoundly conservative policy. The National Curriculum in England (differences in Wales are slight, in Northern Ireland and Scotland they are considerable) now consists of 13 subjects taught across all or some of four Key Stages. Children follow nationally set and graded tests at the end of each Key Stage in some or all of the three foundation subjects of English, mathematics and science. These three subjects are compulsory at all Stages, as are design and technology, information and communication technology (ICT) and physical education (PE). Religious education, although controlled by local rather than national documentation, is nevertheless compulsory at all Key Stages and is thus counted within the 13 subjects. A modern foreign language is compulsory at

Key Stage 3. The newly introduced subject of citizenship is compulsory at Key Stages 3 and 4 only. History, geography, music and art and design are compulsory at Key Stages 1 to 3 and the documentation provides no guidance on these subjects at Key Stage 4. Control of the curricula in these subjects has effectively reverted to the GCSE examination boards.

The National Curriculum is not meant to constitute the entire curriculum for schools in England. Schools are free to teach other subjects – a second modern foreign language, social sciences or classics – if they so wish. However, even such a brief outline as this makes clear that this is a highly demanding and time-consuming curriculum. Children in England are taught with a vast amount of stipulation. The introduction of citizenship, Labour's forlorn attempt to radicalize a structurally conservative policy, into the third version, without substantial reduction in content in the other subjects, means that the third version of the National Curriculum is if anything more crowded than the second.

In turning to consider the place of Classical Greece within this curriculum it is important, then, not to overemphasize the space that it takes. Those who have not seen the two lavishly published spiral-bound documents might be surprised at the extent and prescriptiveness of the National Curriculum. Within this, Classical Greece forms a small if significant part. Certainly the days are gone when the learning of Ancient Greek language, literature, philosophy and history formed an indispensable part of the education of the male section of the English elite.

There are opportunities for reference to Greece at several points in the National Curriculum, for instance in the 'myths, legends and traditional stories' which children must study in English at Key Stage 2 (p. 54). However, it features most prominently in history at Key Stage 2. Here pupils have to study five topics: a local history study; three British history studies (Romans, Anglo-Saxons and Vikings; Britain and the wider world in Tudor Times; Victorian Britain or Britain since 1930); a European history study; and a world history study. It is the European history study that involves Classical Greece. Classical Greece thus comprises one component of five in one of the 11 compulsory subjects studied by English children in the three junior years. It is, however, a component that all children in state schools in England must study.

In the compulsory section of the documentation it is stipulated that children most study 'the way of life, beliefs and achievements of the people living in Ancient Greece and the influence of their civilisation on the world today' (p. 106). The programme of study spells this out in more detail:

> *Aspects of the way of life*: arts and architecture; houses, cities and public buildings; citizens and slaves; education for girls and boys;

language; medicine, health and hygiene; games and leisure including the Olympic Games; plays and the theatre; ships and trading;
soldiers and warfare.

Beliefs and achievements: the city states of Athens and Sparta; gods
and goddesses, myths, legends, beliefs and customs; Pheidippedes
and the battle of Marathon; Pericles and the building of the
Parthenon; the conquests of Philip of Macedon and Alexander the
Great; great scholars and discoverers.

(p. 107)

This, then, is the version of Greece to be studied by all English children.
If it is tainted by the extremes of nineteenth-century classicism this is not
glaringly evident, though civilization and contemporary influence are
both taken for granted. It is not the intention of the chapter to conduct
a lengthy piece of murderous deconstruction on this apparently
innocuous paragraph. The main point, after all, is that this element of
the curriculum in England has remained intact; that Classical Greece is
part of the cultural foundations of all English children. And the context-
ualizations specified in the opening section of this chapter are all clearly
there: citizens and slaves, girls and boys, soldiers (were there no
Athenian sailors?) and warfare.

Inevitably, in one paragraph, if sufficiently heavily scrutinized, difficulties will emerge. But then this is a risk taken by those who take
upon themselves the task of laying down compulsory school knowledge
for an entire nation. Even the most Hellenophilic English primary teacher
might be excused for needing to consult Encarta at the reference to
Pheidippedes. Taken along with the mention of the Olympics, the writer
of the paragraph might be seen to have an enthusiasm for sport
unmatched by, say, any interest in mathematics or sculpture. Or is fifth-
century Athens actually being reduced to the level that this curriculum
writer considers to be appropriate for junior-age children? Cute little
stories about Pericles and Marathon? Despite the contextualization, the
hard issues about Athens – the massacre on Melos, the attack on Syracuse, the death of Socrates or, for that matter, homosexuality – are
overlooked. What is being offered is a superficial and acceptable version
of Athens that is commensurate with English taken-for-granted knowledge: the London Marathon and the tourist visit to the Acropolis.

Greece is only one component of this history curriculum. An examination of other history units at Key Stage 2 would show an encouraging
trend towards international studies. Four out of six units are of course
British. Greece provides the fifth. The sixth, however, is a world history
study: 'A study of the key features, including the everyday lives, of men,
women and children, of a past society *selected from*: Ancient Egypt,
Ancient Sumer, the Assyrian Empire, the Indus Valley, the Maya, Benin,

or the Aztecs' (p. 107). (The italics are in the original and seem to be designed to prevent some astonishingly ambitious primary teacher taking on all of this huge range of civilizations.) While the majority of schools will probably opt for the familiarity of Egypt, where published materials and the British Museum offer sound support, as new publications and CD-ROMS are developed a wider range of topics may be offered.

The English history curriculum, like the National Curriculum as a whole, remains Anglocentric (Aldrich, 1988; Coulby, 2000a; Coulby and Ward, 1996; Lawton, 1988; White, 1988). In its third version its actual xenophobia appears to be reducing. There has been, however, little attempt to Europeanize the history curriculum. If the UK's role in the European Union and a wider Europe is to be seriously addressed, surely this cannot be done exclusively through studying fifth-century Athens.

Classical Greece is still studied as a civilization of origin in England. The goddess is white.

Conclusion

The processes of globalization are leading to a homogenization and Westernization of culture. Part of this process, begun a long time before the political and economic forces of globalization described in the Introduction, has been the emergence of a narrative of civilization. This narrative privileges the achievements of Western civilization and especially Classical Greece. This narrative has been highly influential on the school and university curriculum both during the period when classics were perceived as the elite subject and subsequently. The enhanced economic and cultural power of the triad states mean that this narrative is likely to continue to influence curricula in a wide range of states despite the dismantling of the formal structures of imperialism. Educational institutions need to challenge this narrative in at least three sets of terms: first, that there have been many civilizations with significant achievements in all parts of the world; second, that the Greek achievement was based on that of antecedent civilizations, not least those of Egypt and Phoenicia; and, third, that Western civilization is a contested and far from exclusively beneficent process and that it was the product of a range of intellectual and cultural influences from all five continents.

Acknowledgements

The idea for this chapter emerged from discussion with Crispin Jones. An earlier version was presented at the Comparative Education Society in Europe Conference in Bologna, 2000.

References

Aldrich, R. (1988) 'The National Curriculum: an historical perspective', in D. Lawton and C. Chitty (eds) *The National Curriculum*. London: Institute of Education.

Arnold, M. (1960) *Culture and Anarchy*. Cambridge: Cambridge University Press.

Bernal, M. (1987) *Black Athena: The Afroasiatic Roots of Classical Civilisation. Volume 1: The Fabrication of Ancient Greece 1785–1985*. London: Vintage.

Bernal, M. (1991) *Black Athena: The Afroasiatic Roots of Classical Civilisation. The Archaeological and Documentary Evidence*. London: Free Association Press.

Braudel, F. (1989) *The Identity of France. Volume 1: History and Environment*. London: Fontana.

Braudel, F. (1990) *The Identity of France. Volume 2: People and Production*. London: Fontana.

Cartledge, P. (1993) *The Greeks: A Portrait of Self and Others*. Oxford: Oxford University Press.

Colley, L. (2003) *Captives: British Empire and the World 1600–1850*. London: Pimlico.

Coulby, D. (2000a) *Beyond The National Curriculum: Curricular Centralism and Cultural Diversity in Europe and the USA*. London and New York: Routledge-Falmer.

Coulby, D. (2000b) *Old Knowledge, New Societies: Schools and Universities in Europe*. Lewes: Falmer.

Coulby, D. and Jones, C. (1995) *Postmodernity and European Education Systems: Centralist Knowledge and Cultural Diversity*. Stoke on Trent: Trentham.

Coulby, D. and Jones, C. (2001) *Education and Warfare in Europe*. Aldershot: Ashgate.

Coulby, D. and Ward, S. (eds) (1996) *The Primary Core National Curriculum: Education Policy into Practice*, 2nd edn. London: Cassell.

Department for Education and Employment and Qualifications and Curriculum Authority (1999a) *The National Curriculum: Handbook for Primary Teachers in England: Key Stages 1 and 2*. London: Department for Education and Employment and Qualifications and Curriculum Authority.

Department for Education and Employment and Qualifications and Curriculum Authority (1999b) *The National Curriculum: Handbook for Secondary Teachers in England: Key Stages 3 and 4*. London: Department for Education and Employment and Qualifications and Curriculum Authority.

Diaz-Andreu, M. and Champion, T. (eds) (1996) *Nationalism and Archaeology in Europe*. London: UCL Press.

Euripedes (1972) *The Bachae and Other Plays*. Harmondsworth: Penguin.

Fairbank, J. K. and Goldman, M. (1998) *China A New History*, enlarged edn. Cambridge, MA, and London: Harvard University Press.

Fernandez-Armesto, F. (2001) *Civilisations*. London: Pan Books.

Hale, J. (1993) *The Civilisation of Europe in the Renaissance*. London: HarperCollins.

Hall, P. (1998) *Cities in Civilisation: Culture, Innovation and Urban Order*. London: Phoenix Giant.

Hamnett, B. (1999) *A Concise History of Mexico*. Cambridge: Cambridge University Press.

Herodotus (1972) *The Histories*. Harmondsworth: Penguin.

Hicks, D. and Slaughter, R. (eds) (1998) *The World Yearbook of Education 1998: Futures Education*. Series edited by D. Coulby and C. Jones. London: Kogan Page.

Joseph, G. G. (1992) *The Crest of the Peacock: Non-European Roots of Mathematics*. Harmondsworth: Penguin.

Koliopoulos, J. S. and Veremis, T. M. (2002) *Greece: The Modern Sequel. From 1831 to the Present*. London: Hurst and Company.

Lawton, D. (1988) *Education, Culture and the National Curriculum*. London: Hodder & Stoughton.

Mazower, M. (2001a) *The Balkans: From the End of Byzantium to the Present Day*. London: Phoenix Press.

Mazower, M. (2001b) *Inside Hitler's Greece: The Experience of Occupation, 1941–44*. New Haven, CT, and London: Yale Nota Bene.

Mumford, L. (1966) *The City in History: Its Origins, Its Transformations and Its Prospects*. Harmondsworth: Penguin.

Norwich, J. J. (1982) *A History of Venice*. Harmondsworth: Penguin.

Orr, D. (1992) *Ecological Literacy: Education and the Transition to a Postmodern World*. Albany, NY: State University of New York Press.

Persianis, P. (1998) '"Compensatory legitimation" in Greek educational policy: an explanation for the abortive educational reforms in Greece in comparison with those in France'. *Comparative Education* 34 (1): 71–84.

Psomiades, H. and Thomadaki, S. (1993) *Greece, the New Europe and the Changing International Order*. New York: Pella Publications.

Rice, M. (1997) *Egypt's Legacy*. London: Routledge.

Said, E. (1995) *Orientalism: Western Conceptions of the Orient. With a New Afterword*. Harmondsworth: Penguin.

Saunders, A. N. W. (ed.) (1970) *Greek Political Oratory*. Harmondsworth: Penguin.

Thucydides (1972) *The Peloponnesian War*. Harmondsworth: Penguin.

Usher, R. and Edwards, R. (1994) *Postmodernism and Education*. London: Routledge.

White, J. (1988) 'An unconstitutional National Curriculum', in D. Lawton and C. Chitty (eds) *The National Curriculum*. London: Institute of Education.

Young, R. (1990) *White Mythologies: Writing History and the West*. London: Routledge.

Young, R. (1994) 'Egypt in America: *Black Athena*, racism and colonial discourse', in A. Rattansi and S. Westwood (eds) *Racisms, Modernity and Identity: On the Western Front*. London: Polity Press.

Young, R. J. C. (1995) *Colonial Desire: Hybridity in Theory, Culture and Race*. London: Routledge.

Zambeta, E. (2000) 'The curricular construction of Greece', in *Comparative Education Society in Europe Conference: The Emergence of the 'Knowledge Society': From Clerici vagantes to the Internet*. Bologna: Comparative Education Society in Europe.

11 Globalized history in a nationalist context

The curricular construction of Greece

Evie Zambeta

Introduction

Global knowledge is socially constructed. The perception of concepts such as Europe, civilization and art are deeply inscribed by powerful discourses which dominate Western science and culture. These discourses, which have been globalized through colonialism and cultural imperialism, have been generalized through state education systems. The recognition of Homer, Aristotle, the Parthenon temple, Shakespeare or Goethe as indisputably valued features of the global cultural heritage is the outcome of the specific interpretation of the world, and the past in particular, that took place in imperial cities and countries, especially during the eighteenth century. The establishment of the British Museum in 1753, for instance, was a manifestation of both European Enlightenment (Sloan, 2004) and imperial power. The collection of ancient artefacts or objects of usage and their transformation into objects of display, public admiration and universal worship was at the same time a classification of preceding human endeavour and a theorization about the past. Ancient Greek art had an exceptional place in the way the European Enlightenment constructed knowledge and interpreted the past. The power of this discourse, which is intensified by the forces of globalization, is reflected in educational systems today.

The image of Greece as the roots of European civilization had not emerged in Greece. It is an ideological elaboration, which is related to the way the European Enlightenment constructed the idea of Europe through the reinterpretation of ancient Greece (Koliopoulos and Veremis, 2002; SMGSGP, 2003). The rediscovery of ancient Greek art, architecture and literature in the eighteenth century gave rise to the movement of 'the Greek revival'. This movement was consolidated in neoclassicism, which, in many European countries and especially in the UK, became associated with the revival of liberty and art (Knox, 2003). The Greek past, and particularly that of the fifth and fourth centuries BC, was considered and classified as the 'classical' period of art and civilization, representing an ideal expression of both. The development of classical studies in Western universities or the place of ancient Greece in European school curricula (Coulby, 2000b) offer some indicative examples of the considerable influence that this elaboration has exercised throughout Europe and the world.

It was within this ideological and cultural context that the 'Greek achievement' has been used as the foundation stone for nation-building on the part of the modern Greek state. Greek intellectuals who studied in European universities during the nineteenth and early twentieth centuries and who formed the elite of the modern Greek state, or European archaeologists and architects – mainly German and English – have significantly contributed to the elaboration of this image.

Antiquity has been a crucial component of national narratives and nation-building in general. This was a construction of eighteenth- and nineteenth-century historiography that is reproduced in curricular systems today. This specific restoration of antiquity and the construction of historical continuity presents nations as ahistorical transcendental entities that existed long before the establishment of modern states. This is particularly the case regarding the curricular construction of Greece, which is mainly intellectual artefact of romantic historiography. In the case of Greece, however, this process has been more complicated since it has been mediated by the way the European Enlightenment elaborated the idea of Europe. The interpretation of ancient Greece as the root of European civilization is contested; it leads to Eurocentrism and potentially to racism. This chapter argues that the deconstruction of Greece in terms of originality (something which is attempted in Chapter 10) should not be perceived as being 'anti-Greek', and it is not a sufficient way to fight racist knowledge either. It is further argued that tradition, modernity and, perhaps, postmodernity are political forces in conflict in the Greek curricular system. School knowledge continues to be a major strategy for identity politics on the part of the state. Historical accuracy then might be seen as an alternative to the arbitrary and authoritarian imposition of constructed memory.

This chapter examines the curricular construction of Greece as a form of identity politics exercised by the Greek state. Focusing on the current history curriculum, it argues that, in Greece, ethnocentricity and Eurocentrism are the Janus face of the school curriculum. This specific curricular construct of Greece reflects the coexistence of tradition and modernity in Greek society and is the intellectual product of the nineteenth-century Romantic historiography that has served the task of nation-building. This version of history continues to be influential in the context of a Eurocentric approach that provides historical and cultural links between Greece, Europe and the world.

'The making of Europe' and the legacy of ancient Greece

The above heading derives from a book published by Helene Ahrweiler (2000). The idea of Europe as a coherent geographical, historical and cultural unit is highly contested. The boundaries of Europe are rather obscure and related more to geopolitics than to any meaningful definition of geography. As has been argued, all maps are fictions (Heffernan, 1998). The definition of space is not a self-evident and uncontested empirical detail referring to physical facts. Geographical premises are predominantly historical. They change over time and they reflect the ideas of boundaries, territoriality, commonality and difference that are prevalent in their historical, political and cultural contexts. The Mercator projection of the world is an indicative example of a Eurocentric approach to geography, reflecting the worldview of the beholder.

The idea of Europe as a meaningful historical concept has become the subject of both intellectual enquiry and political debate. Nevertheless the project to define the historical distinctiveness or unity of Europe has not been an easy task. Many attempts at writing a comprehensive history of Europe have been assessed as not avoiding sins of omission and commission or even prejudice. Duroselle's attempt to grapple with the question of the meaning of Europe was perhaps the least fortunate one. Duroselle's book identifies Europe with the West and, ironically, came out just after the fall of the Berlin wall. This book was the outcome of a history research project funded by the European Commission in Brussels. The project was met with discontent in many countries and the European Commission was obliged to dissociate itself from it (Davies, 1997; Heffernan, 1998). Perhaps the political context that this intellectual endeavour emerged from was not fortunate. The political goal of the researchers to write a history of Europe that went beyond the continent's national fragmentation was ambitious indeed. It should be noted, however, that any attempt to write history will meet with criticism.

In his magisterial work on the history of Europe, Norman Davies acknowledges that he has preferred 'to describe it rather than define it', since any definition raises more questions than it answers (Davies, 1997). Any description of Europe, however, unavoidably involves questions such as where is Europe? when does European history start? what are its distinctive elements? In this respect the meaning of Europe is a matter of interpretation. Helene Ahrweiler, in an article titled 'What Europe Means To Me', argues:

> Humanism is, and has always been, the foundation of every European culture. Although it is rather difficult to define a European cultural identity and, therefore, European identity as such, there can be no doubts about European humanism, which ought to be preserved; a humanism born in Europe, a unique humanism that

finds expression through various languages and traditions, within different cultures, and which constitutes the hard core and very heart of Europe. This humanism, as Paul Valery put it, is the combined fruit of the Greek spirit, Roman law and Jewish–Christian spirituality, and provided the grounding for Enlightenment learning that led the way for Europe both in the past and today.

(Ahrweiler, 2000, p. 274)

Nonetheless, this definition, although it might be well intentioned, projects on to Europe the image of the great and the good. This image is the product of an eclectic abstraction that understands European culture as being of supreme and universal value. Ahrweiler, by using the term culture in the plural, celebrates European cultural diversity as being one of the characteristics of European identities, but she understands this as an internal European matter deriving from the Enlightenment. It should be added, however, that Ahrweiler does recognize cultural diversity within Europe. In an article titled 'Roots and Trends in European Culture', she writes:

And meanwhile fresh human resources were always being grafted on to these zones from outside, fertilizing or strengthening the original kernel of the Graeco-Roman world – as, for example, the various peoples of Central Europe (such as the Hungarians) and the Jewish and Muslim communities. These communities flourished in the atmosphere of unity created by the cultural and political tolerance, which is the hallmark of multi-ethnic entities such as Empires; and they lived an almost entirely peaceful existence within the confines of the Byzantine and Ottoman Empires – as indeed they did later within the Austro-Hungarian Empire of Central Europe. Are we therefore to conclude that the symbiosis between peoples, which exists within multi-ethnic wholes, represents an object lesson in tolerance and humanism? If so, that fact alone would be enough to make us all convinced Europeans.

(Ahrweiler, 2000, pp. 66–7)

Of course, there are as many ways of looking at the past as there are identities. For example, the extent to which the 'kernel' of the above-mentioned Empires was exclusively 'Graeco-Roman' or 'the atmosphere of unity' within them might be questionable. Also, phenomena such as the Inquisition or the Crusades should recall that tolerance and respect for otherness was hardly the case in the European past. Moreover, perceptions of European humanism might be totally different on the part of the victims of the Holocaust, colonial exploitation or the slave trade. Europe had many faces in the past and tolerance has scarcely been the dominant political practice.

The above conceptualization of Europe, however, is of crucial importance since it forms a representative example of Eurocentrism that prevailed in European intellectual thought in the past and continues to be influential at the present time. In a recent book titled *The Europeans* (Ahrweiler and Aymard, 2003) and originally published in French, the argument that is constructed refers exactly to the same premises that understand Europe as a distinct cultural entity (Kokkinos, 2003). The volume starts with an introductory chapter by Paul Valery, which offers an indicative paradigm of a Eurocentric approach:

> Everywhere where the European spirit dominates, one sees the greatest of the needs to emerge, the greatest of labour, the greatest of capital, the greatest of performance, the greatest of ambition, the greatest of power, the greatest of transformation of the external nature, the greatest of the relationships and transactions. This ensemble of greatest rates is Europe or the image of Europe.
>
> (Valery, 2003, p. 22)

Based on the idea of supremacy and universality of European culture, Eurocentrism tends to understand the world through the European spectrum. Europe is associated with the idea of scientific and social progress which are the outcome of a civilization based on the political and epistemological principles of the Enlightenment (Coulby and Jones, 1995). In this respect Europe develops the self-consciousness of a society of rational reasoning and social contract. This construction of the historical and cultural continuity of Europe emphasizes the contributions of ancient Greece, Rome and Christianity.

Greece has an exceptional place in this image of Europe, since the European enlightenment recognized in the ancient Greek civilization, particularly that of the fifth century BC, the roots of European civilization (Sloan, 2004). Philhellenism, developed in Europe during the eighteenth and nineteenth centuries, was an admiration of what has been called the 'Greek achievement'. Ancient Greece exercised a particular enchantment on Romantic poetry, philosophy, literature and art, not least in the Humboldtian idea of the university, which gave particular emphasis to classical studies. Archaeologists like Schliemann and Evans were committed to revealing the richness of this civilization that they perceived as the dawn of Europe. The concepts of harmony, measure and beauty that are expressed in Greek architecture and sculpture have influenced, if not shaped, the modern ideas regarding the body and beauty. Interestingly the term 'classical' civilization, as a way of referring to fifth- and fourth-century BC Greece, continues to be widely used not only by historians (Davies, 1997; Roberts, 1997), but also by the writer of *Black Athena* (Bernal, 1987).

The identification of the origins of Europe with ancient Greece has become the subject of harsh criticism and attack on the part of Martin Bernal. *Black Athena* has seriously divided the academic world. Although the hard core of Bernal's linguistic argument that the Greek language has links to Coptic and Western Semitic has been questioned, the view that ancient Greece had close connections and cultural debts to earlier civilizations, such as that of Egypt, Babylon and Phoenicia, is widely accepted (Goody, 1997). What Bernal adds is that the way European Romanticism reinterpreted ancient Greece is Eurocentric and fails to acknowledge the contribution of earlier non-European civilizations. In doing so, Romanticism forms the ground for racism. Europe has suffered in the past from ideologies such as Aryanism, which are based on the alleged Indo-European purity of European languages and cultures. Many historians, however, continue to follow this Eurocentric view, which understands Greece as the origin of European civilization. It is argued, for instance: 'Of these basic sources of Europe, Greek culture always remains first in time and first in importance' (Ahrweiler, 2000, p. 118).

Antiquity and nation-building

The reinterpretation of ancient Greece that took place in Western Europe during the eighteenth and nineteenth centuries has been transferred to modern Greece and has been used as a foundation stone for nation-building. The establishment of the modern Greek state in the early nineteenth century was accompanied by the process of building national identity. Nation-building presupposed the construction of cultural and historical continuity. Romanticism provided the ideological background for both.

The European and Western orientation of the Greek state and the related attempt to 'regenerate' ancient Hellas have been key elements of the nation-state formation and the construction of Greek modernity (Koliopoulos and Veremis, 2002). Perhaps nothing can describe more vividly the interconnectedness between nation-building in Greece and the Romantic image of Europe, than Dionysios Solomos (1798–1857), considered to be the national poet of Greece, who in 1823 composed the long poem that was later turned into the country's national anthem. The little poem that follows is a scarcely known one, but illuminating regarding the perception of Europe by the early nineteenth-century Greek intellectuals and public consciousness:

> *Hellas*
> Europe is looking at her; how is she going to act?
> She is looking towards Europe;
> Without the face losing its countenance

She puts her hand on the sword
Royally, and in warfare order
She nodded, saying: Wait.
And she frowns fiercely on Asia;
She shakes the forefinger and strikes with horror.

(Solomos, 1960, p. 148)*

Of course, the philhellenic image of Europe is not just a fiction of public imaginary. Byron and Schiller were eminent European intellectuals who admired and idealized Greece. The involvement of the European 'great powers' in the Greek war of independence did not reflect just philhellenism of course, but also their competing interests in the dissolution of the Ottoman Empire (Skopetea, 1992). The enlightened Europe is also a Europe that identifies itself with Greek antiquity and subsequently denigrates the Ottomans as the 'barbarian conqueror'. The European matrix of the modern Greek rejection of the 'Turk' can be traced in Voltaire's references to 'the barbarianism of the Turks' or in Victor Hugo's view that 'every move of Turkey is against civilisation' (Pesmazoglou, 2003, p. 190). European thought has been part of this polarity that marks the modern trajectory between Greece and Turkey.

In the nineteenth-century Balkans, within the context of a declining Ottoman empire, there was a strong antagonism between the various populations for territorial domination. The competitive nationalisms of the nineteenth- and twentieth-century Balkans were investing in the linguistic, religious and cultural mosaic of the peninsula. Greek nationalism was not an exception to that. In its early origins, after 1821, the modern Greek state was characterized by an ideological and political division. On the one hand, intellectuals and politicians who were influenced by the ideas of the European Enlightenment were oriented towards a Western-type constitutional democracy. The Greek bourgeoisie in Istanbul in particular, the Phanariots, had been influenced by the ideas of the European Enlightenment and the French Revolution and they formed the hard core of the Greek enlightenment (Dimaras, 1983). So did many Greek intellectuals in other cities such as Odessa, Bucharest, Vienna and Venice. On the other hand, the military officers who had taken part in the Greek war of independence and a class of rich merchants and former local officials of the Ottoman regime were interested in maintaining their own privileges and hoped to exploit the 'national lands' which used to belong to the Ottoman ruling class in the past. The first turbulent years of the new state, and the oppressive policies that followed, expressed the weakness of the central political power to deal with this internal conflict (Veremis, 1983).

* All translations from Greek are by the author.

Within this context Greek nationalism was developed as a means to ensure internal stability and expand the sovereignty of the state. The main mechanisms used on the part of the state for building national consciousness and cultural coherence were the army and the educational system (Kitromilides, 1997). The army, in particular, contributed to nation-building not only through its main function, warfare, but also by performing 'educational activities'. The most important of these were the generalization of the Greek language and the integration of the agrarian population. Education and the army both served as ideological state apparatuses that contributed to the political socialization of the new citizenry and to the generalization and dominance of the Greek language. Education, however, also served the expanding strategy of Greek nationalism. During the nineteenth century a network of Greek schools was developed throughout the Ottoman Empire which aimed at the linguistic Hellenization of the Orthodox populations living in the Balkans or in Asia Minor. The Greek schools contributed to the revival of the Greek language in places where it used to be spoken in the past, but also where it had been superseded during the Middle Ages by Albanian, Aromounic (the language spoken by the Vlachs (Sella-Mazi, 1997)), Slavonic, Turkish or Armenian (Kitromilides, 1997). Languages, as well as alphabets, were the main means of the cultural war that took place in the Balkans during the past centuries (Tsitselikis, 1999). The revival of the Greek language formed the ground for building ethnic identities and the cultivation of memories regarding the ancient past. The transformation of religious affiliation to national consciousness then was mediated by language.

The content of knowledge transmitted through the Greek schools aimed at the construction of Greek national identity and it was the intellectual product of the University of Athens. The University of Athens, being the first university in the Balkans, has been one of the key ideological mechanisms of the modern Greek state. The first Rector of the University of Athens, in a speech given in 1837, said that 'one of the roles of the University was to transmit the western civilisation to the East' (Kitromilides, 1997, p. 84). By the end of the nineteenth century the University was attracting students coming not only from within but also from outside the Greek state. These students became the intellectuals that disseminated the ideas of Greek nationalism in Macedonia, Thrace and Asia Minor. Though it has been argued that the University of Athens was not that effective in creating a national ideology, since it took it so long to develop a national version of history (Skopetea, 1994), the fact is that it finally did so.

Though there have been different political versions of Greek nationalism (Veremis, 1983), there was one central point at which they converge: the understanding of the modern Greek state as the natural heir of ancient Greece. The modern Greek enlightenment, as it has been called, considered the links between ancient and modern Greece as being unquestionable. However, Byzantium and the period of Ottoman rule were considered as the dark ages between the two periods of Hellenism. The Greek enlightenment used to distinguish the 'Greek nation' from the medieval empire, while some of the representative figures of this intellectual movement expressed derogation for the cultural legacy of Byzantium. This was particularly the case when Romanticism started developing the idea of historical continuity and of the 'Greek Byzantium'. When Zambelios first used the term 'Greek-Christian', Kaligas replied: 'The Greek nation has never mixed religion with politics!' (Dimaras, 1983, p. 399). This position, however, has met with strong resistance in the formation of the Greek state.

It was within this context that the official Greek history thesis was formulated. The historical continuity of the Greek nation that was constructed by Romantic historiography in the decade of 1850s was based on the idea of the 'Greek Byzantium'. Zambelios first and later Paparigopoulos, a historian and a professor at the University of Athens, restored Byzantium to the official history. In doing so they added the missing link in the continuity of the nation between ancient and modern Greece. The periodization of Greek history as ancient, medieval (Byzantine) and modern is the historical canon that by the end of the nineteenth century prevailed in the conceptualization of Greece in the school curriculum.

The understanding of historiography as a political project towards building national consciousness is reflected in the work of Kontantinos Paparigopoulos. In 1853, Paparigopoulos authored the *History of the Greek Nation*, which was a history textbook to be used in schools. In 1860, he published the *History of the Greek Nation from Antiquity to Modern Times* as a two-volume work for the general public. In the same year, he started publishing a much more detailed version of this work that in 1872 numbered five volumes. In his attempt to construct national continuity, Paparigopoulos was faced by two main challenges. First, he had to establish arguments supporting the view that the inhabitants of modern Greece were direct descendants of the ancient Greeks, a view assertively opposed at that time by Fallmerayer, a Bavarian historian (Skopetea, 1997). Second, and perhaps most importantly, Paparigopoulos had to argue against the historical view of Edward Gibbon (Gibbon, 2000), which was influential not only in many parts of Europe, but also among many Greek intellectuals. Gibbon was rather unsympathetic to Byzantium, considering it a deterioration of classical Greek civilization. If these arguments were valid, then not only the bonds between ancient and modern Greece would be obscure, but also the links between modern Greece and Europe would be questionable. For both these arguments the restoration of Byzantium as a Greek Empire was of crucial importance. In 1859, in his introductory lecture at the University of Athens, Paparigopoulos notes:

During this year we intend to study *the history of medieval Hellenism* [his emphasis], or in other words what is usually called Byzantine history. I had many times the opportunity to expose the scientific and national reasons which oblige us to draw special attention particularly to this period of the history of the Greek Nation. . . . We have certain evidence regarding the prejudices of the western world regarding this important period of Greek history. . . . We should not forget that we are the most direct descendants of medieval Hellenism, or of what is called the Byzantine epoch. Of course, first and foremost, we are bonded with ancient Greece through the language that we speak, through the country that we live in, through the traditions that we have, through the sentiments that we cherish, through the name that we bear. But we are bonded even more closely with medieval Hellenism, not only through the above mentioned bonds, but also through religion and through the polity, through the more recent political interests and through the more recent origins. Of course the names of Themistokles, Kimon, Alexander are alive in our memory, but the experiences of our medieval life are particularly alive in our nation's consciousness. . . . Passing through Roumeli you will very often listen to the fall of the Constantinople still being sung in the folk song:

They took the City, they took it! They took Salonike!
They took Hagia Sophia, the great monastery!
. . .
When Madonna listens to this, the icons burst into tears.
'Stop Madonna! Don't cry, don't be in tears.
In the fullness of time, they will be yours again'.

And you will see the old men crying. . . . In the nation's consciousness, the belief is clear that if Hellenism has been rescued from the enormous Ottoman cataclysm, it is owed to the . . . monarchy in Constantinople. Our fate is intrinsically connected with them. . . . It is our duty to restore their reputation. . . . Their condemnation is our condemnation. Their vindication is the vindication of ourselves.
(Paparigopoulos, 1955, volume A1, pp. 73–7)

Taking into account that the mid-nineteenth-century Greek state was limited to a small part of the mainland on the south of Thessaly, this speech could be read as a prelude to Greek expansionism. The Greek nation is constructed as a continuous identity, defined as 'Hellenism', which emerges in ancient Greece and is further elaborated in Byzantium. Paparigopoulos uses the term 'nation' even when he refers to antiquity, or, in other words, for periods long before the formation of nations. 'In the most ancient times of history we find the Greek nation under the common name of Hellenes' (Paparigopoulos, 1955, vol. A1, p. 51). The identification of 'Hellenism' with the Byzantine Empire implies that the territory of the Greek state did not correspond with the historical space of 'Hellenism'. In a clear way Paparigopoulos literally acknowledges that the modern Greek state shares common 'political interests' with Byzantium. As Dimaras notes, 'Greece loved romantic historiography' (Dimaras, 1982). Paparigopoulos managed to formulate a scientific legitimization for the so-called 'Great Idea', or, in other words, for the expansion aspirations of Greek nationalism. The modern state acquired a nation with a long history, a noble past and a common future. Antiquity and Byzantine Christianity were shaped into a historical continuum that links the new state to ancient Greece and Europe. The nation now had a new mission: to liberate the 'non-freed brothers who were still in bondage'. The myth of historical and cultural continuity was then unquestioned and had become the 'national truth'.

If the 'Great Idea' has been hopefully buried with the victims of the Asia Minor war of 1923, the myth of continuity and cultural purity is still alive. Ahrweiler (2000) distinguishes Greece from the rest of Eastern Europe, arguing that, while Eastern European states consisted of ethnically mixed populations, this was not the case for Greece. Greece by contrast preserved cultural continuity with its past and the 'perennial nature of the spirit of Greece, birthplace and home of freedom'. Historical Romanticism is, in a way, still alive:

> The fact that Eastern Europe almost uninterruptedly formed a part of multinational Empires is no doubt the explanation for the weakness of the national states of which it is composed, which have not yet had the time to consolidate their allegiances and their own cultural traditions, as their populations are often ethnically mixed. It goes without saying that this does not apply to Greece, whose cultural traditions, as we have seen, are fundamental to the European spirit, whose medieval Empire of Byzantium, by its civilizing action, permitted the assimilation of the newcomers – in practice Slavs – into Christian Europe. The population of Greece, welded together by the lessons of thousands of years of history, has remained firmly united and at one over the essential fact of its Hellenic identity. Doubtless this is why the Greeks were the first to throw off the Ottoman yoke in 1821, so giving the signal for the emancipation of the other Balkan states. They captured the admiration of the Westerners – the 'Europeans' as they used to be called – who finally became conscious of the debt they owed to Greece, as the inspirational exploits of the war of the Hellenic liberation showed them the perennial nature of the spirit of Greece, birthplace and home of freedom.
>
> (Ahrweiler, 2000, pp. 67–8)

In this text Greece is constructed as a historical and cultural entity that existed uninterruptedly for 'thousands of years'. For all these years Greece preserved its distinct 'spirit', its 'Hellenic identity', and it was able to transmit it to others and to Europe, which, interestingly, tends to be identified with the West. The ethnic mixture that took place in the area has not influenced the cultural purity of the Greek people. This is exactly where the cultural superiority of Greece rests. Europe owes its gratitude to the Greek cultural legacy, which is recognized as fundamental for the construction of Europe as such. But what is even more important here is the interpretation of modern Greece. While nineteenth-century Romantic historiography was committed to the task of nation-building, twenty-first-century Eurocentrism continues to perceive nations as ahistorical, almost transcendental, eternal entities, which existed long before the establishment of modern states.

Antiquity in the Greek history curriculum

The Greek history curriculum is almost exclusively about 'Greece and Europe'. The devaluation of the present and the continuous reference to the noble past are some of the general characteristics of the history textbooks (Avdela, 1997). The perceptions of Greek antiquity presented in school knowledge are mediated through the image of Europe. Europe, which is basically identified with the West, is associated with the idea of cultural and scientific progress. Greek antiquity, on the other hand, is presented as an ideal civilization, the supremacy of which is presumed from the fact that Europe recognizes in it its own cultural roots. Consequently, the fact that Greece is constructed as part of Europe is another route leading, once again, to ancient Greece (Frangoudaki, 1997b).

However, the construction of the historical continuity of the Greek nation on the basis of its uninterrupted existence from antiquity to present times has serious political implications. The construction of the cultural superiority of Greek identity is accompanied by the ideology of its strength and sustainability and the fear for its fragility. This construct prepares the ground for racism and xenophobia (Frangoudaki, 1997a).

Greek children, however, do not learn at school that ancient Greek civilization does not have roots in earlier civilizations. But, of course, this aspect of the curriculum is not the central one. Definitely, the Greek history curriculum is ethnocentric and does not present any sort of cosmopolitanism. The history textbook taught in the first grade of Gymnasium (lower secondary education and part of compulsory education) starts the historical account from the Stone Age by making references to findings in North and Central Europe, Greece and Mesopotamia. The next chapter refers to the 'People of the East':

The first great civilisations in the history of humanity originated and developed in the area of the eastern Mediterranean Sea, in Egypt and Mesopotamia in particular. . . . The people that lived in these areas of the eastern Mediterranean Sea, like the Egyptians, people of Mesopotamia, Phoenicians, Hebrews, Medes, Persians, are well known in history under the general title 'People of the East'. The ancient Greeks took many cultural elements from them, in the beginning of the creation of their great civilisation. Of course, in ancient times notable civilisations have been developed also in other parts of the globe, as for example in China and India. Those civilisations, however, remained isolated and became well known in modern times mainly.

(Tsaktsira and Tiveriou, 1999, p. 15)

Though the contribution of earlier civilizations is acknowledged, the reference to them takes 20 out of 300 pages of the whole book. Practically, this is the only direct systematic reference to civilizations earlier than those in Greece that is made within the nine years of Greek compulsory schooling. The 'People of the East', as they are called, are presented as having remarkable cultural and scientific achievements. For example, it is acknowledged that medicine was well developed in Egypt and the Egyptians were able to perform very difficult and sensitive operations (Tsaktsira and Tiveriou, 1999, p. 23). It is noted, however, that those achievements were mainly the outcome of 'practical needs' (p. 30), while the achievements of Greek civilization are usually associated with pure intellectual inquiry and not with the 'technicalities' of everyday life. After this brief and selective presentation of the ancient civilizations of Egypt and the Middle East, the book moves to Bronze Age Greece. But before actually doing so, there is one page showing the map of Greece, which is titled 'The metropolitan Greek space'. The small text that follows under the map refers to the description of the geophysical structure of the land and the climate that allowed the Greeks to turn to the sea:

The centre of the ancient Greek world was the space that surrounds the Aegean. . . . The shape of the coasts and the many islands have facilitated the development of navigation, which had as a consequence the Greeks turning to the sea.

(Tsaktsira and Tiveriou, 1999, p. 37)

This page is followed by the presentation of the Cycladic, Cretan (Minoan according to the book) and Mycenean civilizations. The book does not literally identify the civilizations that flourished in Bronze Age Greece as being Greek. But the impression that it gives to the students is that they were Greek, since 'we have already started discussing the Greeks and their "metropolitan" space'. In the text, however, it is clear that at least the Cycladics and the Cretans were not Greeks. They are identified as 'people of the Mediterranean Sea'. When the book refers to the Cretans it raises the issue of 'race': 'The Minoans belong to the so-called Mediterranean race. They were of medium height, slim and dark-skinned' (Tsaktsira and Tiveriou, 1999, p. 47). It is also mentioned that there were relationships between these civilizations and Egypt and the Middle East. It is implied, however, that even if there has been cultural exchange in the area there was no imitation. These civilizations were not just a cultural transfer but a creative cultural innovation:

> There is no area of Art where the Minoans have not put their own touch. Perhaps the Art of their neighbouring civilisations many times has influenced them. But they have never made an exact imitation of foreign creations. Their pieces of art are distinct for their originality.
>
> (p. 53)

In the case of the Mycenean civilization, the book adopts the view that it was 'the first great Greek civilisation' (p. 70). The only cultural transfer from the East that is acknowledged is that of the Phoenician alphabet that took place within the Geometric period (p. 84).

At the level of the Lyceum (the post-compulsory upper secondary education), there is a limited reference to the ancient civilizations before Greece. A relatively detailed reference, in comparison to earlier books, is made in the latest history textbook, which was introduced in 2000 and is taught in the first grade of the Lyceum. This book devotes 52 out of 291 pages to the ancient civilizations of the near East, something that had been omitted in the textbooks of the late 1990s. It also devotes 14 pages to India and China, civilizations that were not even mentioned in earlier Greek textbooks. Nevertheless, in school practice, the civilizations earlier than that of Greece are examined only briefly according to the Ministry of Education's guidelines regarding the implementation of the national curriculum. Although this book is much less hellenocentric than the one it replaced, it focuses on ancient Greece and places particular emphasis on the importance of the cultural legacy of Greece for the rest of Europe. In this book the civilizations of the Aegean are examined as part of Greek antiquity. The fifth and fourth centuries BC are considered as 'the epoch in which the values that consist the foundations of western civilisation were formed' (Mastrapa, 2000, p. 98).

A reference to the legacy of civilizations other than the Greek is made in a book titled *History of Science and Technology* (Arambatzis *et al.*, 1999), which devotes the first chapter to the contribution of ancient Egypt and Mesopotamia to mathematics and astronomy. This book is not part of the history curriculum. Its authors work on science, mathematics and epistemology. This textbook, however, makes interesting remarks regarding antiquity that are hardly mentioned in the history textbooks:

> The Egyptian civilisation, along with the Mesopotamian civilisation, was one of the most ancient civilisations and developed five thousand years ago. . . . It seems that it was one of the most peaceful civilisations. . . . From Greek history we know that in ancient Greece warfare was a rather usual phenomenon. Exactly the opposite was the case in Egypt. Neugebauer writes on this: 'Among the ancient civilisations the most pleasant was the Egyptian. . . . Maybe there is no other country in antiquity that preserved for such a long time such a peaceful and secure civilized life.
>
> (Arambatzis *et al.*, 1999, pp. 23–4)

Although it cannot be argued that this book follows a non-Eurocentric approach, since it refers to the history of European and American science, it makes a brief reference also to the contribution of the Arabs and Islamic culture. The reference to Greek antiquity is very detailed, while ancient Greece is constantly present, either as a positive contribution on which later scientific theories are based, or as a theory that is to be revised. In both cases it is presented as a contribution of central importance to scientific progress.

A more confusing account of the Bronze Age civilizations is given in a textbook that is intended to be an in-depth analysis of ancient Greece. The book titled *Social and Political Organisation in Ancient Greece* (Gryntakis *et al.*, 1999) presents Greek history as a continuum that starts from Crete and passes through Mycenae to classical Greece. This book uses the terms 'CretoMycenean Society' and 'post-Mycenean societies' (Gryntakis *et al.*, 1999, pp. 11–17). In doing so it constructs a distinction on the basis of social structures and refuses to make even a single reference to the fact that Crete had a totally different culture in terms of language, alphabet, art or religion. Nevertheless, the issue of culture and identity is raised later when the authors refer to Alexander. 'The kingdom of Macedonia under Alexander the Great will take the limits of hellenism and of Greek civilisation to the depths of Asia' (Gryntakis *et al.*, 1999, p. 143).

The most extreme example of traditionalist, ethnocentric school knowledge is that expressed in the book titled *The Cultural Legacy of Hellenism. From Antiquity to Renaissance* (Asemomytis *et al.*, 1999). This book, which was an idiosyncratic restoration of tradition and Romantic historiography, was withdrawn in 2000 after having received severe criticism on the part of the country's educational and academic community. It started with a chapter titled 'The Indo-European Origins of the Greeks' (pp. 8–16):

The Greeks belong to the big Indo-European family, which means to a group of peoples spread from Europe to India, who were speaking the same language in the beginning. The Greeks ... developed a close relationship with the flourishing Aegean civilisations. .... They assimilated many elements of the Cycladic and Minoan civilisations and, in this way, gradually, a new civilisation was developed that was purely Greek.

(Asemomytis *et al.*, 1999, p. 8)

The above text constructs the idea of cultural purity in terms of race. The race is characterized as being a 'family', a conceptualization that develops connotations of blood bonds and domesticity. The clear and distinct biological origin is the common background that allows the Greeks to preserve their cultural purity even when they develop close relationships with others (see also Konstandinidou, 2000). The outcome will be a civilization 'purely Greek'. The fact of the mixture of populations and cultural transfer is underlined in order to be deconstructed. The mixture simply 'does not matter'. On the other hand it is argued that, even in the cases where 'the Greek element was in a minority, it always made a remarkable contribution in the economic and intellectual life' (Asemomytis *et al.*, 1999).

The demonstration of the importance of the dissemination of Greek culture to the world is the main concern of this book. The anxiety for the recognition of the cultural legacy of Greece leads the authors to extreme and politically dangerous formulations regarding 'the people chosen by God'. The following quotation refers to the situation that, according to the book, resulted from the occupation of Jerusalem by the Romans in 70 AD:

After the catastrophe of the Temple the Jewish people lost their spiritual centre and their religious and historical reference. ... On the other hand, the Hellenized Christian part of the Jews, as well as the Christians of other ethnicities who converted into Christianity through the Greek language, started formulating the idea that, after the fall of Israel, the members of the Church of Christ constituted '*the people chosen by God*' [*sic*, their emphasis]. Hellenism then, alone, became the spearhead of the Christian onset and it (Hellenism), with its ideological arming and synthetic potential, will manifest the Christian universality.

(Asemomytis *et al.*, 1999, p. 201)

The above assumptions are not only historical fiction, or what Coulby (2000a) calls 'lies and nonsense' in school curricula. They also adopt a dangerous Hellenocentric and racist view of history. Moreover, the reference to Christianity throughout the book presents a peculiar denominational type of historiography which does not distinguish historical facts from dogmatic issues, while at the same time taking for granted the 'universal' acceptance of the Christian religion. On the other hand, this history textbook expresses a sort of restoration of the nineteenth-century Greek Romantic historiography, which invented the Greekness of Byzantium. In order to construct the concept of Greek cultural legacy for the world and for Europe the book needs to restore Byzantium. So this legacy is defined as 'Greek-Christian', a fact which implies that the cultural contribution of the Greek people to Europe and the world is not confined only to the achievement of classical Greece, but also to the adoption and preservation of Christianity (Zambeta, 2000c). This formulation does not differ at all from the influence that Paparigopoulos had on late nineteenth-century historiography and was expressed in the history textbooks of that period (Koulouri, 1988).

The above conceptualization of the relationship between 'Hellenic' identity and Christianity as well as the continuity between ancient Greece and Byzantium is the hard core of Paparigopoulos' historical thesis. He argues that Christianity has been preserved and disseminated to the world through the Greek language:

> The Greek language has been the most direct means of interpretation and dissemination of Christianity. It could not have been otherwise. The Greek language was the language of commercial exchanges throughout the Roman state.... Everything had been prepared in order for the Holy Spirit to speak through the Greek language.
>
> (Paparigopoulos, 1955, volume B, p. 363)

Moreover, he claims that Christianity was more widely disseminated in places where the Greeks were prosperous, while as a form of political organization it borrowed elements from the political institutions that emerged in ancient Greece (the type of participatory democracy):

> The political organisation of Christianity is a fact of major importance in the history of the Greek nation. ... Whilst the religious typology comes from Judaism, the political typology comes ... from ancient Greek life. The Churches (ecclesia) of the Christians ... come from the ancient Greek assembly of the city (people ecclesia). ... These institutions were prospering in the East, rather than in the mainland of Greece. The fact that proves the extent to which the fate of Christian Hellenism has depended on the fate of the nation, is that in the places where the national institutions were prospering, which means in the East, the Christian institutions were prospering also.

> ... In the lands of eastern Hellenism the mystery of metempsychosis
> of Hellenism from the ancient to the modern life was taking place
> more vividly.
>
> (Paparigopoulos, 1955, pp. 370–1)

The anxiety to fabricate the continuity, distinctiveness and exclusive
legacy of Hellenic identity is indicative of a racial interpretation of
culture and history. Paparigopoulos himself refers directly to the issue
of race. The following citation is indicative of his views on race:

> The first inhabitants of Greece, and of the rest of Europe, originated
> from Asia, which is considered as the common origin of humankind,
> due to its most ancient civilisation. ... Humankind is subdivided
> into three or five major races, according to certain essential differ-
> ences in colour and in general appearance. Among these races, the
> Caucasian race comes first, not only due to its beauty, but also
> because all the nations that have achieved great things in human
> history belong to this race.
>
> (Paparigopoulos, 1955, volume A, p. 50)

Paparigopoulos' perceptions regarding the legacy of ancient Greece are
in tandem with his views regarding race. When he discusses the possible
relations between ancient Greece and the Phoenicians and Egyptians
his anxiety regarding 'racial' purity and superiority becomes explicit. In
doing so he refers to several German and English historians. In this
particular case he finds the arguments of George Grote particularly
convincing:

> some researchers accept that there have been colonisers in Greece
> coming from Asia or Egypt. ... George Grote ... considers these
> views as lacking historical validity. ... It is possible, however, that
> Phoenicians and Egyptians were installed in Greece and it is quite
> possible that the Greeks have taken some elements of their civilisa-
> tion from those overseas people. But the important thing is to what
> extent Greeks can be considered as being either descendants of
> these colonisers or to have borrowed their entire civilisation from
> these peoples. George Grote rejects this argument, justifiably to our
> account. If, he says, we compare the character and the nature of the
> Greeks to those of the Egyptians and the Phoenicians it is evident
> that there is no analogy between them. ... But, above all, he
> exclaims, it is impossible for us to accept that the Greek language,
> the most noble of all human languages, which has symmetry and
> harmony, has emerged from the contribution of two external
> barbarian languages, the Phoenician and the Egyptian.
>
> (Paparigopoulos, 1955, pp. 53–4)

In sharp contrast to the Asemomytis *et al.* textbook is the one titled *European Civilisation and its Roots* (Liakos *et al.*, 1998). This book is offered as an additional, optional course of the history curriculum in the first grade of the Lyceum. The students that choose this optional course, however, have to take also the compulsory history course and textbook, which till the year 2000 was the one on *The Cultural Legacy of Hellenism* (Asemomytis *et al.*, 1999). In practice, the authors of the book on Europe deconstruct the argument the compulsory book tried to establish. For example, it is argued that 'Modern Europeans discover in ancient Greece elements by which they elaborate an ideal image and they attempt to resemble this image. ... Admiration, of course, is not the best way to understand Greek antiquity' (Liakos *et al.*, 1998). One of the fundamental issues dealt with is the conceptualization of Europe and the demythologization of stereotypic knowledge and xenophobia:

> People tend to perceive reality not as this actually is, but as they think or imagine that it is, according to their limited experience. Consequently, this imaginary reality becomes so powerful that people act by being based on that. This is what happens in the case of identification of Europe with western Christianity. It was a fantasy that led to stereotypes that have lasted for centuries, limiting European citizenship exclusively to the inhabitants of western Europe. However, what we should keep in mind for this period is the following: the presence of the Turkish threat created a very deep rupture within Europe and the inhabitants of western Europe were rallied round the concepts of (western) Christianity and Europe, concepts that in their mind became identical.
>
> (Liakos *et al.*, 1998, pp. 31–2)

One of the discussion questions for the students was: 'Across time who were the "others" that have critically contributed to the construction of European identity?' (Liakos *et al.*, 1998, p. 32). Unfortunately only a marginal number of students have the opportunity to read this textbook. Given the intensive character of Greek education at the level of the Lyceum, very few students take an additional course in history as an option.

School knowledge is not coherent. It is contradictory. As has been argued, traditionalism, modernity and postmodernity are political forces in conflict in European curricular systems (Coulby, 2000a). This is certainly the case for Greek education. In fact, the conflict as well as the symbiotic relationship between tradition and modernity is a constant characteristic of modern Greek society that is projected also on education (Zambeta, 2000b). School knowledge offers an illuminating example of that. In 2000, in Greek education for instance, in the first grade of the Lyceum, school knowledge was clearly divided into two paradigms.

On the one hand, there was an extreme case of traditionalist, ethnocentric, Hellenocentric and racist knowledge (the textbook by Asemomytis *et al.*, 1999). On the other hand, there was a surprising example of critical knowledge that distanced itself from the traditional national narratives and prejudice (the textbook by Liakos *et al.*). Ironically these books both contained state-endorsed knowledge, since the Pedagogical Institute, the central institution which appoints the curricula and the textbooks, approved them both. To what extent then there is still space for an effective central control over school knowledge remains an open question. Knowledge is genuinely uncontrollable, despite anguished attempts for its control on the part of totalitarian regimes, school systems or agents for public opinion formation (such as opinion polls, mass media, cultural industries). In times of globalization, dissemination of information and communication technologies and increasing cultural fusion, knowledge becomes even harder to control. However, regarding the two conflicting paradigms of knowledge it should be noted that, at least in Greece, that of tradition and ethnocentricity is by far the most powerful one. Knowledge control has been a key strategy for nation-building in the past and continues to be one of the most contested areas for identity politics at present times.

Cracks in the mirror: and now, what will become of us without the barbarians?

Antiquity has been of central importance in building national identities. Present territorialities seek for legitimization in ancient legacies. The construction of the past in terms of the nation's continuity in time and space has been the concern of nineteenth-century historiography. It could be argued that Romantic historiography was an intellectual response to the process of nation-state formation and nineteenth-century nationalism. It seems though that the restoration of antiquity continues to be a strategy for nation-building, as the case of the post-communist Balkan states indicates. Ethnocentricity, selective memory and oblivion, competitive claimants of ancient legacies, reflect the aspirations of competitive nationalisms that are expressed in curricular systems. For example, in Albania the new history textbook refers also to the history and ancient past of places that are not part of the Albanian state, such as Kosovo, Macedonia and Thrace. This has been interpreted as strengthening the nationalist orientation of the new textbook (Vouri, 2000). In fact Kosovo, Macedonia, Thrace, the Aegean and Asia Minor can be the historical landscapes of many states' history textbooks. The question is to what extent this is to underline cultural richness and a perspec-tive of peaceful coexistence or whether it is a curricular construct that develops hostility, xenophobia and hatred or even prepares for war (Coulby and Jones,

2001). Despite the attempts at modernization, the Greek history curriculum reflects both continuity with the traditional formulations of Greek historiography on the one hand, and the conflicting process of change on the other. Nineteenth-century Greek historiography understood history as an epistemological and political project towards nation-building, which eliminates the possibility of alternative approaches to the past. The interpretation of the past through the political interests and goals of the present times, however, is a questionable method of doing history. The present Greek history curriculum cannot claim that it has abandoned the epistemological and political project of tradition.

As Davies notes, 'Distortion is a necessary characteristic of all sources of information' (1997, p. 5). Probably this is also true for any possible historiography. It is certainly true for state-endorsed knowledge and curricular systems, which attempt to narrate history through the nation-state's perspective. In the case of Greece, Eurocentrism and ethnocentricity form the national narrative. Europe is important for Greece. It is important in terms of both geopolitics and identity. The classicist interpretation of Europe, which places the origins of European civilization in Greece, implies the universality of the value of European cultural products and, in this respect, the cultural superiority of European civilization. The reference to Europe on the part of the Greek history curriculum, then, is another way to express and underline the cultural legacy of Greece to the world. It is not only the school curriculum that makes this Eurocentric and ethnocentric construct of Greece. The same is performed by the ideological discourse of conservative intellectuals, the Greek Orthodox Church or even reputable historians of our times.

It is worth wondering, though, why Europe needed Greece in the past. Why did Europe interpret Greece as the origin of European civilization? Was it the modernist construction of Europe that needed the roots of Europe to be in Europe and white? This is what Bernal would argue. Bernal places himself against the idea of progress, which argues that 'the later is better' (Bernal, 1987, p. 27). By raising the issue of originality of civilizations Bernal implies that the origin matters. The argument of origin, though, does not form any stable epistemological ground for fighting racism. Bernal is right at least on one point: that the systematic omission of acknowledgement leads to oblivion and prejudice. However, the rejection of historical oblivion and cultural arrogance should not lead to the devaluation of any new level of exegesis and synthesis. The Industrial Revolution would have been impossible without the wheel, but it is not of less value because it did not reinvent it. Any new social stage of civilization is the outcome of interaction and mediation among cultures. At the same time, any new social stage forms a new level of human enquiry, which in some cases revolutionizes social reflexivity and practice. The almost unavoidable fact that any civilization is based on previous human endeavour and knowledge should not lead to the devaluation of its particular character and distinct contribution. The question of whether the former or the latter stage of civilization is more valuable is an invalid question. In this respect the deconstruction of Greece in terms of originality should not be seen as an 'anti-Greek' thesis. In fact the idea of originality per se is a myth. There is no 'original' civilization in terms of cultural purity. Culture is always an osmotic process and the stranger is always within.

School knowledge, history in particular, identifies itself with the collective memory. This is an arbitrary abstraction. Perhaps historical plausibility and the dialogue between different knowledge paradigms could offer an alternative to the authoritarian imposition of memory (Avdela, 1998), which unavoidably leads to discrimination, racism and hatred. The example of the curricular construction of Greece is only one among the many paradigms of school knowledge worldwide that reflect a distorted image of the past. It is an important example though, because, for reasons alien to Greece as a country, it has been used as the canvas for building Western knowledge and self-consciousness. The globalization of the idealized image of Greece through Western knowledge systems is part of their inherently imperialistic nature.

Acknowledgement

The idea for this chapter emerged from discussion with David Coulby. An earlier version of it was presented at the Comparative Education Society in Europe Conference in Bologna, 2000 (Zambeta, 2000a).

References

Ahrweiler, H. (2000) *The Making of Europe*, Athens: Nea Synora.
Ahrweiler, H. and Aymard, M. (2003) *The Europeans*, Athens: Savvalas.
Arambatzis, T., Gavrolou, K., Dialektis, D. *et al.* (1999) *History of Science and Technology (Lyceum, Grade C)*. 2nd edn, Athens: Ministry of National Education and Religions, Publishing Organisation of School Textbooks.
Asemomytis, B., Gryntakis, G., Katsoulakis, St. *et al.* (1999) *The Cultural Legacy of Hellenism. From Antiquity to Renaissance (Lyceum, Grade A)*. 3rd edn, Athens: Ministry of National Education and Religions, Publishing Organisation of School Textbooks.
Avdela, E. (1997) *Time, History and Identity in Greek School*, Athens: Alexandria.
Avdela, E. (1998) *History and School*, Athens: Nissos.
Bernal, M. (1987) *Black Athena: The Afroasiatic Roots of Classical Civilisation. Volume 1: The Fabrication of Ancient Greece 1785–1985*, London: Vintage.
Coulby, D. (2000a) *Beyond The National Curriculum: Curricular Centralism and Cultural Diversity in Europe and the USA*, London and New York: Routledge-Falmer.

Coulby, D. (2000b) 'Greek civilisation as curricular construct: overview and an illustration from England', in *Comparative Education Society in Europe Conference: The Emergence of the 'Knowledge Society': From Clerici Vagantes to the Internet, Bologna*: Comparative Education Society in Europe.

Coulby, D. and Jones, C. (1995) *Postmodernity and European Education Systems: Centralist Knowledge and Cultural Diversity*, Stoke on Trent: Trentham.

Coulby, D. and Jones, C. (2001) *Education and Warfare in Europe*, Aldershot: Ashgate.

Davies, N. (1997) *Europe: A History*, London: Pimlico.

Dimaras, K. T. (1982) *Greek Romanticism*, Athens: Ermis.

Dimaras, K. T. (1983) *Modern Greek Enlightenment*, Athens: Ermis.

Frangoudaki, A. (1997a) '"Descendants" of Greeks "from the Mycenean era": analysis of history textbooks', in Dragonas, T. (ed.) *'What's Our Homeland?' Ethnocentricity in Education*, Athens: Alexandria, pp. 344–400.

Frangoudaki, A. (1997b) 'The political implications of the unhistorical presentation of the Greek nation', in Dragonas, T. (ed.) *'What's Our Homeland?' Ethnocentricity in Education*, Athens: Alexandria, pp. 143–98.

Gibbon, E. (2000) *The History of the Decline and Fall of the Roman Empire*, London: Penguin.

Goody, J. (1997) 'Early links between East and West', in *Synchrona Themata*, pp. 105–11.

Gryntakis, G., Dalkos, G. and Chortis, A. (1999) *Social and Political Organisation in Ancient Greece (Lyceum, Grade B, Theoretical Course)*. 2nd edn, Athens: Ministry of National Education and Religions, Publishing Organisation of School Textbooks.

Heffernan, M. (1998) *The Meaning of Europe: Geography and Geopolitics*, London: Arnold.

Kitromilides, P. (1997) '"Imagined Communities" and the origins of the national issue in the Balkans', in Veremis, T. (ed.) *National Identity and Nationalism in Modern Greece*, Athens: National Bank Educational Foundation, pp. 53–131.

Knox, T. (2003) 'The King's Library and its architectural genesis', in Sloan, K. (ed.) *Enlightenment: Discovering the World in the Eighteenth Century*, London: The British Museum, pp. 46–57.

Kokkinos, G. (2003) *Science, Ideology, Identity: The History Curriculum in the Constellation of Supranationalism and Globalisation*, Athens: Metechmio.

Koliopoulos, J. S. and Veremis, T. M. (2002) *Greece: The Modern Sequel. From 1831 to the Present*, London: Hurst & Company.

Konstandinidou, E. (2000) 'The changes in the Greek history textbooks: how effective are they in "improving" the image of the national other?', in A. Kapsalis, K. Bondidas and A. Sipitanou (eds) *The Image of the 'Other'/ Neighbour in the Balkan States History Textbooks*, Athens: Typothito-Dardanos, pp. 376–87.

Koulouri, C. (1988) *History and Geography in Greek Schools (1834–1914)*, Athens: Historical Record of Greek Youth, GSY.

Liakos, A., Gaganakis, K., Gazi, E. *et al.* (1998) *European Civilisation and its Roots (Lyceum, Grade A, optional)*, Athens: Ministry of National Education and Religions, Publishing Organisation of School Textbooks.

Mastrapa, A. (2000) *History of the Ancient World: From the Pre-historical Civilisations of the East till the Justinian Times (Lyceum, Grade A)*. 1st edn, Athens: Ministry of National Education and Religions, Publishing Organisation of School Textbooks.

Paparigopoulos, K. (1955) *History of the Greek Nation* (Introduction, comments and notes by N. Bees), vols A1, A2, B, C, D, E, F, Athens: Seferlis.

Pesmazoglou, S. (2003) 'The European matrix for the modern Greek rejection of "the Turk"', in SMGSGP (ed.) *Europe and Modern Hellenism*, Athens: Society of Modern Greek Studies and General Paideia, pp. 187–96.

Roberts, J. M. (1997) *The Penguin History of Europe*, London: Penguin.

Sella-Mazi, E. (1997) 'Bilingualism and less spoken languages in Greece', in Christopoulos, D. (ed.) *The Minority Phenomenon in Greece*, Athens: Kritiki, pp. 349–413.

Skopetea, E. (1992) *The Setting of the East. Images from the End of the Ottoman Empire*, Athens: Cnossi.

Skopetea, E. (1994) 'Balkan national histories', in SMGSGP (ed.) *Nation – State – Nationalism*, Athens: Moraitis School, pp. 305–17.

Skopetea, E. (1997) *Falmerayer: Tricks of the Awesome Adversary*, Athens: Themelio.

Sloan, K. (2004) *Enlightenment: Discovering the World in the Eighteenth Century*, London: The British Museum Press.

SMGSGP (2003) *Europe and Modern Hellenism*, Athens: Society of Modern Greek Studies and General Paideia.

Solomos, D. (1960) *Collected Works*, Athens: Galini.

Tsaktsira, M. and Tiveriou, M. (1999) *History of Ancient Times till 30 BC (Gymnasium, Grade A)*. 20th edn, Athens: Ministry of National Education and Religions, Publishing Organisation of School Textbooks.

Tsitselikis, K. (1999) *Languages, Alphabets and National Ideology in Greece and the Balkans*, Athens: Kritiki.

Valery, P. (2003) 'Characteristics of the European spirit', in Aymard, M. (ed.) *The Europeans*, Athens: Savvalas, pp. 59–67.

Veremis, T. (1983) 'State and nation in Greece: 1821–1912', in Tsaoussis, D. (ed.) *Hellenism and Greekness*, Athens: Estia, pp. 59–67.

Vouri, S. (2000) 'Antiquity as source of national trace in the Balkan history textbooks (1991–1996)', in A. Kapsalis, K. Bonidis and A. Sipitanou (eds) *The Image of the 'Other'/Neighbour in the Balkan States History Textbooks*, Athens: Typothito-Dardanos, pp. 101–15.

Zambeta, E. (2000a) 'The curricular construction of Greece: ethnocentrism and Eurocentrism', in *Comparative Education Society in Europe Conference: The Emergence of the 'Knowledge Society': From Clerici vagantes to the Internet*, Bologna: Comparative Education Society in Europe.

Zambeta, E. (2000b) 'Greece: the lack of modernity and educational transitions', in Jones, C. (ed.) *The World Yearbook of Education 2000: Education in Times of Transition*, London: Kogan Page, pp. 63–75.

Zambeta, E. (2000c) 'Religion and national identity in Greek education', *Intercultural Education*, 11: 145–55.

12 The global and the national

Inclusive knowledge and linguistic diversity

Jagdish Gundara

Globalization and exclusions

The pressures on nations during the post-colonial period have led to intense strains on many national governments. One of the problems has been the difficulty of holding together socially diverse polities not only in the post-colonial states but also in other parts of the world. Relevant knowledge systems and sound language policies can lead to social integration and strengthen the democratic legitimation of institutions and the national and international social order. This chapter suggests that, in educational terms, knowledge and language policies need to be reconsidered in most polities. This consideration ought to take place at national, regional and global levels.

One of the main problems confronting national integration is the way in which state systems are being disaggregated by the dual pressures of globalization and calls for autonomy or devolution. Part of the problem lies in the way in which the articulation of global visions is not democratic and certain societal features are excluded by the way in which globalization is currently constituted. The globalized satellite information and entertainment systems are not free or democratic and a rational appraisal of the role of diverse voices at national and local levels has not been worked out or planned in any region of the world. Reactive stances to Western media control, information and linguistic neo-colonialism are not adequate. For example, within the economic domain, since the transnationals, the World Bank and the International Monetary Fund (IMF) determine capital flows and devise structural adjustment programmes, they do not necessarily take cognisance of the significance of social markets or national sovereignties. Richard Falk suggests that they administer snake oil and have not rescued failing economies. The use of English as the main communicative language is not only a threat to various forms of local or regional English but to other commercial languages and linguistic systems generally. The issues therefore are of developing greater levels of consensus on language policies, which will avoid exclusion, and the negative reactions of various linguistic communities.

Likewise, knowledge systems based on other cultural and linguistic systems become subordinated to dominance by those who use the English language. The substantive exclusions of knowledge and languages cannot be labelled merely as an issue of political correctness. These issues need to be considered to redress substantive exclusions of the histories and knowledge of subordinated civilizations. In democratic polities such a redress presents the possibility of developing strong shared and common values within the public domain and institutions, which provides a basis for good governance.

It is not surprising that issues of political correctness and opposition to 'multiculturalism' have deep roots in conservative and reactionary academic circles in the USA. This is the case because economic liberalization entails a strict control of dominant group knowledge within academic institutions to provide a systematic institutional basis for global control. This American and European dominance of the globe was strengthened during the racialized and exclusionary phase of nineteenth-century colonialism and imperialism.

Discussions in certain circles (Waters, 1995) view globalization as a concept of the 1990s and see it as less controversial than postmodernism. While the term 'global' is 400 years old, 'globalization' began to be used in about 1960, and has been extensively used since the 1980s in academic discussions (Robertson, 1992). There are obvious ways in which economic and social processes are subject to fewer geographical constraints than in the past, largely through capitalist developments emanating from the USA, the European Union and Japan. As a result of these developments, nation-state structures governing diverse societies are increasingly under stress and at times have a limited role in controlling the impact of globalization. This stress has undermined the certitudes of the state-centric world. The neo-liberalization of economies has meant that many state systems have little control over the flows of capital and most of their efforts to control economies and societies are accomplished through coercion and violence towards their populations. As early as 1914, the social relations of production, the variety of what was produced and semi-autonomous ecological zones had been fractured into a massive tessellated pavement. This has led over the period of a century to the negation of a consensual view at the global scale of the community of states.

Most of the state systems in the southern hemisphere and east of the Elbe are peripheral or semi-peripheral to the dominant players (the European Union, Japan and the USA). Their political, economic and linguistic integration and development does not result from a democratic process of consultation and engagement, but is largely a result of dominant aggressive capitalist expansion. Corrupt and autocratic national regimes and elites exacerbate the situation for the masses of poorer citizens and minorities in such states.

Increasingly, marginalized societies are also more vulnerable to global forces of terrorism, lawlessness and crime. The more authoritarian the societies, the greater the likelihood that the forces of democratization are curbed as are those of the legitimate and diverse market forces. The economic crisis represents a crisis of ethical values in the economic domain, partly since there are few interculturally derived ethical values in the world of business. It also represents aspects of corruption in the wake of international capital flows that are autocratic not democratic and conspiratorial not transparent, as well as embodying low levels of accountability and therefore reflective of bad governance. The darker side of undemocratic economic globalization also entails a great deal of criminal activity, which nets $750 billion to $1 trillion a year. The technocratic global cannot be equated with the democratic global. In many cases there has been an increased divide between the information rich and the information poor.

Globalization as it has currently taken shape, largely through the massive control of technological, financial and natural resources, media and communications by transnationals is worrying for national governments. These monolingually operated transnational empires have few moorings or accountabilities. This massive harnessing of resources without any democratic mandate and largely relying on an increasingly monopolistic market is inimical to universal human needs. The negative features of globalization do not liberate humanity from the menace of war, nor do they provide access to global resources for equitable sharing and distribution. The monopolies of financial and technological resources remain intact and there are no political institutions at a world level which can provide 'social interests on a global scale' (Amin, 1997, p. 6). They therefore give rise to xenophobia, chauvinism and fundamentalism in many local and national contexts. The assumption being made here is that, unless globalization processes are undertaken within the democratic political realm, the alienations, inequalities and disadvantages felt by various groups, communities and nationalities as a result of purely economic liberalization will inevitably have negative consequences. In the absence of egalitarian goals to bring about equality and fraternity there can be no stability. The only agencies which have the legitimacy to undertake these processes are the national governments.

Current economic forces have led to 20 per cent of the world's peoples controlling 80 per cent of its resources and tensions at local levels in many parts of the world have been heightened. The expansion of capitalism in global terms cannot be seen as being conducive to development because it does not necessarily lead to full employment or greater levels of equality in the distribution of income. Instead, expansion is guided by the search for profits by corporations and the consequences of their activities for local communities are seldom an important consideration. Most transnationals pay lip-service to issues of equity, environment and ethics, but these accountabilities are not translated into action at national levels.

Instead of the current globalization imposed by capital, there is a need for processes which take the social, economic, cultural and political needs of peoples as their central focus. In the absence of such a complex process a disjuncture between globalization based on capital and localization based on xenophobia, communalism, chauvinism, fundamentalism and racism is likely to increase. This can be seen in many countries, which have become peripheralized because of the differentiation between the semi-industrialized third world and the de-industrialized fourth world.

In areas which have become peripheralized and have not become industrialized, there are vast pools of reserve armies of labour with no prospect of productive capacity or of migration (African Development Bank, 1995). As the project of nation-building and integration becomes remote for many of the socially diverse polities, the previous unifying tendencies turn sour. Forces become centrifugal and the state begins to disaggregate in many parts of the world: 'The political crisis is founded on this breakdown, on this disintegration of the state and the accompanying rise of ethnic movements and religious fundamentalism' (Amin, 1997, p. 60).

The disintegration of many countries is a living example of this process and ethnic renewals take the place of the previous forces of modernization and integrative nation-building. The unification of nations as diverse as India, Indonesia and the Philippines has been challenged and there is rising linguistic and religious fervour in many countries (Naipaul, 1998). In general the weaker and more peripheral the state the more vulnerable it is to global crisis and especially the negative aspects of market forces. Globalization as it currently operates, therefore, is not based on rational or equitable principles and nor does it have a universalist character. Therein lies the real challenge of how to bring about inclusive global forces, which will lead to the universalization of equitable relations at an international level.

While there are no frontiers for the transfer of capital, there is obviously no such freedom for the migration of labour, so that labour can follow the flows of capital. The vulnerability of the three million or so South Asian migrant workers in the East Asian tiger economies and the rough treatment meted out to Indonesian refugees in Malaysia by the Malaysian Government are typical consequences. The fall of the Suharto regime in Indonesia resulted from the combination of the IMF's enforced economic medicine and the garnering of vast national resources by one corrupt and autocratic family. Even under the new government, the Chinese or the Ambon as minorities have been scapegoated for Indonesia's problems. What is missing in current regional relations are ways in which collective regional bodies can consolidate the needs of diverse groups in different regions. These needs are not just economic but also for greater democratization, the protection of rights and progressive social policies.

One important issue is how to reconfigure international relations to ensure that disaggregative tendencies of religious, linguistic, territorial and other diversities do not pull apart societies which have previously held together. At one level this poses a political and ideological issue, and at another level calls for the implementation of public and social policy measures to assist in reshaping diversity into unity. To turn diversity into unity can only work if democratic forces can prophylactically plan towards unity. As Amin states:

> Bourgeois revolution is not a viable solution because it does not permit these societies to go beyond the boundaries of peripheral capitalism, while socialist revolution is not the order of the day, because the local social forces do not have sufficient maturity.
>
> (Amin, 1997, p. 78)

It is the contention of this chapter that liberalization of economic forces and economic globalization has paradoxically led to greater control of the knowledge systems which form the 'canon' within dominant educational institutions. This necessitates the revisiting of the modern project to strengthen inter-subjectivity in terms of the knowledge used within educational institutions. The solution demands the political wisdom to strengthen and develop modern constitutional nations based on equality, fraternity and liberty. This presents a major challenge to education system and schools (Axtman, 1998; King, 1998). Developing inclusive knowledge systems and optimum bilingual and multilingual policies (which differ according to contexts) should be used to enhance the process of developing inclusive polities.

Many of the civic movements attempting to create democratic governance need to use the global informational systems in order to develop their capacities to establish more cooperative mechanisms for democratic and sustainable development. This version of the 'global village' in participative terms, however, currently remains in its infancy.

The nation state under duress

The political map of the world consists largely of sovereign nation-states and is an aspect of the way in which the political organization of the world is globalized. This political globalization is reflected in the way in which a broad range of public and social policies are the responsibility of the state through constitutions and legislation.

At the international level most of the states are connected with each other through intergovernmental organizations (IGOs). There are about

300 global IGOs and more than a thousand regional or sub-regional IGOs. While the United Nations' system of organizations largely forms the world's political forum, the World Trade Organisation, the World Bank and the IMF manage the economic infrastructure. Nevertheless, within this IGO system there are markedly different power relationships.

There is a continuing tension between the legitimacy of the United Nations-based state system and the assertion by others that state institutions and boundaries are irrelevant. As the general welfare of citizens becomes eroded through increased global economic power there is increased unemployment and poverty. These are leading to the state systems becoming destabilized. Citizens' and workers' rights have become increasingly eroded as the transnational corporations, through free trade and capital flows, erode wages. The consequent erosion of the ability of the state to make social provision is one aspect of the liberalized economies. There is at the present time little balance between the power of the global and liberal economic forces and the role of the state to regulate its internal public and social policy provision.

Many multilingual polities have not been able to support the diverse languages of the old or new linguistic minorities. As national languages and cultures come under threat and face uncertainty from commodified global cultural factories there is an attempt to undermine the 'other' languages within the state. This largely happen to languages and cultures of racialized groups. Racism and neo-fascist violence has led to ethnic cleansing in countries as far apart as Rwanda and southeast Europe. Languages, cultures and ethnicities have been obliterated by this globalized racism, which is perpetrated within nation-state contexts. Minorities within national boundaries have been increasingly ethicized and racialized and accused of being the cause of crisis confronted by the nation. These multiple forms of exclusion through racism take place in national contexts and undermine the human and citizenship rights of groups.

During this period of globalization it is increasingly difficult to reconcile notions of nationality and citizenship. Those who are minorities and are poor are excluded in terms of being both a national as well as a citizen. These issues can only be reversed if the social contracts at the level of the state can be globalized to maximize the gains, which accrued from social democracy's labour movement struggles so that a transnational and global ethos can be actualized.

Linguistic diversity

At the national and the global level the issue of linguistic diversity needs to be seen in the context of the other kinds of diversity which can be identified in human societies: ethnic diversity, religious, social class and territorial diversity. In different geographical and political environments these get formulated in different ways, depending on the decisions made by national, regional or local authorities. An understanding of these different kinds of diversity is important to an understanding of most societies, both in historical and in contemporary terms (Gundara, 1982). These diversities, however, are not mutually exclusive. There are considerable overlaps. As a consequence it is not possible to consider one kind of diversity – linguistic diversity – without touching on other kinds of diversity. Inevitably then, in addition to linguistic issues, social and economic matters impinge on language teaching.

At policy formulation levels, governments in different countries respond differently to linguistic diversity. In many countries a privileged position is given to autochthonous languages, which are considered indigenous, and a lower status to allochthonous, or non-indigenous, languages. This creates an arbitrary division between such languages. Such a division in the European context not only divides the languages from each other but is inimical to the development of cohesive language policies and practices in schools. At the European level such a stance could reinforce notions of 'Fortress Europe' as a 'linguistic fortress', with a greater importance being attached to major European languages. This is particularly true for the elite personnel in the European Union being trained in the official European languages both for the public and private sector, while the less powerful European languages and non-European languages are relegated to the margins (Sögren, 1997). The British Government's antipathy to other languages was reflected in the two schedules of languages proposed for the National Curriculum. The subsequent reversal of this position did not substantively change the status of non-European languages in the curriculum.

Governments which favour integration, like the USA or France, do not accord full recognition to languages other than that of the majority community, while others like China and India recognize a number of languages. Hitherto, the saffronization of the Indian education system not only privileges the Hindi language but the primacy of knowledge about the Hindu majority. This can further exacerbate tendencies towards the fragmentation of India and it is to be hoped that, with the election of the Congress Party, the marginalization of the large Muslim community will be reversed. Other countries involved in nation-building may use only one national language, to minimize problems of disintegration. In terms of official educational policy, some governments favour bilingual education as a reflection of their acceptance of a pluralist society; others offer bilingual education in order to facilitate sending migrant workers back to their countries of origin. However, language policies, which are not based on consent of the linguistically subordinated groups, have great potential for national disintegration.

These various responses are indications of the power relations between the different linguistic groups in different societies. They also reflect the security or insecurity of different groups in a society. In the former Soviet Union, the pressure for centralization resulted in the teaching of Russian as the first language, while pressures for the teaching of languages of the nationalities remained. The collapse of the Soviet Union was partly the result of the way in which Russians dominated the languages and cultures of the other nationalities and republics after Stalin. It has led to a narrow nationalistic and linguistic reaction within a number of ex-Soviet and Baltic states.

In India, pressures on the one hand to learn Hindi as a national language, and on the other to maintain the local and regional 'link' languages, continue. This involves the issue of a balance between national integration on the one hand, while allowing for regional autonomy on the other. At the level of the elites in all sectors of national life, English retains a pre-eminent role. In eastern Africa, particularly Tanzania, the use of Swahili as a national language and a language of national integration is not based on economic considerations but more on political grounds. In the East African region, Swahili is increasingly becoming a lingua franca because it is not associated with the domination of any particular group. Similarly the turnabout of the British Government in September 1980, in granting Wales a television channel – in Welsh – was a result of political pressure. This has been followed by recognition of the Welsh language (Morris and Ghuman, 1995) in the National Curriculum for Wales and the setting up of the Welsh Language Board. As devolution develops, Scotland and Wales will increasingly turn to the Gaelic and Welsh languages in their respective legislative assemblies and other aspects of national life. Will this give a new lease of life to various forms of regional English in the various regions of England? Will such linguistic diversity enrich local lives and also create friendships between different linguistic communities?

In describing linguistic factors, it is important to start from a description of the particular speech communities and their communicative networks. In some parts of the world the linguistic issues are extremely complex. Each district in Micronesia has a different language. The Solomon Islands, with a population of 480,000 spread across 1,000 islands, has over 70 languages. In Papua New Guinea, two million people speak 700 languages. A country like Indonesia adopts a national language, which is not that of the majority population, while the Philippines has several major languages with a national status.

In sociolinguistic terms, a world language is one used over wide areas of the world, providing access to modern science, technology and economic life. A standardized language is used within a particular political unit like the state and is used to express a wide range of cultural, scientific, technological and economic notions within that unit. A local vernacular is both more regional in nature and has the character of a social dialect. If this typology is used of various types of languages, they should be looked on as a continuum so that no value judgements about their relative importance are made. At a global level demographic changes can lead to different languages becoming dominant. By 2050 it is estimated by some that Arabic, Hindi and Urdu will be spoken more widely than English.

Language planners in bilingual contexts try to make certain choices, relating to maintenance, shift or revival of a language. If a language has to be maintained, this requires that a value judgement be made, and a decision taken on whether that language is to be used to a limited extent or given equal value with the standard language. Similar decisions need to be made on reviving a language. French in Quebec (cut off as it is from France) has continued to be used in schools, colleges and universities and in all aspects of Quebec's life. Its role is different from that of Spanish in the USA, despite the demographic changes, where it is a minority language not largely used in public life. The Maori language in New Zealand was widely used in 1900 and more material was published in it than in English. Now, over a century later, it is used infrequently. However, with the infusion of Polynesian languages in New Zealand, there is a strong demand for the revival of the Maori language (Kennedy and Dewar, 1997). Similarly, the revival of Irish as a national language has increased with the rise of political nationalism.

In sociological terms, immigrants in Europe and the USA basically face assimilatory policies since their languages are accorded low status. In economic terms, bilingual programmes are expensive to implement. First, teachers need to be educated so that they can work with more than one language. Second, these programmes necessitate the availability of two sets of materials. Third, there are extra costs involved in language planning and language modernization. In some countries this is implemented by law. For instance, in the USA some projects have received funding from the Federal Government under the Bilingual Education Act. This Federal intervention, in turn, has made it necessary for state governments to allocate additional funds. In the recent past some states have negated the impact of this Act.

The major economic factor needing consideration is that, in the long term, some parents may see bilingual education as providing preparation for employment, while others may feel their children's job prospects are only improved if they are effective speakers and writers of standard English or the dominant language. In many European countries, stress on mother tongues is used to keep a reserve pool of low-paid migrant labour, which is taught more in mother tongues and less in the standard dominant language lest the 'migrant' group becomes more mobile. This also facilitates their return to their countries of origin. In Australia (Bianco, 1987), where the minorities do not feel as vulnerable as some migrants in certain European countries, the demand for and provision for 'community languages' is more firmly based in the school system and in teacher training. This is helped by large numbers of teachers and teacher trainers who come from countries which are bilingual and even trilingual.

Educational options and outcomes

The concept of mother tongue teaching or bilingual education may give rise to two linguistic programmes: it may involve *pure language mainte-nance*, and it may involve *development of the language*. The goals may vary: they may be transitional bilingualism, partial bilingualism (i.e. mono-literate bilingualism) or full bilingualism.

The education of children at primary school level may change dra-matically if their first languages and dialects are recognized by teachers and supported in school (Granville, 1996) and subsequently by the exam-ination system at the end of secondary school level. This would have a significant effect on their performance in reading, writing, the national language(s) and other subjects. In London there are at present few policies in place and insubstantial resources expended in this field and the linguistic wealth of the city is being depleted. Supplementary and other voluntary schemes continue to provide patchy support to bilin-gual learners. These have no consistent pattern of involvement with the schools. Since such classes are out of school time, they do not become part of the work in the school or the classroom. Unless these languages are used in school, they will not become an integral part of the cur-riculum. In London, again, local education authorities have produced 40 bilingual cards for newly arrived secondary school pupils (in Chinese, Spanish, Greek, Turkish, Bengali, Punjabi, Gujarati and Urdu). Also, the Smile Maths Project produced and translated versions of Smile Maths Cards (in Chinese, Turkish and Bengali). In general, however, issues of mother tongue in London have only received superficial attention given the potential presented by linguistic diversity. More positively, in many cases languages continue to be used socially by peer groups and form part of a network of intercultural friendships (Hewitt, 1986; Rampton, 1995).

These issues and the partial policy solutions mentioned indicate that progress in this field in London has been limited when compared to some of the work done, for instance, in Quebec. Studies there showed children who were totally functional in subject studies either in French or in English. The research established that, by the time children were in Grade 4, they had suffered no intellectual deficit or retardation. Children in Grades 2 and 3 were less ethnocentric and had a healthy self image as the self-concepts of children were not confused. Children also devel-oped a higher order of skills in reading and calculating, and had a fuller capacity for learning as a two-way concept (O'Brian *et al.*, 1986).

If bilingual education is implemented nationally, bilingual children benefit from this education, and there is no evidence of any disadvantages. In fact such children have advanced conceptual frames of reference. Problems arise only if social factors or issues of social adjustment are not taken into account. For instance, in Quebec, for long periods the French Canadians learnt English but the English did not learn French. However, now that the Québécois have changed attitudes most of the English children learn French without any obvious adverse effect psychologically or educationally. Quebec realities have to a great extent changed the low status that previously accrued to the French language. The Welsh language similarly faces issues of authenticating itself as having a public culture, associated with world literature or with the educational system. But, over a period of time, both the Welsh language in Britain and French in Canada will be accorded a status relative to the dominant language, which accords with their relative political and economic power.

In the UK, if the linguistic minorities remain relatively linguistically powerless and continue to occupy a low socio-economic status, their languages and culture will be ascribed a similarly low status. Among some first-generation immigrants, one commonly found a tendency to accept assimilationist aims for their children. Maintenance of their language and culture could then keep open opportunities for the second generation to learn the language formally, and this can be important where the second generation rejects parental acceptance of assimilationist tendencies and asserts a more positive identity. This is particularly the case as the younger generation realizes that assimilationist policies are superficial because widespread discrimination demonstrates continued segregation. The racial minorities in Britain have moved from a position where parents would regard the teaching of the mother tongue as a marginal activity. Problems of parent–child communication are obvious. These spill over into communication within families and with members of the family in the countries of origin. This generation, in a devolved Britain, also recognizes that, if the Welsh people can be both Welsh and British and the Scots both Scots and British, the logic of other minorities establishing dual identities is strengthened. Also, as power relationships change in the world, the low status of what were once languages and cultures of the Empire continues to change. This change involves the acceptance by popular British culture of its own changed position relative to its former colonies.

Issues of mother tongue use and bilingualism lead on to the wider question of bicultural or intercultural education. After all, languages cannot be taught without accepting their cultural basis. This raises curricular issues in subjects like history and social studies, areas which are dealt with more easily at primary school level but give rise to greater difficulties at secondary school level because of the inflexibility of the examination system. In many instances, religious instruction in Hebrew or Islamic instruction in Urdu or Arabic may also increase the demand for bilingual education.

Bilingual education and its success demand the use of relevant materials that are meaningful to all children. Imported materials do not always meet this criterion and the need for local variation calls for local initiatives. The issue of teacher education needs to be stressed again if balanced bilingual programmes are to be implemented. More use should be made of teachers from minority communities who are fluent in more than one language. Their skills can be updated through both initial and continuing education programmes.

Linguistic domination and conflict

Educational policies can optimize the advantages of linguistic diversity. If such policies are devised prophylactically they can take the sting out of the negative features attributed to subordinated languages by dominant linguistic groups. Most societies have an enormous potential for maximizing advantages of local, regional and national languages.

For much of the modern period, languages have been disappearing at a seemingly ever increasing rate. Colonization and modernization has resulted in the demise of a large number of languages. Even today, when many accept the importance of maintaining such languages, decisions have to be taken, on the grounds of cost if nothing else, to remove governmental support from those indigenous and tribal languages with only very small numbers of speakers and/or only adult users. All over the globe, small languages are disappearing, particularly if economically or politically powerless groups use them. At the same time, other languages are rapidly growing in terms of numbers of speakers, particularly Chinese and English, the latter mainly as a second language. This language loss is, of course, not new. Even the linguistic landscape of Europe, which to an extent escaped the linguistic power of European colonialism, is dotted with the memories of dead languages. Perhaps the most famous of these is Latin, but even countries so seemingly linguistically homogeneous as England have Cornish and Manx as dead or nearly dead languages. In many countries the pressures of modernization, national unity and integration lead to further pressures. Furthermore, the important role of an official Mandarin class, as in China, which used a common language with an ideographic script, provides a written unity in a nation of mutually unintelligible languages and dialects.

If language history shows that languages are constantly disappearing, it also shows that other languages are growing, both in terms of numbers of speakers and in terms of adequately dealing with the vast explosion of knowledge that has characterized the last few centuries. A key example of this is the way in which English dominates scientific

discourse: scientists who wish to be at the forefront of their area ha\
to have access to the scientific journals, some 80 per cent of which ai_
published in English. This linguistic domination raises the question
that, apart from reasons of sentimentality, why should languages that fail
to compete survive? Do not languages follow a path of social Darwinism,
leading to the survival of the fittest? Such questions seem harsh, but, as
many languages continue to decline in terms of the number of speakers,
such questions need to be addressed. As Pattanayak has written: 'Many
languages form a national mosaic. If some petals wither and fall off
or some chips are displaced from the mosaic, then the lotus and the
mosaic look ugly. With the death of languages, the country will be
poorer' (1987, p. 10). Such views are powerful and of a long-standing
nature and need increasingly to be accepted by state governments internationally. Furthermore, smaller linguistic communities whose languages are not in common usage in society are more likely to have their
human rights diminished.

Many states do not teach minority languages because they fear that it
will lead to demands for separation. In such cases the issue requires
national agreements and appropriate educational responses. The enormous resources or skills to teach other languages may also become
an impediment. In educational terms the following issues are worth
considering: (1) the avoidance of language loss as mentioned earlier;
(2) that the first language provides the child with the best medium to
learn at the early stages, and so literacy in the first language precedes
literacy in the second; (3) that the acquisition and development of the
first language assists in the successful acquisition of the second (dominant, national majority or link language) – hence, the first language
enhances and does not detract from learning the second language;
and (4) enhancement of belongingness to a group, its knowledge and
values in a school. The use of the first language is useful in developing
an inclusive ethos. It is more difficult to marginalize children with other
languages, cultures and histories from the school and its curriculum if
their languages and cultures are used in the school.

There is a continuum of bilingualism, from language loss at one end
to a more sustained learning of a second language and the curriculum
in that language. Language loss is reflected by transitional bilingualism
in many countries. The other response is shelter or maintenance programmes (akin to state languages in India). In some countries, many
schools use immersion programmes in which high-status language users
learn the alternative language, as well as the curriculum in this language.
In Canada, for example, dominant English-speaking children learn
French, as well as the curriculum in French. The Mauritian example of
using Creole, French and English as well as Hindustani presents another
model of multilingualism. In an understated way, multilingualism is

viewed as a national asset in literary, cultural, economic and national integration terms. A similar response is necessitated in Asian countries so that languages like Tamil in Sri Lanka or Urdu in India remain vibrant languages with dynamic literatures. Yet, they can be used for purposes of political mobilization. Linguistic assimilation may increase demands for national disintegration and separation, but enlightened linguistic policies can enhance national integration and not the reverse. For instance, an enlightened policy on the question of teaching Punjabi language may have obviated the Sikh/Hindu religious divide on linguistic grounds. In the Punjab even rural peasants and not just urban groups embody multiple identities, and schools need to validate these broader notions. At the inter-state level, Hindu and Sikh Punjabis in India also share cultural symbols with Punjabi speakers in Pakistan who are Muslims. With the opening up of the border between the two countries their regional linguistic and cultural affinities may help re-establish peace in the region.

In general, linguistic dominance prevails and is a major cause of ethnic tensions among groups whose languages are being excluded from the globalizing educational process. An international collation and replication of good practices could help in minimizing conflicts in some states. Examples of good educational practice from one context have relevance to others internationally.

References

African Development Bank (1995) *African Development Review: Special Issue on Africa and the Future*, Vol. 7. No. 2.

Amin, S. (1997) *Capitalism in the Age of Globalization*. London: Zed Press.

Axtman, R. (1998) *Globalization and Europe*. London: Pinter.

Bianco, J. (1987) *National Policy on Languages*. Canberra: Commonwealth Ministry of Education.

Granville, M. (1996) *Supporting Bilingual Learners in Schools*. Stoke-on-Trent: Trentham Books.

Gundara, J. S. (1982) 'Issues of Linguistic Diversity', in Russell, R. (ed.) *Urdu in Britain*. Karachi: Urdu Markaz, pp. 11–28.

Hewitt, R. (1986) *White Talk, Black Talk*. Cambridge: Cambridge University Press.

Kennedy, S. and Dewar, S. (1997) *Non-English Speaking Background Children: A Study of Programmes and Support of New Zealand Schools*. Wellington: Ministry of Education.

King, A. (ed.) (1998) *Culture Globalization and the World System*. London: Macmillan.

Morris, J. B. and Ghuman, P. S. (eds) (1995) *Bilingualism, Educational Identity*. Cardiff: University of Wales Press.

Naipaul, V. S. (1998) *Beyond Belief: Islamic Excursions among the Converted Peoples*. London: Little Brown.

O'Brian, K. G., Reitz, J. G. and Kuplowska, O. M. (1986) *Non-Official Languages: A Study of Canadian Multiculturalism*. Ottawa: Ministry of Multiculturalism.

Pattanayak, D. P. (1987) *Multiculturalism: Britain and India.* Occasional Paper No. 6. London: International Centre for Intercultural Studies, Institute of Education, University of London.

Rampton, B. (1995) *Crossing Language and Ethnicity Among Adolescents.* Harlow: Longmans.

Robertson, R. (1992) *Globalisation.* London: Sage.

Sögren, A. (ed.) (1997) *Language and Environment.* Botkyrka, Sweden: Multicultural Centre.

Waters, M. (1995) Globalisation, London: Routledge.

13 Negotiating nation

Globalization and knowing

Zane Ma Rhea and Terri Seddon

In education, and in much popular commentary, nationalism and globalization are often seen to be opposing forces. In the modern world,
education has been fundamental to nation-building and the construction
of national identity (Readings, 1996). In a globalizing world this construction of nation is challenged by global developments relayed through
economic, political, social and cultural processes. The reach and power
of transnational corporations, the growth of cross-national experience
through immigration, refugee movements and tourism, and the flow of
knowledge, global policies, commercial signage and media images all
feed the sense of nation under siege.

Yet to see this confrontation between nationalism and globalization as
a simple opposition is a mistake. It presumes that nations and their
nationalisms are coherent and established features of the social landscape
rather than recognizing their inherently contested character. It suggests
that contemporary globalism is a unique development that marks a
new era of human history, rather than one of many globalizing forces –
the spread of communism, the growth of capitalist market ideology, the
reach of the Catholic Church, the travelogue of Marco Polo, the global
endorsement to Greece as being the symbolic marker of civilized
knowing, government and beauty (see Chapters 10 and 11) – that have
challenged historically specific constructions of nation. And it implies
that the clash of nationalism and globalism has its most significant
impact in the impersonal world of the economy, politics and culture
when, in fact, its most significant impacts are felt in the spatial registers
that frame our everyday experience and ways of knowing.

In this chapter, rather than assuming an opposition between nationalism and globalism, we see their relationship more like grinding tectonic
plates disturbing and realigning identity. The construction of nation and
national identity is a political process that fabricates the institutional
arrangements and consolidates the horizons of our experience in ways
that shape understanding and collective action. These processes constitute distinctive, national, ways of living. Globalization shifts the horizons
of the everyday, opening our eyes not just to developments on the world

stage but also to features of the local that were previously obscured. It destabilizes loci of decision-making, shifting decisions and defining constituencies across spatial registers in ways that differentially empower or disempower individuals and groups in governance. It fuels a politic around the making of the Australian nation and the direction of its future development. If, as Benedict Anderson (1991) suggests, tales of Marco Polo's travels contributed to the formation of the imagined communities of modern nation-states, todays re-spatialization of experience creates the conditions for both the destabilization and reconstruction of established understandings and practices of nation and nationalism (Djelic and Quack, 2003).

Our particular focus in the chapter is on the grinding tectonic plates that have constituted, and are reconstituting, Australia as a nation and as a global actor within a turbulent world. Unlike other chapters in this book which have focused on old countries (Greece, Sweden, Japan) in the core of the globalizing world, Australia is seen (from a Western frame of reference) to be a young country (only 217 years old). Yet this focus allows us to problematize the crafting of Australia as a nation and to acknowledge the significance of education and the politics of knowledge in the metaphoric grinding between nationalism and globalization.

In telling this story, we recognize that Australia may be a 'nation born modern' (Pusey, 1992), but it is also a very old country with cultural continuities that reach back between 40,000 and 60,000 years. Like others (Tsolidis, 2001; Attwood, 1996), we also recognize that Indigenous Australians have become a critical flash point between these grinding tectonic plates. Indigenous Australians bear a disproportionate responsibility in providing Australia with its distinctive national identity (for example, in the synonymity of 'Australia' with 'Aboriginal art' and 'didgeridoos' and as was apparent at the opening ceremony at the Sydney Olympic Games) and are central to debates about the contemporary reconstruction of national institutional arrangements and citizenship. Yet, the challenge of continued Indigenous presence to a colonial settler history, and the more recent challenges brought to Australian identity by diverse immigrant populations that now settle in these lands, continues to problematize the fabrication of Australia.

Globalization encourages diversity and pluriculturality and is unsettling. It grates against an old White Australia longing for sameness, monoculturality and certainty. It also grates against an Aboriginal longing for a return to sovereignty and control, even as Australian Indigenous scholars join with Indigenous scholars from around the world to articulate a global Indigenous agenda (see, for example, Battiste and Henderson, 2000; Brady 1992; Williams and Stewart 1992; Bishop 1996; Kawagley and Barnhardt, 2001; Langton, 1998; Morgan, 2003; Rigney 1997; Nakata 1998; and Smith 1999). This grating globalization confronts nationalism not as an opposition but as a contested overlapping of horizons, ways of knowing, and their institutionalization as official knowledge practices.

These politics of knowing are fundamental to the politics of education. As Williams (1976) argues, education is the social institution that effects an inter-generational selection, organization and distribution of knowing. As localized processes of knowing become distanced from their local sources and are endorsed, authorised and credentialled as official ways of knowing, they become the official curriculum, the official history, the official way of knowing in that place. Such authorization remainders other ways of knowing and delegitimizes other knowers. This means that questions about who has the authority to define and authorize official knowledge, the veracity of Indigenous and 'Other' knowledge, and its place in education systems that struggle to address the limits of their monocultural past, have become fundamental issues. These questions underpin more familiar concerns about Indigenous education: How might Australia as a nation, under identity pressure from globalization, teach its Indigenous peoples? And how might it teach its settlers about Indigeneity and Indigenous knowledge?

We approach these issues by first considering the fabrication of Australia as an interplay between colonialism, nation-building and the positioning of Australia in a turbulent global world. We then consider three issues that are being thrown into particular relief by the grating relation between nationalism and globalization with respect to Indigenous presence in Australia. These are the issues of citizen status and practical reconciliation, Indigenous knowledge and its place in public education. We conclude by reaffirming our position that globalization today, like previous globalizing dynamics, shifts the spatial register of everyday experience and collective action, reconfigures the horizons of knowledge, and therefore fuels an active politics of knowing within specific locations with their established institutional arrangements. These processes challenge us all as citizens of a nation but they also create openings for building a better world than that of the past.

Fabricating Australia: the weft and warp of national identity

Recent archaeological evidence indicates that Indigenous Australians have lived on the island continent of Australia for at least 40,000, and possibly 60,000, years. Yet Australia is widely seen to be a young country; a new nation that has been formed within the experience provided by the modern market economy, industrial capitalism and colonialism. This representation of a 'youthful' Australia highlights commonly held cultural horizons (both in and beyond Australia) that are rooted in the history of British colonization and colonialism and yet continue to shape everyday experience. This colonial history sedimented particular institutional arrangements in Australia that have structured social action through regulatory arrangements and through the endorsement of particular normative and cultural frames.

The process of British colonization broke up the geographic space that is now Australia, beginning with convict settlements dispersed on the edges of the land mass. Eventually, these developed into six separate colonies (now States), which were, by the end of the eighteenth century, given a degree of administrative latitude because of the distance between the Colonial Office in London and the Colonial Governors in the separate Australian colonies. Each colony's natural and human resources shaped its economic and cultural character in different ways (Greenwood, 1974). For instance, the growth of manufacturing in the high-population States of New South Wales (pop. 5.5 million) and Victoria (pop. 4.1 million) contrasted with the continuing emphasis on primary production (agriculture, forestry, mining) in less densely populated Western Australia (pop. 1.5 million) and Queensland (pop. 2.6 million). In a parallel way, the challenges and cultural consequences of farming in the island colony of Tasmania, an area of 68,000 square kilometers located in the temperate Roaring Forties, are very different from those associated with agricultural production in Western Australia, which has an area of 2.5 million square kilometres stretching, in the southern latitudes, from a tropical 13° to a temperate 35°. Yet, on 1 January 1901, these rather different, albeit English-speaking, colonies federated, creating Australia as a Commonwealth of States (Crowley, 1980). At Federation, the self-governing colonies agreed to a division of powers in which the federal government was given responsibility for defence, trade and tariffs and immigration. All other responsibilities, including education, remained within State jurisdictions.

When Federation constituted Australia as a nation, it was conceptualized as 'nation' in the sense of the men with citizen rights belonging to the same white race (female suffrage was generalized in the early twentieth century). There are now newer meanings of nation in the global world, well-described by Anderson (1991, pp. 6–7) as 'a deep, horizontal comradeship'. Yet the extent to which Australian identity and polity has moved towards this newer meaning and the extent to which it remains faithful to the old is illustrated by a number of abiding historical legacies. For instance, the persistence of States as autonomous administrative entities means that the construction of a national narrative or national curriculum remains highly contested (Seddon, 2001). Britain retains sovereign power over Australia and the process of nation-building is cleaved by a politics that is manipulated by those who are unwilling to separate from Britain and become a Republic. Indigenous people are also concerned about the issue of what entity might hold administrative sway over the landmass called Australia. Most do not recognize the British claim and yet are wary of an Australian Republican movement whose vision of independence for Australia as a sovereign nation does not recognize pre-existing Aboriginal claims to land, water and resources. It is argued that there needs to be a treaty or negotiated settlement between Indigenous and non-Indigenous Australia before the shape of a new Republic might emerge (Dodson and Strelein 2001; Langton, 2001a).

The connection between geography and administrative separateness between the States that is central to colonization also institutionalized a fracture line between Indigenous Australians and the colonial settlers. Britain occupied and claimed the Australian landmass but did not acknowledge the existence of the Indigenous peoples who already lived there. As the separate colonies became States and moved towards Federation, Langton argues that 'the background to the apparently parliamentary manner of the [Federation] conventions was a world of violence – racist violence'. Unlike in New Zealand, where a treaty acknowledged the Maoris' former occupancy of the country, Australian Aborigines and Torres Strait Islanders were denied any existence under the legal convention of *Terra Nullis*. Australia was purportedly empty land into which the British introduced their culture, institutions and practices unimpeded. The history of White settlement is a history marked by the appropriation of land, water and resources and by government policies which sought to manage settlement and assimilate (some would say destroy) Indigenous cultures (Reynolds, 2000).

This history of British colonization, immigration and Indigenous dispossession produced distinctive relations between government and civil society. Settlement of the Australian landmass was contingent upon government activity and enterprise (Butlin *et al.*, 1982), but went hand in hand with a vigorous settler society which frequently resolved its own problems well beyond the reach of public authorities. One consequence of this social and political history has been the development of a participatory politics which has shaped Australia, as a nation and national identity, from the bottom up. Such grass-roots democratic politics, developing through the nineteenth and early twentieth centuries, has been described as an 'Australian Way' in institution-building (Smyth and Cass, 1998). Governments negotiated settlements that addressed divisions within the White population but which rested on the dispossession and denial of rights of Aboriginal and Torres Strait Islander people.

A potent example of this is the way that Commonwealth and State laws combined to effectively exclude Indigenous people from the emerging concencus on political rights. As Indigenous leader, M. Langton shows:

> the Constitution drafted in 1901 did not formally exclude Aboriginal and Torres Strait Islander people from either citizenship or the vote, [but] two sections did discriminate against Aborigines and establish

the conditions – and powers – for the States to deny Aborigines the
franchise among many other rights of citizenship.

(2001b, p. 8)

In 1967, a referendum was put to the non-Aboriginal voters of Australia that fundamentally changed the national response to Indigenous
issues within the nation. As Langton describes:

> The 1967 referendum changed two aspects of the Constitution. First,
> it amended the race power to allow the Commonwealth to pass laws
> for the Aboriginal people. Secondly, it deleted section 127 of the
> Constitution, which had stated that in taking the census, 'Aboriginal
> natives were not to be counted'. Few constitutional referendums
> have succeeded in Australia. Thirty years later, it is difficult for one
> to believe that the 1967 referendum was passed by almost 90 per cent
> of Australian voters, easily the highest 'yes' vote ever.
>
> (2001b, p. 8)

There is much to applaud in nineteenth- and twentieth-century
institution-building which consolidated what has been described as a
progressive 'workingman's welfare state' (Castles, 1988). This achievement was described as 'socialism without doctrine' (Metin, 1977),
because of the way it provided social protections for all citizens and
ensured social and economic resources to support citizenship (Davidson,
1997). This social protection was centred on the concept of the basic
wage – the wage which was sufficient to support a male breadwinner,
his wife and three children. Institutionalizing this basic wage through
a system of industrial awards (to protect working families), comple-
mented by tariff protection (to protect businesses from international
competition) and the White Australia policy (limiting the import of
cheap labour), provided security in terms of basic standards of living
for the working population and their dependants. It also encouraged a
commitment to full employment – a principle that was formalized after
1945 (Boreham *et al.*, 1999). This welfare safety net developed at a time
when 'the inclusive ethics of citizenship and social democracy' were
in the ascendant (Roe, 1998, p. 71). It provided a practical realization of
a 'fair go' for all, being structured around citizen entitlements that
'were universal in principal and selective in practice' (Roe, 1998, p. 75).
These entitlements were available to 'categories' of recipients (e.g. the
aged, infirm and unemployed) who were all equally entitled to take up
their benefits and encouraged to collectively pursue grievances or seek
redress for mistreatment. But it did not include women who were seen
to be dependent on male breadwinners and it was blind to non-citizens.
This institutional framework also excluded the majority of Indigenous
Australians who were not landholders, who were managed as a

dependent population of State wards through a system of State- or Church-administered reserves.

Education insitutions developed within this broad institution-building framework and duplicated its exclusion both of Indigenous Australians and their life worlds. This history meant that Indigenous cultures and languages were not recognized in the curriculum until the 1970s (Beresford, 2001). Such cultural exclusion also had an impact on Indigenous participation in education and training. For example, in 1996, 71 per cent of Indigenous secondary schoolchildren had dropped out of school before Year 12 (the final year of schooling), compared to 26 per cent of non-Indigenous students. In the same year, only 14 per cent of Indigenous Australians had a post-school qualification compared to 34 per cent of all Australians (NCVER, 1998). By 2001, levels of drop-out had fallen to 67 per cent, still unacceptably high.

Nationalism and globalization

Since the late 1960s, these institutional arrangements that fabricated Australia have been subject to increasing challenge. Destabilizing forces were mediated by external agencies such as global policies, transnational corporations, the media, markets and social movements in ways that challenged the established patterns of institutionalization, in relation to both structural and cultural frames of reference. They were also mediated by internal agencies in both dominant and fringe locations. As governments and other dominant voices engaged in energetic institutional redesign, more marginalized voices renegotiated the established and challenged frames as activists and agitators (Djelic and Quack, 2003). The upshot was not a simple confrontation between nationalism and globalization but an extended renegotiation of national institutional arrangements with flow-on effects in terms of the social action they constitute.

The oil shocks, then growing unemployment and the retreat from Keynesianism, were early signs of contemporary 'globalisation' (Sheil, 2001), but attitudes had begun to change before that. For instance, there were growing signs of social movement activism, bipartisan political moves away from the White Australia policy and the 1967 referendum which indicated popular support for the recognition of Indigenous Australians as citizens. By the 1980s, a more confident and cosmopolitan culture prevailed which was actively contesting the exclusions and silences in prior institution-building. Equality of access to opportunities for women, non-English-speaking background migrants and Indigenous people was advocated. But there was also growing policy convergence around an economic rationalist policy agenda that affirmed balanced budgets, privatization, deregulation, tax reform, reducing public services and the scope of the public sector (Marginson, 1993; Pusey, 1992). While governments of different political complexion varied in the extent to which they committed themselves to social justice and a social safety net, all governments have reoriented their work so that they increasingly 'govern through regulated choices made by discrete and autonomous actors' (Rose, 1996, p. 327).

As in earlier periods, the politics that have accompanied these developments have taken different forms. Public opinion suggests that there is an uncomfortable acquiescence to the remaking of Australian institutions and society. Yet Pusey's (2003) study of the impact of economic reform on 'middle Australia' indicates that middle Australians are uneasy about the changes that have been pursued on their behalf. For instance, while wealthy Australians are more positive than those on lower incomes, for many Australians economic reform has 'gone sour' (p. 170). Nine out of ten respondents (n = 400), across all income levels, identified the rich, big business and those close to government as the winners in economic reform, and people on low incomes as losers. In 2000, 86 per cent of respondents (n = 195) indicated that the income gap was too high or much too high. Given a choice between economic growth at any cost and a smaller gap between rich and poor, 70 per cent (across all income groups) opted for the latter. Pusey concludes that 'After twenty years of economic reform, middle Australia does not, on balance, accept the overriding priorities of reform and wants to conserve the hard-won institutional innovations of a successful past' (p. 173).

Formal political debate has been undercut as the major parties have converged around economic rationalist policies, reducing public language to what Watson (2003) describes as verbal 'sludge' that defies normal understanding. Yet there is an ebb and flow of counter positions and there has been a proliferation of minority parties. Pauline Hanson's (now marginalized) One Nation movement advocated re-regulatory economic nationalism and reactionary restrictions on social spending for those who were not 'White Australians'. Politicians from the Green Party and independent (non-aligned) politicians have raised issues such as the environment and a range of special interest concerns. They have been significant in both contesting and blocking legislation. Through such formal political processes and activism there is growing evidence of efforts to reconceptualize and re-imagine Australia as a nation. This re-imagining contests the old view of Australia as a White outpost in the Pacific or British branch office, and is moving towards a more cosmopolitan sense of Australia as a tolerant multicultural nation, a part of Asia, a Republic with an Australian head of state, and as a place where Indigenous and non-Indigenous people are reconciled. The governmental articulation of these cosmopolitan aspirations reached a high point under the Labour government led by Prime Minister Paul Keating (1990–6). The many gains made during this period have been systematically stymied under the subsequent Liberal–National Party Coalition (i.e. conservative) government led by Prime Minister John Howard (1996–present). The Howard government has been returned to office twice, suggesting that a substantial proportion of voting Australians want their government to shift the focus back to the majority at the expense of the Indigenous minority. They want the old White Australia back (Hage, 1998).

These cultural politics mark key struggles in the contemporary fabrication of Australia that is being played out across all levels of society. Alongside attempts to redefine the Australian nation within a conservative politics, the impacts of globalization continue to destabilize the structural and cultural framing of Australia and what it means to be Australian. In this space, there is evidence of an active politic aimed variously at remaking Australia in the image of the past or pressing forward towards an unknown future. The question of Indigenous existence is a lynchpin in these debates.

The reality of Indigenous existence in Australia foregrounds the turbulent, constantly shifting alignment and realignment between national and global identity formation. Within the national spatial register, sovereign Indigenous peoples have been coralled, administratively defined and controlled. Indigenous identity in the Australian national space has been twisted and bent to suit the colonial settler psyche. When mediated through global frames, such as a seemingly global organization like the United Nations, Indigenous Australians are considered alongside other Indigenous peoples who exist within nation-states and have struggled to defend their rights that pre-existed contemporary nation-building (Battiste and Henderson, 2000). This globalized space is able to be imagined as a global world free of nation-state curtailments and consequently offers relatively unfettered places, in comparison to nations, that can be generative for activism. The negotiation about the shape of existence of Indigenous Australians in global and national spaces, thus, becomes critical.

Negotiating Indigenous existence

The historical fabrication of Australia has disregarded and excluded Indigenous Australians. While this state of affairs was partially addressed by the 1967 referendum, the formal recognition of Indigenous citizenship has been treated, in practical terms, as an administrative addendum to existing institutional arrangements. Aboriginal and Torres Strait Islander people are recognized as categories in policy and in welfare provision, but only ambiguously as active citizens, land and knowledge owners, and as participants integral to processes of defining national institutions and national culture. The following three illustrations highlight these contemporary arguments about Indigenous existence and the way protagonists draw from different spatial registers in developing their positions. They give some feeling for the way the contemporary practices of nation in Australia, and the determination of authorised ways of knowing, are being contested in different political contexts.

Citizen status and practical reconciliation

Citizenship defines the 'we' of modern Australia. Historically this 'we' of citizenship was White: first, White English-speaking men, then White women, and later non-English-speaking migrants. The formal inclusion of Indigenous Australians under the administrative remit of the Commonwealth has not displaced this lived sense of who 'we' are in Australia. Prime Minister Paul Keating made this point in a landmark speech launching the International Year of Indigenous People in 1992. In this speech Keating publicly acknowledged the wrongs done to Indigenous Australians and the responsibility of non-Indigenous people in perpetrating these injustices. He went on:

> the starting point might be to recognise that the problem starts with us non-Aboriginal Australians. It begins, I think, with the act of recognition. Recognition that it was we who did the dispossessing. We took the traditional lands and smashed the traditional way of life. We brought the disasters. The alcohol. We committed the murders. We took the children from their mothers. We practised discrimination and exclusion. It was our ignorance and our prejudice. And our failure to imagine these things being done to us. With some noble exceptions, we failed to make the most basic human response and enter into their hearts and minds. We failed to ask – how would I feel if this were done to me? As a consequence, we failed to see that what we were doing degraded all of us.
>
> (Keating, 1992)

His challenge was for Australia to 'bring the dispossessed out of the shadows, to recognise that they are part of us, and that we cannot give Indigenous Australians up without giving up many of our own most deeply held values, much of our own identity – and our own humanity'. This, he said, was 'the fundamental test of our social goals and our national will: our ability to say to ourselves and the rest of the world that Australia is a first rate social democracy, that we are what we should be – truly the land of the fair go and the better chance'.

Subsequently, on taking office, Prime Minister John Howard stepped back from Keating's position and refused to apologize for the wrongs that non-Indigenous Australians had done to Indigenous Australians.

He also committed his government to 'practical reconciliation': to addressing practical issues of health, housing and education in Indigenous communities. At Corroboree 2000, which opened Reconciliation Week, Howard called on all Australians 'to honour the contribution' of Indigenous Australians to the life of the country; 'to honour the special character of their cultures'; to 'thank them for the generosity of their spirit'; and to 'recognise the richness that their cultures bring to modern Australian life' (Howard, 2000).

Where Keating affirmed Indigenous Australian's as part of the 'we' of modern Australia, Howard delineated 'them' and remaindered them as 'one of many cultures' that make up Australia and as a 'profoundly disadvantaged' group. 'Disadvantage', not citizen right, was the justification for policy action aimed at addressing this group's social disadvantage. Where Keating sought to construct an inclusive understanding of 'we' in Australia by building on the legal framework of citizenship, Howard indicated that his government would target funds to support health, education and housing initiatives for disadvantaged communities – funding that was, in any case, a citizen entitlement that 'every Australian should enjoy' (Dodson, 2000).

As Indigenous leader M. Dodson (2000) stressed in his speech at the same event, 'Reconciliation is about the blood and flesh of the lives we must lead together not the nuts and bolts of the entitlements as citizens we should all enjoy'. This reaffirmation of practical reconciliation alongside the continuing undercutting of land rights and denial of Indigenous activism highlights the historical failure of non-Indigenous Australia to acknowledge Indigenous Australians. It also shows that the continuing challenge of reconciliation goes beyond interpersonal or even cultural recognition to a reworking of legal and institutional frameworks with their inherent blindness to Indigenous Australians (Grattan, 2000). Dodson and Strelein (2001, p. 832) suggest that the problem with 'practical reconciliation' is that it 'seeks to address Indigenous peoples' place in Australian society within a liberal democratic model of unitary government and individual responsibility'. While this acknowledges the practical failures of institution-building, including the failure of the education system to attract Indigenous students and ensure their success, it does not accept Indigenous Australians as active citizens in the defining of modern Australia. Dodson and Strelein argue that practical reconciliation 'does not admit Indigenous peoples' autonomy to address these issues collectively [and] . . . it certainly does not admit an underlying constitutional issue' (2001, p. 833). Yet Pearson, other Indigenous leaders and welfare reformers have criticized the established welfare regime for its effect of inducing passivity among Indigenous welfare dependants. Their argument is that Indigenous communities (and others) have been damaged by becoming passive citizens and welfare receivers rather than being active citizens who can build their lives and communities within a real economy and exercise their legal rights to participate in the shaping of an inclusive Australia.

Institutionalizing Indigenous education

There are a number of settler states, like Australia, that have White majorities and which have historically deployed their authority over Indigenous peoples as part of their nation-building processes. Education has been an important conduit for ensuring Indigenous participation in such nation-building processes, even when this participation has ultimately undermined the full recognition of Indigenous rights within the nation-state. Currently, education is promoted by Australia's federal and State governments to educate Indigenous peoples in education systems that are predominantly based on a Western model. Within these systems, statistics and anecdotal evidence shows that schools are failing Indigenous students. Yet this institutionalization of education for Indigenous peoples is contested.

In Australia, there is significant difference between the terms 'Indigenous Studies' and 'Indigenous Education' that is central to federal government policy formulation and has been a central distinction for many years. Indigenous Studies has been developed as a field of study at school and university levels to research and teach about Indigenous issues in the broad arts curriculum, including law, sociology, anthropology, archaeology, philosophy, politics and psychology. By distinction, Indigenous education is framed by National Aboriginal and Torres Strait Islander Education Policy. Indigenous peoples' participation in the definition of good educational practice has also informed the development of professional development initiatives for teachers on issues relating to Indigenous education under this and other bodies, such as the Ministerial Council for Employment, Education, Training and Youth Affairs (MCEETYA) Taskforce on Indigenous Education.

Many aspects of Australian government policy formulation with regard to Indigenous peoples point to a role for education. For example, the Australian National Biodiversity Strategy affirms the need to integrate Indigenous and Western knowledges in school curricula to promote understanding and appreciation of Indigenous knowledges and cultures. Section 1.8.6 on Ethnobiological Education seeks to ensure that curricula at all levels in Australia promote an understanding of the importance of traditional knowledge and the social and economic benefits of ethnobiology. This will include:

- an understanding of Aboriginal and Torres Strait Islander practices that have been instrumental in shaping the biological resources of Australia; and

- an appreciation of the cultural heritage of biological knowledge in Aboriginal and Torres Strait Islander communities.

However, this integration poses many challenges because of the way Western-style education is seen to have failed Indigenous peoples. Teasdale and Ma Rhea (2000) argue that the hierarchical school system has promoted narrow, memorised forms of learning. Such learning places Indigenous learners in the position of being able to reproduce Western knowledge, but lacking the skills to critically analyse or test such knowledge. Similar observations have been made about European aid, development and colonization, where Western-based education systems have traditionally required Indigenous learners to know more about the geography, history and culture of the colonizing people, which tends to be regarded as 'better' than locally focused knowledge.

Rigney (2002) argues that these limitations in the institutionalization of education arise because Indigenous Australians have had limited jurisdiction over education programmes. By 'jurisdiction' he means 'the inherent right of Indigenous peoples' authority over their own affairs that was not given over at contact'. This situation has meant that 'Indigenous Australians have struggled hard to gain access and control over Indigenous education against state and national authorities'. Yet there is a growing global awareness of the need for protocols to protect Indigenous knowledges and provide legal frameworks to ensure just incorporation of Indigenous knowledges into Western-based education systems (see, for example, Langton, 1998 and Ma Rhea, 2002b).

Despite their complexity, a number of protocols are emerging around the use of traditional knowledge in Western science and technology education. One approach, of particular relevance to countries with both Indigenous and non-Indigenous communities, is premised upon the development of collaborative learning partnerships, like that developed to support curriculum development in science and technology education (Ma Rhea, 2002a). The basic framework for these partnerships establishes that:

- Indigenous and non-Indigenous knowledge can be taught together within a Western-based science and technology curriculum;
- both Indigenous and non-Indigenous collaborators have a clear understanding of their rights and responsibilities regarding the inclusion of traditional knowledge in the curriculum;
- the intellectual value of Indigenous peoples' knowledge is credited: teachers should convey to their students that Indigenous knowledge is as important as Western science;

- there is sound and accurate documentation of local knowledge, particularly traditional ecological knowledge, that has been verified by both knowledgeable Indigenous leaders and Western scientists;
- the traditional resource rights and intellectual property rights of the Indigenous collaborative partners are recognized, for example through a *sui generis* system.

Indigenous and local community leaders and teachers take equal responsibility in devising methodologies for curriculum development and teaching, and in shaping the partnership. Teachers may undergo a period of learning within the local or Indigenous community before being entrusted with traditional knowledge that could be taken back to the classroom.

These approaches rely on a formal agreement between the parties about their rights and responsibilities. They are commonly guided by global charters (such as the Draft Declaration on the Rights of Indigenous People) and implemented at a national level under *sui generis* protection. It might, for example, take the form of a Memorandum of Understanding between a government education department and an equivalent Indigenous body (for example, a Council of Elders education committee.) (See, for example, UNESCO, 2001 and Kawagley and Barnhardt, 2001.)

Yet such Indigenous/non-Indigenous collaborations are difficult to develop due to the diversity of Indigenous experience in Australia, limited agreement on what constitutes Indigenous knowledge and lack of understanding in relation to how Indigenous students learn (Craven and Mooney, 2000). Assessment of student performance and measures of teaching quality relevant to Indigenous education are also undeveloped. Yet many Indigenous students report that school tests do not accurately measure what they know and there are no recognized standards by which to measure whether a teacher has effectively taught an Indigenous student except correlationally through assessment results. These issues constitute an agenda for the future, for as Hesch (1999) comments in relation to Canada, we need to know whether Native people are being educated to fit into White society (in which case, do we want teachers to be better at doing this?) or whether they are being educated to be part of the nation but not the same as others (in which case, is school the best place for this to occur?).

Recognizing language, culture and Indigenous knowledge

Nation-state absorption and assimilation of Indigenous peoples' lands, waterways and resources, and assertion of ownership and control of their knowledge systems for commercial and national purposes, pose a great threat to the capacity of these peoples to sustain their social and economic systems and even, in some cases, to the continued existence of these groups. Langton and Ma Rhea (2003) observe in their Report on Article 8j for the Convention on Biological Diversity (CBD) that the tendency, in nation-state responses to Article 8j, to dismiss Indigenous knowledge systems as viable human ways of life in the expanding global economy is a threat to traditional knowledge systems. They argue that it is a threat that should be addressed in the future development of measures under the CBD to protect and retain biodiversity-related knowledge and natural resource management systems of Indigenous peoples and local communities.

Possibly the most significant incentive measure to support the promotion, protection and facilitation of use of traditional knowledges is nation-state recognition of the *sui generis* rights of traditional knowledge holders within the legislative framework of the nation. The term *sui generis* is a legal concept that means *unique* and frames the development of a custom-made national or local system of intellectual property. The recognition of *sui generis* rights enables the protection of intellectual property and traditional resource rights of particular Indigenous peoples in such a way as to give clear indication that the nation recognizes these rights.

Those involved in Western science and technology are beginning to recognize the value of traditional knowledge in terms of gaining an insight into managing ecological sustainability and resource biodiversity. For example, global policies endorse the integration of Indigenous knowledge within national education systems, arguing that such education provides a critical building block in fostering positive attitudes about human rights, equitable resource management and development, and the preservation of the Earth's biodiversity (Brundtland Report, 1988). In one sense, Indigenous peoples might welcome this interest as a chance to preserve their knowledge systems and secure acknowledgement of their rights under international legal protocols. On the other hand, many are suspicious of business people, scientists, teachers and government officers – whether foreign or local – trying to elicit their traditional ecological knowledge, for example, while refusing to recognize their fundamental human rights. As Morgan explains:

> rather than Indigenous scholarship being pursued through Indigenous methodologies in higher education institutions, it is still Western methodologies that are perpetuated. In many cases when Indigenous communities are researched and their knowledges recorded, the higher education institutions retain copyright or patents for the information gathered. The intellectual property from thousands of years of Indigenous scientific endeavour is not recognised, and the economic rewards are given to those who appropriate from and exploit Indigenous peoples. While the rhetoric espouses

accommodation within higher education institutions, the actuality often encompasses continued exploitation of Indigenous intellectual property.

(2003, p. 45)

Negotiating nation

This chapter has argued that nationalism and globalization are not in simple opposition to one another. Rather, like grinding tectonic plates, globalizing dynamics and the processes of building and positioning the nation rub up against each other in ways that destabilize and restabilize the structural and cultural frames that are sedimented in the fabrication of nation. Within this metaphoric grating, spaces open which not only accommodate dominant voices that support or contest change but also admit marginal and activist voices that seed and negotiate alternative futures.

These processes have been illustrated with reference to the systematic exclusion of Indigenous Australians in the fabrication of modern Australia and the way contemporary globalism facilitates the opening up of spaces for the assertion of preferred futures which rest upon a reconciliation of Indigenous and non-Indigenous Australians. What is fundamentally at stake in these politics is the character of Indigenous existence in Australia – as a passive presence, as formal citizens locked in dependency or as active citizens who mobilize their resources as they participate in the making of a reconciled Australia.

The nature of globalization and its endorsement of diversity and pluriculturality has shifted the cultural horizons of Australian nation-building in ways that enable the positive assertion of Indigeneity and Indigenous rights. This is illustrated in the growing global networks of Indigenous scholars and the significance of the work of international organizations, such as UNESCO and the CBD, which encourages nations, such as Australia, to think about Indigenous education beyond the confines of their established national agenda. Similar stories about the politics that open up as globalization and nationalism grate against one another could have been told in relation to other cultural groups within Australia – women, or ethnic and class communities – but Indigenous exclusion is the most stark and systematic. It shows most clearly the continuing and ongoing influence of colonialism in contemporary Australia, as well as the way the implications of a White past are being challenged at the level of global identity formation in both Indigenous and White communities.

Without doubt, continued and strengthening Indigenous existence within Australia poses problems for the old Australian 'nation'. Concurrently, the demands by Indigenous peoples that globalizers act locally while they think globally, taking into account Indigenous presence and custodianship of land and resources, places a strain on that aspect of the emerging Australian polity that sees itself as sophisticated, worldly and cosmopolitan. It is a constant reminder that settlers have no real country. They are 'surface dwellers', walking cautiously on the eggshells of only faintly discerned cultural practices.

Even so, Indigenous people continue to face complex problems, not least when they approach the Western education system. As Rigney so eloquently writes:

> In the midst of writing this paper our eldest daughter demanded my immediate attention. Dressed in her uniform with a beautiful smile, it was to be her first day at a white controlled school. As a family we have equipped her with a Narungga education since birth. This education develops qualities and values such as respect for Elders, care for country, love and compassion for others and all things, and a strong sense of pride and respect for Narungga community, culture and family. This education involves marinating the child in her ancient Narungga language, customs and culture, which brings cultural responsibility and obligation. Equally important is for her to develop the skills of the dominant education to understand the technically globalised world in which the Narungga now live.
>
> (2002, p. 73)

References

Anderson, B. (1991) Imagined communities: reflections on the origin and spread of nationalism, London: Verso. Available at http://images.lib.monash.edu.au/gsc3423/04115513.pdf.

Attwood, B. (ed.) (1996) *In the Age of Mabo: History, Aborigines and Australia.* St Leonards, NSW: Allen & Unwin.

Battiste, M. and Henderson, J. Y. (2000) *Protecting Indigenous Knowledge and Heritage: A Global Challenge.* Saskatchewan: Purich Publishing.

Beresford, Q. (2001) Creating educational disadvantage: the impact of Aboriginal Affairs policy on the education of Aboriginal students in Western Australia, *Australian Journal of Education*, 45 (1).

Bishop, R. (1996) *Collaborative Research Stories: Whakawhanaungatanga.* Palmerston North, NZ: Dunmore Press.

Boreham, P., Dow, G. and Leet, M. (1999) *Room to Manoeuvre: Political Aspects of Full Employment.* Melbourne: Melbourne University Press.

Brady, W. (1992) Beam me up Scotty! Communicating across world views on knowledge principles and procedures for the conduct of Aboriginal or Torres Strait Island research, in C. White (ed.) *National Aboriginal or Torres Strait Island Higher Education Conference Proceedings.* Toowoomba, Australia: University of Southern Queensland, pp. 104–15.

Brundtland Report (1988) *Our Common Future.* World Commission on Environment and Development. Oxford: Oxford University Press.

Butlin, N. G., Barnard, A. and Pincus, J. J. (1982) *Government and Capitalism: Public and Private Choice in Twentieth Century Australia*. Cambridge: Cambridge University Press.

Castles, F. (1988) *Australian Public Policy and Economic Vulnerability*. Sydney: Allen & Unwin.

Craven, R. and Mooney, J. (2000) Teaching the teachers to understand and teach Indigenous Australian Studies: new models, teaching strategies and resources to empower and educate a nation. Paper presented at AARE, New Orleans, LA.

Crowley, R. K. (1980) *A New History of Australia*. Melbourne: Heinemann.

Davidson, A. (1997) *From Subject to Citizen: Australian Citizenship in the Twentieth Century*. Cambridge: Cambridge University Press.

Djelic, M-L. and Quack, S. (2003) *Globalization and Institutions: Redefining the Rules of the Economic Game*. Cheltenham: Edward Elgar.

Dodson, M. (2000) Inspirational Speech, Corroboree 2000. Available at www.reconciliation.org.au/media/Dr%20Mick%20Dodson.htm (accessed 17 December 2003).

Dodson, Michael and Strelein, Lisa (2001) Australia's nation building: renegotiating the relationship between Indigenous peoples and the State, *UNSW Law Journal* 24 (3): 826–39.

Grattan, M. (2000) *Reconciliation: Essays on Australian Reconciliation*. Melbourne: Black.

Greenwood, G. (1974) *Australia: A Social and Political History*. Sydney: Angus and Robertson.

Hage, G. (1998) *White Nation*. Sydney: Pluto Press.

Hesch, R. (1999) Indigenous teacher education in neo-liberal settler societies. Paper presented at the World Indigenous People's Conference, New Mexico.

Howard, Hon. J. (2000) Address to Corroboree 2000: 'Towards Reconciliation', May 27. Available at www.australianpolitics.com/news/2000/00-05-27.shtml (accessed 17 December 2003).

Kawagley, Angayuqaq Oscar and Barnhardt, Ray (2001) *Education Indigenous to Place: Western Science Meets Native Reality*. Available at www.ankn.uaf.edu/EIP.html.

Keating, Hon. P. (1992) *Australian launch of the International Year for the World's Indigenous People, the Redfern Speech, 10 December*. Available at www.australianpolitics.com/executive/keating/92-12-10redfern-speech.shtml (accessed 17 December 2003).

Langton, M. (1998) *Burning Questions: Emerging Environmental Issues for Indigenous Peoples in Northern Australia*. Darwin: Centre for Indigenous Natural and Cultural Resource Management, Northern Territory University.

Langton, M. (2001a) A treaty between our nations? Inaugural professorial lecture. Available at www.Indigenous.unimelb.edu.au/lecture1.html (accessed 20 January 2004).

Langton, M. (2001b) *The Nations of Australia*. Available at www.abc.net.au/rn/deakin/stories/s300007.htm (accessed 11 February 2004).

Langton, M. and Ma Rhea, Z. (2003) *Convention on Biological Diversity (CBD) Report: Australia, Asia and the Middle East*. Regional report on the status and trends concerning the knowledge, innovations and practices of Indigenous and local communities relevant to the conservation and sustainable use of biological diversity, UNEP/CBD/WG8J/INF/4. Available at www.biodiv.org.

Marginson, S. (1993) *Education and Public Policy*. Melbourne: Cambridge University.

Ma Rhea, Z. (2002a) *Raising Awareness of Indigenous Knowledge in Science and Technology Education*. Available at www.scidev.net/dossiers/index.cfm?fuse-action=policybrief&policy=35&dossier=7.

Ma Rhea, Z. (2002b) The economy of ideas: colonial gift and postcolonial product, in A. Quayson and D. T. Goldberg (eds) *Relocating Postcoloniality*. Oxford: Blackwell, pp. 205–16.

Metin, A. (1977) *Socialism Without Doctrine*. Sydney: Alternative Publishing Cooperative.

Morgan, D. (2003) Appropriation, appreciation, accommodation: Indigenous wisdoms and knowledges in higher education, *International Review of Education* 49 (1–2): 35–49.

Nakata, M. (1998) Anthropological texts and Aboriginal or Torres Strait Island stand points, *Australian Aboriginal Studies Journal*, 2.

NCVER (1998) *Indigenous Students, 1996: An Overview*. Adelaide: NCVER.

Pusey, M. (1992) *Economic Rationalism in Canberra: The Nation-building State Changes its Mind*. Cambridge: Cambridge University Press.

Pusey, M. (2003) *The Experience of Middle Australia: The Dark Side of Economic Reform*. Cambridge: Cambridge University Press.

Readings, B. (1996) *The University In Ruins*. Cambridge, MA: Harvard University Press.

Reynolds, H. (2000) *Why Weren't We Told?* Melbourne: Penguin.

Rigney, Irabinna-Lester (1997) Internationalization of an Aboriginal or Torres Strait Island anti-colonial cultural critique of research methodologies: a guide to Indigenist research methodology and its principles, research and development, in *Higher Education: Advancing International Perspectives, Higher Education Research and Development Society of Australasia (HERDSA) Annual International Conference Proceedings*, Vol. 20, pp. 629–36. (Available on CD-ROM, PC and Mac compatible, and in PDF and HTML versions.)

Roe, J. (1998) The Australian way, in P. Smyth and B. Cass (eds) *Contesting the Australian Way: States, Markets and Civil Society*. Melbourne: Cambridge University Press.

Rose, N. (1996) The death of the social? Refiguring the territory of government, *Economy and Society* 25 (3): 327–56.

Seddon, T. (2001) National Curriculum in Australia, *Pedagogy, Culture and Society* 9 (3): 307–31.

Sheil, C. (2001) *Globalisation: Australian Impacts*. Sydney: University of New South Wales Press.

Smith, T. L. (1999) *Decolonizing Methodologies: Research and Aboriginal or Torres Strait Island Peoples*. London: Zed Books.

Smyth, P. and Cass, B. (1998) *Contesting the Australian Way: States, Markets and Civil Society*. Cambridge: Cambridge University Press.

Teasdale, G. R and Ma Rhea, Zane (eds) (2000) *Local Knowledge and Wisdom in Higher Education*. Oxford: Elsevier Pergamon.

Tsolidis, G. (2001) Cultural identifications: young people extending understandings of Australianness. Paper presented at the Australian Association for Research in Education conference, December. Available at www.aare.edu.au/01pap/tso01223.htm (accessed 20 January 2004).

UNESCO (2001) Collaborative learning partnerships, in *Teaching and Learning for a Sustainable Future*. Available at www.unesco.org/education/tlsf/index.htm.

Watson, D. (2003) *Death Sentence: The Decay of Public Language*. Sydney: Random House.

Williams, R. (1976) *The Long Revolution*. Harmondsworth: Penguin.

Williams, S. and Stewart, I. (1992) Community control and self-determination in Aboriginal education research: The changed roles, relationships and responsibilities of Aboriginal and non-Aboriginal researchers and Aboriginal communities, in C. White (ed.) *National Aboriginal or Torres Strait Island Higher Education Conference Proceedings*, December. Toowoomba, Australia: University of Southern Queensland, pp. 90–8.

14 Cultural relativism and cultural imperialism in a globalized economy and monopolar polity

David Coulby

Introduction

This chapter concentrates on the curricula of schools and universities. It begins by outlining the power of cultural relativism as a concept for understanding the construction of knowledge in international terms and its crystallization into curricular systems. It then restates the importance of cultural relativism and post-colonial discourse theory in understanding curriculum formation and reproduction. It contrasts the pluralism and hybridity of this approach with trends towards homogenization evident within the shift to globalization and a monopolar polity. There then follow sections on both cultural imperialism and on the persistence of imperialism itself within the globalized economy. The focus remains on curriculum formation and in particular on the possibilities for international and intercultural approaches to inform this process. It concludes by suggesting that a critical interculturalism may have a part to play even within the tightening constraints of globalization.

The chapter is interspersed by four italicized extracts from a Spanish account, written by one of the conquistadors, of the conquest of Mexico and the destruction of Aztec culture and the enslavement of the indigenous people. The purpose of this narrative device is to exemplify the process and consequences of colonization and the attitudes of both parties involved. It demonstrates that colonization is not about theory but about the massive processes of world history. The chapter asserts that these processes of colonization are still at work within the economics of globalization and the politics of the 'war on terror'. The differences (and similarities) between the Aztecs and the Habsburg Spanish alert us to different dimensions of superiority – cultural, economic and military. Both cultures engaged – to varying degrees – in artistic creation, cultural and actual imperialism, religious intolerance and human sacrifice. Only one had the economy and the technology to build ocean-going galleons; only one possessed horses, metal weaponry, armour and cannons.

Theorizing cultural relativism

To restate briefly the case for cultural relativism, it is possible to take two examples of a similar genre, derived from the same space and time – two early nineteenth-century French Romantic poems, say, or two contemporary American popular songs. There may be ways in which it is possible to arbitrate between these products. It may be possible to enumerate which poem has been the most widely anthologized for instance, or which translated into the greatest number of foreign languages. It may be easy to discover which popular song has sold the greatest number of recordings or sheet music. Again, international sales and translations would provide another way of discriminating between the relative success of two similar cultural products. These extrinsic modes of comparison may point to intrinsic worth. The 'best' poems become the most well known, the 'best' popular songs sell most recordings and the 'best' academic articles receive the most citations. As suggested in Chapter 1, popularity may become a default mode of discrimination, particularly in a context of superabundance.

Each person's subjective preferences, however, suggest that this is not always the case. The personally dearly held artwork or genre may be one which is far from widely appreciated even among contemporaries. Historically, new movements in the arts frequently commence with, or become associated with, a rejection of the previously accepted critical cannon. Alternatively, as in the Renaissance, they may be associated with the installation of a revived canon, the invention of tradition. Popularity has not been an overriding cultural criterion either in historical or personal, subjective terms.

Searching for criteria to determine between cultural products, there is, on the one hand, the solipsism and subjectivity of personal preference, and, on the other, a chaos of popularity contests or non-discrimination. And this is between very similar works of art. How, in that case, might one compare the relative worth of Milton's epic with a contemporary lyric of Marvell's? How compare Joyce's *Ulysses* with the linguistically related but chronologically remote *Canterbury Tales*? And these putative comparisons would still be within one language and geographical space. Is it possible to discuss the relative merits of *The Epic of Gilgamesh* with those of *One Hundred Years of Solitude*? Even this question is too easy since both are ultimately literary productions. Is it possible to discuss, in any meaningful way whatsoever, the relative merits of Van Eyck's Ghent triptych and Gaudi's Sagrada Familia? The Easter Island statues and *Cosi Fan Tutte*? The suggestions are absurd.

> *'My lord Malinche (Cortes)', Montezuma replied, 'these arguments of yours have been familiar to me for some time. I understood what you said to my ambassadors on the sandhills about the three gods and the cross, also what*

you preached in the various towns through which you passed. We have given you no answer, since we have worshipped our own gods here from the beginning and know them to be good also . . .'.

(Diaz, 1963, pp. 222–3)

Different cultures have different manifestations. Some value epic poetry, some folk dance, some the delicacies of ritual human sacrifice. It is not possible to discriminate between cultures in terms of the magnitude or meaningfulness of their achievement. Of course, there are ways in which one may arbitrate at the extreme edges of cultural activity, as the provocative examples of Aztec ritual sacrifice or the punishments of the Spanish Inquisition suggest. One may prefer those cultures in which people and other living creatures were and are not systematically harmed, though, in this case, the slavery and slave trading of Periclean Athens and Renaissance Spain would present the argument with considerable paradoxes. One may doubt for the viability of those cultures within which the number of tools in use is actually declining across the centuries, though the systematic genocide of indigenous Tasmanians points to more ruthless factors than technological decline in the decay of cultures. Consequently, the only rational, non-particularistic perspective from which to regard different cultures or cultural products is that of cultural relativism. Despite human sacrifices (indeed partly to facilitate them) the Aztecs built Tenochtitlan; despite the slave trade (indeed partly with the profits it generated) England built Bath. Socrates was wrong: goodness, beauty and truth are unfortunately not a unitary project. Beauty, even the spiritual beauty of the Most Catholic Monarchs, is compatible with evil and so, most regrettably of all, is truth (if truth is conceived in the limited, but workable, sense of science).

The argument is not that the Aztecs and the English can be forgiven their barbarity because of their spectacular achievements in architecture. It is rather asserting for culture what Braudel, writing of the Most Catholic Monarchs, insisted with regard to historical judgement: that one cannot only stand on the moral high ground of the present in order to understand the past (Braudel, 1992). The present is heir to an astonishingly rich legacy of cultures and cultural products and it has no rational way to arbitrate between them.

Literary or musical critics may contrive a discourse which can arbitrate which poem or song gives most pleasure and/or enlightenment to most people over the greatest range of time and space, but their arguments to construct and defend their canons tend to be nationalistic or tendentious or both. There have been many attempts at this arbitration, some of them of a high scholarly order (Leavis, 1962, 1963; Pound, 1938, 1954). But to exemplify the criteria and referents of these arbitrations readily reveals their flaws. Does this culture ascribe to the same religion as

I do? Is this culture of the same language or geographical space as I am? Is this culture knowledge (science)-seeking? (The greatest slave traders and the progenitors of the Industrial Revolution are bounded by the same time and space.) Is this culture popular with a lot of people? Did I learn this culture in my school, family, workplace, place of worship, trade union? Is this culture endorsed by (or, alternatively, opposed to) the state or global capitalism?

There remains a surprising reluctance on the part of serious commentators on the school curriculum to adopt an approach based on cultural relativism (Lawton, 1988, 1997). Cultural relativism would surely provide a decentred and impartial way of understanding the processes and consequences of curricular selection. Curricula are a minute selection from the magnitude of human knowledge. It is primarily by adopting a position of cultural relativity that it is possible to assess these curricular systems, and in some cases the processes of their selection (Bash and Coulby, 1989; Coulby and Bash, 1991). The assessment might consider the extent to which they are informed by nationalism, say, or whether they enhance or endanger intercultural understanding or an internationally progressive response to the forces of globalization. The reverse, of course, is also the case: those who adopt a position of cultural superiority, of confidence in the greater humanity, beauty or truth claim of one particular culture, are unlikely to be well qualified to comment on the curricular issues within international education. Yet, as the following section makes clear, imperialism is still a pervasive force in curriculum construction as well as in culture more generally.

There are wider arguments within the theory of cultural relativism that may be mentioned, if not resolved, at this stage. Some commentators have asserted that knowledge too is relative. Epistemological relativism is particularly associated with the sociological and philosophical critique of Western science ('truth') (Feyerabend, 1975, 1978a, 1978b). The implications for the teaching of science and technology in schools and universities are profound but beyond the scope of this chapter (Coulby and Jones, 1995). The wider issues of ethical and political relativism may perhaps more appropriately be briefly addressed here. Does cultural relativism imply no disapproval of, say, the Taliban's policy with regard to women in Afghanistan? The trouble with these kinds of ethical-political condemnations is that they tend to be of distant, often poorly understood, others. Indeed, in the context of the 'war on terror', these condemnations seem to be predominantly directed at the beliefs and practices of Islamic groups. These Islamophobic commentators tend not to address the problematic ethical-political practices within their own cultures: the prevalence of paedophilia in the USA and the UK; the connections between right-wing fundamentalist Christianity in the USA and the daily atrocities of the Israeli armed forces in the West Bank and

Gaza; or institutional racism on the part of police forces and judiciaries throughout Europe and the USA. The biblical injunction to remove the beam from one's own eye before starting on the mote in someone else's is germane here. To be more emphatic, the point is that there is no clear ground on which the critic of culture, ethics or political practice can stand. Any attempt to occupy such ground will ultimately be that of the cultural supremacists, the nationalists who believe, no matter how indirectly, in the primacy of their own beliefs and practices.

More recent developments within the paradigm of cultural relativism have provided great power for the educational evaluation of curricular systems. Postmodern and post-colonial approaches to knowledge, not least school and university knowledge, adopt a position which not only refrains from cultural judgements but also examines the conditions and contexts under which anterior judgements came to be made. More simply these positions examine knowledge systems based upon cultural imperialism and cultural supremacism (Bernal, 1987, 1991; Bhabha, 1990; Diaz-Andreu and Champion, 1996; Said, 1995; R. Young, 1990, 1994, 1995; R. J. C. Young, 1995). This facilitates further levels of cultural deconstruction and historical decentring. In particular, these approaches suggest the relations of particular types of knowledge with particular political and economic arrangements. This does rather more than revive the theories of Marx's *On the German Ideology* because it pays particular attention to the role of knowledge in the processes of colonization. In educational terms this has implications for both the colonizers and the colonized in terms of the construction and deconstruction of all areas of the school and university curriculum (Arnonowitz and Giroux, 1991; Coulby and Jones, 1995; Usher and Edwards, 1994).

While the discourses of critique may have been refined, this does not, of course, imply that the processes of actual colonization have ended. Post-colonialism, unfortunately, describes a discourse theory rather than a political reality. Not all colonialism ended in 1947. The process of colonization is still ongoing in many places: for example, Famagusta, Lhasa, Aceh, Grozny, Hebron and Derry. A later section of the chapter briefly examines some of the new forms of colonialism. Before that, it is necessary to consider the more specific process of cultural imperialism and in particular its curricular manifestations:

> *Cortes answered them (the Aztec ambassadors) through our interpreter somewhat sternly. He reminded them, with a show of anger, how often he had requested them to keep the peace, and said that they had committed a crime and now deserved to be put to death, together with all the inhabitants of their towns. He then pointed out that we were vassals of a great king and lord named the Emperor Charles, who had sent us to these parts with orders to help and favour those who would enter his royal service. This*

we would do, he continued, if they were now as well-disposed as they said, but if they were not, something would jump out of those (cannon) . . . which would kill them, for some of these (cannon) were still angry with them for having attacked us.

(Diaz, 1963, p. 79)

Globalization and cultural and linguistic imperialism

The potential of education to constitute a form of cultural imperialism has long been recognized (Carnoy, 1974; Matherson, 1996). The process whereby a politically strong group uses the school curriculum to impose its religion on a weaker group is not hard to identify. In the history of actual imperialism it was not only religion but culture more generally and also science and the doctrine of progress that were imposed by imperial powers through schools and universities on a large part of the globe. Colonialism in this sense may be both internal (Catalonia, Soviet Latvia) or external (Mexico, Peru). The continuation of cultural imperialism beyond the period of colonialism (though see the next section for its survival and continuation) involves the complex interplay between cultural, economic and political forces within the emerging and conflicted pattern of globalization.

The contemporary perpetrators of cultural imperialism, unlike the missionary schools, are themselves major economic players. Films, books and magazines, television and media, newspapers and electronic games are increasingly the products of large transnational corporations based mainly, but not exclusively, in the triad states. Moreover, other commercial products carry important cultural significance: pharmaceuticals, mobile phones, music players and fashion items. While schools and universities struggle, with varying degrees of success, to free their curricula from earlier layers of cultural imperialism, their pupils and students are exposed to the globalized culture that simultaneously acts as colonizing agent and profit maker. In the face of these global forces other chapters in this volume show how school curricula in particular have often retreated to a back-to-basics and nationalistic core.

Cultural messages have political purposes as well as economic motivations. The inscription of the school curriculum by nationalism, described in Chapters 3 and 11, is only one, though probably the most powerful, of these. Reassertions of nationalism can be made by other mechanisms such as the codification of archaeological discoveries (Diaz-Andreu and Champion, 1996) or the presentation of museums or exhibitions. In the early 1980s, memories of the Second World War were still fresh in London. At the same time, the UK was being overwhelmed with imported manufactured products from Japan: motorbikes and cars, cameras and electronic goods. Sponsored by the Japan Foundation and ultimately the Japanese government, the Royal Academy at this point staged its lavish Edo exhibition of art and cultural products from the Shogunate period. The conflicts of recent war and current economic failure were mollified by this exhibition of silk kimonos, screen paintings and decontextualized samurai swords. The population of London were given an alternative view of Japan, an opportunity to reconceptualize, which set economic and political conflict against a would-be international appreciation of the apparent richness of Shogunate culture.

Linguistic imperialism is perhaps the most prevalent current curricular manifestation of cultural imperialism. The English language, like capitalism itself, is both a vehicle and a manifestation of globalization. The penetration of school and university curricula across the world by English has been described in Chapter 2. At this point it is appropriate to stress two factors: first, that this penetration has met with resistance in many forms and places; second, that, in the context of globalization, the English language and its teaching in schools and universities have political and economic dimensions. The EU has resisted the ubiquitous use of English and has tried, with dubious success, to encourage the teaching of the languages of the smaller states of the Union (European Commission, 1996, 2002). The European Bureau for Lesser Used Languages, by contrast, has campaigned on behalf of those European languages which are not represented by state power (European Bureau for Lesser Used Languages, 1993, 1995a, 1995b, undated). Each time a school system or individual school elects to have a different or even a second foreign language they are resisting the hegemony of English. This resistance has clear political significance in France as well as in the Arab world. Each time a young person on the West Bank refuses to function in English the political power of the USA is resisted.

The spread of the English language generates a preferential market for commercial and cultural products which operate in English. An obvious and prevalent example is popular music, but English is also widely used in advertising and marketing to give an international cachet to a range of banal products. This process is mutually reinforcing. As well as marketing the product the language itself is given another leverage of power and influence. Furthermore, the English language embodies a set of political and cultural assumptions about, among others, madness and sanity, black and white, sickness and health, male and female, the uniqueness of the individual identity, the superiority of the historical role, political systems and cultural products of the UK and the USA (Bhabha, 1990; Hodge and Kress, 1993; Watson, 1997). The inculcation of individualism and identity, itself a widely exported Western cultural preoccupation, for many children and young people takes place within a context where English is a compulsory and high-status school subject and where the language's links to political power, economic success and cultural hegemony are manifest in an increasing number of contexts.

Educational institutions are among the most important sites where the hegemony of the English language is spread, reproduced, but also contested.

Current colonial manifestations

After Christmas 1991 there was only one world power. While the USA might not willingly confront China or even Russia or India, all other major military powers are dependent on the USA for aid and/or technology – the UK as well as Israel, Pakistan and South Korea. By a combination of bullying and bribery the USA was able at the end of 2002 to command a unanimous vote in the Security Council in favour of intervention in Iraq. This happened in the teeth of strong and vocal opposition from the populations of many of the Council's member states.

This military and political power is based on great national wealth and on an economy which continues to create jobs despite the near destruction of its manufacturing sector. Almost all the major transnational corporations have their headquarters in the USA. The globalization of culture is surely benefiting American products and values more than those of any other single state. The centring of media industries in the USA ensures that the propaganda of CNN and the atavistic values of the Hollywood film are widely distributed throughout the world. The USA invariably privileges the safeguarding of domestic profit over such issues as human welfare, the reduction of international inequalities, the equitable and sustainable use of resources, the preservation of the biosphere, or even the independence, peace and safety of other states.

The current forms of colonialism cannot be understood then without the background of globalization, outlined in the Introduction, and the emergence of American hyperpower. While other forms of cultural, economic and technological ascendancy now form major aspects of the process of domination, actual military intervention remains widespread. This has involved the USA in an interventionist foreign policy even after the ending of the Cold War. Military colonialism now takes the forms of intervention by the USA itself (former Yugoslavia, Colombia, Afghanistan, Iraq) or by those other states that can legitimate their imperialism on the basis of the 'war on terror' (Russia in Chechnya, Indonesia in Aceh and West Papua, Israel in Palestine, the UK in Sierra Leone). In the main, these interventions require the tacit or explicit approval of the USA. In extreme cases, notably Israel, much of the finances and munitions to support military action are supplied by Washington.

From the point of view of this chapter and indeed this volume, the point is that the processes of colonialism, reflected and reproduced in school and university curricula, are not merely items in the past. They are part of the contemporary context of pupils and students.

Understanding the literature, culture and history of Habsburg expansion in America or of English imperialism might give access to an understanding of the present as well as of the past. Conversely, curricula which serve to conceal, disguise or glamorise the histories of imperialism and slavery, subservient, as this volume suggests, to nationalistic and traditionalistic influences, will seriously hinder an understanding of contemporary events as well as of the past. British armed forces are currently in Iraq not for the first time in the last hundred years. The nature of the understanding gained at schools and universities, in London and Baghdad, as to why they were there, and with what political, economic and cultural consequences, in the past will inform the attitudes of pupils and students to their presence there in 2004. Were the earlier invaders 'throwing off Ottoman tyranny'? Are the current ones 'eliminating weapons of mass destruction' or securing energy supplies for the UK and its allies?

> So, with luck on our side, we boldly entered the city of Tenochtitlan or Mexico on 8 November in the year of our Lord 1519.
>
> (Diaz, 1963, p. 218)

Intercultural education and the prospects for optimism

Against this background of globalization and monopolarity it is difficult to see what opportunities there are to be sanguine. Aids has joined corruption, civil war and genocide in the misery of sub-Saharan Africa. India and Pakistan are only beginning to ease their nuclear stand-off. There seems to be no end in sight to the occupation of the Palestinian lands. But there are other straws on the global wind. Progressive governments have come to power in Ecuador and Venezuela as well as Brazil, while popular movements in Argentina might hold the promise of democracy and reform (Klein, 2003). The gradual emergence from abject poverty of large populations in China and India mean that the proportion of the world's population living in dire want has reduced considerably over the last 20 years (Wolf, 2003).

Throughout this volume authors have needed to lurch between the apparently massive forces of globalization and nationalism on the one hand and the apparently less significant institutions and processes of education on the other. The difficulty is to sustain a rational discourse which can hold together the explosive economic development in eastern China and changes in the pattern of infant education. There is a constant danger of appearing to relate great things to those which seem much lesser. Nevertheless, in the expansion of intercultural and international approaches to education there may be real cause for optimism. This may yet be one of the beneficial, if far from central, aspects of globalization. This is not to deny, and indeed to regret bitterly, that there are areas of the world where a basic level of schooling, let alone a university education, are an unimaginable luxury. That said, this section will attempt to outline and assess the ways in which international and intercultural changes to school and university curricula may be able to assist in the understanding and even the modification of those processes of globalization described elsewhere in this volume.

Post-colonial theories and understandings have given students and some pupils in many parts of the world new insights into the ways in which school and university knowledge has been part of the processes whereby one set of states have exploited the populations of another set. Intercultural education, certainly at university level, does offer the opportunity to engage with colonial legacies – in London as well as in Mumbai and Dublin. The Korean and Chinese governments, for example, as well as enlightened Japanese academics, now see that the Japanese history school curriculum is an affront to those who suffered in the first half of the previous century (Ienaga Saburo, 2001). The governments of Spain, South Africa and, more remarkably, France have become attuned to the linguistic rights of their national minorities. It is important to stress that in terms of developing intercultural and international knowledge all areas of the school and university curricula need to be kept under continuous review, not least so that the current, mutated forms of colonialism taking place within the processes of globalization can be understood. Curricular change in the Baltic States, while throwing off the previous Soviet (Russian) colonialism, can yet manifest other forms of nationalism (Lieven, 1993; Vetik, 1995).

Earlier in this chapter it was suggested that culture was personal and often dearly held (as well as contested at all sites). This is actually derived from one of Ezra Pound's aphorisms, mentioned in Chapter 1, to the effect that 'civilisation is individual'. In order to see why this insight is helpful it is necessary to relinquish, at least temporarily, the sociological framework and to operate at the level of the individual. Again, there is no high ground in terms of intercultural analysis. The very notion of individuality is a central concept of Western, modernist culture. It is far from equally prevalent or important in more traditionalistic cultures. That said, it can be seen that, at least in Western (and Westernized) society, each person makes a huge range of cultural choices every day: what to wear, what newspaper to read, what music to listen to or make, what to eat, whether to go to the theatre or watch television. In some states or cities the choices in just these diurnal activities is exceptionally rich and internationally derived. We have to decide, for example, which three of the British Museum's hundred galleries we can take in this afternoon. Now, of course, there is an element of consumerist fetishism for the over-privileged here and sociological perspectives can never be utterly eschewed. But think of the dimension of the cultural choices made by academics: what body of literature to study, which journals to subscribe to, which courses to design for students, which languages to read, write and speak in, which conferences to attend, which books to write. It is hard to believe that all these choices are culturally or economically determined. And these choices go well beyond fetishism to the actual shaping of identity, that of pupils and students as well as teachers and academics.

Identity, then, as well as culture can be self-directed, though clearly not self-determined. The context is given and yet individuals act. They act as groups and against groups. Above all, they act differently and thereby demonstrate the extent to which context does not entirely define them. And this offers the possibility for a culture, for a series of identity formation processes, which might, while encircled in context, be self-consciously eclectic and international. The culturally fetishistic tourists in Bloomsbury make the decision to visit the Mexican gallery and those which exhibit the civilization of ancient Persia. They decide, on this occasion, not to see the Egyptian collection or to take a walk in Russell Square. And, if identity and identity formation for a growing number of people can, as a matter of choice, or of decision, become international and intercultural, might not that, in its turn, impact upon wider patterns of social and political change?

This is by no means to deny that social and political patterns in turn impact even more generally and relentlessly on identity formation, even on the concept of identity itself. Without inverting Marx, however, it is possible to recognize that the spread of post-colonial discourses within the curriculum might itself impact not only on the understanding of past colonialisms but also on responses to the current processes of globalization and associated current colonialism.

Chapter 2 outlines four characteristics of knowledge: accessibility, superabundance, marketization and internationalization. The purpose of focusing on each of these characteristics in turn again here is to examine the extent to which they offer possibilities for contestation (as well as more obviously confirmation, reproduction and legitimation) of the processes of globalization and unipolarity within education systems.

Accessibility is the first characteristic in analysing the ways in which knowledge and its curricular formations are changing. Satellite broadcasting, the internet and the explosion of specialist journals all result in large and ever-increasing amounts of data being available internationally, at home, at work or on the move. Despite the Chinese government's attempts to limit access to the web, or the gestures of some American states to silence Darwinian accounts of evolution, it is becoming increasingly impossible to exert political or academic censorship. In educational terms this has led to a rich range of learning resources available across many states. At post-school level it has facilitated the development of open and distance learning. Leaving aside the distressing ubiquity of the

English language, discussed earlier, the potential for internationalization and interculturalization of learning has never been greater. In some ways national school curricular systems can be seen as a forlorn attempt to control young people's access to knowledge. Meanwhile, digital imaging and broadcasting make prison atrocities in Baghdad and events on the West Bank available throughout the world. The political consequences of this level of accessibility are yet to be fully discovered, but the secrecy which has so often shrouded atrocities in the past, and thereby secured their perpetuation, is being steadily removed.

A second characteristic is the tendency towards superabundance: of information, analysis, entertainment. While the criteria of school and university curricular selection become ever more arduous, the possibilities for variety, plurality and hybridity expand. That this is particularly so at university level is partly because so many states, wedded to modernist versions of nationalism, are hidebound by centralized curricula at school level. The criteria in the selection of knowledge become increasingly visible at higher education level. Modularization and student choice further facilitate the individualization (fetishization) of knowledge already suggested. It may be that superabundance itself will encourage relativism and exploration as people and groups become self-conscious of the way they obtain, organize and evaluate knowledge and culture.

The third characteristic is the trend towards a market-driven knowledge formation. The popularity of a book, journal, school, website or university course is seen as a legitimate estimation of their quality as well as a prediction of their survival. A criterion of knowledge formation becomes literally the head count: the number of hits on a website, the number of sales of a set of course books, or the number of applicants for a university degree course. If people do not want a range of knowledge then it closes down, as indeed has happened to several science departments at universities in the UK or to Junior Colleges in Japan beset with demographic decline. In terms of wider marketization, given the increasing control of publication and media by a few transnational corporations, this trend must be seen to be as much a threat as an opportunity for the development of international and intercultural approaches to education. There will be a danger that marginal voices will be less likely to be heard within the clamour of globalized media.

The fourth and final characteristic in knowledge formation is that of internationalization. Knowledge and culture at all levels are becoming international. The globalization of finance and the globalization of knowledge have taken place simultaneously. People are tending to enquire about events, histories and cultures in a wider number of states. Student and scholar movement is a further manifestation of internationalization. ERASMUS, SOCRATES and TEMPUS have provided an impulse for the Europeanization of higher education in the EU and beyond. One and a half million Chinese students have sought degrees in other countries in the last ten years. This trend is partly to do with the spread of English and certainly this has facilitated internationalization and student movement in many regions. But it involves more than language: hybridity and fusion in many forms and domains are actively pursued at both the individual level and that of educational institutions. At curricular level the positive impact and potential of the internationalization of knowledge involves the erosion of nationalist knowledge and the facilitation of relativistic perspectives. The enhanced possibilities for student movement may also serve to break down nationalistic knowledge paradigms and to develop a critical interculturalism.

Some aspects of knowledge, however, remain, for the moment, unchanged:

- the unavailability of even basic education in some parts of the world, especially for girls;
- the tendency towards nationalism and xenophobia in the curricula of a vast majority of school systems;
- the continued, and in some cases, increased penetration of schools and even universities by traditionalistic forces often associated with religious institutions;
- elitist hierarchies of schools and particularly higher educational institutions;
- hierarchies of knowledge, differing between states, but often associated with a gendered differentiation of personal reward and status.

Optimism must then be tempered. Furthermore, this chapter has shown that imperialism is not only cultural and that the hegemonies of global exploitation in terms of culture, economics and politics are all mutually reinforcing. Nevertheless, as patterns of knowledge formation are increasingly characterized by trends towards access, superabundance, marketization and internationalization, the potential for knowledge to be emancipatory may be explored. At least at university, or indeed at the autodidact level, it may be that knowledge can liberate as well as enslave. Internationalized and intercultural individuality, solidarity and knowledge might counter the globalized economy and the monopolar polity. This is not to assert that, if the mode of the music changes, the walls of the city will fall. The reverse is ever more likely to be the case. It is to insist that the processes of globalization are conflicted and contested at all levels. In these conflicts the assertion of international and intercultural approaches to school and university knowledge has a significant, if by no means determining, part to play.

It is by no means determining, however, as imperialist processes persist, modified but relentless. Wells' contest between education and disaster continues. Here is Diaz's version of *derinda est Cartaganea*:

When the news spread through all these distant provinces that (Tenoch-titlan) was destroyed their (leaders) and lords could not believe it. However, they sent chieftains to congratulate Cortes on his victories and yield themselves as vassals to His Majesty, and to see if the city of (Tenochtitlan), which they had so dreaded, was really razed to the ground. They all carried great presents of gold to Cortes, and even brought their small children to show them (Tenochtitlan), pointing it out to them in much the same way that they would say: 'Here stood Troy'.

(Diaz, 1963, p. 413)

Cultural relativism then provides the necessary theoretical position to understanding the processes and consequences of cultural imperialism. Its insights into the formation of school and university curricula remain essential if children and young people are to understand the ongoing process of globalization in the context of hyperpower politics. To the extent, certainly limited, that these insights can be incorporated within school and university knowledge, there are possibilities for emancipatory education and identity formation. These identities will also be actors in progressing and resisting globalization.

References

Arnonowitz, S. and Giroux, H. A. (1991) *Postmodern Education: Politics, Culture and Social Criticism*. London: Routledge & Kegan Paul.

Bash, L. and Coulby, D. (1989) *The Education Reform Act: Competition and Control*. London: Cassell.

Bernal, M. (1987) *Black Athena: The Afroasiatic Roots of Classical Civilisation. Volume 1: The Fabrication of Ancient Greece 1785–1985*. London: Vintage.

Bernal, M. (1991) *Black Athena: The Afroasiatic Roots of Classical Civilisation. The Archaeological and Documentary Evidence*. London: Free Association Press.

Bhabha, H. K. (ed.) (1990) *Nation and Narration*. London and New York: Routledge.

Braudel, F. (1992) *The Mediterranean and the Mediterranean World in the Age of Phillip II*. London: HarperCollins.

Carnoy, M. (1974) *Education as Cultural Imperialism*. New York: David McKay.

Coulby, D. and Bash, L. (1991) *Contradiction and Conflict: The 1988 Education Act in Action*. London: Cassell.

Coulby, D. and Jones, C. (1995) *Postmodernity and European Education Systems: Centralist Knowledge and Cultural Diversity*. Stoke on Trent: Trentham.

Diaz, B. (1963) *The Conquest of New Spain*, trans. J. M. Cohen. Harmondsworth: Penguin.

Diaz-Andreu, M. and Champion, T. (eds) (1996) *Nationalism and Archaeology in Europe*. London: UCL Press.

European Bureau for Lesser Used Languages (1993) *The Sound of Europe*. Brussels: EBLUL.

European Bureau for Lesser Used Languages (1995a) *Feeling at Home in Your Language: Intergenerational Language Transmission*. Brussels: EBLUL.

European Bureau for Lesser Used Languages (1995b) *Key Words: A Step Into the World of Lesser Used Languages*. Brussels: EBLUL.

European Bureau for Lesser Used Languages (undated) *Language Rights, Individual and Collective: The Use of Lesser Used Languages in Public Administration*. Brussels: EBLUL.

European Commission (1996) *Teaching and Learning: Towards the Learning Society*. Brussels: European Commission.

European Commission (2002) *A New Impetus for European Youth*. White Paper. Luxembourg: Office for Official Publications of the European Communities.

Feyerabend, P. (1975) Poppers 'Objective Knowledge'. *Inquiry* 17: 465–507.

Feyerabend, P. (1978a) *Against Method*. London: Verso.

Feyerabend, P. (1978b) *Science in a Free Society*. London: Verso.

Hodge, R. and Kress, G. (1993) *Language as Ideology*, 2nd edn. London: Routledge & Kegan Paul.

Ienaga Saburo (2001) *Japan's Past, Japan's Future*, trans. R. H. Minear. Lanham, MD: Rowman & Littlefield Publishers.

Klein, N. (2003) Out of the Ordinary. *The Guardian Weekend*, 25 January, pp. 14–24.

Lawton, D. (1988) *Education, Culture and the National Curriculum*. London: Hodder & Stoughton.

Leavis, F. R. (1962) *The Great Tradition*. Harmondsworth: Penguin.

Leavis, F. R. (1963) *New Bearings in English Poetry*. Harmondsworth: Penguin.

Lieven, A. (1993) *The Baltic Revolution: Estonia, Latvia, Lithuania and the Path to Independence*. New Haven, CT: Yale University Press.

Matherson, D. (1996) Imperial Culture and Cultural Imperialism. *European Journal of Intercultural Studies* 7(1): 51–6.

Pound, E. (1938) *Guide to Kulchur*. London: Peter Owen.

Pound, E. (1954) *Literary Essays of Ezra Pound*. London: Faber.

Said, E. (1995) *Orientalism: Western Conceptions of the Orient. With a New Afterword*. Harmondsworth: Penguin.

Usher, R. and Edwards, R. (1994) *Postmodernism and Education*. London: Routledge.

Vetik, R. (1995) The Relationship between Ethnic and Security Issues in the Baltic States, in ICCEES (ed.) *Fifth World Congress of ICCEES*. Warsaw: ICCEES.

Wolf, M. (2003) Economic Globalisation: An Unfinished Revolution. *Financial Times Special Report: The World 2003*, 23 January, p. III.

Young, R. (1990) *White Mythologies: Writing History and the West*. London: Routledge.

Young, R. (1994) Egypt in America: *Black Athena*, Racism and Colonial Discourse, in A. Rattansi and S. Westwood (eds) *Racisms, Modernity and Identity: On the Western Front*. London: Polity Press.

Young, R. (1995) Liberalism, Postmodernism, Critical Theory and Politics, in R. Smith and P. Wexler (eds) *After Postmodernism: Education, Politics and Identity* (series). London: Falmer Press.

Young, R. J. C. (1995) *Colonial Desire: Hybridity in Theory, Culture and Race*. London: Routledge.

Index

210; exchange/entitlement 122; fee-paying schools 195; foreign languages and 243; immigrants 247; imperialism 205; Internet 64; Iraq War 5, 280; Japanese imports 277; local authorities 165–6; managerialism 158–9; Manx 248; National Curriculum (England) 42, 179, 183, 195, 207–10, 243, (Wales) 244; nationalism 9, 68; New Labour 130; nurseries 78; Office of Standards in Education (Ofsted) 179; paedophilia 275; privatization of education 167; recruitment 33; religion 69, 80; salaries 48; schools 48; Scotland 68, 117–27, 137; secondary-school catchment areas 166–7; Sierra Leone 279; teachers 45, 51, 53; unemployment 41; university course closures 43, 283; USA and 12; welfare state 120; Welsh language 244, 247; Welsh TV 244

United Nations 9, 64, 242, 260, 279

United Nations Educational, Scientific and Cultural Organization 267

United States of America 3, 4, 5, 6, 8, 24, 38, 39, 41, 42, 46, 50, 148, 277; Americanization 1, 2, 12, 14; anti-Americanism 16; Belgium and 12; Bilingual Education Act 245; capitalism 238; Christianity 92, 96, 275; Civil Information & Education Section 96; Colombia 5; cultural dominance 12–13; Darwinism and 282; economy 39; education 23, 71, 74, 78, 158; English language 278; EU and 4, 12; France and 12; Germany and 12; global dominance 64, 79; 'heir' of classical Greece 194; hyperpower 9, 12, 279; ICT and 26; Internet and 26; Iraq War 5, 203, 279; Islamophobia 67; Japan and 12; Kyoto 63; languages 245; liberal democracy 183; managerialism 158–9; multiculturalism in 238; NAFTA 10; 'Nation at Risk' 98; neoliberalism 179; paedophilia 275; Panama 5; Pentagon 11;

productivity 98; racism 107, 276; recruitment 33; 'Ron-Yasu alliance' 99; salaries 48, 52; schools 48; State Department 95; State-War-Navy Coordinating Subcommittee for the Far East 95; teachers 53; Turkey and 12; UK and 12; unemployment 41; World Bank 12; WTO 62, 63

universities 41–4; autonomy 183; ICT and 44–8; importance of 78; workplace and 48

Unknown Soldiers 90

Ur 201

Uusitalo, H.: *Nordic Welfare States* 151

Vagabond 107

Valery, P.: 'Characteristics of the European spirit' 217

Van Eyck, Jan: Ghent triptych 273

Venezuela 3, 10, 280

Venice 197, 204, 219

Verdi, Giuseppe 199

video 30

Vienna 219

Vietnam War 186

Vitruvius 204

vocational education and training 41–4, 139, 150, 153, 156, 182

Vogel, J.: *European Welfare Production* 151

Voltaire 199, 219

vouchers 78, 156

Wagner, Richard 199

Wall Street Journal, The 32

Wal-Mart 8

Ward, R.: 'Legacy of the Occupation' 97, 98

warfare 1, 60, 63, 64, 90, 186, 196–7, 199, 209, 232, 239, 272, 275

Watson, D.: *Death Sentence* 259

wealth production: knowledge and 176

Weber, M. 43, 69, 92; *Economy and Society* 180

welfare state: EU and 129, 130, 151

Wells, H. G. 284